Darrell Kauffman

THE COVENANT

A Theology of Human Destiny

by

JAKOB JOCZ

Professor of Systematic Theology
Wycliffe College
University of Toronto

WILLIAM B. EERDMANS PUBLISHING COMPANY
GRAND RAPIDS, MICHIGAN

Library of Congress Catalog Card Number: 67-13984
Printed in the United States of America

CONTENTS

FOREWORD

New insights come by laborious and slow degrees. The present work has taken a long time to mature. No theologian writes in independence from others. Much that he has to say has already been said before. His modest contribution is frequently limited to a re-arrangement of material and a shifting of emphasis. Those who strain to produce a completely new theology, because novelty is the fashion, never succeed to do justice to the discipline. No theology can be written that signifies a radical breach with the past. Historic continuity is an essential feature of theological endeavor. For this reason much of recent "theology" is a misuse of the term.

This writer has endeavored to remain true to tradition yet open to the cross-currents of our age. Biblical revelation in the historical context was his main concern. His effort was directed towards coherence with the concept of Covenant as a guiding principle. This work would have been impossible without the contribution of many writers both ancient and modern. The footnotes to the text and the bibliographical index bear ample witness to the extent of the author's indebtedness.

Amidst the vagaries of shifting opinion about man and his destiny we are pressed to acknowledge that there can be no ultimate answer from within the human situation. The conviction that the Covenant as witnessed to by Holy Writ provides an answer *extra nos* to the question regarding human destiny, and that it is a valid answer, is the contention of this work.

There is yet another debt the author wishes to acknowledge: without the help of willing friends and members of his own family this book would not have beeen written. His thanks are specially due to an ever-patient wife who spent many hours at the typewriter and assisted with the indices; to his colleague, the Rev. Norman Green, who kindly read the galley proofs; to Mrs. Harold Bohne of Wycliffe College Library, who never failed to respond to the call for help; and last but not least, to Elisabeth Anne, who made herself responsible for the main index.

— J. J.

Wycliffe College
Toronto

ABBREVIATIONS

AV	Authorized (King James) Version (1611)
BR	*Biblical Research*
CD	Karl Barth, *Church Dogmatics*
CE	*Catholic Encyclopedia*
CJT	*Canadian Journal of Theology*
ET	*Expository Times*
HDCG	Hasting's *Dictionary of Christ and the Gospels*
HUCA	*Hebrew Union College Annual*
IB	*Interpreter's Bible*
JE	*Jewish Encyclopedia*
INTERP	*Interpretation*
JQR	*Jewish Quarterly Review*
NZST	*Neue Zeitschrift für systematische Theologie*
RGG	*Religion in Geschichte und Gegenwart*
RSV	Revised Standard Version (1952)
RV	Revised Version (1881-85)
SJT	*Scottish Journal of Theology*
TDNT	G. Bromiley's translation of *TWNT*
TT	*Theology Today*
TWNT	G. Kittel, ed., *Theologisches Wörterbuch zum Neuen Testament*

CHAPTER ONE:

INTRODUCTION

The problem of finding a unifying principle or concept underlying the diverse material of the Bible has occupied many writers. The present work was undertaken on the presupposition that such a unifying principle is given us in the concept of the covenant. This principle arises naturally from the biblical theme of the divine-human relationship. The basic assumption of the biblical documents, no matter how diverse, seems to be that Israel stands in a peculiar relationship to YHVH his God. The whole concept of election derives from the principle of a covenant relationship between man and God. It is therefore no exaggeration to say that covenantal theology is at the root of biblical thinking.

But once we admit a theological principle behind the biblical documents we have to make room for diversity of expression. "Theology" means engagement on an intellectual plane, and when such a stage is reached the results are never uniform. Man's thought is inevitably conditioned by cultural environment and political and social circumstances. Extraneous influences, the needs of society, the moral milieu, religious convictions and prejudices, and a thousand other contributing factors help to shape theological thought. A basic presupposition, therefore, can be expressed in a variety of ways depending upon circumstances. This is exactly the case with the concept of covenant in the biblical setting. But what is so impressive to the present writer is the fact that behind the obvious diversity of approach, the basic assumption of a covenant relationship persists throughout the whole literature and is never called in doubt.

Though the present writer is not committed to the "source theory" or any other theory that purports to explain wholesale the complexity of the biblical literature, he is indebted to the results of scholarly investigation that are established by facts. One of these facts is the great diversity of outlook we meet in the Old Testament. This raises obvious difficulties in the way of a consistent theological approach. But Walter Eichrodt has shown without violence to the text that the covenant concept is a basic category providing the varied material with an overall pattern. Modern scholarship has tended to overemphasize the diversity and overlook the underlying unity. It may well be that some of the basic assumptions that govern scholarship will have to be rectified in order to do better justice to the ancient texts.

Scholars have been trying to explain the origin of the religion of ancient Israel by relating it to the surrounding cultures of the East. There is no denying that Egyptian and Canaanite influence, and later, Persian and even Greek influence, left their mark upon the religious views of the Hebrew people. But this must not obscure the other fact that the Old Testament bears witness to a gigantic spiritual struggle against foreign influence in any form.

In search for the origins of Hebrew religion, scholars turned to Canaanite society with its hierarchic structure, tribal laws, and priestly lore. They assumed therefore that a similar pattern persisted in primitive Israel. But oddly enough, no aspect of Canaanite society entirely fits the ancient Hebrews. Over against the "cultic prophets" we also meet rebel prophets who stand in opposition to the cult; over against the priestly hierarchy we come upon traditions of a nonpriestly nature; over against the sacrificial system, we meet a simple piety entirely independent of the sacrifices; over against the idea of sacral kingship we also encounter a tribal system organized on democratic lines. These contradictory aspects make it next to impossible to accept a theory of correspondence in the sense that what applies to one ancient community equally applies to another.

The source theory presupposes a wide range of diversity which only by slow degrees and over a long period resulted in a more unified pattern. But at the same time, scholars have fastened upon the idea of cultic kingship as an overall principle to explain the general pattern of the Hebrew cult. To do this, however, they must first succeed in providing proof that our records derive from a very primitive stage of society; that the Hexateuch was left untouched by prophetic influence; that the religious tradition the Hebrews brought with them to Canaan was in no essentials different from the Canaanite cult.

Without entering into detail we take the view (1) that even our most primitive records already bear evidence of a highly developed cultural level. Even patriarchal society cannot be termed primitive in any sense. Be it noted that Abraham himself came from an important cultural center; (2) that the Hexateuch is under strong prophetic influence. The so-called "J" sections in the Pentateuch show a broadness of vision, a high spiritual concept of God, great emphasis upon *ḥesed,* all typical features of the prophetic attitude. Specially the early chapters of Genesis reveal an outlook and spirit much more akin to the book of Jeremiah than to pagan society; (3) that the central story of the Pentateuch, the epic of the flight from Egypt, the covenant at Sinai, the Ten Words, as the covenantal document, all bear testimony to the fact of the utter difference between ancient Israel and the Canaanites in respect to religion.

If these considerations carry any weight, then von Rad's contention that Israel's ancient faith presents a unified system has to be questioned. He says: "The faith of Israel cannot possibly be divided into two forms of religion which are so completely different and so entirely foreign to each other."[1] On this assumption he feels compelled to contradict E. Sellin's position that in addition to the prophetic faith in YHVH there was in existence in ancient Israel a "priestly cult religion." But it seems to us that the whole weight of Old Testament evidence is on the side of Sellin against von Rad. Admittedly, von Rad's view is the more appealing one, for it provides a more ready explanation. It is only a question of whether we submit to the evidence of the text or import principles derived from the history of religion.

---

[1] Gerhard von Rad, *Old Testament Theology,* I (1962), 260.

The Bible, from beginning to end, presents a battlefield of opposing views. For this reason we may rightly call it a *theological* document. To prove our contention we point to an instance by way of an example: according to the sacrificial code, the penalty for deliberate sin is death or excommunication.[2] Von Rad takes the so-called "P" document seriously and constructs a whole theory of the social concept of sin in ancient Israel on the basis of this document.[3] But we would ask: how primitive has society to be in order to punish sinners with such severity? The fact is that Leviticus is *not* a code that was ever enacted under ordinary conditions, but is a purely theological document deriving from a particular priestly school of thought.[4] Sin in this document is certainly conceived in a cultic sense, and in a way it expressed the views of the priestly caste; but to treat it as a legal enactment is a great mistake. The distance between daily life and the Temple cult is too great to be spanned by theological definition. Only on the assumption that society was entirely dominated by the priesthood can the "P" document be taken literally, but this is a point still to be proved.

A somewhat comparable situation is provided by the New Testament. It is widely recognized that early Christianity was hostile to the sacrificial cult. It is enough to mention the speech of St. Stephen (Acts 7) and the letter to the Hebrews to prove the point. Jesus is reported to have spoken against the Temple, and this was the major charge before the Sanhedrin.[5] Here we have an instance when radically opposed views are held by two factions and both claim to be faithful Israelites. There is no reason to suppose that a somewhat similar situation could not develop at an earlier period, especially under conditions of cultural and religious tension when two different traditions clashed head-on.

The assumption that Israel's religious situation can

---

[2] Cf. Norman H. Snaith, *The Distinctive Ideas of the O.T.* (1944), pp. 66f.

[3] *Op. cit.*, p. 258.

[4] Cf. Robert H. Pfeiffer, *The Books of the O.T.* (1967), p. 60: "The Priestly Code is just as dogmatic and detached from reality as the apocalypses." In view of this statement it is more than a surprise to read that these stringent laws were observed literally (*ibid.*, p. 93)!

[5] Cf. J. Jocz, *The Jewish People and Jesus Christ* (1954), pp. 159ff.

be gauged from conditions obtaining among his neighbors must be treated with greatest caution. Without discounting the fact of reciprocal influence we must pay equal attention to the great differences in tradition and outlook. In our approach to the Old Testament we are therefore determined to treat the internal evidence seriously, bearing in mind all the time the "theological" nature of the document. It is impossible to do justice to the Old Testament literature unless full weight is given to the immense ideological conflict that serves as the background.

The writer desires to confess that he is not approaching his subject in "scientific detachment." The more he reads what others have to say, the more he is convinced that no writer is devoid of predilections and prejudices, though he seldom confesses it. He therefore decided to write as a partisan of definite convictions. His thesis is founded upon several basic presuppositions:

(1) that the Bible in most of its sections is first and foremost a theological document.[6] This is to say, it is heavily biased ideologically and on moral and religious issues it is never neutral.[7]

(2) that the Bible is the result of a religious conflict that stretches over centuries. It reflects a battlefield of diametrically opposing views. The major cause of such tension derives from the opposing attitudes of prophet and priest. Expressed in theological language, the Bible bears witness to a dialectical tension resulting from the confrontation between religion and revelation. Here man and God, prophet and priest, law and grace stand in an unresolved challenge to each other.

(3) that from beginning to end biblical theology is founded upon the premise of the covenant. This is the overall pattern that gives substance and meaning to the biblical concept of grace. It is here that we come upon the unifying principle that binds and keeps together this fascinating and widely heterogeneous literature.

---

[6] Cf. Pfeiffer, *op. cit.*, pp. 112ff. For the difference in religious outlook between Israel and his neighbors see Th. C. Vriezen, *The Religion of Ancient Israel*, 1967, pp. 71ff.

[7] W. Macneile Dixon has shown how impossible it is not only for the theologian but also for the scientist to achieve objectivity. Cf. *The Human Situation* (The Gifford Lectures, 1935-37), pp. 13, 17, 21, etc.

No writer who engages in a biblical subject these days can escape the embarrassment of the present situation. On the one hand, as a Christian theologian, especially if within the Protestant tradition, he is tied to Holy Writ. But on the other hand, he is accused of obscurantism if he treats the text seriously, paying scant attention to the conflicting opinion of scholars. But whom is he to believe? If he takes sides he finds himself opposed by the whole weight of opposite opinion; if he refuses to take sides, he is left in the confusion of opposing views. This is a special problem for the systematic theologian today. The disintegration of the authority of the Bible cuts at the root of theological endeavor and reduces theology to metaphysical speculation. The result is that the theologian and the biblical scholar move in opposite directions and are increasingly losing touch with one another.

The chaotic state of biblical studies makes it next to impossible to use the Bible effectively and to interpret the text unequivocally unless the theologian is prepared to make his own decision. Frequently he is pressed to put a construction upon the text which runs contrary to scholarly opinion but which provides meaningful theological content. In such cases he is left with an uneasy conscience until he has worked out a compromise. In one sense such pressure is a wholesome experience in that the theologian is prevented from taking the Word of God for granted. He is forced to reconsider the meaning and the limits of historic revelation. But on the other hand, he is tempted to give way to the *Zeitgeist* and escape the control of Scripture, a fact that leaves him without anchorage.

The dichotomy between biblical scholarship and systematic theology becomes most apparent in the pulpit. Here the difference between the text as preached and the text as handled by critical scholarship is such that no effort of imagination can unite the two: if God speaks in the pulpit and only J, E, P, or D in the study, an ambiguous situation is created that verges upon hypocrisy.

The solution to our problem, it seems to us, is not a choice between theology or scholarship, but a more thorough integration of theology *and* scholarship. This can only come about when scholars will pay more attention to the fact that the Bible is essentially a theological document.

It is a biased document, or a collection of documents, which has one and only one major concern, namely man's relation to God. Unless this premise be granted, the divergence between biblical scholarship and systematic theology cannot be overcome.

The present writer has endeavored to treat biblical scholarship seriously but only on condition that the major premise be respected, namely, that behind the Bible is the speaking God. He therefore reserves for himself the right to listen to dissenting opinion and ultimately draw his own conclusions. His conclusions are not outside and apart from faith but within the context of faith. It means that the writer is first a believer who humbly listens, before he is a scholar who tries to speak. Such a position is dictated to him by his theological commitment. He cannot see how otherwise he can be a theologian who by definition is a confessor before he is a scholar. This explanation will account for the fact that he has had sometimes to make decisions against the prevailing view of scholarship.

A word to the biblical expert may not be amiss. Theologians have patiently listened to the divergent and frequently extravagant views of biblical critics.[8] Is it asking too much that the biblical scholar pay some attention to the theologian? It is not impossible that while listening he may become aware of the Voice he failed to hear while engrossed in the minutia and detail of the text.

Unless the scholar, like the theologian, is able to discern the *other* Voice that is assumed in the text, he will fail to do justice to the text itself. It is at the point when the *other* Voice becomes audible that the scholar ceases to be a critic and becomes a servant in the response of faith. At this point theology and scholarship unite.

---

[8] Cf. *CJT*, Oct. 1967, pp. 225ff. Prof. N. E. Wagner points to "the current chaotic situation" in Pentateuchal studies. The same can be said about most of O.T. studies, as evidenced from H. Ringgren's book, *Israelite Religion*, 1966, trans.

CHAPTER TWO:

THE OLD TESTAMENT CONCEPT OF COVENANT

1. DEFINITION OF COVENANT

In certain scholarly circles it is recognized that there is an important difference between Greek and Hebrew thought-categories. Dom Gregory Dix stresses that while the Greek is concerned with being, the Hebrew concentrates upon action.[1] This difference in basic concern results not only in a difference of approach and attitude but in an important difference of perspective. Some writers look upon the preponderance of Greek influence in the West as over against the Hebrew as an unfortunate mistake;[2] others glory in the synthesis achieved by Western culture within the Judaeo-Christian tradition.[3] Again, some scholars, though acknowledging the difference of approach and thought-forms, yet hold that these two aspects are supplementary and lead to the same results.[4] This is a question-

[1] Dom Gregory Dix, *Jew & Greek*, 1953, pp. 12f, 77ff, etc.

[2] Cf. Claude Tresmontant, *A Study in Hebrew Thought*, 1960.

[3] W. R. Inge, *"Religion" in the Legacy of Greece*, 1921, pp. 28ff. Cf. also P. T. Forsyth, *Christ on Parnassus* (n.d.), pp. 82, 84f, 252f.

[4] Thorlief Boman, *Das Hebräische Denken im Vergleich mit dem Griechischen*, 1952, pp. 166ff. Cf. also Robert D. Crouse, "The Hellenization of Christianity: A Historiographical Study," *CJT*, Jan. 1962, pp. 22ff; also Wm. D. Geoghegan, "Should the Bible be De-Platonized?" *TT*, April 1960, pp. 39ff. For the historical significance of Hellen-

able conclusion. Those who distinguish between the two thought-forms are convinced that if pursued to the end they would yield two divergent theologies. But such a radical revision has never been attempted. It is almost next to impossible to unwind the skein and to separate the Hebrew and the Greek strands that make up Christian theology. All we can do is to go back to the Hebrew Scriptures and to re-emphasize certain aspects that have been toned down as a result of the synthesis.

The difference between the Greek and Hebrew *Weltanschauung* need not lead us to the conclusion that Greek thought is irrelevant and of no consequence. No theologian can blind himself to the fact of the immense Greek contribution to philosophy, science, and logic.[5] The theologian's problem arises at the point where Greek and Hebrew thought-forms diverge. It is at this point that the question of the normative aspect of the Bible springs into prominence. This is the most severe test of theology. The question immediately arises: Is it at all possible to apply the presuppositions of one system to the premises of another?

There is no easy answer to our problem. It must, however, be acknowledged that an undiluted biblicism is not only an impossibility to the Western mind steeped as it is in Greek thought-forms, but also an undesirable undertaking. The Western mind has been molded by the two traditions, the Greek and the Hebrew; and at this stage a disentanglement would mean a complete break with the past. The very fact that dogmatic theology rests upon a propositional basis, even when reduced to a minimum, testifies to the subtle influence of Greek intellectualism.

Not only Christianity, but Judaism itself had to yield to the pervasiveness of Greek influence and reluctantly allow for a credal formulation of its faith.[6] Such a credal

---

ization, see R. D. Crouse, "The Hellenization of Christianity," *CJT*, Jan. 1962, pp. 22ff.

[5] In addition to the *Legacy of Greece*, ed. by R. W. Livingstone, Oxford, 1921, cf. also Philip Leon's article: "The Greek Professors and the Modern Mind," *The Listener*, June 9, 1955. For Greek influence upon Judaism, see *Commentary*, August 1962, pp. 108ff. Cf. also C. H. Dodd, *The Bible and the Greeks*, 1935, pp. 243ff; L. A. Garrard, *Athens or Jerusalem*, 1965.

[6] Max Weber's contention that in the last resort all logico-theological systems of belief demand a "sacrifice of the intellect" may equally

deposit is inevitable if faith is to extend beyond ceremonial observance and emotional appeal. A faith that has never acquired an intellectual content belongs to the realm of superstition, or else is so tied to personal experience as to become incommunicable. Theological endeavor is only possible where coherence and logic are taken seriously. To that extent theology depends upon the Greek tradition.

But the issue is not clearly understood if we are led to assume that philosophy and theology are natural allies and complement each other. The only element they have in common is the human subject, otherwise the two disciplines rest upon different suppositions and are governed by different rules. This becomes apparent when we come to consider the basic biblical category out of which all theological concepts arise. This category is the covenant relationship between God and man. Biblical theology is covenantal theology; all dogmatic theology is determined and governed by this fact. The logic and the method of theology is predetermined by the givenness of the covenant relationship. The covenant, in biblical terms, spells out God's condescension to man; and all theology has to do is to grasp the significance of this fact. No theologian treats his subject seriously unless he pays full attention to this fundamental supposition. But if he does take the biblical concept of covenant seriously, there comes a point when his philosophical premises begin to collide with the odd logic of biblical revelation.

Our task is to examine the biblical aspect of covenant and to show how it forms the underlying presupposition of all aspects of Christian theology.

a. The Problem of Unity in the Bible

There was a time when the Bible was treated as a monolithic structure. With the advance of biblical criticism the idea of unity in which every part of the Bible fitted and supplemented every other part, fell into disrepute.

---

well apply to all set systems of thought (cf. Max Weber, *Ancient Judaism*, with introduction by Hans Gerth and Don Martindale, 1952, p. XIII). For the revival of theological interest in Judaism, see Eugene B. Borowitz, "The Jewish Need for Theology," *Commentary*, Aug. 1962; also Jakob J. Petuchowski, "Faith as the Leap of Action," *Commentary*, 1958; also Joseph H. Gumbiner, "Revelation and Liberal Jewish Faith," *Judaism*, Spring, 1961. For Jewish Creeds see *Jewish Encyclopedia*, 1905.

Scholars went out of their way to prove how ill assorted was the material, especially of the Old Testament. In the end it became impossible even to contemplate a coherent Old Testament theology, unless a scholar was prepared to jeopardize his reputation. At best he could confine himself to the exegesis of a single document always bearing in mind its isolated position. As one writer put it: "The task of Old Testament theology is not primarily the writing of books which will hope to come as near as possible to expressing this consensus (i.e. of a unifying principle in the O.T.). It is primarily an exegetical science and its reference is no narrower than the totality of the text to be interpreted."[7]

It was therefore a memorable event in the theological world when a scholar of Walter Eichrodt's stature published the first volume of his *Theologie des Alten Testaments* in 1933. James L. Mays in reviewing the English translation made the following remark: "Its production and influence broke the long dry spell in O.T. theology which reached from the beginning of our century into the thirties."[8] Prof. Eichrodt has shown the way of a new approach to the Old Testament and recovered for us an underlying theme in the covenant that gives unity to the great variety of texts. Prof. H. H. Rowley acknowledges the importance of the covenant in ancient Israel: "Mosaic religion was (therefore) a religion of the Covenant grounded in the prior election and deliverance of God."[9] But, unfortunately, he does not draw the ultimate consequences from the above statement. It is important, however, to notice that Rowley admits that there is in the Old Testament "a remarkable unity about its teaching"; that it carries a common message; and that the framework is governed by a common pattern. Against this stands the authority of Gerhard von Rad who denies a common denomination and sharply distinguishes between the various professions of Yahvistic faith.[10] But even he admits: "the belief that Jahweh took Israel as his

[7] James Barr, "The Problem of O.T. Theology and the History of Religion," *CJT*, July 1957, pp. 148f.

[8] *TT*, Oct. 1962, p. 430.

[9] H. H. Rowley in his *Unity of the Bible*, London, 1953 (W. T. Whiteley Lectures for 1951/52), p. 27.

[10] Cf. Gerhard von Rad, *Old Testament Theology*, 1962 trans., I, 115ff, 124ff.

own peculiar people is, of course, very old."[11] After careful reflection we have decided to take our stand with Eichrodt against von Rad. Our reasons are theological: the covenant provides us with a principle that covers both Testaments and provides an inner unity to an otherwise wide diversity of views. We repudiate J. N. Schofield's criticism that Eichrodt appeals to a "static" unity whereas he himself prefers a unity through "action and interaction,"[12] as if the covenant relationship can be understood as anything but a living relationship between God and man.

b. THE COVENANT IN ANCIENT CUSTOM

The idea that the covenant tradition was a later invention is now dismissed by most scholars. It is assumed, however, that the concept of a covenant with God derives from the sociological structure of ancient society, which was amphictyonically constituted. Tribal life depended upon the co-operation within the related groups and tribal leagues came about under political pressure. George E. Mendenhall has shown that such co-operation was customary "long before the time of Moses." He notes, however, the sudden growth of Israel, originally "a small religious group of clansmen," which soon developed into a formidable organization. Such a phenomenon cannot be explained by natural reproduction. Mendenhall therefore suggests that the religious community of the ancient Hebrews was joined by extraneous groups who preferred the social and political system of Mosaic law to that of pagan society. Such a confederation of tribes would be based upon a solemn covenant agreement. These covenantal pacts would be rooted in Mosaic religion, which was the "foundation of all tribal organization,"[13] as far as Israel was concerned. The covenantal pact was widely practiced in the ancient world and carried religious implications. In the case of Israel it meant submission to the overlordship of YHVH and acceptance of Mosaic law. Mendenhall makes the interesting suggestion that the replacement of the covenant bond by that of blood relationship is a later development that points to the loosen-

---

[11] *Ibid.*, I, 178.

[12] J. N. Schofield in *The Modern Churchman*, April 1962, pp. 240f.

[13] George E. Mendenhall, "Biblical History in Transition," in *The Bible and the Ancient Near East*, Essays in honor of Wm. Foxwell Albright, 1961, pp. 43f.

ing of religious ties. Originally, political confederations were founded upon religious loyalties rather than biological kinship.

The custom of forming a covenant on the basis of a solemn oath is as old as history. A *coniuratio* or oathbound league is mentioned in the Amarna letters. Max Weber provides the following explanation: "In Antiquity every political alliance, in fact almost every private contract was normally confirmed by an oath, i.e. the curse of self. . . . Above all, Israel itself as a political community was conceived as an oathbound confederation."[14]

We have the testimony of Gerhard von Rad, who compared the ancient Hebrew custom with other Near Eastern treaties; he concludes that there is a remarkable similarity between them.[15] It is therefore obvious that the religious motif and the social custom are closely connected. At the same time there are aspects of the biblical concept of the covenant relationship between God and Israel that require special elucidation. Von Rad readily admits that the "history of the conception of the covenant" is a very involved one and that there is considerable divergence of opinion among scholars on the subject.[16] We will have opportunity to see something of the complexity of the problem as we proceed.

c. THE COVENANT AND MOSAIC LAW

Whatever conclusions we may reach with regard to the place of covenantal pacts in the ancient East, it appears that the Old Testament concept of the covenant relationship does not seem to cover the general picture satisfactorily. The reason for the discrepancy, as we see it, seems to lie in the peculiar biblical concept about God.

Mendenhall's approach to the covenant is based on an assumed analogy between "the suzerainty treaty by which a great king bound his vassals to faithfulness and obedience to himself,"[17] and YHVH's dealing with Israel.

---

[14] Max Weber, *Ancient Judaism*, 1952 trans., p. 75.

[15] *Op. cit.*, I, 132 and notes. Von Rad specifies the items that make up the formal legal document and quotes the appropriate literature.

[16] *Ibid.*, p. 133.

[17] George E. Mendenhall, *Law & Covenant in Israel & the Ancient Near East*, The Biblical Colloquium, Pittsburgh, Penna., 1955, p. 20. For criticism of Mendenhall's view see Th. C. Vriezen, *op. cit.*, 1967, pp. 145f.

But on Dr. Mendenhall's own admission the analogy does not always fit. In the case of the Abrahamic covenant, for instance, "no obligations are imposed upon Abraham," whereas the whole idea of covenant in the ancient setting presupposes reciprocal obligations. Genesis 17:2ff makes no demands upon Abraham whatsoever though it abounds in promises. This is an odd situation, which is puzzling to Old Testament scholars.[18] But the fact remains that according to the text the Abrahamic covenant is absolutely conditionless. As far as we know this is a unique situation and has no parallel in custom either in ancient Israel or the Near East. Within the political setting of ancient society a conditionless covenant is meaningless. We come here upon an aspect of the biblical covenant relationship that demands not a sociological but rather a theological explanation.

Mendenhall explicitly contradicts Wellhausen's position that the Bible assumes a "natural" relationship between Israel and YHVH so that "there was no interval between Him and His people to call for or question."[19] On the contrary, modern scholars are convinced that the covenant relationship between YHVH and Israel was anything but conditionless. There were definite obligations on both sides.[20] The Sinaitic covenant is explicit on this score: "Now therefore, if you will obey my voice and keep my commandment, you shall be my own possession among all peoples..." (Exod. 19:5). Obedience to God's will is here the *sine qua non* condition of the covenant relationship. This, of course, solves a difficult moral problem, namely the question of election. There is no favoritism with God;[21] God only elects

---

[18] My friend and colleague R. K. Harrison assumes, as a matter of course, that reciprocity is implied and makes the promises conditional upon "undivided allegiance and worship," but there is no warrant for it in the text (cf. R. K. Harrison, *A History of O. T. Times*, 1955, p. 67).

[19] Quoted by Mendenhall from the *Prolegomena to the History of Israel*, 1885, pp. 24, 417.

[20] Cf. Mendenhall, *The Bible and the Ancient Near East*, p. 47; R. E. Clements, *Prophecy & the Covenant*, 1965, where the covenant is understood to be conditional throughout. But Clements lapses from a consistent position when he suddenly states that "obedience was not the presupposition of the covenant, but its consequence" (p. 74). This statement ill accords with his general view that a covenant has always a condition attached to it.

[21] Cf. G. Ernest Wright, "The Faith of Israel," *IB*, I, 353b.

those who deserve it. Prof. Rowley quotes C. H. Dodd to the effect that God's covenant is a *diatheke*, and not a *syntheke;* that is to say, God fixes the terms of the covenant and offers it to man that he may accept it: the acceptance is also essential.[22] But this is not the whole story. There is another side to election that is determined by the concept of grace, where the covenant assumes a different aspect and makes election independent of desert or merit.

d. The conditionless covenant

Once we allow the theological aspect to determine the meaning of the text we are forced to see the concept of the covenant in conjunction with the biblical concept of God. These two aspects are interrelated in such a way that they cannot be treated separately. The sociological approach to the covenant, helpful as it is, ceases to suffice at the point where the specific biblical understanding of God comes into play.

Scholars usually regard the decalogue as the document *par excellence* of the Sinaitic covenant; von Rad attaches great importance to this text. He says: "There can be no doubt that it is the proclamation of the Decalogue over her which puts Israel's election into effect."[23] Let us then consider the conditions that attach to the Sinaitic covenant.

The decalogue, be it noted, is a strictly ethical document. Von Rad finds the fact that it is completely devoid of a cultic note difficult to explain. He falls back upon the naive suggestion that the Ten Words were addressed to the laity "with reference to their everyday affairs," hence the noncultic character.[24] It would be wrong, he thinks, to conclude from the Ten Commandments that Moses was the founder of a noncultic religion. If, however, we are prepared to accept the more complicated reasoning of Martin Noth we find ourselves in a completely different position.

Noth suspects that the revelation at Sinai goes back to an older tradition than the story of the Exodus. Only

---

[22] H. H. Rowley, *The O. T. Interpretation of History*, 1946, p. 47, note 1. This is a typically Jewish understanding of election and found classical expression in the talmudic story that God offered the *torah* to the nations, but they refused it because of the Ten Commandments; Israel, however, accepted (cf. C. G. Montefiore and H. Loewe, *A Rabbinic Anthology*, 1938, p. 78).

[23] *Op. cit.*, I, 192.

[24] *Ibid.*, p. 193.

at a later stage were these two traditions conjoined. He thinks that the older tradition of the covenant at Mount Sinai became gradually superseded by the more recent tradition of the Exodus: the covenant tradition was thus pushed in the background as the Exodus tradition took its place. Noth explains that the reason for this is due to the fact that not all the tribes were involved in the flight from Egypt. This would explain the reason why the tradition regarding the revelation at Sinai remained undeveloped while the Exodus story is so much in prominence. After considering all the facts Noth concludes that "Israel's community consciousness is much older than the origins of the Pentateuchal tradition and presupposes it."[25]

The change of emphasis that placed the covenant in the general theme of the Exodus and the occupation of the Promised Land, thus reducing it to a mere episode, is difficult to explain. Noth thinks, however, that the unity underlying the Pentateuch tradition is somehow connected with the cultic profession: "Yahwe, who brought Israel out of Egypt." This, however, does not explain the puzzling question: "What brought about the unity of Israel, and Israel's community consciousness?"[26]

It may well be that Martin Noth managed to penetrate beyond the secondary tradition of the Exodus, and hit upon an *"Urdatum"* that precedes the cultic tradition of the covenant.[27] If Noth is right, such a discovery of a primary tradition would confirm the view of those scholars who still hold that the earliest Hebrew faith was noncultic.[28] This view is confirmed by Prof. Mendenhall, who has grave doubts about the present tendency among Old Testament scholars to overemphasize the importance of the cult. To quote his own words: "There is certainly little justification for the idea that early Israelite religion consisted primarily

---

[25] Martin Noth, *Überlieferungsgeschichte des Pentateuchs*, Stuttgart, 1948, p. 274.

[26] *Ibid.*, p. 279.

[27] *Ibid.*, p. 273.

[28] Cf. J. Jocz, *The Spiritual History of Israel*, 1961, pp. 86f. If Albright is right about Samuel's attitude to the cultic sacrifices, as no doubt he is, then Samuel constitutes an important bridge between the faith of the ancient Hebrews and the later O. T. prophets; cf. Wm. F. Albright, "Samuel and the Beginnings of the Prophetic Movement," the Goldenson Lecture for 1961 (Hebrew Union College Press, Cincinnati), p. 17.

of sacrifice or other cultic acts."[29] In view of the fact that religion dominated the life and attitude of most communities in the ancient world, we may well ask: If not the cult, what else constituted the center of ancient Hebrew religion? It seems to us that the problem of the covenant is linked to this question.[30]

It is important for us to take notice of the fact that cultic and moral aspects of religion do not easily coalesce. Once the covenant relationship is interpreted in cultic terms, the moral element inevitably takes a secondary place.[31] We know both from experience and history that the sacral-magical approach to God results in a toning down of ethical demands. But because the God of Israel was primarily conceived in moral terms the conditions of the covenant are therefore set forth in the form of moral obligations. Neither Mendenhall's explanation that the priests had little to do with judicial procedures nor von Rad's that the decalogue was primarily addressed to "laymen" is convincing.[32] According to the context, the Ten Words are addressed to a "kingdom of priests and a holy nation" (Exod. 19:6). Chapter 19 is the obvious preamble to chapter 20. The decalogue is addressed to the whole nation and the condition is the same for priests and people: "if you will obey my voice and keep my covenant." Here is a definite condition laid down for the covenant relationship, and on the basis of the Sinai tradition we would have to conclude that the covenant is conditional. But there still remains the puzzling fact that the Abrahamic covenant is different.

Aage Bentzen takes the view that every covenant car-

---

[29] George E. Mendenhall, *Law & Covenant in Israel*, 1955, p. 15.

[30] Johann Jakob Stamm, *Der Dekalog im Lichte der Neueren Forschung*, 1962, tries to cope with the fact of the complete lack of cultic reference in Exod. 20. He arrives at the complicated result that Exod. 20 is older than Deut. 5, but Deut. 5 is more original than Exod. 20 as we have it now (cf. p. 9f).

[31] Clements appears to assume a straightforward connection between the cult and the decalogue and refers to Mowinckel and others who take this view (cf. *op. cit.*, pp. 73ff). In reference to Mowinckel, Stamm regards the connection cult and decalogue as "endgültig bewiesen" (*op. cit.*, p. 21), but we are still unconvinced.

[32] This seems to us a more adequate explanation than Mendenhall's, which holds that the "secular nature of the Covenant Code" (i.e. the Ten Commandments) is due to the fact that the "religious personnel" played no important part in judicial procedure. This is quite an unwarranted assumption. Cf. *op. cit.*, p. 15; von Rad, *op. cit.*, p. 193.

ries legal significance. This view is held by most scholars. It is based on the prevailing custom in ancient society. But once we admit a "theological motive" in the Pentateuch as Bentzen does,[33] we cannot avoid the further conclusion, namely that the covenant relationship is determined not by legal custom but by theological presupposition. This does not mean that we need discount ethnic custom altogether, and only allow for modification when theology and custom diverge. It means that we must make allowance for what von Rad calls the "third dimension"[34] and interpret the text on its own merit.

We are inclined to the view that the idea of a conditionless covenant is an *innovation* and is of prophetic provenance. Behind it is the supposition of the utter faithfulness of the God of Israel. An outstanding example of the modification that has taken place under prophetic influence in the understanding of God's character is the text in Exodus 34:6f. Here God is both merciful, gracious, slow to anger, abounding in covenant love and faithfulness, but also punishing transgression and sin and visiting the iniquity of the fathers upon the children. The compromise between mercy and judgment must be understood in a parainetic context — this is more a sermon than a legal statement.[35] The question arises, What happens when Israel breaks his promises and becomes faithless to the covenant? Does God cease to be Israel's God? This is the problem that the prophets had to puzzle out. It is at this point that the analogy between the despot and his subject breaks down, for YHVH remains the God of the covenant even in the face of Israel's faithlessness.

According to the legal understanding of the covenant relationship the two parties in question enter upon a contract of mutual obligation: the king offers protection, the

[33] *Op. cit.*, p. 193. Cf. Aage Bentzen, *Introduction to the O. T.*, 1948, II, 78.

[34] G. von Rad, *Das Formgeschichtliche Problem des Hexateuchs*, 1938, p. 72.

text on its own merit.

[35] Clements finds it difficult to reconcile the contradictory attitude, especially on the part of the prophets, where grace and judgment alternate (cf. *op. cit.*, p. 50), but he overlooks the exhortatory nature of prophetic speech. For the prophetic position in respect to covenant see D. N. Freedman, "Divine Commitment & Human Obligation," *Interp*, Oct. 1964, p. 430.

subject offers loyal service. Pedersen points out that the inequality between the partners of the compact is almost always assumed: "In reality," he says, "the covenant rarely contains full equality. Within the community of the family, it is the man to whom the others subordinate themselves, and within the community where peace reigns, it is the chief to whom they submit. And when the two parties unite in covenant, the one will generally be a greater giver than the other. The covenant is always a psychic community, but within it everybody must give and take as much as he can."[36]

What happens, however, when the weaker party fails in its fealty? To this Pedersen's reply is: "Friend wholly, or enemy wholly, this is the moral law of the ancients." To substantiate the verdict Pedersen points to II Kings 10:12-14, the account of Jehu's merciless dealing with the kinsmen of Ahaziah. But does YHVH ever so deal with Israel as Jehu dealt with his enemies?

A crucial case is Israel's involvement in the worship of the golden calf in the wilderness. Here is an instance of a clear breach of loyalty. Yet despite Israel's faithlessness, YHVH remains His people's protector and guide. This is the theological motif behind Exodus 32 and 33.

Some scholars maintain that there was the practice of an annual renewal of the covenant in which the decalogue played an important part.[37] Such a festival of renewal by its very nature presupposes God's willingness to be reconciled and to forgive all expressions of the people's disloyalty. The act of renewal related to the original covenant at Mount Sinai and was a reaffirmation of loyalty to the God of the fathers.[38] The assumption that God is readily propitiated and exercises mercy rather than judgment is another instance where the analogy of the covenantal relationship between ruler and subject breaks down. The principle of reciprocity on a legal basis cannot easily be maintained within the biblical context, though perhaps sometimes it comes near it. Pedersen's statement that "Yahweh occu-

---

[36] Johs. Pedersen, *Israel*, 1926 trans., I-II, 294.

[37] "The Decalogue formed the mid-point and climax of a very solemn event, namely, the festival of the renewal of the covenant at Shechem ..." (von Rad, I, 192).

[38] Cf. Noth, *op. cit.*, p. 65; also W. Harrelson: "Covenant Renewal Ceremony in Joshua 24" ("Worship in Early Israel," *BR*, III, 1-14, 1958).

pied the same position in the covenant as the king in the western Asiatic communities,"[39] is an oversimplification of the case. Sometimes, it would appear, YHVH occupies the position of a tribal chief or national savior; but this is only a peripheral view. The more prevalent attitude, expressed in Hebrew piety, is that "He does not deal with us according to our sins, nor requite us according to our iniquity" (Ps. 103:10). The unconditional aspect of the covenant therefore is as indigenous to the Old Testament as is the conditional one.[40]

We have mentioned the unconditional aspect of covenant relationship in the case of Abraham. But this is not the only instance of such a covenant in the Old Testament. Surprisingly, a similar situation obtains in the case of Noah: God makes a promise, institutes the rainbow as a token of that promise, but requires nothing in return. The same can be said about the messianic renewal of the covenant that God initiates according to Jeremiah 31:31. Here YHVH binds Himself to deal mercifully with His people on no other basis than His own faithfulness: "for I forgive their iniquity and will remember their sin no more" (Jer. 31:34). In direct contradiction to the prevalent view, Martin Buber has contended with impressive plausibility that "the original meaning of *berith* is not 'contract' or 'agreement'; that is, no conditions were originally stipulated therein, nor did any require to be stipulated."[41] A similar view is taken by Prof. Norman H. Snaith.[42]

Martin Buber sees in the "Book of the Covenant" not a legal document that expresses conditions of agreement, but rather a royal manifesto. By this Buber means to say that this document does not lay down the conditions for reciprocal obligations but rather the rule of life for those *already* under the covenant. We encounter a similar situation in the case of the Sermon on the Mount: Matthew chapters 5 to 7 are not the conditions of discipleship but the messianic

[39] Pedersen, *op. cit.*, p. 612.

[40] It seems to us that Clements grossly overstates his case when he interprets Amos' message in the radical sense that God is breaking off His covenant relationship by reason of Israel's failure (cf. *op. cit.*, pp. 40ff, 50, 69).

[41] Martin Buber, *Moses*, 1946 trans., p. 103. For the opposite view see W. Eichrodt, "Covenant & Law," *Interp*, July 1966, pp. 320ff.

[42] Cf. *The Distinctive Ideas of the O. T.*, 1944, pp. 135ff.

manifesto that the disciple of Jesus would accept as his rule of life.

In ancient society the covenantal relationship took on a variety of forms, depending upon circumstances. Sometimes an alliance between two people would be formed on the ordinary human level, as in the case of David and Jonathan. Buber calls it a "covenant of brotherhood." Again, there could be the contractual relationship between a person in power and a group of subordinates, as in the case of David and the elders of the Northern tribes (II Sam. 5:3). Buber describes this as the "royal covenant."[43] God's covenant with Israel is more like the second and utterly unlike the first. But the likeness is only superficial. David did not debase his majesty by entering into a covenant relationship with the Northern tribes; on the contrary, he enhanced it. In the case with God and Israel the situation is reversed: God humbles Himself to Israel's level to dwell in his midst.

Had Max Weber been more of a theologian he would have avoided the contradiction in which he found himself: on the one hand he holds that "the confederate people had chosen him (i.e. YHVH) through *berith* with him, just as later, it established its king by *berith*"; but on the other hand he affirms that the choice was action on God's part and was a one-sided pledge offered as a mark of privilege. This, he thinks, was at any rate the attitude of the priestly code (P) as instanced in the case of Noah, Abraham, and Phinehas (cf. Num. 25:12). In all these instances God's promises were conditionless.[44] It seems to us that Weber's namesake, Otto Weber, is nearer to the more general biblical position when he affirms that the covenant in the Old Testament setting is "essentially determined by one side" and that it is God who acts as initiator. It is therefore not a "contract" in the usual sense, "implying two partners, but an arrangement made solely by the one who determines it."[45]

At a later stage of our discussion it will become appar-

[43] *Moses*, p. 103; cf. Max Weber, *op. cit.*, p. 441 and notes. Weber speaks of a *foedus iniquum* and *foedus aequum*. Cf. also Walter Harrelson, *Interpreting the Old Testament*, 1964, p. 329.

[44] Cf. Max Weber, *op. cit.*, p. 130.

[45] Otto Weber, *Ground Plan of the Bible*, 1959 trans., p. 25. Cf. also J. G. Harris, "The Covenant Concept Among the Qumran Sectaries," *Evangelical Quarterly*, April - June, 1967, pp. 86ff.

ent how the one-sided nature of the covenant relationship is decisive for a theological understanding of the Bible.

2. COVENANTAL HISTORY

Much if not all of biblical theology is grounded upon the covenantal relationship between God and His people. In fact, the Bible is best viewed as the history of the covenant, or covenants. The question of the historicity of the covenantal experience is a matter of dispute. Martin Buber insists upon the objective historic aspect of the Sinaitic covenant.[46] Johs. Pedersen on the other hand doubts "whether we can take for granted such an uncorrupted tradition from the wilderness period in a cult communication in the Pentateuch. . . ."[47] But in either case the theological aspect is not vitally affected, for what matters here is the theology based upon a supposition that God condescends toward man in the promise of grace.

Within the Old Testament tradition there is a record of a series of covenants. The question arises whether these covenants are to be viewed in separation as special acts on the part of God, or whether these are only manifestations of a general principle in God's dealing with man. The answer to this question will determine the meaning of election and the relationship of Israel to the rest of mankind.

Martin Buber showed great insight into the intricacy of biblical thought when he decided for a primary covenant relationship that determines and precedes the Sinaitic covenant. Moses, he tells us, is not the initiator of the covenant at Mount Sinai but enters only into an already established covenantal tradition. The Sinaitic covenant is not an innovation, an *ab initio* attempt for a *modus vivendi* between a tribe and its god, but rather a reaffirmation of an already existing relationship.[48] Martin Buber rightly points to the case of Joshua by way of example: Joshua "did not establish a new covenant but renewed the one which was in existence between Israel and YHVH, just as it was repeatedly renewed during the ensuing period after having been seriously broken, in accordance with the practice of the Ancient

---

[46] Cf. M. Buber, *Königtum Gottes*, 1932.

[47] Pedersen, *op. cit.*, III-IV, 677 (note to p. 85).

[48] Martin Buber, *Moses*, p. 103: "YHVH & Israel enter into a new relation to one another by making the covenant, a relation which had previously been in existence."

Orient, where a covenant entered into with a God always admitted of renewal."[49]

What happened at Sinai was a confrontation with the "God of the fathers," who reaffirmed His promises given to the patriarchs. Moses does not introduce a new God whose name is YHVH, but the God of Abraham, Isaac, and Jacob (Exod. 2:15), who as an act of special intimacy reveals His Name.

If Buber's assumption is acceptable — and there is much to support it — it appears that the concept of covenant that intends to formalize a theology based upon the principle of God's gracious condescension toward man, is older than the tradition of the Pentateuch itself. The book of Genesis may well embody a concept of covenant that is uniquely biblical and differs radically from the legal concept in terms of reciprocal obligations. We have therefore every right to assume that there is a history of development behind the theological concept of covenant and that the line of development was determined at least to some extent by sociological and political factors. There are vestiges of a primitive view of covenant which express the intimacy of patriarchal society and which is quite different from the later monarchical relationship between overlord and subject. The classical example is Exodus 24:9-11, which North regards as the most primitive expression of the concept of covenant:[50] Moses, Aaron, Nadab, Abihu, and the Seventy Elders ascend the Mount to eat and drink in the presence of God. YHVH is here very close to His people in condescension and love. The intimacy of the relationship is akin to the piety of the Psalter and the spirit of the prophets, but the tradition itself is much older and goes back to the very beginning of YHVH worship.

Though the main attention of the covenant relationship is focussed upon Israel we must not overlook the more universalist aspect, of which traces have survived in the Pentateuch. There is the fact of the Noachidic covenant to which the Rabbis have paid considerable attention.[51] Here not only Noah and his descendants but "every living creature," birds, cattle, beasts, and reptiles, indeed, the

---

[49] *Ibid.*, p. 113; cf. also p. 203 and II Kings 23:3.

[50] C. R. North, *The O. T. Interpretation of History*, 1946, p. 30.

[51] Cf. *Midrash Gen. R.* to 8:17; also J. H. Hertz, *Commentary to Pentateuch*, 1938, p. 33.

earth itself, is included in the covenant promise: "never again shall there be a flood to destroy the earth" (Gen. 9: 11).[52] It is obvious that for the writer of Genesis world history is covenantal history. The spirit behind the Noachidic covenant brings us close to the attitude of the prophets.

For most of the writing prophets the nations surrounding Israel constituted a problem and a challenge. Because YHVH was not just a national God but Creator of heaven and earth, the *benēy nēkar*, the "foreigners," were somehow part of God's purpose and had to be brought under His dominion. The prophetic hope that the nations will "join themselves to the Lord" and that God's house will become "the house of prayer for all peoples" (Isa. 56:6f) was the logical inference of the claim that YHVH only is God. The logic of monotheism demanded the inclusion of the Gentiles under God's providence. Even Egypt, the archenemy of Israel, could therefore be designated as "God's people," and Assyria "his handiwork" (Isa. 19:25). Israel's task, as the prophets saw it, was to tell the nations that "YHVH reigns"; therefore "let the earth be glad and the many islands rejoice" (Ps. 97:1). That God's reign over His whole creation is the expression of His providential love is the natural conclusion for the psalmist, brought up in the tradition of covenantal grace. When the psalmist says that the young lion seeks his food from the hands of God (Ps. 104:4) and that the young raven cries to Him when hungry (Ps. 147:9), he gives expression to his belief that the whole creation is under the care of Almighty God. Providence is here not a detached, impersonal principle, but the expression of personal oversight over all God's creatures. It is He "who gives food to all flesh," says the psalmist (Ps. 136:25); "He gives and they gather; He opens His hand and they are all well satisfied" (Ps. 104: 27). In this His care for His creatures, He reveals Himself as the covenant-keeping God "who keeps faith for ever" (Ps. 146:6). The Hebrew: *shomēr 'emeth leʿolām,* lit.:

---

[52] Cf. G. von Rad, *Genesis*, 1956 trans., pp. 129f; cf. also Jakob J. Finkelstein, "Bible and Babel," *Commentary*, Nov. 1958, p. 442. Occasionally even Adam is conceived as a strictly Hebrew person (cf. David Hoffmann, *Judaism*, Fall, 1958, p. 302 n. 2). This derives from the fact that so much of Jewish Theology is "Jewishology" (cf. *ibid.*, p. 305).

"keeper of eternal faithfulness," is even more expressive: He is the One who remains faithful forever. This is the finest definition of what the Bible means by covenant loyalty. *'Emeth* is here not truth in the Greek sense, but faithfulness, which can only be circumscribed by the elusive Hebrew term *ḥesed.* God is described as *rab ḥesed we-'emeth:* "great in mercy and faithfulness" (Exod. 34:6). Israel's history, as the Bible sees it, is the expression of YHVH's covenant loyalty to His people. All the incidents in Israel's history, both good and ill, are demonstrations of God's goodwill. All Israel's blessings and privileges derive from God's covenantal promises: underneath God's people are "the everlasting arms" (Deut. 33:27).

a. "NATURAL" LAW

Some scholars seem to think of Mosaic law as the codification of the priestly cult. But even a casual reader will notice the strange intermixing between Levitical rules and moral principles that indicates more than a purely cultic concern. It is the moral side of the *torah* that takes Israel's faith outside the tribal context and gives it universal application. In the area of inter-human relations the difference between Israel and the Gentiles shrinks to a minimum. If Eichrodt is right in his exegesis of Deuteronomy 4:13, 23, then the basis of the covenant, at least for the writer of Deuteronomy, is to be seen in the Ten Words with all their moral implications.[53] It would seem that the *hukkîm, mitsvoth* and *mishpatim* in this context refer to the Ten Commandments rather than the cultus.[54] If this is the case there is even a broader base for the covenant than the purely inter-human relationship. Here fields, seeds, and animals, as well as man, are taken into the area of God's protective care. Certain acts are prohibited because they are understood as a violation of God's ordering of the universe. The curious prohibition of *sha'atnēz* (mixing, weaving) is probably connected with this sentiment. The law that forbids the platting of different kinds of threads, the interbreeding of different species, and the mixing of different seeds is not necessarily a ceremonial or cultic law,

---

[53] Cf. also I Kings 8:21 where the Ark is synonymous with the covenant.

[54] Cf. Walter Eichrodt, *op. cit.*, I, 54.

but may equally be a moral law.[55] As such it would not only apply to Israelites but it would have universal application. There are many such aspects of "natural" law in the Old Testament that apply to man in general. A case in point is the conjugal law of marriage: Genesis 2:23f presupposes a union between a man and woman that runs contrary to polygamistic society of the ancient world. This cohesion of husband and wife so that they become one flesh is such a novel aspect of the marriage union that R. H. Kennett has tried to interpret it to mean adoption of one partner into the tribe of another. But this is hardly the case, for intertribal marriage would be a rarity rather than the rule. Kennett himself admits that in Genesis 2:24 we have "more primitive strata ... of which there is no evidence at a later date."[56] Prof. Driver's understanding of the passage comes nearer to the intention of the text: "marriage — and moreover monogamistic marriage, — is thus explained as the direct consequence of a relationship established by the Creator."[57] Man and woman were originally one and therefore belong to each other. The attachment between them is even closer than that of mother to child. This is understood as a "natural" law and goes back to the beginning of creation. It therefore holds good for all mankind and not only for Israel. Kennett's conclusion may be well founded that polygamistic practice entered Israelitic society at a later stage and that we have in this law the *mores* of a primitive and less sophisticated community.

We can see now that the Rabbis continued within an old tradition when they set themselves the task to work out the *mitsvoth beneȳ Noaḥ* (Noachidic laws): "The Jews could no more conceive a world in the past without a revelation of God's will for man's life than in the present and the future. Accordingly they believed that certain laws for all mankind were given to Adam."[58]

In order to find the necessary text the Rabbis resorted to some exegetical ingenuity in their effort to deduce the Adamitic laws, six in all. In the case of Noah they had no

[55] Cf. J. Jocz, *The Spiritual History of Israel*, pp. 78f. J. M. Powis Smith is unable to find any reason behind these laws (*The Origin & History of Hebrew Law*, 1960, p. 63).

[56] R. H. Kennett, *Ancient Hebrew Social Life & Custom*, 1933, p. 19.

[57] R. S. Driver, *The Book of Genesis*, 1909, p. 43.

[58] G. F. Moore, *Judaism*, 1927, I, 274.

less difficulty. The text in Genesis 9 refers only to a single prohibition, that of shedding blood; or perhaps to two: shedding and eating of blood. But with the help of some textual wrangling they managed to distill seven moral laws that form the minimum of basic human behavior.[59]

There would be no justification for the prophets to pronounce judgment upon the nations had there been no conviction that a common moral law underlies all of humanity. In this connection G. F. Moore's remark is most pertinent: "In the Bible it is affirmed, or consistently assumed, that God has taught men what is right and what is wrong, set before them consequences of the alternatives, and left them to choose between them."[60] When Amos denounces the sins of Damascus, the transgressions of Gaza, Tyre, and Edom as he does of Judah and Israel, he assumes that the laws of equity and justice are as applicable to the nations as they are to Israel (cf. Amos 1 and 2).

A basic moral law is embedded in the universe and governs all life. It is the tragedy of man that because of his special position he is able to pervert that law and thus fall below the instinctive behavior of the animal. "The ox knows his owner and the ass his master's crib," but Israel does not know his Creator, is Isaiah's lament (Isa. 1:3). The prophet Jeremiah makes a similar comparison: "Even the stork in the heavens knows her time; and the turtledove, swallow and crane keep the time of their coming — but my people know not the ordinance of the Lord" (Jer. 8:7).

We have described this basic law of life as "natural" law but we do so with some caution. "Natural law" is more a Greek than a biblical concept. The Bible understands the implanted laws within creation not mechanically as if they were the results of impersonal principle. The basic law that governs all existence is of a personal and covenantal nature; it expresses God's eternal faithfulness to His creation. It is a mark of His covenant loyalty that God's creatures are endowed with instincts that make for the preservation of life. His protective hand covers both man and beast: the covenant is "between God and every living creature of all flesh that is upon the earth" (Gen. 8:16). In Eichrodt's view the rainbow serves as a sign of "Yahweh's everlasting

---

[59] J. Jocz, *The Jewish People & Jesus Christ*, p. 69 & references.
[60] *Op. cit.*, p. 453.

grace towards the Gentiles. . . ."[61] In this wider context theologians rightly speak of common or universal grace.

b. THE TORAH

In the rabbinic understanding of the situation Mosaic law in its detail puts only Israel but not the Gentiles under obligation. According to a talmudic fable the *torah* was offered to the Gentiles before it was offered to the Israelites. But the Gentiles rejected the offer, whereas Israel accepted it.[62] The purpose of the story is not so much to indict the nations as to extol Israel's merit. As far as the Gentiles are concerned the basic moral laws were known to them and therefore sufficient. The Rabbis held that the *torah* was of a supererogatory nature to mark Israel as a special people but at the same time the righteous of the Gentiles will have a share in the world to come.[63]

Israel, as God's special people *('am segullāh)* was put under additional obligation as a privilege. The Rabbis made much of the text: "I have separated you from the nations, that you should be mine" (Lev. 20:26). C. G. Montefiore comments on the rabbinic attitude as follows: "Israel is a holy nation, severed from the others to be holy and pure and separate, even as God is holy and pure and separate. Stress is laid upon passages such as Lev. 20:22-26, and the holiness and separateness of Israel are to be shown both by the outward and the ceremonial laws as well as by inward and moral laws."[64] By an application of exaggerated casuistry the Rabbis elaborated the text of the *torah* and deduced from it 613 precepts, but it was all done on the understanding that the gift of the *torah* is a privilege and a token of God's special grace to His people. To observe the commandments, ordinances, and judgments is Israel's peculiar dignity. Although "in content and intention the Law is universal,"[65] yet Israel is under special obligation by reason of the covenant. The Rabbis understood the covenant as a contractual undertaking that spelled out the mutual relation-

[61] Eichrodt, *Theology of the Old Testament*, 1961, I, 429n. Cf. also C. H. Dodd, "Natural Law in the Bible," *Theology*, May and June, 1946.

[62] Cf. G. F. Moore, *op. cit.*, pp. 278, 453.

[63] For details see Moore, *op. cit.*, II, 386; I, 279.

[64] C. G. Montefiore & H. Loewe, *A Rabbinic Anthology*, 1938, pp. 104f.

[65] Moore, *op. cit.*, I, 278f.

ship between God and Israel. This is perhaps classically expressed by R. Simeon ben Yoḥai: "Like as when a man who brings together two ships, and binds them together with ropes and cords, and builds a palace upon them; while the ships are lashed together, the palace stands; when they drift apart, it cannot stand. So only when Israel does God's will is his heavenly palace secure. . . ."[66] There are other rabbinic utterances that express the same sentiment: God depends upon Israel as Israel depends upon God. This is not to deny that they were not equally aware of God's sovereignty, which owes nothing to man. But they also knew and knew with remarkable persistency of God's unfailing loyalty to His people: "The world was created for the sake of the *torah*," said R. Yudah; "for the sake of the tribes of Israel," said R. Yoshua ben Nehemiah.[67] On these utterances Montefiore comments: "God created the world for the sake of the Torah or for the sake of Israel, the people of His choice, the people of His special and overwhelming love. In a way this last reason for the world's creation coalesces with the reason that He created it for His glory, seeing that Israel's function is to display His glory."[68] But the question arises: If Israel does not display God's glory, what then? The Rabbis still held on to God's unflinching loyalty: "The Lord appeared of old unto me, saying: 'I have loved thee with an everlasting love' (Jer. 31:3). It does not say 'with abounding love,' but with 'everlasting love.' For you might think the love with which God loves Israel was for three years or two years or a hundred years. But it was a love for everlasting and to all eternity."[69] The token of God's eternal love for His people the Rabbis saw in the *torah:* "If it were not for my Law which you accepted I should not recognize you, and I should not regard you more than any of the idolatrous nations of the world."[70] Montefiore regards this passage as "fundamental" for Jewish self-understanding as a religious people.[71] It means that Israel and *torah* are inseparable. What makes Israel God's people is obedience

[66] C. G. Montefiore & H. Loewe, *op. cit.*, p. 35.
[67] *Gen. R., Bereshit*, 12, 2.
[68] C. G. Montefiore & H. Loewe, *op. cit.*, p. 37.
[69] *Op. cit.*, p. 63.
[70] *Ex. R., Ki Tissa*, 47, 3.
[71] C. G. Montefiore & H. Loewe, *op. cit.*, p. 116.

to the way of life as prescribed by the law.[72] This is amply borne out by the tractate *Pirke Avot* where every page is a paean to the greatness of the *torah.*

The rabbinic attitude regarding Israel's position is not without a paradox but it is the inevitable paradox that derives from faith both in God's sovereignty and man's freedom. The Rabbis held that Israel chose the *torah* of his own free will. But they also held that man cannot contradict God's will successfully. Commenting on the text: "Is He not thy Father and thy Owner?" (Deut. 32:6), the *Midrash Exodus Rabba* explains: "When the Israelites do God's will, He has pity upon them, as a father has pity upon his children. When they do not do His will, He rules over them, as an owner over his slaves. As the slave, whether voluntarily or involuntarily, has to serve his master, and even against his will, so will you accomplish God's will, whether willingly or unwillingly and even against your will."[73] In the same vein the *Sifra* explains: "When the Scriptures say: 'For I am the Lord your God who brought you out of the land of Egypt to be your God' (Lev. 11:45), 'to be your God' means even against your will."[74] Strangely enough, the same passage in the *Sifra* continues to explain that God brought out the children of Israel from the house of bondage "on condition" that they would receive the yoke of the commandments: "On condition I brought you out of Egypt: namely, on the condition that you should surrender yourselves to the sanctification of my Name."

It is obvious that the contradiction arising from man's free will and God's sovereignty ultimately leads to the second contradiction, namely that the covenant is both conditional and unconditional. Seen from God's side it is the latter; seen from the human side it is the former. That these two aspects appear side by side arises from a parainetic need bound up with the human condition. We find the same situation in other biblical contexts: God decrees, but man is expected to respond; God offers unconditional grace, but man is put under obligation. The reconciliation of these paradoxes can only take place when full attention is paid to the biblical concept of election. The Rabbis were right when

---

[72] Cf. *ibid.*, p. 81 (218).
[73] *Ex. R.*, *Beshallah*, 24, 1.
[74] C. G. Montefiore & H. Loewe, *op. cit.*, p. 117.

they insisted that the *torah* is the token and pledge of Israel's special position as God's chosen people. *Torah* and covenant are inseparably linked.

c. Election

Election in the Bible is a basic theological concept and is inseparable from the biblical doctrine of God. It must be understood in terms of responsibility rather than privilege and refers to divine decree as the expression of God's saving will. But in this context, election is only another aspect of the covenant, for it bears witness to God's unfailing grace toward mankind.

It is a grave mistake to separate election from the covenant as has been done by G. Ernest Wright.[75] Wright himself admits that these two aspects are interrelated.[76] It is our view regarding election that will ultimately decide whether we see the covenant as conditional or unconditional. Election in biblical terms expresses God's sovereign initiative, and it is part of His sovereignty that He does not fail when man refuses obedience. On this score there is considerable confusion among Old Testament scholars for the simple reason that the paradoxical aspect of election and free will cannot be resolved logically. Prof. Rowley is right when he says that "election is for service," but he is wrong when he declares that "when the service is withheld the election loses its meaning, and therefore fails."[77] His theological inconsistency derives from his indecision regarding the covenant relationship. On the one hand he admits that the covenant is not just a "bilateral contract" that can be terminated by either party "on due notice." But on the other hand, he holds to the idea that the covenant is conditional upon Israel's loyalty. He fortifies his position with a quotation from R. B. Y. Scott to the effect that "there was nothing necessary or final about Israel's election, should she fail to serve the divine purpose."[78] It is on this premise that Prof. Rowley is able to write a chapter under the heading "Election without Covenant." The very phrasing of the title is a theological impossibility, for it makes light of the nature of God as we know Him from the Bible. Here covenant means election and election is for covenant. But if

---

[75] Cf. G. Ernest Wright, "The Faith of Israel," in *IB*, I, 335b note 14.
[76] *Ibid.*, p. 356b.
[77] H. H. Rowley, *The Biblical Doctrine of Election*, 1950, pp. 49, 52.
[78] Cf. R. B. Y. Scott, *The Relevance of the Prophets*, 1944, p. 121.

covenant depends upon man's loyalty, then God has chosen the wrong partner.

If we are to take God seriously, then we will have to allow that He does not proceed by trial and error. If we believe with the Bible that He is the God of grace, then we will have to admit that He does not repay tit for tat. If we confess that He is almighty, we will have to say that He does not fail in the face of human disobedience. If we believe that God is faithful, then we will have to insist that He does not break faith on Israel's faithlessness. The fact is that we cannot have it both ways, either God is God or man is God — *tertium non datur*.

To take election seriously we will have to put greater emphasis upon God's wisdom and His power. This aspect of God's character will assume special importance when we come to discuss the meaning of messianic renewal. In this respect the Rabbis can teach us an important lesson. With due regard to God's sovereign power they denied that God's purpose could be frustrated because of Israel's failure. In the last resort God does not depend upon man, though He invites man's co-operation. Prof. Rowley's concept of election suffers from an inherent contradiction: on the one hand, he holds that Israel's election was due to his special suitability for purposes of revelation; on the other hand, he affirms that God chooses a weak and downtrodden people in order to demonstrate His divine compassion.[79] The ambiguity here expressed leaves us puzzled: does God choose because of man's "suitability" or man's need? That Israel is an unsuitable instrument is the theme of the prophetic indictment and is borne out by the evidence of history. Prof. Rowley further complicates the situation by spiritualizing the concrete historical fact of election as understood in the Bible. He readily admits the unconditional, everlasting, and irrevocable nature of Israel's election and quotes the following texts in support of this view: Exodus 32:13; Leviticus 26:42; Deuteronomy 1:8; 4:31; 6:10; 9:27; 32:9; II Kings 13:23; I Chronicles 16:16-18; I Samuel 12:22; Psalm 33:12. But at the same time he introduces a proviso that bypasses the historic concreteness of election and makes it dependent upon human desert.[80] Prof. Rowley's concern that election

[79] H. H. Rowley, *op. cit.*, p. 42; cf. p. 39.
[80] Cf. *ibid.*, p. 33 n. 1.

should not be understood as an impersonal principle and purely biological has much merit. There is no privilege attached to it, except the privilege of service. Election has nothing to do with favoritism; it is "summons to a task exacting and unceasing."[81] But at the same time we must not lose sight of the irrational nature of election as far as man is concerned: there is nothing within man himself that warrants God's grace — it is utterly gratuitous. Election means that God binds Himself to man, and this His covenant-keeping loyalty is historically demonstrated by His attitude to Israel. It is for this reason that we must insist upon a conditionless covenant: unless the covenant is conditionless election depends upon merit.

At this point, and regrettably, we have to part from the majority of scholarly opinion. Most scholars hold to the idea of a conditional covenant. Even Eichrodt himself, with all the immense importance he attaches to the covenant, rejects the minority view: "The idea that in ancient Israel the *berith* was always and only thought of as Yahweh's pledging of himself, to which human effort was required to make no kind of response (Kraetzschmar), can therefore be proved to be erroneous."[82] We notice, however, Eichrodt's guarded words: "always and only." Kraetzschmar has obviously overstated his case by declaring the covenant unconditional throughout. This is not the situation we meet in the Old Testament. As already observed, both aspects are present, and are sometimes present side by side. The best example is the book of Deuteronomy: here the covenant is certainly not conditionless, yet God is described as *shomēr ha-b^e^rîth w^e^-ha-ḥesed* (Deut. 7:9, 12): "the keeper of the covenant and of grace." The parainetic juxtaposition of God's faithfulness and man's response cannot be easily resolved but once we allow the full scope of *ḥesed* the balance immediately changes. God's grace goes beyond man's faithfulness and this finds its fullest expression in the prophetic attitude "where the free action of divine love is the prominent feature."[83]

Election then is the inseparable concomitant of the cov-

---

[81] *Ibid.*, p. 59; cf. p. 137.

[82] Eichrodt, *op. cit.*, I, 37 and note 3.

[83] *Ibid.*, p. 54; Cf. also Walter Harrelson, *Interpreting the O.T.*, 1964, p. 329. Also Eichrodt's article in *Interp*, 1966, pp. 314f.

enant as the conditionless and the irrevocable will of God to be present to His people. The heart of the *torah* is the declaration that the Creator of the universe condescends to take man under His protection and to become Israel's God. This is the Great Manifesto of man's franchise: "I am YHVH thy God."

We will misread the message of the Bible if we define the covenant in narrow national terms: the covenant with "man" precedes the covenant with Abraham and the covenant with Abraham *includes* mankind. There is an unbroken continuity of God's condescension toward man of which covenantal history, as recorded in the Bible, is a demonstration. The promises to Adam, to Noah, to Abraham, and to Israel, all amount to one promise, that YHVH wills to be our God.

In the last resort there is only one covenant in which the "new" covenant in the blood of the Messiah is nothing else but a renewal of the "old" that God wills to be present to His people. Election stands for the Presence of God.

3. THE PRESENCE

The law as the basis for covenant suggests a legal and impersonal relationship. But this is contradicted by the repeated emphasis of God's Presence in the midst of His people. To give to the "law" a purely legal aspect is to miss an important point.

The Presence of YHVH is built into the structure of Mosaic law in which the covenant relationship is already presupposed. At a critical juncture in Israel's history, Moses refuses to proceed toward the Promised Land unless the Presence of God accompany His people (Exod. 33:15). The Presence of YHVH is the guarantee of the covenant promise not only to remain Israel's God but also to remain in Israel's midst.

a. THE ARK

The *mishkān*, the "Place of Abode," was the visible symbol of God's Presence. It is not possible any more for us to assess the original significance of the Ark, and there is a large variety of scholarly opinion to choose from. We can, however, say with some reasonable certainty that the Ark goes back to a very ancient tradition and that it played a prominent part in the history of Hebrew religion. Scholars naturally connect the Ark with similar objects in other ancient religions, but the similarity must not blind us to the peculiarly biblical significance given to this object.[84]

Under pagan conditions, i.e. in societies where the gods found visible representation, shrines like the Ark would be used for the housing of idols. Referring to the pre-Islamic *qubbah,* Dr. R. K. Harrison observes: "The *qubbah* possessed an innate sanctity which was slightly inferior to that of the sacred cultic objects which it housed."[85] The sanctity of the *qubbah* derived from the sanctity of the contents it carried. It is reasonable to assume that the same applied to the Ark: it could not have been an empty box revered for its own sake. As we have to exclude any suggestion of a visible representation of YHVH[86] we have to assume that it contained the "testimony" as stated in Exodus 25:16: "And thou shalt put into the ark the testimony which I shall give thee."

Because the law was engraved upon stone there is no need to jump to the conclusion that it carries reminiscences of the stone worship of animist religion as do Oesterley and Robinson.[87] This does not discount the fact that the Ark acquired a magical character (cf. I Sam. 5:1ff; 6:1ff) and was used for superstitious purposes. In compliance with ancient custom the law was hewn in stone, which symbolizes durability, and there is no need to go beyond this simple explanation.[88]

John Garstang describes the Ark as a "wooden coffer" enclosing the sacred stones, which the Israelites had adopted as emblems of YHVH's revelation on Mount Horeb. It "formed the cultural feature of the cultus and occupied a

---

[84] For the whole subject see J. Morgenstern, *The Ark, the Ephod and the Tent of Meeting,* 1945, pp. 77ff; 95ff. Also *HUCA* (1928), V, 81ff; (1942-43), XVII, 153ff; (1943-44), XVIII, 1ff; see also R. E. Clements, *God & Temple,* 1965, pp. 28ff.

[85] *The Zondervan Pictorial Bible Dict.,* 1963, p. 822a; for a description of the Kubbe and similar articles, see Morgenstern, *op. cit.*

[86] Cf. Clements, pp. 64f; this against Morgenstern, *op. cit.,* p. 78. Morgenstern depends entirely on Arab customs in his interpretation of the Ark. For a more positive view see Th. C. Vriezen, *op. cit.,* 1967, pp. 151ff.

[87] Cf. W. O. E. Oesterley & T. H. Robinson, *Hebrew Religion,* 1930, I, 44f.

[88] For the carving of the law on stone see *JQR,* 1963, pp. 28ff.

special tent detached from the rest."[89] He holds, however, that the description of the Tent as portrayed in the book of Numbers is an addition by a priestly hand and conveys a picture of the Tabernacle as it obtained at the time of David.

The story of the Ark is a complicated one and scholars are not altogether sure what part it played in relation to the Tabernacle. Johann Maier regards the "Lade-Erzählung" as belonging to the Temple tradition of Jerusalem and closely related to the Davidic dynasty.[90] According to Maier it never played any important part in early Hebrew history and is of little consequence for an understanding of ancient Israelite religion.[91] He suspects that the tradition recorded in Joshua 3 and 6 was taken over from the book of Samuel, and he looks upon I Samuel 3:3 as the oldest substratum of the Ark legends. The aetiological explanation for this he sees in the Levitical priesthood, which is typical of the Deuteronomic spirit. There is no historic connection between the Ark and the Tent, though the Ark played an important part in the *Hoftheologie* at the Solomonic temple.[92] The process as Maier sees it developed in this fashion: at first the Ark served as a symbol of an amphictyonic covenant; later it was used by the Davidic dynasty as a symbol of the double election, namely of David and of Jerusalem; finally it emerged in the Deuteronomic tradition as the symbol of YHVH's covenant with Israel at large.[93]

Whether it is now possible to disentangle the skein of tradition is for scholars to decide. Some associate the Ark with the primitive idea of the throne or the bark of a god.[94] Others regard it as a typical cultic object and associate it with the P document.[95] Maier does not exclude the possibility

---

[89] John Garstang, *The Heritage of Solomon*, 1934, p. 187; for the historic process see Clements, *God & Temple*, pp. 120ff. Cf. also G. Henton Davies, "The Ark of the Covenant," *Annual of Swedish Theol. Institute*, V, 1967.

[90] Johann Maier, *Vom Kultus zur Gnosis*, 1964, p. 43 n. 135; pp. 56, 82.

[91] Maier speaks of the "Winkeldasein der Lade," *op. cit.*, p. 60. Cf. p. 56. The opposite view is taken by R. E. Clements in *God & Temple*, but cf. the review of the book in *Times Literary Supplement*, Aug. 19, 1965.

[92] *Ibid.*, p. 50f and note 182.

[93] Cf. *ibid.*, pp. 49f, 61, 87, 93.

[94] Cf. Maier's Excursus: *Die Keruben*, *op. cit.*, pp. 64ff.

[95] Cf. *ibid.*, pp. 86f; Morgenstern, *op. cit.*, p. 79.

that it actually served as a container for a document as is the case with the Bedouin Arabs.[96] On these complicated matters only an expert can decide. But whatever the origin of the Ark, there is general consent as to its significance: it stood as a symbol of the Presence of YHVH. Maier sees special significance in the fact that there is within the tradition a close connection between Ark, covenant, and *'ēdûth* (testimony). He stresses that the Ark is not to be conceived as the locale of God's Presence but as the "testimony" or symbol of it.[97]

There can be little doubt that behind the Ark tradition are some historic facts of great antiquity. That the Ark retained its mobile character long after the settlement in Palestine we know from I Samuel.[98] In I Samuel 5 and 6 it appears to have been used as a totem for magical or superstitious purposes. This need not surprise us as religion and magic are frequently close allies. But on the other hand there is evidence of an almost conscious effort to interpret the Ark in the spirit of Israel's best prophetic tradition.[99] We are inclined to believe that the more magical aspects in connection with the Ark are due to Canaanite influence. The original tradition connected the Ark with the "testimony" as the visible sign of the covenant.

Here, as elsewhere, we come upon the major theological supposition that dominates our theme: the transcendental God, remote as Creator of heaven and earth, is yet immanently present to His people.

b. THE TENT

The Hebrew *'ohel mo'ēd* is wrongly translated "Tabernacle" if the latter is understood as a congregational place

---

[96] *Ibid.*, p. 59 n. 12; cf. Morgenstern, *op. cit.*, pp. 131ff.

[97] *Ibid.*, p. 85. Cf. also Johann Jakob Stamm, *Der Dekalog im Lichte der neueren Forschung*, 1962, p. 44. R. E. Clements takes a similar view (cf. *God & Temple*, pp. 63f, 110, 112, 114, 116); Morgenstern, pp. 151ff.

[98] Cf. Garstang, *op. cit.*, pp. 239, 257, 259. G. Henton Davies points to a number of concealed references to the Ark to be found in the Psalter; cf. *Promise & Fulfilment:* Essays presented to Prof. S. H. Hooke, ed. by F. F. Bruce, 1963, pp. 51ff.

[99] What Maier attributes to priestly and Deuteronomistic influence the present writer prefers to attribute to the prophets with greater emphasis upon ancient Hebrew tradition than cultic worship; for Maier, cf. *op. cit.*, pp. 85f; for J. Jocz, see *The Spiritual History of Israel*, pp. 71f; for Clements see *God & Temple*, ch. VII, pp. 100ff.

of meeting. "The root of *mo'ēd,*" says McNeile, "signifies 'to appoint' or 'fix' a time or place so that the name was understood to mean 'the tent where Yahweh will meet his people by appointment'. . . ."[100] Scholars therefore speak of "the tent of tryst"; Ewald refers to it as *Offenbarungszelt.* Von Rad's considered opinion is most important: "The Tabernacle is neither the dwelling place of Jahwe himself nor of his name, but the place on earth where, for the time being, the appearance of Jahwe's glory meets with his people. ['*ohel mo'ēd*], Tent of Meeting, is the proper designation most corresponding with the facts."[101] Von Rad associates this interpretation of the Tent with the "Priestly Document," but however the case may be it certainly rules out a crude concept of a localized deity imprisoned in a tent. Sometimes the effort is made to avoid every semblance of representation, as in Exodus 19:19, where it is explicitly stated that "Moses spoke and God answered him by a voice."[102] Exodus 33 presents a difficulty: verse 11 is contradicted by verse 20; in the first instance God speaks to Moses "face to face," but this is later denied: "thou canst not see my face: for no man can see me and abide alive."[103] The suggestion that the latter is an interpolation does not solve the problem, for the question arises why these two contradictory texts were not reconciled. It seems that we have to fall back upon the "root-idea" as Vriezen calls it, namely "that communion between the Holy One and man" is the essential Old Testa-

[100] A. H. McNeile, *The Book of Exodus,* 1917, p. 213. Keil & Delitzsch refuse to identify the Tent with the Tabernacle. The Tabernacle they hold to be a later development. The Tent was only a temporary arrangement; it was the ordinary tent of Moses which became a sanctuary "by the fact that the pillar of cloud came down upon it" (C. F. Keil & Franz Delitzsch, *Biblical Commentary on O.T.*, II [Exodus], 1882), p. 233. For a historical approach to the Tabernacle see K. A. Kitchen: "Some Egyptian Background to the O.T.," *The Tyndale House Bulletin,* April 1960, Nos. 5-6.

[101] G. von Rad, *Studies in Deuteronomy,* 1953 trans., p. 38. Von Rad distinguishes between the Tent and the Ark: cf. pp. 42f; also *O. T. Theology,* I, 235: "Tent and Ark were two different cult objects existing independently of each other."

[102] It is difficult to see why the RSV translates "thunder"; cf. the RV which translates literally.

[103] So the Targum. The translation: "for man shall not see me and live" (AV, RV, RSV) says the opposite and rests upon a misunderstanding.

ment message about God.[104] Keil and Delitzsch are therefore close to the spirit of the text when they aver on Calvin's authority that God spoke to Moses not from the distance of heaven and not by means of mediation but "mouth to mouth" as in Numbers 12:8,[105] yet at the same time ruling out any suggestion of a visible presence.[106] Thomas Aquinas has already warned against the use of Exodus 33:11 in a literalist sense.[107] Here is a clear case where a theological decision is necessary in order to do justice to the text. In theological perspective the two opposing statements express an inner logical consistency: God is and remains invisible but at the same time He is and remains a real Presence. Man is always *coram Deo* — *vis-à-vis* God.[108]

The contradiction between "seeing" and "not seeing" in the prophetic context resolves itself on a higher plane. The prophet is a "seer," but unlike the false prophet his vision is always beyond and above the visible. Vriezen rightly regards Exodus 33:11 (together with Exodus 24:10f and Deuteronomy 34:10) as comparable to the Pauline "mystical" experience as related in II Corinthians 12.[109] The intention of the text in Exodus 33 is to establish two facts: (a) that Moses was uniquely privileged to be admitted into the Presence of YHVH; (b) that this Presence relates to the covenant, which is mediated by God's law.

Incidentally, there is an obvious ambiguity about the position of the Tent in relation to the rest of the camp. According to one tradition the Tent is in the midst of the camp (cf. Num. 2:2, 17, etc.); but according to another tradition, the Tent is removed from the camp (cf. Exod. 33:7). The difference is obviously dictated by theological motives.[110] Schol-

---

[104] Cf. Th. C. Vriezen, *An Outline of O. T. Theology*, 1959, p. 134. Cf. also Th. C. Vriezen, *op. cit.*, 1967, pp. 74, 152.

[105] Keil & Delitzsch, *op. cit.*, p. 234.

[106] For the subject of the Invisibility of God, cf. J. Jocz, "The Invisibility of God and the Incarnation," *CJT*, IV, No. 3 (July 1958).

[107] Cf. *Summa Theologica*, pt. II/2, Q. 98 art. 3.

[108] If this statement is acceptable we will have to revise the "evolutionary" concept of revelation. We meet here as high a view of God as anywhere in Deutero-Isaiah, in spite of Oesterley & Robinson who hold that in the latter "we reach the zenith of Hebrew religious belief." We are assuming, of course, that Exodus and Deutero-Isaiah are separated by a considerable period of time.

[109] Vriezen, *op. cit.*, p. 135.

[110] Cf. J. Jocz, *The Spiritual History of Israel*, p. 91.

ars suspect it is priestly interest that places the "tent of meeting" outside the camp.[111] But there is no need to go to the extreme and deny any historical reality to the Tent as Maier does.[112] It seems to us that the Tent and the Ark are inseparably connected. Once we allow evidence for the Ark we have to accept the Tent, as it would be difficult to visualize either an empty Tent or a perpetually exposed Ark.[113] These two prerequisites obviously presuppose each other. But for us the main importance lies in the idea behind the Tent. Driver attributes the placing of the Tent in the midst of the camp to a "conscious effort to give sensible expression to certain ideas or truths." He has no difficulty in interpreting the symbolic act as signifying "Jehovah's presence *in the midst of His people*."[114] Both Ark and Tent express the Presence and condescension of the God of Israel. These form, as it were, the framework for the covenant. These objects are the symbolic representations of YHVH's determination to be Israel's God.

c. The Name

The name YHVH has an air of mystery about it. When we turn to the classical passage for an explanation of its meaning we are confronted with an ambiguous situation. The first impression is that the *Tetragrammaton* spells out one plain answer: "I am that I am"; but on closer examination the problem becomes complex.

Moses asks the question: "What is thy (his) name?" (Exod. 3:13). The reply he receives is veiled and complicated: there are three possibilities supplied by the text: God's name is *'Eheyeh;* or *'Eheyeh 'asher 'Eheyeh;* or else YHVH. Because of the lack of clarity scholars have suspected a conflation of several sources. This is a possibility; but there is also an alternative, namely that the three expressions of the Name are correlated and are meant to explain each other.

M. Reisel has raised the question: "What is the relation

---

[111] Cf. S. R. Driver, *An Introduction to the Literature of the O.T.*, 1894, p. 120; also F. V. Winnett, *The Mosaic Tradition*, 1949, pp. 58ff.

[112] He writes of the "grossartige Fiktion" on the part of the priestly document (cf. *op. cit.*, p. 87); but cf. Clements, *God & Temple*, pp. 36ff.

[113] Clements regards the question of the original relationship between Ark and Tent "a very vexed one," *op. cit.*, p. 38.

[114] *Op. cit.*, p. 128 (Driver's italics).

between these three answers?" Reisel accepts the traditional answer that the clue to the puzzle is the expression *'Eheyeh* and that there is a connection between it and the recurring statement: *"I am the God* of your father(s)."[115] Such an answer places the Name directly in the context of the covenant. Here God declares Himself to be the God of Israel supremely concerned with His people's destiny, and this concern is rooted in the promises given to the patriarchs of the race. There is still, however, the question, What is the relation between *'Eheyeh* and the verb *hayah?*

Traditionally, as Reisel has shown, the verb *hayah* is understood in the "static" sense, expressing God's aseity: *Ego sum qui sum.* This is the sense in which Maimonides understood the text according to Reisel's rendering: "The Existing One whose typical characteristic is that He exists."[116] But some other Jewish commentators and an increasing number of Christian scholars prefer to read the text in the active sense. In this case, the phrase *'Eheyeh 'asher 'Eheyeh* is a typical example of *paronomasia,* a characteristic feature of Hebrew as of other Semitic languages. If this is so, then the meaning of the phrase has to be rendered in English: the One who is actively engaged in revealing Himself as the God of creation and the covenant.[117]

Reisel favors a compromise between the static and dynamic mood for the following reason: "On the one hand the Revelation of the absolute and external Existence of God must be considered the *conditio-sine-qua-non* of the Revelation and of His continuous Readiness to fulfil His Promises. On the other hand, it is inconceivable in the Biblical atmosphere and particularly within our context that the formula אהיה אשר אהיה should only denote God's Existence, without simultaneously denoting His Readiness."[118]

This seems to us sound exegetical reasoning on the accepted rule that the text must be determined by the context. But we are still left with a problem: according to Exodus 6:3, the patriarchs knew God as *El Shaddai* and not as YHVH. Reisel, after careful examination of the text,

---

115 M. Reisel, *The Mysterious Name Y.H.W.H.,* Assen, 1957, p. 6.
116 *Op. cit.,* p. 12.
117 For other definitions in the dynamic mood as proposed by scholars, see *ibid.,* pp. 14ff.
118 Reisel, *op. cit.,* p. 18.

contradicts the traditional reading of this passage. First, he denies that YHVH was a new name, unknown to the patriarchs. Then, on linguistic grounds, he suggests that the phrase שם יהוה means more than the literal translation: "Name Yahweh." Furthermore, he holds that ידע means not just "to know" but "to acknowledge," and that נודעתי does not mean "I have made known" but rather "I have manifested." With these corrections in mind, Reisel holds that the text ought to be understood in the sense that the promises made to the fathers are now being realized.[119] If Reisel's reading is correct, it means that the revelation given to Moses is not the revelation of a name but the revelation of the covenant-keeping God who reveals Himself as the One acting out His promises given to the fathers. The Name of YHVH was already known before the time of Moses. The central idea permeating the text is the covenant loyalty of the God of Israel who keeps His promises.[120]

We may therefore conclude that the Name YHVH is not a magical formula or the result of metaphysical speculation. The Name YHVH is inseparable from the covenantal relationship which precedes Mosaic legislation and which stands as a token of God's utter dependableness as the God who keeps faith. *'Eheyeh 'asher 'Eheyeh* requires more than a grammatical approach; it has to be read theologically: what God was to the fathers He will also be to their descendants.

In the context of Exodus 3 God's Name is more than a token; it is also a pledge of His Presence. This is the very message Moses is called to bring to his enslaved people; the Name YHVH stands for the awesome Presence of the living God.

George Foot Moore has shown how the theme of God's Presence dominates rabbinic thinking. The Rabbis held to the principle that wherever the people of the covenant were,

---

[119] Cf. *ibid.*, pp. 27f.

[120] *Ibid.*, p. 29. Against this Clements seems to suggest a variety of gods under different names (cf. *op. cit.*, pp. 67 & 91 note 1). He also regards the connection between patriarchs and covenant as a post-exilic development. But these are extreme views which scholars would find difficult to substantiate on the basis of our documents. To regard Bethel as a separate deity requires as much imagination as to interpret Hamor (ass) the father of Shechem because of the custom of slaughtering an ass (!) *Op. cit.*, pp. 90f and notes. Similar extravagance is displayed by H. Ringgren, *op. cit.*, 1966, pp. 19ff.

there was also the God of the covenant.[121] This is not to be understood in the sense that God became the captive of His people, but rather that He freely and out of love ties Himself. Outside the covenantal context YHVH would appear to be a national God whose influence is confined to an ethnic group. But within the context of the covenant the situation is different: here YHVH chooses Israel and not Israel YHVH.[122] According to Deuteronomy 7:6-9 the reason for Israel's election is not to be seen in the people's merit but in God's faithfulness.

The Name therefore stands for God's Presence, and "His Presence is not something else than God," and yet not completely so, for it remains "but a reverent equivalent for 'God.' "[123] The dialectic between invisibility and Presence persists through most of the Bible: the Name of God is equivalent to His Presence but at the same time His Presence is never exhausted in His Name. This is especially evident in Exodus 33 and Exodus 34: Moses asks for an assurance of God's Presence, and YHVH spells out the meaning of His Name: "a God merciful and gracious, abounding in mercy and faithfulness, keeping mercy for thousands. . . ." The phrase: *notsēr ḥesed lā'alāphîm* has a covenantal ring about it; it expresses God's undeviating loyalty.

We thus have every reason to conclude that the Name has definite covenantal associations and stands for God's abiding Presence with His people.

4. THE COVENANTED PEOPLE

There is a startling similarity of perspective between the Pentateuch and the Fourth Gospel. In both cases it is not just history that is recorded, though there is a definite historical background to the story, but history in theological terms. To put it differently: both the Pentateuch and the Johannine Gospel attempt a theological interpretation of history. The primary supposition for both is the covenantal interrelation between God and His people.

a. The March through the Wilderness

The story of the quest of the Promised Land as pre-

[121] G. F. Moore, *op. cit.*, I, 435ff.

[122] Cf. *ibid.*, I, 219ff.

[123] *Ibid.*, I, 436; cf. also von Rad, *Studies in Deuteronomy*, 1954, pp. 38f. Cf. also J. J. Stamm, *op. cit.*, p. 47. Stamm discounts any sugges-

sented by the Hexateuch is not meant to be a factual but a theological narrative. Though based on traditions originating in historical events, the journey through the wilderness is fashioned for a theological purpose. There is no fundamental theological difference between the various documents, though there is considerable difference of style and background. They all want to affirm God's special care for and loyalty to His people. The reason for this unmerited providence is not seen to lie in Israel's worthiness; these books unanimously affirm the opposite. The intention is to stress God's constancy to His promises.

The story of Israel's experience in the wilderness is punctuated with incidents that are skillfully used to emphasize God's care over His people. There is a moving passage in Exodus that sets the tone to the "theological dimension" of the whole epic: "The Lord will fight for you, and you have only to be still" (Exod. 14:14). Von Rad places this text, as he does the corresponding texts in Deuteronomy (Deut. 31:3-6, 7f), in the institution of the "Holy War."[124] But even if we accept von Rad's main argument, there is still the unmistakable fact that YHVH is seen as Israel's Lord Protector. The pillar of cloud by day and the pillar of fire by night is a most descriptive way of expressing God's unfailing care (Exod. 13:21f). Rabbi Hertz quotes the medieval Jewish exegete Abarbanel to the effect that these two pillars "were symbols of and a witness to, God's providence."[125] This is exactly the intention of the text; in the words of the *Interpreter's Bible:* "The pillar of cloud and the pillar of fire set forth in mythological language the statement of vs. 17 that God led Israel. These are symbols of the divine presence."[126] The Presence is here tantamount to providential care. YHVH by promising to be Israel's God undertakes to care for His people's need: He feeds, He guides, He protects. YHVH fights on Israel's behalf and shields His people from the dangers of the desert. The march through the wilderness is a dramatization of the theology of God's providence and is summarized in the words of Deuteronomy: "the eternal God is your

---

tion of magic in connection with the Name. Cf. also "The Ṭetragrammaton in LXX," *JTS*, July/Oct., 1944, pp. 158ff.

[124] G. von Rad, *op. cit.*, pp. 56ff.

[125] J. H. Hertz, *The Pentateuch & Haftoras*, 1960, p. 265.

[126] *IB*, I, 931.

dwelling-place and underneath are the everlasting arms" (Deut. 33:27).

There is rich symbolism in the story that the Ark of the Covenant went three days' journey ahead of the people "to seek out a resting place for them," while the people remained overshadowed by "the cloud of the Lord" (Num. 10:33f). Even while the Ark is absent, Israel does not remain without God's protecting Presence. The connection between the Hexateuch and the historical books on the one hand, and the Prophets and Psalter on the other, lies in the common assumption that Israel's history takes place under the guiding hand of the Lord of Hosts. The perspective of biblical history, from beginning to end, is the perspective of purposeful providence. The Psalter, by reason of its liturgical provenance,[127] expresses this conviction with greater clarity and emphasis than any other book of the Bible. The bards of Israel never tire in reciting God's gracious dealing with His people: "The things which we have heard and known, that our fathers have told us — we will not hide from their children, but tell the glorious deeds of the Lord and his might, and the wonders which he has wrought" (Ps. 78:3f). The characteristic term of God's fatherly care, especially in the Psalter, is the *ḥesed* concept. This noun expresses the main motif of most of the Psalms: "I will sing of the loving mercies of YHVH for ever, with my mouth will I proclaim thy faithfulness from generation to generation" (Ps. 89:1). This verse can also be translated: "I will sing of the eternal mercies of YHVH. . . ." *Ḥesed* is here in the plural; it extends over all generations and is equated with God's faithfulness. It is a particular feature of Psalm 89 that God's faithfulness covers not only times of prosperity but also of adversity: even though Israel be cast off, the king rejected, his crown defiled and humbled to the dust, and even though the covenant be removed,[128] God remains blessed forever and ever.[129]

That God should utterly break faith and renounce His

---

[127] Provided S. Mowinckel is right in his insistence that the Psalter is primarily a liturgical creation; cf. *The Psalter in Israel's Worship*, 1962, II, 75f, 79ff, 98f, etc.

[128] Ps. 89:39 : נארתה from נאר, *Piel*, to reject.

[129] Even if we interpret v. 52 as a liturgical doxology, the triumphal note of faith in the persistence of God's mercy remains unchanged; cf. Artur Weiser, *The Psalms*, 1962, p. 593.

promises is unthinkable to ancient Hebrew piety. If Psalm 89 suggested to scholars that the covenant is conditional they have overlooked the psalmist's concept of *ḥesed*. Norman H. Snaith has established it as a matter of principle that *ḥesed* is inseparable from the idea of the covenant. "The root" of *ḥesed,* he tells us, means "eagerness, steadfastness," and then "mercy, loving-kindness," but all this within the covenant context.[130] He therefore suggests that *ḥesed* is best rendered: the covenant love of God for Israel. When Psalm 89 is read with the peculiar concept of *ḥesed* in mind, it becomes apparent that the bard is not questioning God's loyalty but wants to affirm that in spite of Israel's defeat YHVH is still his God and therefore faithful to the covenant.

Perhaps the finest expression of God's providential care is to be found in Psalm 105, where in more than forty verses the story of Israel's history is recounted. Beginning with Abraham and the patriarchs, it proceeds to tell the whole story of the people's experience of God's guiding hand from the day they left Egypt to the day they reached the Promised Land. God fed His people with bread from heaven and water from the rock "which flowed through the desert like a river"; and why? "For He remembered His holy promise and Abraham His servant" (Ps. 105:42).[131] Part of this Psalm is quoted in I Chronicles 16:8-22 in a context that according to some scholars seems to suggest an annual cultic festival celebrating the renewal of the covenant.[132] Weiser points out that "the 'offspring of Abraham', the 'sons of Jacob', are addressed as the bearers of the covenant tradition" (cf. v. 10).[133] Indeed, such a remarkable recitation of *Heilsgeschichte* would be unthinkable without the covenant background.[134] This only confirms our assumption that the narrative of the Pentateuch is in the

---

[130] Norman H. Snaith, *The Distinctive Ideas of the O. T.*, 1944, p. 98. Cf. also *Interp*, Oct. 1964, pp. 419ff.

[131] Weiser, perhaps more correctly, translates: "to Abraham his servant" (*op. cit.*, p. 672).

[132] Clements: "The covenant festival was the centre of the entire people's religious devotion" (*op. cit.*, p. 87). It would be interesting to know on what basis this statement rests. This is an instance of scholarly "exaggeration" as serious as the one the author is accused of (cf. Clements, *op. cit.*, p. 15 n. 1).

[133] Weiser, *op. cit.*, p. 673.

[134] *Ibid.*, pp. 674f.

first place a theological exposition, and that historical data are secondary. The intention of the Pentateuch is to set forth God's faithfulness, who in spite of provocation brought His people across the desert into the Promised Land.

Once we have established the theological intention of the Pentateuch (or Hexateuch) we are naturally led a step further: the journey through the wilderness is not only a historical incident in the experience of God's people but carries at the same time a parabolic reference to human life. In the community every individual is himself a pilgrim to the Promised Land. Man is on a journey: he is a stranger and sojourner (Ps. 39:12) as Abraham was (Gen. 23:4). To achieve his goal man needs the guiding hand of God. The covenant promise extends from the nation to each individual; no member of God's people travels alone, God is with him. The covenant spells out God's Presence in the wilderness of human life.

b. The prophetic indictment

N. H. Snaith stresses the difference between *ḥesed* and *'ahᵃbāh* in the Old Testament; whereas *ḥesed* ("lovingkindness") presupposes the covenant, *'ahᵃbāh* (love) forms the basis of the covenant.[135] For this reason he likes to translate *'ahᵃbāh* as "elective love," while *ḥesed* is "covenant love." Though this is only a semantic nicety, for both terms express God's fatherly care, they provide us with nuances within the covenant relationship: the covenant is not just a legal concept, as some scholars would have it, but a personal involvement on the part of God and man, with an emotional content.

The prophetic indictment against Israel must be viewed from the deeper aspects of the covenant relationship. As the prophets saw it, Israel's disloyalty amounted to spurning the love of God. To treat God in this way was for them an act of *laesa majestas* and therefore nothing short of treason. This will explain the vehemence of prophetic language in the annunciation of God's judgment upon His faithless people. The enormity of the crime had to be matched with the appropriate invectives. Ezekiel 16 is per-

---

[135] *Ibid.*, p. 95. It is difficult to see why Wildberger assumes the attitude that *ḥesed* was not originally associated with covenant. The logic of his argument is entirely dialectical (cf. Hans Wildberger, *Jahwes Eigentumsvolk*, 1960, p. 112).

haps the most outstanding example of prophetic indictment, though Isaiah is not far behind. In the case of Ezekiel there is, however, the repeated reference to the constancy of God's covenantal love in spite of Israel's faithlessness, which is not so pronounced in the opening chapter of Isaiah.

Ezekiel begins his address to Jerusalem by reminding her of her early origin: she was born in Canaan, the land of idolatry; her father was an Amorite, her mother a Hittite. Jerusalem is a mongrel who cannot brag about her parentage; even worse, she was a foundling exposed to perish in the open field, had not God seen her misery and taken pity on her. But He did more than this: He watched over her till she grew up and then took her to "wife": "I plighted my troth to you and entered into a covenant with you, says YHVH God, and you became mine" (Ezek. 16:8).

The prophet's description of God's tender care over His people to the point of raising it to the "regal estate" (v. 12) is the most moving aspect of this chapter. But in spite of all the lavished care, Jerusalem turned from Him to commit adultery with pseudo-lovers. The reference is mainly to idolatry.[136] For a theological assessment of the covenant verses 59-63 are of special importance, for this passage reveals the dialectic of judgment and grace in all its acuteness. Because Israel has broken the covenant, God says: "I will deal with you as you have done." But such an attitude obviously contradicts the prophet's understanding of *ḥesed* and *'ahabāh*. Verse 60 therefore presents a *volte-face* which comes utterly unexpectedly: "I will remember my covenant with you in the days of your youth, and I will establish with you an everlasting covenant — *b^erîth 'ôlām*."

c. THE EVERLASTING COVENANT

B^erîth 'ôlām can mean either, in reference to time, "everlasting covenant," or else, in reference to God's constancy, an unalterable covenant.[137] Another striking feature about the passage in Ezekiel is the all-inclusiveness of the covenant: it embraces not only Jerusalem and Samaria, but even Sodom. The context makes it obvious that the prophet has in mind not a new covenant, but the reestablishment of the broken covenant. This is made clear

[136] Cf. *IB*, VI, 145.

[137] Cf. Lev. 24:8 where the situation is similar.

in verse 62: "I will establish my covenant with you and you shall know that I am YHVH." "My covenant" is the covenant that on God's part was never broken, and the Name YHVH in the text guarantees His irrevocable decision. Because YHVH spells faithfulness,[138] Israel receives the promise of restoration: "When I forgive you all that you have done, says the Lord God."[139]

We have discussed Ezekiel 16 in some detail because this chapter is characteristic for the prophetic attitude in respect to the covenant. The situation in Isaiah is similar: a faithless people and a faithful God. The indictment is written large in all the prophetic books: "They have forsaken YHVH, they have despised the Holy One of Israel, they are utterly estranged" (Isa. 1:4), but here as in the later Prophet Ezekiel this is not the last word. God extends His invitation to Israel: "Come now, let us reason together" (v. 18). Not all is lost: God will yet restore His people and His mercy will triumph; Jerusalem shall be called "the city of righteousness, the faithful city" (v. 26).[140]

Underlying the prophetic attitude is the unfaltering conviction that God's *ḥesed* triumphs over His justice and that His faithfulness extends from generation to generation. The RSV was right in adopting the expedient of translating *ḥesed* by "steadfast love," though the phrase is cumbersome. Snaith has shown that *ḥesed* is at the very heart of the covenant and that it carries the connotation of "steadfastness."[141]

---

[138] Cf. the phrase *'erek 'appayim* in Exod. 34:6.

[139] It would seem that the exegete in *IB* failed to appreciate the meaning of Jerusalem's dumbness in v. 63: Jerusalem stands confounded and dumb not because God puts her in this condition but because she is dumbfounded at His mercy (cf. *IB*, VI, 151).

[140] Ernst Jenni refuses to see in the prophets mere preachers of repentance. Grace does not just follow judgment so as to sweeten the blow. For him grace in the prophetic message carries eschatological significance in that God promises to renew His covenant with His people by reason of His faithfulness. He therefore contends that the proclamation of judgment is a real annulment of the covenant, but because of God's faithfulness to election promises the prophets are able to speak of renewal of the covenant in the future. (Cf. Ernst Jenni, *Die alttestamentliche Prophetie*, 1962, pp. 15ff.)

[141] Snaith, *op. cit.*, p. 106. Aubrey R. Johnson explains that "the primary meaning of the term" *(ḥesed)* is loyalty, but he adds, "it is *bᵉrîth* loyalty" (*Interpretationes ad Vetus Testamentum partinertes Sigmundo Mowinckel*, 1955, pp. 101f).

No prophet has so intimately grasped the meaning of "covenant love" as has Hosea. This moving little book may be called an exposition of *ḥesed* in depth. His own love for an unfaithful wife becomes for him a simile, "even as YHVH loves the people of Israel, though they turn to other gods . . ." (Hos. 3:1). God's infinite patience in wooing back the faithless spouse seems to have no limit: "I will allure her, and bring her into the wilderness, and speak tenderly to her" (2:14). The prophet is inspired by the vision of God's ultimate triumph over the broken relationship. But this is a triumph of love and not of judgment. Even nature co-operates in the establishment of peace between God and His people, so that the bow, the sword, and war are abolished from the land; and God's people at last dwell in safety (2:18). The last verses of chapter 2 are a veritable paean to the triumph of love over sin and failure: "I will betroth you to me for ever; I will betroth you to me in righteousness and in justice, in *ḥesed* and in mercy (*raḥammîm*), I will betroth you to me in faithfulness and you shall know YHVH" (2:19f).

The Rabbis have shown great perspicacity in associating the above text with the daily liturgy. Every pious Jew, as he winds the thong of the phylactery three times round the middle finger of his left hand, repeats these words of promise and hope.[142] In this way he is reminded that the covenant stands under the promise of *hesed* and *rahammîm* — covenant love and abounding mercy.

Scholars have noticed the difference between *syntheke* and *diatheke:* the former is the usual Greek term to describe "league" or "agreement" among equal partners, but the latter is a juridical term meaning "testament" or "will." Whenever the LXX uses *diatheke* it describes the covenant between God and man; here it is not a matter of mutual agreement but of God's disposal. A will or a testament is not an "agreement"; "the conditions of a will are not made on equal terms. They are made by one person and accepted by the other, who cannot alter them and who could not have made them."[143] Prof. Barclay draws atten-

[142] Cf. Lewis N. Dembitz, *Jewish Services in Synagogue and Home*, 1898, pp. 314f.

[143] William Barclay, *A New Testament Wordbook*, 1955, p. 31. Cf. also Wm. M. Ramsey, *A Historical Commentary on St. Paul's Epistle to the Galatians*, 1899, pp. 356ff.

tion to Philo's definition of *diatheke:* "the covenant of God is an allegory (or symbol) of His gifts of grace, and it may not be that any of His gifts should be imperfect...."[144] Though Philo insists that God benefits only those who are worthy,[145] yet he never forgets that God's grace goes beyond human desert: "For the life of man appears virtuous not because they are without weaknesses from beginning to end, but when they are inspired (to rise) from weakness to health (or wholeness)."[146] In another passage Philo equates the covenant with God Himself: "...'My Covenant', this is nothing else but Me, for I am that same covenant by which pacts are made and formed...." He explains that "this is the archetypal form of covenant," which serves as the basis of all moral principles among men.[147] This "givenness" of the covenant is somehow connected with Philo's typical Hebrew conviction of the "unchangeableness of the deity,"[148] which is in some measure bestowed on those whom He chooses: "He imparts to chosen natures a share of His steadfastness to be their richest possession."[149] In this emphasis of the gratuity of God's grace as bestowed in the covenant Philo strikes a truly prophetic chord.[150] "The very word 'covenant', *diatheke,*" says Prof. Barclay, "is a word which in itself sums up our 'debt' and our 'duty' to God."[151] It is the reminder to God's people that it stands unalterably under the promise of God; as a modern Jewish writer puts it: "The loyal relationship between God and Israel cannot be dissolved. He will never dissolve the union with Israel (Isa. 50:1), and He is eternal."[152] This is the meaning of Jeremiah 31:37: YHVH will not cast off His covenanted people in spite of all that they have done.[153]

---

[144] *De Sacrificiis Abelis et Caini,* p. 57 (to Deut. 9:5). Prof. Barclay's quotation is a paraphrase, as the text is ambiguous; but the translators of the Loeb Classical Library append the following explanatory note: "The argument seems to be: The covenant means God's gifts, God's gifts are perfect; virtue is perfect; therefore virtue is God's gift, and not man's merit" (The Loeb Classical Library, *Philo,* II, 1929, p. 491).

[145] Philo, Gen. II, 10.

[146] Gen. III, 40.

[147] Gen. III, 42.

[148] μὴ τρέπεσθαι τὸ θεῖον (*De Somniis,* II, 222).

[149] *De Somniis,* II, 223.

[150] Cf. *TWNT,* II, 131.

[151] *Op. cit.,* p. 31.

[152] Benno Jacob, *Judaism,* Winter, 1964, p. 9.

[153] In spite of a somewhat rigid eschatological interpretation E. Jenni

5. THE COVENANTED KING

There is a division of opinion regarding the autumnal festival in ancient Israel. Some scholars think that the ceremony was mainly centered upon the enthronement of YHVH as King, while others see in it the annual renewal of the covenant.[154] Mowinckel strongly advocates the former view. With H. Gunkel and H. Gressmann he believes that the Israelites inherited from Canaanite civilization ideas about kingship that have affinity to the Babylonian cult, which was continued in the New Year Festival of the Hebrews. The "enthronement of Jahweh as king of the world" was the theme on these occasions, and Mowinckel is able to detect traces of this festival in the Old Testament, mainly in the Psalter.

The school of thought that adheres to this view speaks of a definite cultic institution in which the king was enthroned as the vice-regent of YHVH. Like the Egyptian king, though not a god himself, he was on these occasions "endowed with a divine vocation and with a superhuman power and quality." A similar situation obtained in Babylon, where the king by reason of his office was looked upon as partaking of the supernatural, which distinguished him from all other men. There is, however, one difference: in Egypt the king ultimately acquired the status of an "incarnate god" while in Babylon he was in the position of "deified man," but in either case he was "superhuman." This school holds that, as a result of the Hebrew contact with Canaanite society, the king's person acquired a somewhat similar position among the Israelites. Mowinckel puts down the rule: "It is in the light of the fundamental thought of the king's divinity that all other features in the conception of the king have to be understood."[155]

With this rule in mind Mowinckel feels justified in assuming a ceremony by which the king as YHVH's anointed is by a cultic act installed to office. From Psalm 110:7

---

finds it difficult to postpone grace indefinitely. He therefore admits the possibility of grace not only for the future but for the generation under prophetic judgment (cf. *op. cit.*, pp. 20f).

[154] Cf. A. R. Johnson, *Sacral Kingship in Ancient Israel*, 1955; but cf. von Rad, *O. T. Theol.*, pp. 10, 17f, 88f, 192, 220.

[155] S. Mowinckel, *He That Cometh*, 1956, p. 63. For the preceding ideas see Chapter 3: "The Ideal of Kingship in Ancient Israel." Cf. also E. O. James, *Christian Myth and Ritual*, 1933, pp. 21ff, 318ff.

Mowinckel deduces that the ceremony of installation "included a rite of purification at the spring and of drinking its water which was imbued with power and able to bestow increases of strength."[156] Psalm 110:7 reads: "He will drink from the brook by the way, therefore will he lift up his head." Admittedly, it is a difficult text; and Weiser, as many before him, is baffled by it. Weiser suspects that the psalm is incomplete; yet in spite of the "difficulties," which he admits, he still feels justified to connect the king with the sacred fountain on *Ras Shamra* evidence. In a footnote he fortifies his position by a reference to I Kings 1:9, 45. But the fact that Adonijah sacrificed at En-rogel can hardly serve as proof that he also drank from the brook. (!) This only goes to show how quickly scholars jump to conclusions, especially when in need of a text to justify a theory.

Von Rad is clearly dubious about the sacral kingship as presented by A. Bentzen, A. R. Johnson, H. Ringgren, and many others. He also reserves his judgment on the "royal psalms" as interpreted by Mowinckel.[157] Henri Frankfort is even more outspoken: he flatly denies that in Israel kings were a divine institution. He points especially to I Kings 12:16, which is an important text in this connection: "When all Israel saw that the king did not hearken to them, the people answered the king, 'What portion have we in David? . . . Look to your own house David.' So Israel departed to their tents." Frankfort draws attention to the fact that there was "no voice raised to decry the rejection of David's grandson as an impious act."[158] Weiser has tried to resolve the difficulty in a compromise by modifying Mowinckel's theory: on the one hand he rejects the "hypothesis of a separate Enthronement Festival of Yahweh," on the reasonable grounds that such a festival is never mentioned in the Old Testament; but on the other hand, he is willing to combine the annual renewal of the covenant with the cult of the sacred kingship: the renewal of the covenant was, "so to speak, a single scene within the whole drama

[156] *Ibid.*, pp. 63f.

[157] G. von Rad, *O. T. Theology*, 1962, I, 317 and notes 15 & 16. Ringgren has since greatly modified his position; cf. his *Israelite Religion*, 1966 trans., pp. 234ff.

[158] Henri Frankfort, *Kingship and the Gods*, 1948, pp. 340f. H. Ringgren: "Never was he thought of as a god, not even in theory," *op. cit.*, p. 237.

of the cult."[159] The assumption is that the annual renewal of the covenant is an established fact.[160] But this too is a conjecture based upon form-criticism, and some scholars allow it only as a "probability."[161]

Against all this scholarly ingenuity we have to put down some obvious facts: nowhere does the Old Testament seem to ascribe as great an importance to kingship *per se* as we are made to believe by the cultic school; Israelite society is mainly theocratic even while there is a king; there are instances of plain hostility to kingly rule, which must not be overlooked. J. L. Koole, who belongs to the school advocating a cultic theory of kingship in the Old Testament, yet has to admit the democratic character of Psalm 15. The democracy we meet in Psalm 15 Koole regards as characteristic for the Old Testament idea of kingship.[162] He further concedes that the king in Jerusalem knew himself dependent upon God and that kingship implied election for service.[163] When compared with the divine rule of Egyptian Pharaohs or the absolute autocracy of Babylonian kings, the king of Israel is a pale figure whose power rests upon general consent. The kingly office derives from God and is therefore rooted in the covenant relationship between YHVH and Israel. In this respect Koole saw aright: "The Davidic covenant is included in the Sinaitic covenant and the Davidide plays the same part as Moses at Sinai and Joshua in the amphictyony."[164] In this view he does not stand alone: von Rad has already expressed a similar view in respect to the book of Deuteronomy, [165] and so have Noth and Fohrer in respect to kingship in general.[166] There is

[159] Weiser, *op. cit.*, p. 62.

[160] Cf. Martin Noth, *Überlieferungsgeschichte des Pentateuchs*, 1948, p. 64. But cf. H. Ringgren, *op. cit.*, pp. 234, 236. He questions the whole venture on methodological grounds.

[161] Cf. G. Ernest Wright, "The Faith of Israel," *IB*, I, 355 n. 11. Hans Wildberger provides reasons derived from a careful exegesis of Deut. that such a festival undoubtedly existed; cf. Hans Wildberger, *Jahwes Eigentumvolk*, 1960, pp. 56ff.

[162] J. L. Koole, "Psalm 15—Eine königliche Einzugsliturgie?" *Studies on Psalms*, Leiden, 1963, p. 110; cf. Deut. 17:15ff; Jer. 22:13ff.

[163] *Ibid.*, p. 111.

[164] "Der Davidbund ist in den Sinaibund eingegliedert und der Davidide spielt die Rolle Moses am Sinai und Josuas in der Amphictyonie" *(ibid.)*. Cf. also Clements, *op. cit.*, p. 62.

[165] Cf. von Rad, *op. cit.*, I, 220.

[166] Cf. Koole, *op. cit.*, p. 111 n. 2.

therefore some considerable consent that the kingly covenant derives from the Sinaitic covenant. It means that the source of the king's authority lies in God's covenant relationship to His people. In a sense, the king performs a priestly function in that he represents the covenanted people before YHVH. This is the meaning of biblical theocracy, not that the king represents God, but that God deals with the king as the elect representative of His people.

Noth's hesitation regarding the covenant as the underlying principle of Old Testament faith need not be taken altogether seriously. Noth suggests that the Exodus and not the revelation at Sinai is the leading theme. He thinks that these two themes were linked later. But he also admits that the tradition of the covenant and the revelation at Sinai is much older than the Exodus. He even attempts to give a reason why the older tradition receded in the background, namely because not all the tribes were involved in the flight from Egypt. The more recent events, Noth suggests, seem to have supplanted the older tradition of the covenant at Sinai. On the whole he leans toward the conclusion that the covenant tradition has something fundamental and primordial about it.[167]

Once we accept the overall inclusiveness of the covenantal relationship between Israel and YHVH we find ourselves in a better position to assess the kingly office in the Old Testament, with the result that the messianic function becomes clearer. The question of kingship on the one hand and of messiahship on the other largely depends upon our interpretation of the covenantal relationship.

It has been noticed that at the coronation ceremony of Joash the newly instituted king receives the crown and the "testimony" (II Kings 11:12) as symbols of his office. What does *'ēdûth* mean in this connection? Scholars have

---

[167] Noth's words are emphatic: "jenes Fest der Bundesschliessung, und Bundeserneuerung, von der das Überlieferungsthema 'Offenbarung am Sinai' herkommt (macht) den Eindruck von etwas Ursprünglichem und Grundlegendem" (The Festival of the entry into and renewal of the covenant, which carries the traditional theme "Revelation at Sinai," gives the impression of something that is primordial and fundamental). (Martin Noth, *Überlieferungsgeschichte des Pentateuchs*, Stuttgart, 1948, pp. 65f.) Both Noth and von Rad are puzzled by the fact that the tradition about the revelation at Sinai is left comparatively undeveloped in the O.T., though it is very old (cf. *ibid.*, p. 156).

suggested that "testimony" here stands for *torah* or its equivalent. Koole ventures the suggestion that the term stands for "covenantal obligations" (*Bundesverpflichtungen*) which go with the office of kingship.[168] We would like to see the suggestion expanded in the sense that the king as Israel's representative *par excellence* took upon himself the responsibility for the rest of the people. *'Edûth* signifies the solemn promise whereby king *and* people bear "witness" before God to their loyalty to the covenant. This conclusion we reached on the premise that the king's person is a collective personality representative of the rest of the nation.

This brings us to the crucial problem of II Samuel 7, the chapter that Koole calls the "magna charta of the kingship."[169] Von Rad calls it the Succession Document and ascribes to it artistic, cultural, and theological significance of great importance.[170] He suggests that II Samuel 7 "once existed by itself as an independent story." Though von Rad sees in the document a conglomeration of ideas with the intention of extending the promises made to David to include his posterity, and then by further extension to embrace the rest of Israel (cf. II Sam. 7:22-24),[171] the theology behind the document is uniform: YHVH will act as Father to David, because YHVH is God and Father to His people. It would be a mistake to interpret the *hasedēy David* (cf. Ps. 89:1-4; Isa. 55:3) as a reference to a separate covenant with the house of David unrelated to the overall covenant that is the foundation of Israel's relation to YHVH. Von Rad admits that behind the text of II Samuel 7 there is an older tradition which must be treated as the source of the "historical origin and legitimation of all messianic expectations."[172]

Von Rad has worked out with great skill the theological aspect of the "Succession Document." Behind it is the characteristic Old Testament understanding of history that

---

[168] Koole, *op. cit.*, p. 111; for a discussion on the subject of "testimonies" in this connection, see A. R. Johnson, *op. cit.*, 1955, pp. 20f and notes.

[169] *Op. cit.*, p. 107. M. L. Newman is able to distinguish two opposing covenantal traditions, the "dynastic" and the "kingdom of priests." Cf. *The People of the Covenant*, 1962, p. 188.

[170] Von Rad, *op. cit.*, I, 321.

[171] *Ibid.*, p. 310.

[172] *Ibid.*, p. 311.

sees in all the vagaries of daily occurrence the hidden hand of God. Here Providence does not intervene directly by way of miracle but works upon the hearts of men to accomplish God's eternal purpose. Von Rad points out that this document deals specifically with the "messianic problem" in the strictly Old Testament sense, i.e. with the Davidic dynasty and its right to the throne by divine appointment.[173] The story of David's life, his failures and successes, his humiliation and suffering, and the "happy ending" when Nathan's word is fulfilled in Solomon, intertwines realism with faith in such a way that the guiding hand of YHVH is always apparent. Von Rad holds that this subtle and unique presentation of "theological historiography" has no parallel in the ancient world. Behind this realistic approach to the daily occurrences in the affairs of man is the invincible faith in a positive goal of history under the intelligent and persistent guidance of God.

Kingship in the Old Testament, in contrast to the highly mythological ideas of Israel's neighbors, is not founded upon divine origin but upon moral principles. The king's authority is never absolute and inherent to his own person, but delegated and derivative. He only acts by God's gracious appointment and as His viceroy: "The king on Zion is thus the mandatory of Jahweh himself."[174] The so-called "royal psalms" would seem to point to extravagant claims on behalf of God's anointed king: he shares the throne with YHVH; he rules to the ends of the earth; all the nations serve him. Widengren has drawn extreme conclusions from these utterances.[175] A more reasonable suggestion is that the exaggerated language reflects the courtly manner of the East and is nothing more than a form of stereotyped courtesy. Von Rad connects this kind of language with cer-

---

[173] *Ibid.*, p. 316.

[174] Cf. Geo. Widengren, *Sakrales Königtum im Alten Testament und im Judentum,* The Franz Delitzsch Lecture, 1952, Stuttgart, 1955, p. 57: "Der König ist der Gesandte Gottes und ein Botschaftsträger (Vergl. Jes. 50.4), von seiner Aufgabe ganz durchdrungen." Widengren has difficulty with II Sam. 7 because his whole attention is devoted to the cultic interpretation of kingship. Had he paid greater attention to the covenant he would have arrived at less extravagant results. Cf. also H. Ringgren, *op. cit.*, p. 230. Charismatic kingship was peculiar to the north whereas in the south it was hereditary, *ibid.*, p. 64.

[175] Cf. Widengren, *ibid.*, pp. 44ff.

tain aspects of Nathan's prophecy;[176] in this he comes close to our own position by attributing to the king a special royal *charisma* associated with his office. This is exactly the biblical position: the king by reason of his office is the bearer of the Spirit of God.[177] As God's anointed he stands under the promise and obligation of the covenant, and is the chief representative of God's people. In him YHVH extends his reign over the nations of the world. This is the ultimate logic of monotheism.

Messianism and kingship are closely interlocked in the Old Testament: as the viceroy of God the king acts as savior of his people, but he is no despot who does as he wills. He stands under the law of God and depends upon Him for the Spirit of right judgment and wise rule. Though the covenant with Israel stands forever, the promises to David depend upon the worthiness of his successors: "If your sons keep my covenant" then they "shall sit upon your throne" (Ps. 132:12). In fact Psalm 89 carries an accusation that God has not kept His promise to David and has renounced the covenant with His servant (cf. 89:38f, 51). God's *ḥesed* extended to the king is *ḥesed* to the rest of the people: "If Yahweh's promises and His covenant of 'righteousness', 'wholeness', 'prosperity' and 'salvation', are to be realized at all, it must be through the kings who fulfil Yahweh's righteousness on earth and are the bearers of His blessing for land and people."[178] But the relationship between YHVH and the king is entirely dependent upon moral rectitude. Contrary to Widengren's views Henri Frankfort is nearer the truth when he says: "The Hebrew king never became the necessary bond between the people and the divine powers as was the case in the Near East."[179] According to Psalm 45:6f it is because he loved righteousness and hated wickedness that the king was anointed with the oil of gladness above his fellows.

In history there are no absolutes; no man could possibly live up to the stature of the perfect king as idealized in the Old Testament. The messianic hope was therefore transferred to the future for ultimate fulfillment. But such a hope could only become a matter of faith and conviction

---

[176] Von Rad, *op. cit.*, pp. 320f.
[177] Cf. *ibid.*, p. 323.
[178] S. Mowinckel, *He That Cometh*, 1956, p. 101.
[179] Henri Frankfort, *Kingship & Gods*, 1948, p. 339.

because it was rooted in the covenantal promise of the covenant-keeping God. There could have been no messianic hope without the covenant; the covenant is the very soil of messianism.

6. THE COVENANT AND MESSIAHSHIP

So far we have proceeded on the assumption that the underlying principle of Old Testament theology is the covenant. In this we followed the example of Walter Eichrodt, who rebelled against "the tyranny of historicism in O.T. studies."[180] Eichrodt had the courage to revert to a more traditional position which assumed a definite theological orientation in the Old Testament literature. This seems a reasonable supposition: it will be difficult even for the most ardent historicist to deny theological motives behind the Old Testament documents. The question at issue is whether these motives can be reduced to a single denominator or principle. Eichrodt insists that behind the diverse material is the underlying concept of the covenant between YHVH and Israel. Again, that there is a covenantal theology in the Old Testament no one can seriously doubt. The only question is, How dominant is the covenant concept in the Old Testament? Can it be treated "as the organic theme with which to unify the mass of texts?"[181]

Form-criticism was guided by the fact that the term covenant is only seldom used by the pre-exilic prophets.[182] Von Rad approaches the various confessions of faith in YHVH as sharply distinct in character and lacking a definite focal point. But Eichrodt opposes such a view: "The crucial point is not — as an all too naive criticism sometimes seems to think — the occurrence or absence of the Hebrew word *b^e^rîth,* but the fact that all the crucial statements of faith in the O.T. rest on the assumption, explicit or not, that a free act of God in history raised Israel to the unique dignity of the People of God, in whom his nature and purpose were to be made manifest."[183]

This seems to us so reasonable a statement as to be almost self-evident. J. N. Schofield's criticism that Eichrodt

---

[180] W. Eichrodt, *op. cit.,* I, 31.

[181] *TT*, Oct. 1962, p. 431.

[182] Cf. Brevard S. Childs, *Interp*, July 1962, p. 313.

[183] W. Eichrodt, *op. cit.,* I, 17f. Cf. also Clements, *op. cit.,* pp. 17 and 55.

appeals to a static unity[184] is hardly justified in view of the fact that in the opinion of some the covenant underwent an annual renewal.[185] The issue is of fundamental importance for our understanding of the messianic hope: God's promises, because He is faithful to the covenant, must ultimately find fulfillment. This is the root of all biblical eschatology. There is thus a direct relation between the "foedus uniquum of Mount Sinai" and the Kingdom of God, as Eichrodt rightly points out.[186] Messiahship implies the realization of God's reign upon earth. What the king of Israel was unable to accomplish, namely the establishment of YHVH's overlordship over the nations, is ultimately brought about by God's Anointed at the end of days. The messianic hope in the prophetic writings seems to be sustained by this kind of reasoning. If this is so, then the psalms that have the kingship of God as their theme may be regarded as messianic psalms.

We may ask, however, why God's reign should be made dependent upon the exploits of the ideal king and not upon His determinate will. The answer to this question must be sought in the peculiarly biblical understanding of God in relation to history.

In the Bible, God is both remote and present: these two aspects are always kept in juxtaposition. YHVH speaks, acts, directs, but always indirectly and never visibly. He saves Israel by the hand of Moses and Aaron; He defeats the Philistines by the prowess of a shepherd boy called David; He pronounces judgment by the mouth of His prophets. The other man, God's chosen instrument, is the intermediary. In spite of the almost crude anthropomorphisms, the God of the Bible invariably remains the Hidden One. He is never seen, never described, never given a visible form.[187] Behind these views is the conviction that God's purpose works itself out not by direct interference into the

---

[184] Cf. *The Modern Churchman*, April 1962, p. 240.

[185] Cf. W. Harrelson, *BR*, No. 3, 1958. There may be an ancient connection between the festival of *simḥat torah* celebrated in the synagogue on the last day of Tabernacles (Succot) and the more ancient festival of the renewal of the covenant; cf. Neh. 8:13ff.

[186] *Op. cit.*, I, 40.

[187] Maier has shown how Gnosis tried to overcome the invisibility of God by means of the "chariot" mystic, *op. cit.*, especially pp. 139ff. Ringgren admits that Israel's imageless worship is "unique in the ancient world," *op. cit.*, 1966, p. 39.

affairs of man but by the slow yet inevitable process of the interacting forces of history. A classical example of biblical historiosophy is the life of David as portrayed in II Samuel. Von Rad has shown great insight into the mind of the writer of this book as distinctly advanced from a more primitive position: "For the old narrators," says von Rad, "Jahweh's control of history was principally seen in miracles, in *charisma* of a leader, in catastrophes . . . above all it was tied to sacral institutions." But with the writer of the book of Samuel, a new and hitherto unknown level is reached where all mythology disappears: "The realism with which the anointed is depicted and the secularity out of which it emerges and in which he moves are without parallel in the ancient East."[188] Eichrodt rightly describes this kind of approach as the *"interior attitude to history."*[189] YHVH is here understood to work in the mysterious inwardness of the human heart by trial and error. This, we hold, is the fundamental position of the prophets: the God of history achieves His purpose not by an outward show of strength but by winning the victory over the forces that strain for supremacy within the human heart. This *moral* understanding of history is the peculiarly biblical insight.

The solution to man's problem cannot come by direct intervention on the part of God nor by the manipulation of mechanical forces. God makes Himself available to man only on the basis of the covenant: He is thus not entirely within and not entirely without but is present by *promise*. In this context neither transcendentalism nor immanentism is the answer: the covenant guards against metaphysics on the one hand, and against mysticism on the other. The gap between man and God is kept open; but above it, and in between man's doings, is suspended like a shield the gracious hand of a faithful God.

In the perspective of history God's covenant has a twofold application: it is a covenant with man and a covenant with Israel. But these are only two aspects of the same fact; Israel's election is for the sake and on behalf of mankind. That this is so can be seen from the fact that the biblical covenant concept excludes the widely prevailing notion that the relation between the national god and his worshippers

---

[188] Von Rad, *op. cit.*, I, 316.
[189] Eichrodt, *op. cit.*, p. 41 (Eichrodt's italics).

is founded upon an inherent order of nature.[190] As we have already seen, the covenant is not a pact of mutual agreement and responsibility, but a unilateral act of election.[191] The initiative is entirely God's: Israel is YHVH's people, because YHVH has chosen to be Israel's God.

Messiahship in the more technical sense transcends the historic function of Israel's kings but is never outside the sphere of history. The secret working of God from within remains the inviolate principle of messianic redemption. There is here a logical connection between the covenanted king and the Messiah as he appears in the prophetic writings. Mowinckel suggests that "at certain culminating turning points in Israel's life the prevailing ideal of kingship crystallized into a present expectation and a specific promise of a definite person . . . who was supposed to be the full realization of the ideal."[192] In this quotation the plural is important: the messianic hope is not the invention of a single mind, but is the result of a process which grew and in growing gathered impetus. Here the "culminating turning points" in Israel's history are occasions of disappointment, tragedy, and defeat. Instances of national disaster revealed only too clearly the failure and limitations of Israel's kings and served to emphasize the contrast between God's promises and historical fact. If Buber's philology is correct the very name "Israel" spelled out "God rules over his people"; YHVH is *melek* (king) and Israel is His *mamlākāh* (kingdom).[193] But if YHVH truly reigns how can He be defeated? How can the God of covenant loyalty *(ḥesed)* break His promise? The messianic hope was born out of the anguish of such questions.

Several strains of thought coincided to produce the ideal of the anointed King who would realize Israel's ultimate hope: first, faith in the absolute supremacy of God; second, faith in His covenant loyalty; third, the experiences of history that appeared to contradict the premises of faith.

---

[190] Cf. Eichrodt, *op. cit.*, pp. 42f.

[191] Election in no way diminishes Israel's responsibility toward God and His law: cf. Clements, *op. cit.*, pp. 16, 17 n. 1. For a unilateral view of covenant, see *JE*, IV, 322a.

[192] Mowinckel, *op. cit.*, p. 98.

[193] Cf. M. Buber, *Moses*, 1947 trans., pp. 114, 137. For this Buber quotes as his authority E. Sachsse, *Die Bedeutung des Namens Israel*, 1922.

The Old Testament seems to provide two answers to the question of disparity between promise and fulfillment. The historic books, Deuteronomy, and sometimes the prophets, hold that defeat and suffering are the result of Israel's disloyalty to God and serve the purpose of bringing His people back to repentance. But there is a deeper strain, especially in Deutero-Isaiah, which interprets Israel's suffering in redemptive terms: it is vicarious suffering for the sake of others.[194] Here the Messiah becomes the Suffering Servant of YHVH who sometimes personifies the whole people and sometimes is pictured as an individual.[195] In this context the covenant assumes universal proportions; it stretches beyond Israel to the nations: "turn to me and be saved, all the ends of the earth" (Isa. 45:22). Election is here interpreted in terms of service, witness, and suffering.

From here there is a natural transition to the New Testament, except for one major problem: is the messianic King of the Old Testament in any sense comparable to the Johannine and Pauline Christ?

The answer to this question largely depends upon our theological presuppositions. An interesting example is the case of Adolphe Lods, who for the lack of such presuppositions finds himself torn between two contradictory views. On the one hand he follows the suggestion of Egyptologists that the idea of messiahship is borrowed from neighboring Egypt; in addition he falls for the theory of the "almost divine character"[196] ascribed to the Hebrew kings; lastly, he categorically refuses any connection between the Suffering Servant of Deutero-Isaiah and the concept of a personal

---

[194] This is flatly contradicted by Harry M. Orlinsky; cf. *The So-Called Suffering Servant in Isa. 53* (Goldenson Lecture, 1964), p. 22.

[195] Like Prof. Orlinsky, Miss Morna D. Hooker claims that the concepts of redemptive suffering and service derive not from Isaiah but rather from the apocalyptic literature. She also holds that the "Suffering Servant" was never understood in the O. T. as one particular person (cf. M. D. Hooker, *Jesus and the Servant*, pp. 1, 59). For a similar view cf. H. Wheeler Robinson, *The Religious Ideas of the O. T.*, p. 205. Against these cf. Anthony T. Hanson, *The Church of the Servant*, 1962, pp. 21ff. Also Christopher R. North, *The Suffering Servant in Deutero-Isaiah*, 1948, pp. 3f, 214ff; cf. also his article in *Interpretationes ad Vetus Testamentum pertinentes Sigmundo Mowinckel*, 1955, pp. 140ff. For a summary of the debate see Robert Lennox, "The Servant of Yahweh in the O. T.," *TT*, Oct. 1958, pp. 315ff.

[196] Adolphe Lods, *The Prophets & the Rise of Judaism*, 1937, pp. 70f.

Messiah. For this reason he is forced to deny any messianic meaning to Isaiah 7:14.[197] But on the other hand, he admits a continuous messianic tradition starting with Amos and present with most of the prophets.[198] Lods even allows the possibility that "Isaiah may have attributed special importance to the person of a king who was to usher in better times." And with this possibility in mind, he continues: "Perhaps in his vision of the future he gave a place to the popular expectation of a Messiah, a sovereign more or less divine."[199] At the same time Lods stresses that "ethical monotheism" was the most "original feature of the prophets."[200] It is next to impossible to piece these contradictory statements into a consistent whole. How a fanatical "ethical monotheist" like Isaiah could force himself to believe in a messiah "more or less divine" is a puzzle Lods fails to explain.

It may well be that the effort of the "Scandinavian school" to establish the divine kingship in connection with the Old Testament cult is unconsciously motivated by the desire to uncover the source of "supernatural messiahship" of the New Testament. If Engnell were right that the king's position was such that "on him depend victory, prosperity, rain and fertility, the integrity of nature and of human life, the natural order of the cosmos," and all this because of "the part he plays in the cult,"[201] then there would be an obvious connection between the divine king and the heavenly Christ. But these are extravagant views in no way adequately supportable by evidence. Engnell has good enough reasons not "to distinguish between the cultic and the historical-eschatological Messiah."[202] Had he made such a distinction there would have been no bridge for him from Old Testament to New Testament Christology.

Like Engnell, Ringgren also bases his argument on "the relative uniformity of ancient oriental culture." He thinks that "it would be startling if the kings of Israel had not raised similar claims" to those of Egypt, Assyria, and

---

197 *Ibid.*, pp. 245ff.

198 *Ibid.*, pp. 331ff. (He suspects, however, that these messianic passages were interpolations.)

199 *Ibid.*, p. 111.

200 *Ibid.*, p. 72.

201 Quoted by Mowinckel, *He That Cometh*, p. 451 (Additional Note).

202 *Ibid.*, p. 452 and note.

Babylon, who regarded themselves "as sons of gods and claimed dominion of the world."[203] But this is hardly a convincing assumption in view of Old Testament evidence. The Old Testament never tires of emphasizing the difference between Israel and the nations. But what is more important is the fact that on the theory of the unity of culture biblical monotheism becomes an even greater mystery than it already is. The argument therefore that what applies to Israel's neighbors applies also to Israel is fallacious. Ringgren makes much of the fact that the king is spoken of as God's son but completely overlooks that the people of Israel collectively are addressed in a similar manner.[204] There is an obvious tendentiousness in Ringgren's argument, as can be seen from his treatment of Psalm 8. He uses this psalm as proof of the king's extraordinary relation to God, but on what grounds? The fanciful identification of the king with Adam is an innovation that has no support among scholars. That the king stands as mediator between the people and God and that it is by his mediation that blessing, rain, and fertility are conveyed is so foreign to the spirit of the Old Testament, Psalms included, that only a man with preconceived ideas could arrive at such conclusions.[205] All this goes to show that to do justice to the Bible one must understand it on its own terms.

Ringgren attempts a theological justification for the theory of divine kingship as "part of the preparations that were necessary for the realization of God's plan of salvation."[206] But this presupposes an evolutionary approach to

---

[203] Helmer Ringgren, *The Messiah in the O. T.*, 1956, p. 12.

[204] Ringgren goes so far as to maintain that at least in one instance the king is called God (Ps. 45:6), *ibid.*, pp. 18f, but such a conclusion is not obviously apparent from the text. Moses Buttenwieser understands *kisakha Elohim* as a case of brachylogy (cf. *The Psalms*, 1938, p. 91). To pin a theory on a dubious verse is an audacious undertaking. Mowinckel admits that "Ps. 45 is the only example in the whole of Israelite psalm poetry of a true hymn to the king" *(The Psalms in Israel's Worship*, I, 74. But cf. Ringgren, *op. cit.*, 1966, pp. 195f, 230ff.

[205] Ringgren's example from an Assyrian text (cf. *op. cit.*, p. 22) is unconvincing as evidence even for Assyria itself. That the gods of Shamash and Adad granted the king "a gracious reign and orderly days..." does not in itself constitute evidence for Esserhaddon's divinity. Ringgren now writes more cautiously, preferring "sacral kingship" to "divine kingship," *op. cit.*, p. 233.

[206] Ringgren, *op. cit.*, p. 24.

revelation, the validity of which has never been demonstrated. The efforts of the Scandinavian school, however, are not without merit. It contributed to the discussion of messiahship by fastening attention upon the supramundane aspect of God's Anointed. The divine features of the eschatological Messiah constitute a puzzle. It is for this reason that scholars like Ringgren, Widengren, Mowinckel, and Bentzen have turned for an explanation to the sacral character of kings in the ancient East. But the theory presents difficulties: first, it contradicts the cautious attitude to kings in the Old Testament; second, the evidence from the Psalter is forced and most of the deductions are far-fetched; third, it clashes with the Old Testament concept of God, whose authority is supreme and never delegated—kings, prophets, and priests are only *servants*, never masters. It is an interesting development in Old Testament scholarship that in order to safeguard the theory of the sacral character of kings it had to retreat from a previous position and declare that "the psalms mostly derive from preexilic times."[207] But this only creates new problems, for Gunkel had already shown the extent of prophetic influence upon the Psalter.[208] It is true that Gunkel differentiates between "types" *(Gattungen)* of psalms, and that the "royal" psalms could thus represent an earlier "type"; but in the last resort it is not the date but the content that is decisive. A. R. Johnson's warning is both timely and well put: "We must beware," he writes, "to exaggerate the importance of the fact that in Israelite thought the Davidic king is potentially so closely related to God . . . he is by nature a man; and, as far as his subjects are concerned, he is no more than *primus inter pares*."[209] Over against the sacral aspect of kingship, A. R. Johnson emphasizes the fundamental moral requirements. This brings the king back into the proper Old Testament setting. Without denying extraneous influence, especially of Canaanite provenance,[210] he shows how "the old Canaanite mythology was remodelled in relation

---

[207] Cf. Ringgren, *op. cit.*, p. 8.

[208] Cf. Hermann Gunkel, *Einleitung in die Psalmen* (completed by Joachim Begrich), 1933, pp. 375ff. The present tendency to derive the psalms from the cult and to regard them as cult-hymns indicates the *volte-face* on the part of scholars; cf. Clements, *op. cit.*, p. 19.

[209] A. R. Johnson, *Sacral Kingship in Ancient Israel*, 1955, p. 27.

[210] Cf. *ibid.*, pp. 54f, 128.

to the Hebrew tradition with their focus in the events at Sinai-Horeb."[211]

This presents us with a completely different situation and raises all over again the question of the supramundane features of messiahship that we meet, for example, in Isaiah 9:6. Without violation to the text so as to fit a human king, as Johnson does,[212] we would rather stress the moral aspect of messianic kingship.

The covenant stands for the Presence of YHVH in the midst of His people. Like the Name, the *torah,* the Tabernacle, etc., so is the king a *sign* of God's favor and providence. But no immoral, godless king can represent the Holy One of Israel. In the case of an unworthy king the sign is not for blessing but punishment. This is the principle underlying biblical historiosophy. The *true* Anointed is the one who will fully consummate the prophetic ideal of the perfect king. But because biblical realism prevented such perfection to be expected of a human king, the concept of eschatological messiahship was born.[213]

In this connection A. R. Johnson's concept of the "extended personality" in biblical thinking can help to solve our problem. The classical messianic texts seem to speak of an extraordinary person on the throne of David who represents YHVH in a unique manner. Even when we allow for all the parabolic extravagance of language as employed in the East we are still left with an exalted personage that far transcends the common run of humanity. But on the principle of the "extended personality" there is an identification of Sender and sent that is genuinely biblical. Moses is the mouthpiece of YHVH and therefore carries all the authority of God Himself. Aaron is the mouthpiece of Moses and thus Moses is "god" to him (cf. Exod. 4:15f). According to Johnson, YHVH's personality is extended by the activity of

---

211 *Ibid.,* pp. 59, 69. Even Mowinckel admits modification of style as a result of Israel's own particular religion (cf. *The Psalms in Israel's Worship,* I, 75).

212 Cf. *ibid.,* p. 27 n. 1. Johnson translates the messianic names in Isa. 9:6 in such a manner that the startling effect is completely lost; on the other hand Mowinckel has no doubt that these names mean what they say and that they express the king's intimate relationship to the Deity. He thinks that the Egyptian custom to receive names from the god at the time of enthronement is at the back of this unusual passage (cf. *He That Cometh,* pp. 104f).

213 Cf. Johnson, *op. cit.,* pp. 133f.

His Spirit to the anointed king.[214] This phenomenon, which Johnson sometimes calls "oscillation" of Sender to messenger,[215] is a peculiarly Hebrew thought-form. It explains the prophet's authority as YHVH's "representative" and mouthpiece. In this capacity the prophet is, as it were, an extension of God's personality and in him YHVH is actively present "in Person."[216] The identification of the prophet with God is not inherent to the man but to the office or function. In the New Testament we occasionally meet a similar connection, especially in the Fourth Gospel. Thus Caiaphas by reason of his office is credited with the spirit of prophecy though in himself he is no prophet (cf. John 11:49-52).[217] It may even be that much of Johannine Christology derives from this principle of identification. The transition therefore from the king to *the* King *par excellence* requires no cultic mysticism and is best explained on the moral plane: the Messiah by reason of His moral perfection represents YHVH in a way no earthly king can ever approximate. If God's *ḥesed* and *mishpat* are ever to triumph upon earth then the ideal king is the only possible answer.[218] We submit that this is the seed-bed of New Testament messiahship and that the apocalyptic literature is only a further development from the biblical principle of identification of Sender and sent.

The reader may ask: how does this approach differ from the theory of sacral kingship, as the result is almost the same though achieved on a different principle? The answer is that the difference of approach is of supreme importance: in our case we operate with a biblical concept, namely the mystique of the Word; the others operate with ideas derived from pagan mythology utterly foreign to the Bible.

The messianic triumph of God's *ḥesed* and *mishpat* directly relates to the covenant promises. Only because YHVH Himself is *ḥesed* (covenant love) is there messianic hope not only for Israel but for the world. A. R. Johnson has given sufficient proof that the moral values attached to

[214] *Ibid.*, p. 14.

[215] Cf. *The One & the Many*, 1961, p. 29.

[216] *Ibid.*, p. 33.

[217] Cf. also Acts 23:5 where St. Paul admits the authority of Ananias by reason of his highpriestly office.

[218] Cf. A. R. Johnson, *Sacral Kingship in Ancient Israel*, pp. 65, 128f.

kingship reach beyond the national boundaries of Israel, at least in the Psalms.[219] The king of Israel by reason of his relationship to YHVH extends God's reign to the nations of the world. It is at this point that the *telos* of the covenant becomes apparent — God's reign over mankind. But this is inseparable from the person of the Messiah in whom the covenant promises are ultimately realized.

7. THE COVENANT AND THE INDIVIDUAL

The "synthetic" mentality of the ancient Hebrew expressed itself in a highly developed social instinct.[220] Hebrew society, like other ancient societies, was built upon an amphictyonic structure.[221] In such a social situation the individual was primarily a member of his clan, and his personal rights were subordinated to those of the community. Identification on the part of the individual with the group was so close that it is legitimate to speak of a "corporate personality" in the sense that every individual represented in his person the rest of the tribe. But this enhances rather than diminishes the importance of the individual. There is a tendency afoot to stress the corporate life in ancient Israel to the neglect of the importance the individual played in tribal life.

The Old Testament not only tells the story of a whole people but provides also biographical accounts of individual men and women. These biographical notices run parallel to national history and are part of it. Mowinckel assumes a gradual process of "democratization" or "individualization" in the religious life of the Hebrews. But if we are to follow the biblical tradition, the process seems to be reversed: Israel's history begins with a single man. This in itself would be of small significance, since the ancient sagas of other communities tell of similar beginnings. What makes it significant is the covenant relationship between the individual and God: the covenant with Abram precedes the covenant with the community.[222] Here YHVH and the indi-

---

[219] *Ibid.*, pp. 128f.

[220] For "synthetic mentality" cf. A. R. Johnson, *The Vitality of the Individual in the Thought of Ancient Israel*, 1949, pp. 7f.

[221] Some scholars now question the importance of the amphictyonic hypothesis; cf. Maier, *op. cit.*, p. 49 and notes.

[222] We find it difficult to accept Clements' position that "the patriarchs did not originally form a central part of the covenant tradi-

vidual, in confrontation and encounter, establish a relationship that is both unique and personal. This would seem to contradict Mowinckel's theory that religion is first corporate before it becomes personal.[223]

Mowinckel's theory depends on his interpretation of the so-called "I-Psalms," which according to him refer invariably to the sacral status of the king. For support of the theory he has to go outside the Psalter and the rest of the Old Testament.[224] Mowinckel believes that the "layman" had no other approach to God except by mediation of priest or prophet. But at the same time he points to the case of Abraham's servant and Samuel's mother who pray directly and without mediation. The same applies to the patriarchs and according to I Kings 8:30 to everyone else in Israel. To assume that only the "officials" prayed to YHVH while the people were merely onlookers is to contradict the canons of religion. The inconsistency becomes apparent when Mowinckel is later forced to admit that the "We-Psalms," and not only the more recent but also the older ones, project a personal form of piety.[225]

A. Weiser has shown that private prayer, even within cultic worship, was a practice not only in Israel but also in Babylon and elsewhere.[226] But whatever may have been the theological presupposition of the worshipper to his god outside Israel, in the biblical context the covenantal principle applied to the individual as much as to the community. Weiser well sums up the situation when he says: "To the ancient Israelite way of thinking the individual can enter into a relationship with Yahweh, and can participate in the blessings of the Covenant, only in his capacity as a member of the covenant community."[227] There is indeed an in-

---

tion of Israel" *(op. cit.*, p. 67*)* in view of the fact that the "God of your fathers" is the starting point of the Sinaitic covenant.

[223] S. Mowinckel, *The Psalms in Israel's Worship*, I, 78. He assumes that the great officials, especially under the monarchy, acted as intermediaries between the individual and YHVH. Why they should displace the priests is difficult to see except on the thesis of the divinity of the king.

[224] "The view that the narrative 'I' in the psalms mainly represents the king is supported by the fact that this has been proved to be the case in Babylonian-Assyrian (and Egyptian) psalms" (*ibid.*, I, 78).

[225] *Ibid.*, p. 104.

[226] Cf. A. Weiser, *The Psalms: A Commentary*, 1962, pp. 69f.

[227] *Ibid.*, p. 70.

separable connection between individual and community in the Old Testament; and the "I-Psalms" express both the individual's relationship to God and that of the worshipping community at large.[228]

Weiser warns us against the mistake of identifying too closely the extent of personal involvement on the part of the ancient Hebrew with the prayer-life "of modern individualistic piety."[229] The difference lies, to our mind, in the covenant-consciousness. The Bible knows of no private relationship to God outside the community. It is only within the covenant relationship of the community that the individual participates in the promises. But within this relationship every Israelite is a person in his own right and as such fulfills an important function. If the individual were of no consequence the prophet's position would have lacked a moral basis. In the charismatic individual it is already presupposed that God singles out one person as his tool and mouthpiece. Behind the prophetic call to repentance is the indictment of disloyalty on the part of the nation to the covenant. The prophet addresses himself both to the "house of Israel" and to every individual personally. It could not be otherwise, as "house of Israel" is only a collective noun for individuals in community.

Another aspect of personal responsibility is vouchsafed in the concept of the "remnant." There is here an interchange between corporate and personal life, both negatively in terms of punishment, and positively in terms of grace. Thus Isaiah speaks of him who is left in Zion and remains in Jerusalem as a "holy" person (Isa. 4:3). The reference is to each individual who has survived the national calamity and has been recorded in the book of life. The remnant consists of the sanctified, after God had weeded out the sinners from among His people (cf. Amos 9:10). Such ingathering of individuals to reconstitute God's people finds evangelical expression in the book of Micah: "In that day, says the Lord, I will assemble the lame, and gather those who have

---

[228] Cf. H. H. Rowley, "Individual & Community in Ancient Israel," *TT*, Jan. 1956, pp. 491ff. Prof. Rowley observes that "in no period of the life of Israel do we find extreme collectivism or extreme individualism, but a combination of both."

[229] *Ibid.*, p. 72. A crass example of an overemphasis of the corporate life in ancient Israel is the essay by Raphael Gyllenberg; cf. *Interpretationes ad Vetus Testamentum*, pp. 74f.

been driven away, and those whom I have afflicted; and the lame will I make a remnant; and those who were cast off a strong nation" (Mic. 4:6f). No prophet is as emphatic upon the moral and personal responsibility of each individual before God as is Ezekiel. Ezekiel 18 is a chapter that may be called the biblical manifesto of the moral status of the individual: here God does not deal with a people *en masse* but with each man personally. Although every individual is inevitably caught up in the life of the community so that the sins of the fathers fall upon the children (cf. Exod. 34:7), the moral responsibility before God is borne by each as a responsible person. The individual is not a number or a cog but performs a unique function in society. The importance of the individual is classically illustrated in the story of Abraham's bargaining with God over Sodom and Gomorrah. Here for the sake of ten righteous the whole city might have been saved (cf. Gen. 18:32).

We must take full account of the importance of the covenant in our assessment of the individual in Old Testament thinking. Persons like Noah, Abraham, Isaac, and Jacob are all placed under the covenantal promise prior to the Sinaitic covenant. Even Cain the fratricide is under the protection of YHVH and in token thereof branded with the "mark" to signify that he is God's property (Gen. 4:15). The *imago Dei* concept itself has covenantal significance.[230] Eichrodt has noticed that for the Chronicler the idea of election goes back to the beginning of history and continues from the time of Adam onward.[231] The very thought that man is the result of a free act of God and the expression of His sovereign will ultimately leads to a universalist concept of covenant.[232] Within this wider sweep of universalism the *imago Dei* doctrine stands as the most liberal interpretation of man's status before God. Here "adam" is "man" undifferentiated and unlabelled, who exists by the sovereign will of his Creator. Man is not just a tool, an object, a robot; he is a person marked with a dignity peculiarly his own: he is created in the image, or likeness, or similitude of his Creator. There is here a correspondence between the promise given to "man" and the promise given to Abram: "And God

[230] Cf. von Rad, *op. cit.*, pp. 144ff.
[231] Eichrodt, *op. cit.*, p. 425.
[232] Cf. *ibid.*, p. 431.

blessed them and said: be fruitful and multiply and fill the earth and subdue it" (Gen. 1:29), and: "I will make you a great nation and I will bless you" (Gen. 12:2). Barth is thus well justified in extending the covenant to cover "Adam, the Patriarchs, Abraham and the people of Israel." He regards the covenant with man as the "internal basis of creation."[233] From the very beginning man, as a person, stands under the sign and the promise of the covenant by reason of his origin and by reason of his endowment.

The Bible safeguards man's dignity and equality: God does not create a crowd of men; He creates one single individual. This individual though fashioned from a clod of earth is endowed with the dignity of the image of God. All humanity has a common pedigree and origin; no one can boast superiority. The rest of creation is given to man in trust and he is responsible for it. Eichrodt rightly points out that even the Abrahamic covenant carries the note of universalism and is placed in the general framework of the more general covenant with Noah and his descendants.[234]

This aspect of universalism will prove of special importance when we come to speak of the church as the ingathering of all the nations.

---

[233] *CD*, III/1, 267; cf. pp. 364, 382. Cf. also James Muilenburg, "Abraham & the Nations," *Interp*, Oct. 1965, pp. 387ff.

[234] Eichrodt, *op. cit.*, p. 414. Although von Rad distinguishes between the Noachidic covenant and the one with Abraham and at Sinai his views on universalism are not very different from those of Eichrodt; cf. G. von Rad, *Genesis*, 1961, p. 130.

CHAPTER THREE:

THE BROKEN COVENANT

The account of the creation in Genesis 1 with the refrain "and God saw that it was good" conveys a jubilant note. The *valde bona* at the end of the chapter summarizes the triumph of order over chaos. Behind the phrase, *tob me'od* is the conviction that the Creator is not only perfect in His wisdom but that His purpose is good. This affirmation of the physical world is far removed from the Manichaean aversion to matter as the seat of evil. The reason why creation is good is that God who created it is good.

But the writer of the book of Genesis has a problem: the goodness of God is contradicted by the empirical fact of evil. The evidences of evil are only too apparent to overlook: corruption, misery, suffering, death. This fact has to be accounted for, and in the saga of the Fall the writer tries to trace the origin of evil.

1. THE RELATION BETWEEN EVIL AND SIN

Evil can and has been treated metaphysically. In the metaphysical context it appears as an anti-god, intelligent, pernicious, and destructive. It is outside man but affects him by the influence it exercises, and not only him but the rest of creation. The chief representative of the powers of darkness is the Devil or Satan, whose avowed purpose is to destroy or inhibit the positive powers of good.

In this context evil assumes a cosmic meaning and its appearance antedates creation. Mythology has associated the concept of universal evil with the precosmic fall of angels in the spiritual world, i.e. outside space and time. This rebellion postulates a world of a created spiritual order and of creatures endowed with freedom. Such creatures, it is assumed, will of necessity have finite wills, for otherwise nothing short of divinity would have to be ascribed to them, which in turn would conflict with their status as creatures.

N. P. Williams thinks to follow the Pauline trend of thought in postulating "a mysterious power which vitiates" not only man but the rest of creation.[1] He thinks something has gone wrong outside time and space. "If we face the facts candidly," says Williams, "we must admit that no one of us, if he had been in the position of Demiurge, would have created a universe which was compelled by inner necessity of its being to evolve the cobra, the tarantula and the bacillus of diphtheria." The God we know from the Bible as the God of love, could not have done so: "He did not create such a universe." If He had He could not be the God of love and this would contradict the statement at the beginning of Genesis: "God saw everything that was made, and, behold, it was very good" (Gen. 1:31). The conclusion is therefore obvious: if God is good then evil is an accident outside the purpose and will of God: "To explain evil in Nature, no less than in man we are compelled to assume a Fall — a revolt against the will of the Creator, a declension from the beauty and glory which God stamped upon His work at the beginning."[2] In order to explain the "continuity and homogeneity of evil" from bacillus to man, Williams is forced to assume a "precosmic vitiation of the whole Life-force," of which the human "fall" is only the result but not the cause.

This World-Soul was created by a good God but became perverse of its own free will; it is the Life-Force behind the fallen aspect of nature and man. The "discarnate intelligences," the "fallen angels," and the "Fall of Lucifer" are mythological expressions of this supreme premundane fact.[3] This Gnostic or neo-Platonic answer to the question of evil is very old and traces of it can be found in the

[1] N. P. Williams, *The Ideas of the Fall & of Original Sin*, 1927, pp. 520, 522.

[2] *Ibid.*, p. 522.

[3] *Ibid.*, p. 527.

Bible.[4] Pseudepigraphic literature as well as the Dead Sea documents bear witness that the metaphysical interpretation of evil was widely held.[5]

To invest evil with cosmic power is to create a dualism in the universe; this is the problem of all metaphysics. The way out is to go to the other extreme: evil is an illusion; this is a friendly universe; "the Substance of God is present in every cubic inch of the universe"; man is not corrupt. Man is "the offspring of God; therefore he is primarily a spiritual being." Man's failure is not due to basic evil but only to error. Evil does not exist except "in man's error-consciousness." It is a human invention.[6] Unfortunately, the facts of life make a facile optimism impossible: evil is too obvious a fact to be by-passed lightly. There seems to be more to evil than the mere negation of the Absolute,[7] or as St. Augustine phrased it: *privatio boni.*[8] We cannot avoid the conclusion that "not everything in the universe is very good" and that there is a real distinction between good and evil and this not merely in appearance.[9]

The fact of evil constitutes a major problem to theology in that it challenges the Christian assertion of a loving God who is both good and omnipotent at the same time. Marcion, the great second-century heretic, tried to cope with this problem by postulating two gods. In answer to the question: πόθεν τὸ κακόν (Whence is evil?) he made a radical distinction between the Demiurge who fashioned the universe as the god of the Old Testament, and the God of love who is the Father of Jesus Christ.[10] Evil is the creation of the Demiurge but not of the supreme God. Marcion thus drew a sharp line between law and grace, between the God of judgment and the God of love.[11] Against this Tertullian

---

[4] Cf. Edward Langton, *Good & Evil Spirits*, 1942, p. 52.

[5] For a summary see Werner Foerster, *From Exile to Christ*, 1964, pp. 76ff.

[6] For the above statements see William Le Gant, *Metaphysical Teachings, How They Differ from Orthodox Theology*, 1963, pp. 14-38.

[7] So Franklin J. Matchette, *Outline of Metaphysics*, 1949, p. 91.

[8] Cf. *Enchiridion*, ch. XI; for a discussion of Augustine's view in respect to evil see Gerald Bonner, *St. Augustine of Hippo*, 1963, pp. 196ff. See also D. M. Borcherl, "Beyond Augustine's Answer to Evil," *CJT*, Oct. 1962, pp. 237ff.

[9] Cf. Hastings Rashdall, *The Theory of Good & Evil*, 1924, II, 244.

[10] Cf. E. C. Blackman, *Marcion & his Influence*, 1948, p. 86.

[11] Cf. Tertullian, *Against Marcion*, II, 27.

affirmed "that the God of both law and gospel was none other than the Creator" and that Marcion's *Antitheses* were false.[12] The Christian faith can allow no other conclusion.

More recently Barth has applied himself to the problem of evil, attempting to provide a dialectical solution: evil is not so much reality in itself as a reality arising from the force of the divine No. Barth describes evil as *"das Nichtige,"* which does not mean "nothingness" but rather describes the negative nature of the *Nihil.*[13] As such it does not possess the essence of creation and is not itself a creature but is rather on the shadow side of creation. Creaturely being is "good being," for it exists by the will of a good God. Creation by its very nature, however, is placed in the precarious position of being threatened by "chaos" (*das Nichtige*). Barth postulates "a whole monstrous kingdom, a deep chaos of nothingness, i.e. of what the creator has excluded and separated from the sphere of being. . . ."[14] Barth's own definition of *das Nichtige* may help to elucidate his approach to the problem of evil: *das Nichtige* is "that which is real only in this negativity which through God's decision has been given to it, it is real only in its being denied created being. It is a reality which exists only at God's left hand. But in this sense it is, in its own characteristic way, really relevant and active."[15] Over this negative reality God has pronounced eternal judgment and only in this sense is it real, for whatever is under the judgment of God is real. But the *Nihil* cannot be called the proper work of God; it is not His real work but rather His *opus alienum* as against His *opus proprium.* In other words, Barth has tried to understand evil as the reverse side of what is good, i.e. of all that God has created. At the same time, Barth is aware of the menacing intelligence behind evil and therefore holds it to be more than mere negativity. It is a reality but a phantom reality, a pseudo-power, which has been conquered once and for all upon the Cross. For this reason it must not be taken more seriously than God;

---

[12] *Ibid.*, I, 19.

[13] Cf. Berkouwer's note, *The Triumph of Grace*, 1956, p. 62; cf. also *TT*, Oct. 1956, pp. 311f; cf. also *CJT*, Oct. 1962, pp. 238f where Augustine's views are discussed.

[14] K. Barth, *CD*, III/2, 143.

[15] *Ibid.*, III/3, 73f; cf. pp. 349ff.

it can only be described as the "impossible possibility," which goes to show the absurd character of evil.

That evil is a possibility at all in view of the wisdom and power of God, remains a mystery. Barth postulates that creation was intended by God to have a double destiny: it bears the "weight and dignity" of the Creator, but at the same time it is kept exposed to the peril of nonbeing ("chaos"). Barth tries to derive this double aspect not from metaphysics but from the circumstances of the earthly life of Jesus Christ, who Himself was exposed to both these aspects of existence. It is a question, however, whether Barth has managed to remain within the legitimate confines of historic revelation in his theology of evil. His elaboration of the concept of "chaos" is more reminiscent of a metaphysical approach than of biblical exegesis. But whenever Barth comes to speak of sin in the context of Christology he moves out of the area of speculation and finds himself back on legitimate grounds.

Barth rejects the idea that man was created with the possibility to fall. This *posse peccare* must not be understood as a neutral situation in which the *liberium arbitrium* can function either way, as if God could be taken by surprise and be suddenly confronted with the unexpected. Man can only have one ability: the competence to make his decision in obedience to God's will. Sin therefore is not something consistent with creation; like evil it can only be regarded as the "impossible possibility" because it is outside the will of God. All we can say about sin is that it is an inexplicable mystery which cannot be rationalized by linking it to man's creation or freedom of will. It cannot be denied nor can it be explained: sin can only be described as an enigma, an absurdity, as "chaos." There is no basis for it in creation nor in the nature of man. By reason of the contradictory nature of sin theology must not try to systematize it but must treat it as "logically inconsistent."

Barth contends that the real nature of sin cannot be fathomed outside the area of salvation. What sin is we can only know from underneath the Cross: from here we understand sin as the refusal of grace. But grace precedes sin, and because sin is an "ontological impossibility" we can only understand man when we consider him not under the aspect of sin but under the aspect of grace, the covenant, Jesus Christ.

Berkouwer was quick to uncover the weak points in Barth's structure of evil in relation to sin. He criticizes Barth for rejecting the "step-wise" relation between creation and redemption, which exposes him to the danger of falling into a *monistic* position: he either eternalizes God's works or else he historicizes them.[16]

Barth's difficulty lies in the fact that the initiative of grace tends to absorb the full historical significance of evil; even the wrath of God appears to take on a "form of Grace." The result is a supralapsarian point of view somewhat modified and corrected in the sense that there is a primordial relationship established between guilt and reconciliation.[17]

There seems to be no possible transition from the fact of evil to the fact of sin unless we fall back upon the mythology of fallen angels and a cosmic fall outside history. Barth refuses to believe in the theory of fallen angels and he regards the creation of demons as the result of a "bad dream." It seems to us that by placing the source of evil in a prehistoric setting we do not solve the problem but only defer it. Ultimately, there is no answer to the origin of evil but only an answer to the conquest of evil: Jesus Christ.

Except for a few isolated passages that suggest a mythological attempt, the Bible concerns itself not with a metaphysical explanation of evil but with the existential fact of sin.

As is well known Carl Gustav Jung rejects both the *privatio boni* theory as evasive, and the idea that God is essentially good. He prefers a god who is indifferent to either good or evil. The dictum: *omne bonum a Deo, omne malum ab homine,* Jung regards as utterly unacceptable on empirical grounds. For the same reason, he proposes a deity in whom both aspects are compromised. Such a god, he avers, "puts his actions beyond moral judgment and allows no conflict to arise between goodness and beastliness."[18] This is an ideal solution for those for whom historic revelation is only a meaningless phrase.

The biological approach to evil which sees it in the context of the natural struggle for survival is connected

---

[16] Cf. G. C. Berkouwer, *op. cit.*, p. 253.

[17] Cf. *ibid.*, pp. 256, 260. For Barth's answer to Berkouwer's criticism see *CD*, IV/3/1, 173-180.

[18] Cf. C. G. Jung, *Psychology & Religion*, Bollingen Series, XX, 1958, p. 383 n. 13; cf. also pp. 313, 357f.

with the theory of evolution. Konrad Lorenz, who discusses the "So-called Evil" in the animal world, has to admit that as far as man is concerned he differs from the animal in that his aggressive drives lead to genocide. In this respect, the zoological counterpart to man is the rat, for this is apparently the only animal that engages in total warfare between one group and another.[19]

Konrad Lorenz' explanation that man's bent toward evil is largely a matter of maladjustment does not meet the case. On the other hand to attribute evil to God is a contradiction in terms, for God cannot be good and evil at the same time: "God is not the author of all things, but of good only."[20] For Plato the idea that evil was created by God is a suicidal, ruinous, and impious fiction, and so it is. Evil thus remains a mystery; it belongs to the realm of the irrational. Sin, on the other hand, describes man's willful alliance with evil. By his association with evil man declares himself the opponent of God. He breaks the covenant and takes refuge in the opposite camp. He thus becomes God's fugitive.

2. SIN AS A BIBLICAL PROBLEM

Evil is a philosophical concept and carries an impersonal connotation: it is a metaphysical "principle" rather than an act. Sin, on the other hand, carries the meaning of personal involvement: it is a strictly theological concept and does not exist apart from sinners. Von Rad draws a line of distinction between Genesis 3 to 11, which chapters provide unique insights into the nature of "sin," and the rest of the Old Testament, which apparently only knows of sins in terms of personal deeds.[21] He ascribes this more "psychological" aspect of sin to a source scholars call "J." "The Jahwist" he writes, "makes the reader see temptation as a complex process of tortuous enticement" (Gen. 3:6).[22] It is questionable, however, whether this psychological insight into the human condition is anything other than a dramatized concentration of what is elsewhere exemplified in human acts. For us it is important to notice that in the

---

[19] Konrad Lorenz, *Das Sogenannte Böse:* zur Naturgeschichte der Agression, Wien, 1963; cf. *The Listener,* Aug. 5, 1965, p. 200.
[20] Plato, *The Republic,* II, 380 C.
[21] Von Rad, *op. cit.,* p. 154.
[22] Cf. *ibid.,* p. 157.

Bible sin is understood both as a condition and an act. To speak of "sin" apart from the sinner is to misrepresent the biblical approach: here sin does not exist as an entity; it is rather a condition that inevitably expresses itself in deeds and attitudes. In this way all the three aspects of sin as elaborated by von Rad are accounted for: (1) Sin as a form of *hybris,* which leads man to break out from his creaturely limitation and aspire to the status of God; (2) sin as "a mysterious breach," which somehow permeates man's physical nature and marks him out as a fallen creature; (3) sin as a perverse bent that leads man to a wrong relationship with God, the other man, and even nature itself. In von Rad's own words: "The complete disorganisation of the relationship between man and the earth was affected when the earth had drunk a brother's blood" (Gen. 4:10f).[23]

This strange disruption, which the Bible describes as a permanent taint, as a breach of relationship, and as arrogance, constitutes the basic problem of sin as historical fact.

We will find it impossible to understand the underlying suppositions of the New Testament unless we allow for the basic biblical conviction that man, both individually and corporately, is in the predicament of sin from which he cannot extricate himself by his own resources.

a. SIN AS TITANISM

Von Rad warns against the facile attempt to interpret the Fall and the Tower of Babel as mere myth in the sense that we have here just a repetition of some ancient fables.[24] These stories are skillfully constructed with the definite intention to convey some insight into the complex nature of man. They want to say something of the forces that make man what he is and the driving motives behind his actions. Although the descriptions vary according to circumstances, the biographical notes about individuals and the story of the nations and Israel are so phrased that they serve to emphasize the rebellious nature of human behavior.[25]

---

[23] *Ibid.,* pp. 157-159.

[24] *Ibid.,* p. 154; Robert Eisler suggested that man's transition to violence has something to do with a change from a frugivorous to a carnivorous mode of life. Cf. his *Man into Wolf,* 1951.

[25] When von Rad affirms that "there is absolutely no unity in the ideas of the O.T. about the nature of man" (*ibid.,* pp. 152f), the ref-

The Old Testament appears to see sin in a double perspective: objectively, as a breach of the order of creation; and subjectively as a broken relationship between God and man. These two aspects frequently coincide: thus sins "unwittingly" committed, either by reason of circumstances or ignorance (cf. Lev. 4:2, 22, 27; 5:15; 22:4; Num. 15:27-29) are treated with the same seriousness as sins committed with a "high hand" (cf. Num. 15:30). In the latter case the punishment is greater, but the effect is the same. In both cases sin is understood as rebellion against the majesty of God. Even unwittingly committed acts of transgression are seen as arising from situations that reveal disharmony with God's created order. Von Rad occasionally speaks of a "subjectively guiltless sinner" but he does so on the assumption of a purely cultic concept of sin which would on this understanding carry the connotation of unalterable fate. But this leaves out the profoundly moral aspect of sin so deeply rooted in Old Testament thought. The fatalistic understanding of the human situation ill accords with the fundamental principle of *ḥesed* which determines the Old Testament approach to life and creation. The inveterate optimism of the Old Testament has its source in the conviction graphically expressed in the first chapter of Genesis: "God saw everything that he had made, and, behold, it was very good" (Gen. 1:31).

To "bear guilt" in terms of responsibility and punishment does not mean what von Rad makes it out to mean, namely that man in himself is utterly defenseless against evil and that no moral act can preserve him from it no matter how heroically he may try. If not consciously, then at least "unwittingly he becomes its prey."[26] Such a conclusion regarding evil is only warranted on the understanding of a purely cultic aspect of religion, which some scholars attribute to the source called "P." But oddly enough, even this document never operates on a purely cultic level; the moral principle is always included. The interesting expression for "sin," *pesha'*, which carries the connotation of "revolt," "rebellion," and which according to von Rad "failed to find acceptance among the concepts connected

erence is in respect to the approach and perception and does not affect the above statement.

[26] *Op. cit.*, p. 268.

with the cult,"[27] is not entirely lacking in this document (cf. Lev. 16:16, 21).

Even within the area of cultic atonement, the worshipper does not remain passive, leaving it entirely to the priest to perform the propitiatory ritual. The whole community participates in the action by identifying itself with the victim and by sharing in its suffering: this is the meaning of the expression *teʿannu ʾeth-naphshothēyḥem* —"you shall afflict your souls"— according to explicit injunction (Lev. 16:29, 31). It would be an interesting question to raise whether there could be atonement without this attitude of participation by affliction and humility,[28] purely on the cultic principle of *opus operatum.*

As far as the prophets are concerned *peshaʿ* as rebellion best describes their idea of the root of sin.[29] It is naive to assume that the Levitical Code reflects an accurate picture of a society utterly undifferentiated. All it presents is a particular point of view striving for ascendency. Its very affirmatives betray the hidden fact of contradiction. If P is the kind of document scholars tell us it is, then the Priestly Code must be understood in terms of reaction. We face here a situation where the center of tension revolves round prophetic freedom and priestly legalism. If Pfeiffer's assumption is correct that the Priestly Code derived its inspiration mainly from Ezekiel on the one hand, and Deutero-Isaiah on the other,[30] it would serve to substantiate our contention that none of our Old Testament documents remained unaffected by the struggle between prophet and priest.[31]

The very fact that in the Priestly Code YHVH is "no longer a national deity" but the Creator of mankind[32] re-

---

[27] *Op. cit.*, p. 263; *peshaʿ*, though only mentioned twice in Leviticus, occurs elsewhere 86 times.

[28] Lev. 16:31 reads *weʿinniythem*, which may be translated "and you shall humble yourselves."

[29] Cf. Norman Snaith, *Distinctive Ideas in the O.T.*, pp. 61-68.

[30] Cf. R. H. Pfeiffer, *The Books of the Old Testament*, 1957, p. 61.

[31] Cf. J. Jocz, *The Spiritual History of Israel*, p. 86. In view of adverse criticism on the part of the reviewers of my assumption of a prophetic compromise regarding the cult, I was gratified to discover that Prof. Wm. F. Albright in his Goldenson Lecture, 1961, assumes a similar possibility. Cf. *Samuel and the Beginning of the Prophetic Movement*, p. 17.

[32] Pfeiffer, *op. cit.*, pp. 89f. Much of the universalism ascribed by

veals something of the pervasive influence of prophetism in molding the thinking behind our Old Testament documents. In Pfeiffer's opinion the Priestly Code understands Israel's relation to God on similar terms as "those of subjects to their despotic dictator."[33] This in itself would give to sin the connotation of rebellion even though another word than *pesha'* were used. The important point we must bear in mind is that throughout the Bible, both Old Testament and New Testament alike, "sin," by whatever designation, is always sin *against* God. Whether it be *pesha'*, *'āvon*, or *'āshām*, or their Greek equivalents, makes no difference. "To act perversely," "to go astray," "to become guilty," or "to break faith,"[34] are only different aspects of the same fact, namely that man asserts his will over against the will of God.

Von Rad poses the question: what was sin to ancient Israel? His answer is simple: it was primarily "an offence against the sacral order."[35] But this presupposes too primitive a society. We have no documents to prove such a position except outside the Canon. Even for "P" the "sacral order" has a much wider base than temple worship; it includes the covenant with Abraham, God's providence over the patriarchs, God's noncultic relation to Moses, the story of the Exodus, and the journey to Sinai.[36] It is next to impossible to separate the cultic from the moral aspect of sin within the context of the Old Testament. Sin here is primarily disobedience, of which cultic defilement is only one aspect. Both in the moral and cultic sense sin is always sin against the majesty, holiness, and Lordship of God. We are thus justified to conclude that for the Old Testament sin is primarily rebellion.

That man should dare to stand up and defy Almighty God is such an enormity to the mind of Old Testament writers that it can only describe it as *sākāl* — "folly." *Sākāl* in texts like Genesis 34:7; Judges 19:23; 20:6, 10; I Samuel

---

Pfeiffer to "P" is ascribed by von Rad and Gottwald to "J." (Cf. Norman G. Gottwald, *A Light to the Nations*, 1959, pp. 224f.) Perhaps both views are correct and there is not so much difference between these "documents" after all.

[33] *Op. cit.*, p. 90.

[34] Cf. von Rad, *op. cit.*, pp. 259, 263.

[35] *Op. cit.*, p. 264.

[36] For details see Pfeiffer, pp. 58f.

13:12 — texts quoted by von Rad — is more than "deluded" or ignorant folly.[37] It is rather a premeditated, willful, defiant act against God and society. *Pesha'* means exactly this: presumption, *hybris,* titanism. *Pesha'* is a form of madness and therefore it is "folly."

b. Sin as sickness

Because sin in the Bible is primarily an act that springs from an attitude of rebellion, it carries inevitable consequences. By reason of the close cohesion of the individual with society every sinful act affects the community at large. Gottwald thinks that it is the special intention of the "J" writer to sketch the gradual deterioration of man and society as a result of the Fall.[38] "J" seems to connect skill with sin: in proportion to man's growth of skill grows his independence of God until it turns into rebellion. The situation is summarized in Genesis 6:5: "every imagination of the thoughts of his (man's) heart was evil continually." Noah's drunkenness is here probably used as an illustration of the corrosive effect of sin upon man's character reducing even the righteous to helplessness.

There is a logical interconnection between the sinner and society: sin releases a chain-reaction and has an accumulative effect; one act leads to another and its evil influence affects the rest of the community. Thus the sins of the fathers become the burden of the following generation. Because history is a succession of generations, sin is an inevitable ingredient in society. The events of history are the results of the wrong choices on the part of sinful men. There is here a moral "fatalism" from which man cannot extricate himself except by way of forgiveness.

It is a disputed question whether the Old Testament knows anything about "original sin." Vriezen has shown, however, that sin in the Old Testament is frequently understood as a stain, hence the purificatory lustrations to cope with it. The very meaning of *kipper* may point in this direction; the word may mean as much to "cover" as to "wipe off," to blot out.[39] Sin is here conceived as an uncleanness

---

[37] Cf. von Rad, *op. cit.,* p. 268 n. 185.

[38] Gottwald, *op. cit.,* p. 227.

[39] Cf. Th. C. Vriezen, *An Outline of O. T. Theology,* 1958, pp. 211, 287. For a Jewish criticism of the Christian doctrine of original sin,

not only metaphorically but literally. Both people and objects become contaminated by the impurity of sin and therefore require cleansing by sacrifice to remedy their condition.

The awareness of sin dominates biblical man: he is profoundly aware of its presence and its corruptive influence. For the Bible sin is universal; no human creature can escape it. Genesis 2 to 11 provides us with the classical perspective of sinful humanity as understood in ancient Israel. Vriezen explains that the writer of these chapters "was a man who fathomed the depths of the sinfulness of the human heart and gave expression to his spiritual conviction of the depravity of the human race throughout his history of primeval times."[40] These chapters in Genesis are matched by other utterances that give expression to similar conviction, notably Jeremiah 17:9: "The heart is crooked above all and it is sick:[41] who can understand it?" It is, however, important to remember that the Bible shies from speaking in the abstract. It is not concerned with a theological definition of sin but rather with the concrete fact of sin as demonstrated by the life and experience of sinners. The indictment the prophets hurl against their people opens up the existential predicament of sinful humanity before a holy God. The abstract concept of "sinful human nature" is not a biblical thought-form. The Bible prefers to speak concretely about rebellious men and women who turn their backs upon the Holy One of Israel and dig for themselves cisterns that can hold no water (Jer. 2:13). It is therefore a mistake on the part of Vriezen to affirm that "a chapter like Romans 3 in all its severity is inconceivable in the Old Testament."[42] The tremendous accusation of Isaiah 1 and Jeremiah 9 is no less startling than what St. Paul says in his letter to the Romans; in fact it is more so. But the prophets phrase it more concretely and with greater application to the historical situation.

Occasionally the prophets speak of Israel's departure from God as a disease. It is a form of sickness that requires the healing hand of the physician. This is how Hosea sees the sickness of Ephraim (Hos. 5:13) and Jeremiah the

---

see Roland B. Gittelsohn, "Judaism & Mental Health," *Judaism*, Fall, 1959, pp. 324ff.

[40] *Op. cit.*, p. 210.

[41] *'anash:* incurable, malignant, sick.

[42] Vriezen, *op. cit.*, p. 210.

apostasy of his people (Jer. 3:22): "Return, O faithless sons and I will heal your backsliding." The association of sin with disease finds application also in the Psalms: "God is the forgiver of all thy iniquity, the healer of all thy diseases" (Ps. 103:3; cf. Ps. 41:4).

Oddly enough, God's punishment the prophets understand as a form of healing. He only smites in order to heal "so that they return to the Lord." This applies not only to Israel but to an enemy country like Egypt (cf. Isa. 19:22). It is obvious that more than physical healing is meant; God's chastening of the nations results in a new attitude. Hosea calls to his people: "Come, let us return to the Lord, for He has torn, that He may heal us ..." (Hos. 6:1). It is part of Israel's sickness that he turns for remedy to Assyria and not to God (Hos. 5:13). Behind the rhetorical question of Jeremiah: "Is there no balm in Gilead? Is there no physician there?" (8:22) is the prophet's conviction that Israel's sickness needs the Great Physician who alone is able to heal His people's malady (Jer. 30:17).

c. SIN AS HYBRIS

We have seen that the *torah* distinguishes between two kinds of sin: unpremeditated sin and sin with a "high hand";[43] i.e. sinful acts but which happen accidentally and are, humanly speaking, unavoidable, and acts that are performed as a result of sheer obduracy. It is the latter that bear the character of *hybris* in that they express man's rebellion against God's ordering. In this situation man consistently pitches his defiant will against the will of God. The Bible has a special phrase for this kind of attitude: "hardening of heart."

We will quote an older Old Testament scholar, Gustav Friedrich Oehler, who well describes the defiant attitude: "The O.T. calls the highest degree of sin *obduracy*, or *hardening of heart (ḥizēq lēb)* Ex. 4:21; *('immēts)* 2 Chronicles 36:13; *(hikbîd)*, *(kibbēd)* 1 Sam. 6:6; *(hiqshāh)* Ps. 95:8; Prov. 28:14, for which we also find, to shut the heart, Isa. 44:18, to make fat *(hishmîn)* 6:10; Ps. 119.70, to make the heart like a diamond (Zech. 7:12). This is the condition in which a man, by continually cherishing sin, has (in a

---

[43] Sin: *bishgāgāh*, Lev. 4:2, 22, etc.
Sin: *b^e yād rāmāh*, Num. 15:30.

sense) lost the ability to withstand it; and it is added that God can glorify Himself on such a one only by punishment."[44]

The ability on the part of man to stand up *coram Deo* in order to defy Him is a puzzle to the ancient writer which he can only explain as the height of folly. Such arrogance is the highest form of blasphemy, against which the *torah* never tires to warn. To treat God presumptuously carries the penalty of capital punishment. (Cf. Exodus 22:28. In a parallel passage, Leviticus 24:15, the same verb occurs — *qll* — to treat lightly, presumptuously, to hold in contempt, to defy: "whosoever defies God, shall bear his sin.")

In the case of Shelomith's son, we have an illustration how the law against blasphemy was applied. This half-caste Hebrew (his father was an Egyptian) blasphemed by pronouncing God's holy Name in a defiant manner.[45] This passage is a useful commentary on the meaning of the third commandment: this commandment is not a reference to perjury as is mistakenly held. Leviticus 19:12 prohibits the use of God's Name: "you shall not swear by my name falsely, and so profane the name of your God: I am the Lord."[46] The third commandment carries a much wider implication: it prohibits the use of the Name altogether, and not merely "every wrong, or idle, or irreverent use of God's name."[47] The total prohibition of uttering the Tetragrammaton is assumed in the LXX translation of Leviticus 24:16.[48] According to Jewish tradition only the High Priest, and that only on special occasions in the Temple, was allowed to pronounce the Name. At first, he used to do so explicitly, i.e. within the hearing of everyone, "but when the number of dissolute persons increased, he would say it in a low voice and swallow it in a melody so that even his brother priests were unable to distinguish it."[49]

---

[44] G. Fr. Oehler, *Theology of the O.T.*, 1883, pp. 164f.

[45] *way^e^qallel* cannot mean "and he cursed." It rather is meant to explain the verb *nakab* — *wayyiqqob* — he "pronounced," he "defined" the Name and thus treated it lightly (Lev. 24:11).

[46] R. H. Charles connects the third commandment with this prohibition (cf. *The Decalogue*, 1923, p. 92).

[47] So R. H. Charles. Cf. also J. J. Stamm, *op. cit.*, p. 47.

[48] It translates: *ὀνομάζων τὸ ὄνομα κυρίου* "he named, or pronounced, the Name of the Lord." Cf. also *JTS*, July/Oct. 1944, pp. 158ff.

[49] The Code of Maimonides, Book VIII: *The Book of the Temple*

It is a debatable point whether the third commandment allows the use of God's Name when it is done honestly and not in "vain": *lashshāve'* — *'shāve'* — may mean other than for no purpose; it may mean evil, destruction, calamity. But the more probable explanation is that *lashshāve'* is here an idiomatic expression peculiar to Hebrew. It does not imply that when used other than in "vain" God's Name may be taken. This is in accordance with rabbinic tradition, which under no circumstances allows the pronouncing of the holy Name. According to the Rabbis even hearing the Name pronounced without protest implicates one in blasphemy.[50] When the High Priest rent his garment at the trial of Jesus he was indicating that the prisoner was guilty of blasphemy (Matt. 26:65).[51]

On hearing the Name pronounced by the High Priest on the Day of Atonement all the worshippers in the Temple were expected "to kneel and bow down and fall on their faces and say: 'blessed be the Name of the glory of His kingdom for ever and ever.' "[52] It would appear that the third commandment as well as the law against blasphemy (Lev. 24:15) has in view an extreme case of defiance. Such behavior the Hebrew could not account for by the ordinary laws of reasoning; he therefore fell back upon the concept of the "hardening of the heart" as a sign of God's judgment according to the adage: *quem Deus vult perdere, dementat.* The classical example is the case of Pharaoh, whose "hardening of heart" was the direct result of deliberate defiance (cf. Exod. 7:3; 8:15; 13:15). Oehler points

---

Service, 1957, p. 393. This may be a veiled reference to Jesus of Nazareth, for according to Jewish legend He is supposed to have performed miracles with the help of the *Tetragrammaton* which He had sewed underneath His skin. (Cf. J. Jocz, *The Jewish People & Jesus Christ*, p. 63.)

[50] Cf. Strack-Billerbeck, I, 1007. If one should happen to hear God's Name pronounced in a court of law the obligation is to rend one's garment.

[51] This is denied by Hugo Mantel who maintains that "no good case has ever been made out for the view that Jesus was charged with blasphemy" (cf. Hugo Mantel, *Studies in the History of the Sanhedrin*, 1961, pp. 273-76). Cf. also Paul Winter, *On the Trial of Jesus*, 1961. Against these cf. J. C. McRuer, *The Trial of Jesus*, 1964, but especially the important article by A. N. Sherwin-White, "The Trial of Christ," *The Listener*, June 25, 1964, pp. 1021-23.

[52] Maimonides, *op. cit.*, p. 393.

to the interesting text in Isaiah 63:17: "O Lord, why dost thou make us to err from thy ways, so that we fear thee not?" There is an awesome logic behind this question: to defy YHVH's majesty is so irrational as to be inexplicable except as a demonstration of God's supreme displeasure.

Sin as *hybris* carries the character of utter irrationality and is therefore inexplicable by the ordinary canons of logic. The prophet invites his people to enter into a reasoned discussion with YHVH (Isa. 1:18) so that the more rational side of man's nature can prevail. This appeal to reason is characteristic of the prophetic approach: "Why will you die, O house of Israel?" asks Ezekiel; God has no pleasure in the death of anyone; "turn and live" is his message (Ezek. 18:31f).

This is the distinctive call of the Bible: "turn and live." "Turn, O Israel, to the Lord your God, for you have stumbled by reason of your iniquity" (Hos. 14:1), means that there is a way back to the covenant-keeping God who patiently waits for His people's return. But He does not only wait; He is actively engaged in the task of bringing Israel back under the covenant of grace.

The contention of classical federal theology is that God's covenant with Israel is only an aspect, though an important one, of the wider covenant involving mankind. If this contention is theologically well founded, and in view of the New Testament it appears to be so, then the story of Israel is representative of the story of humanity at large. The writer of the early chapters of Genesis intends to say that *'adam* stands for man and not just for Hebrew. It is man who is expelled from the garden of Eden and finds himself a wanderer in search of his destiny. Man's first-born, Cain, moves one step ahead of his father in the act of defiance and commits fratricide. The rest of the story of mankind is a progression in violence and rebellion, which reaches a climax and ends with the story of the flood. Again, in the story of Noah the covenant is all-inclusive as it is meant to cover the three races: Shem, Ham, and Japheth.

Already in the early days of the Reformation theologians like Andreas Musculus (1514-81) and Szegedinus (Stephanus Kis, 1505-72) extended the covenant to the whole of creation. They distinguished the *foedus speciale*, which had eternal significance, from the *foedus generale*, which was of temporal duration.[53] Most of the classical federal theologians held similar views. Their insistence upon one single covenant covering the whole stretch of history from beginning to end, *ante legem, sub lege, post legem,* puts the whole of humanity under God's grace.[54] The same applies to the Fall, in which all generations become involved. But the *abrogatio foederis per peccatum* never means that humanity is left to fend for itself without the providence of God. The *foedus naturale* by which God graciously extends His mercy to sinners is never abrogated, otherwise mankind would cease to exist.[55] This emphasis upon the universality of God's care greatly promoted the trend toward universalism in spite of the Calvinistic insistence upon predestination.[56]

One of the greatest exponents of federal theology, Johannes Cocceius (1603-69) regards the broken covenant with Adam after the Fall replaced immediately by the better covenant of grace: the *abrogatio* only applies to the *foedus operum.* The *foedus gratiae* between God and sinners is never called into question. It is on this basis that the whole of Scripture, both Old and New Testaments, testifies to one single covenant of grace mediated by Jesus Christ. Reconciliation therefore extends backward even to the patriarchs, who in *promissione sine visione* were kept in an attitude of faith.[57] This, however, would not answer the question regarding the nations who had no vision of the coming Christ.

Cocceius meets the problem with the concept of the

---

[53] Cf. Gottlob Schrenk, *Gottesreich und Bund im älteren Protestantismus, vornehmlich bei Johannes Coccejus,* Gütersloh, 1923, p. 50.

[54] Federal theology is much older than the Reformation. Pope Gregory I (Magnus; 540-604) already said: *Sancti ante legem, sancti sub lege, sancti sub gratia, omnes hi perficientes corpus Domini in membris sunt ecclesiae constituti* (*Ioanni Episc.* [5] 18). Some of the Reformation theologians of the federal school have extended the *foedus* from the *sancti* to humanity at large.

[55] Schrenk notes that the *Helvetic Consensus* of 1675 repudiates the concept of *foedus naturale* in preference to the *foedus operum* as distinct from *foedus gratiae* (cf. *op. cit.,* p. 65 n. 3).

[56] Cf. *ibid.,* p. 67. Schrenk notes the name of Johannes Anastasius Veluanus whose covenant theology led him to repudiate double predestination and to emphasize universal salvation (cf. *ibid.,* pp. 51f).

[57] Schrenk explaining Cocceius' theology writes in italics: "*So war also Christus schon vor der Gesetzeszeit Objekt des Glaubens zur Gewinnung der Gerechtigkeit und des Heils*" (*ibid.,* p. 98).

foedus operum, which was already written into Adam's heart. For this reason he regards the decalogue as an integral part of the law of nature including the Sabbath law.[58] It would mean that man was endowed by reason of the "covenant of works" with a discriminating faculty to recognize right from wrong (cf. Rom. 2:14). This raises the question, On what basis did man obtain forgiveness prior to the death of Jesus Christ?

Cocceius insists that God's forgiveness before and after the Cross can only have one basis and that is the sacrifice of the Son of God, otherwise forgiveness would simply depend upon a despotic act on the part of God. But he makes a distinction between forgiveness in the Old Testament and forgiveness in the New Testament; in the former case it is only *paresis* (Rom. 3:25) as distinct from *dikaiosis,* which is only possible through faith in Christ. But even this "overlooking" of sin was only in view of the coming expiation effected by the Mediator between God and man.[59] It would seem therefore that according to Cocceius forgiveness was not a completed experience but only a keeping in abeyance God's final word of pardon.[60]

Because the covenant of grace applies to the whole of humanity, the covenant with Abraham was only a renewal of God's covenant with Adam after the Fall.[61]

We have quoted Cocceius by reason of the fact that we meet in him a theologian who sincerely strains toward a unified perspective that would embrace both Israel and the nations. Like Augustine,[62] Cocceius does not attempt to answer the question why God allowed the Fall; it remains an inscrutable mystery; but there can be no doubt about the broken covenant and man's need for reconciliation.

---

58 The Sabbath law was regarded by most of the Reformers as a natural law, which served as a means toward sanctification of the person rather than the day. Cf. J. Jocz, "Law & Grace," *Judaica,* Sept. 1965, pp. 175f.

59 Cf. *Moreh Nebochim, utilas distinctionis duorum vocabularum scripturae paresis et aphesis,* 1665.

60 Schrenk: "Der Schuldbrief war noch nicht zerrissen" (*op. cit.,* p. 145).

61 Cf. Schrenk, pp. 128f.

62 Augustine, *Enchiridion,* p. 27: *melius . . . indicavit de malis bene facere, quam mala nulla esse permittere* — "God thought it better to turn evil into good than not to permit evil at all."

CHAPTER FOUR:

COVENANT RENEWAL

Our investigation thus far has shown that the covenant between Israel and YHVH is a fundamental and an ancient concept. It goes back to the very beginning of Israelite tradition. We have also seen that the covenant was variously interpreted depending upon theological insights. Sometimes it was understood as conditional upon the people's loyalty to the national god; at other times it was regarded as a permanent and unalterable fact, no matter how disloyally Israel might behave. The latter view seems to have established itself mainly as a result of prophetic preaching. It is now next to impossible to decide which is the more original interpretation. Both attitudes carry a certain truth and the real difference lies in the emphasis. In either case the principle of YHVH's unfailing loyalty was never at stake. This is vouchsafed by the Old Testament concept of *ḥesed*. The balance between desert and grace is precariously upheld by Israel's prophets. In the prophetic books judgment and mercy alternate in response to the challenge of a given situation.

We must, however, differentiate between motives. When the prophets stress the "everlasting covenant" *(beᵉrîth 'ôlām)* they intend to stress the faithfulness of God. Paradoxically, Israel's punishment somehow relates to YHVH's faithfulness: "I will faithfully give them their recompense, and will make an everlasting covenant with them" (Isa. 61:8). Isaiah

24:5 expresses the paradoxical nature of the situation even more clearly: Israel has "transgressed the laws, violated the statutes and broken the *everlasting covenant,*" at the same time. It is therefore not a matter of chauvinist sentiment, which appropriates YHVH as Israel's national god who will "stick with Israel through thick and thin."[1] Such an interpretation of covenant is a possibility and there may be vestiges of it in the Old Testament literature, but Max Weber is grossly exaggerating when he likens YHVH to the Indian war god Indra.[2] He himself acknowledges the strangeness about YHVH-worship, of a god "from afar": "It was no local or tribal deity familiar of old, but a strange and mysterious form which gave the consecration to the sworn Israelite confederacy."[3] It will be difficult to make out a consistent case for the view that YHVH is nothing more than a "contractual partner" and that Israel had a special right upon him by reason of his vow.[4] This view though not entirely absent is not the dominant view. Max Weber is at fault to quote Deuteronomy 7:8 in support of it. The Pentateuch does not allow so primitive an attitude. It is also a mistake to exhaust the meaning of covenant by tying it to the Levite *torah* with its "fixed divine imperatives." Max Weber's namesake, Otto Weber, seems to us nearer the truth when he differentiates between the book and the covenant: the covenant is something other than the book. The book is only the "written intelligence" about the covenant that transcends it. In this sense the covenant is best understood as a *testament.* It is God's ordering, His disposition for His people.[5] This brings us close to the New Testament.

In the New Testament the balance between judgment and grace is even more difficult to maintain than in the case of the prophets. The equilibrium is constantly upset in favor of grace. Here *ḥesed* acquires additional depth, which profoundly affects the concept of covenant.

New Testament theology operates on the principle that grace is never merited and is utterly undeserving. God gives what man can never achieve on his own merit. This is not

---

[1] Max Weber, *Ancient Judaism,* 1952, p. 119.
[2] Cf. *ibid.,* pp. 127f.
[3] *Ibid.,* p. 124.
[4] *Ibid.,* p. 120.
[5] Cf. Otto Weber, *Ground Plan of the Bible,* 1959 trans., p. 25.

entirely unknown to Old Testament writers but the emphasis is here more pronounced. What is different, however, is the time factor. The Old Testament looks back and looks forward: there is repeated reference to God's gracious dealing in the past and there is promise for the future. In the New Testament the Now of salvation is of greatest importance. The renewal of the broken covenant relates to the immediacy of God's action in Jesus Christ.

1. THE "PLAN" OF SALVATION

There are two possibilities in our approach to *Heilsgeschichte:* either we start with the Old Testament and proceed to the New, or else reverse the process. Traditionally, the first method is regarded as the orthodox one. To start with the promises, the messianic expectation, the law, and to proceed to the fulfillment, advent, and grace, seems the most logical approach. But it is a logic that operates on the purely horizontal line of history. It therefore tends to overlook the vertical aspect of revelation, which always stands in tension with the purely historical.

Jesus Christ is not just the culminating point of Israel's spiritual development. He is not the end-result of a long process. Once we remove the unexpected, unpredictable element of revelation it loses its essential meaning and becomes a purely historical achievement. In order to preserve the true character of revelation we must allow for the disruptive, vertical aspect of God's entry into time.

Christians therefore have to read the Old Testament backward, as it were. They have to read it from underneath the Cross, in the light of the Resurrection, Ascension, and the giving of the Holy Ghost.[6] Their faith in Jesus Christ cannot depend upon Old Testament exegesis, but their Old Testament exegesis depends upon their faith in Jesus Christ.[7]

Seen in this light dispensational theology with its carefully worked out "plan" of salvation, which treats the Old Testament as a blueprint for the New Testament, tends to

---

[6] This explains the radical difference between Christian and Jewish exegesis. Cf. G. L. B. Sloan & Schalom Ben-Chorin, *Das christliche Verständnis des Alten Testaments und der jüdische Einwand,* Jerusalem, 1941.

[7] Cf. J. Jocz, "Das exegetische Problem und die Judenmission," *Judaica,* März, 1956.

reduce salvation-history to a time process.[8] If we speak of a "plan" at all we can only mean God's eternal purpose and determination to be *for* man.

The New Testament *now* of salvation has something to do with God's eternal decree, which the Bible expresses in terms of covenant. In this sense the covenant is never broken: God's promise endures forever. The irrefrangibility of the covenant expresses God's faithfulness — He is God and not man (Hos. 11:9); therefore He cannot deny Himself though man becomes faithless (II Tim. 2:13). For this reason, the prophet tells us, Israel is not consumed, because the God of Israel does not change (Mal. 3:6). In Him there is "no shadow due to change" (Jas. 1:17). *Euangellion,* the Good News, consists in the verification of this fact of which Jesus the Messiah is both token and pledge.

But salvation in time means salvation in history. Revelation cannot be so conceived that the vertical at no point impinges upon the horizontal. If this were the case it would not be revelation. *Heilsgeschichte* means that God acts in history on behalf of man. In this sense we may speak of a "plan," but it must not be conceived as an emergency measure. Traditional orthodoxy understood God's "plan" of salvation in terms of a plot: God created a perfect man; Adam foiled God's purpose by sinning; as a countermeasure God initiated the "plan" of salvation, which culminated in the advent of Jesus Christ.

The schoolmen occupied themselves with the question: *utrum Christus venisset, si Adam non peccasset?* St. Thomas in his wisdom shows reluctance to commit himself either way, but on the whole he sides with St. Augustine: "if man had not sinned, the Son of Man would not have come."[9] But St. Thomas was too good a theologian not to realize that such a position would imply that something happened without the knowledge of God, namely sin; he therefore falls back upon the expediency of predestination: "He predestined the work of the Incarnation to be the remedy of human sin."[10] But this in no way answers the problem; it still leaves the ques-

---

[8] Gabriel Vahanian describes millenarianism as an effort to institutionalize God's sovereignty (*The Death of God,* 1961, p. 23).

[9] Thomas Aquinas, *Summa Theol.,* part III, Q. 1, art. 3, quoting Augustine, *De Verb. Apost.,* VII, 2.

[10] *Ibid.,* reply to objection 4.

tion of evil, if not purposed, at least foreseen by the Creator. To this Thomas has a ready answer: "God allows evils to happen in order to bring a greater good therefrom," and he quotes Romans 5:20: "Where sin abounded grace abounded all the more." He concludes his argument: "Hence too, in the blessing of the Paschal candle we say: *O felix culpa quae tantum et talem meruit habere salvatorum.*"[11]

This raises more problems than it answers. St. Thomas was right in hesitating to commit himself to an answer posed by a hypothetical question. We cannot argue from what is, to what would have been if things were different. But the Pauline text in Romans cannot legitimately be used as a vindication of evil. To sing *O felix culpa* may be an expression of pious sentiment but cannot serve as justification for evil. Evil is too terrible a fact to be glossed over by liturgical chanting. The Fall must not be made a condition of grace and the Incarnation its ultimate purpose. There must be nothing contingent about grace, otherwise both God's goodness and sovereignty become questionable. No theologian has grasped the meaning of this fact in greater depth than has Karl Barth. We cannot do better than quote him: "The eternal will of God in the election of Jesus Christ is His will to give Himself for the sake of man as created by Him and fallen from Him."[12] This sentence is meant to emphasize God's eternal purpose, which is independent from the contingency of history. Barth makes the "election of grace" the beginning of all things in God's self-giving. This does not minimize the fact of Gethsemane and Golgotha. But it does mean that "the eternal history in God's bosom is *salvation* history."[13] In other words God is not taken unawares and His purpose with man is from eternity. The question therefore with which St. Thomas struggles requires a more theologically orientated answer: Christ, the Eternal Word, is man's Elder Brother with or without the Fall. But He need not have died upon the Cross had He come to a different world than ours. I Peter speaks of Him as "destined" (προεγνωσμένον) before the foundation of the

---

[11] *Ibid.*, reply to objection 3.
[12] *CD*, II/2, 161.
[13] Robert W. Jenson, *Alpha & Omega*, A Study of the Theology of K. Barth, 1963, p. 114.

world but made manifest at the end of times for our sakes (I Pet. 1:20).[14]

This still leaves the problem of sin an open question. We can have no ultimate answer, for our faith in a loving God conflicts with the fact of evil. This has always been an embarrassment to the Christian believer and will remain so to the end of time.[15] There are, however, provisional answers without attempting a theodicy in order to justify God before man. Some of these answers lie near at hand. Once we accept the biblical premise that God created man for partnership,[16] then we must presume that moral choice and personal freedom are necessary conditions for such a relationship. Attributes of choice and freedom would require the possibility of a negative attitude. There can only be meaning in man's "yes" if "no" is an alternative. Freedom, though in a limited sense, because circumscribed by man's creatureliness, is thus a gift that accompanies man's existence as man. Barth rightly says: "God in His freedom bestows human freedom," and he continues: "Here we must point to so-called *natural* freedom which constitutes and characterizes human existence in its creatureliness, and to

[14] Cf. K. Barth, *The Humanity of God*, 1960, p. 45. Rev. 13:8 reads according to AV: "The Lamb slain from the foundation of the world." But this is a mistranslation: RSV translates more accurately "foundation of the world" as a reference to the book and not to the lamb.

[15] Celsus the denigrator of the Christian faith and Origen its defender are both agreed on the difficulty of the mystery of evil, though Origen pretends to know the answer. Cf. *Contra Celsum*, IV, 65, 66. Origen falls back upon the demonic nature of the devil and his angels. Later he explains evil as a means of correction for man's blessing (*ibid.*, VI, 56-57). In *De Principiis* Origen accepts the orthodox position that the wicked spirits were not so created "but have obtained these degrees in evil in proportion to their conduct, and the progress which they made in wickedness" (*De Principiis*, VIII, 4). This, however, does not answer the question why God would allow it to happen unless He did not foresee the results. It is difficult to avoid the argument by Carneades later taken up by Sextus Empiricus that God lacks either in omnipotence or omniscience: He either is impotent to forestall evil or did not foresee it (cf. Bertrand Russell, *History of Western Philosophy*, 1946, pp. 261f). No one has grappled with the problem more assiduously than did Augustine, who was placed in the difficult position of opposing the Manichaeans, who overestimated the omnipotence of evil, and the Pelagians, who underestimated it (cf. Gerald Bonner, *St. Augustine of Hippo, Life & Controversies*, 1963; and also Anna S. Benjamin and L. H. Hackstaff, *St. Augustine, On Free Choice of the Will*, 1964, especially the Introduction).

[16] Cf. K. Barth, *The Humanity of God*, 1960, p. 45.

the freedom of eternal life promised to man."[17] If this is granted, moral evil, if not physical evil, becomes the responsibility of man. This, at any rate, is the orthodox answer to the fact of sin.[18] Theophilus of Antioch in his treatise against Autolycus explains that man's sin has even affected the venomous beasts who became evil with the fall of Adam — "for nothing was made evil by God, but all things good, yea, very good" (II, 17). But such reasoning is prompted by apologetic motives and only goes to show the extent of our embarrassment in view of the stark facts. In spite of Leibniz we have to admit that this is not a perfect world where good is in excess of evil,[19] but rather a world where good and evil are in unremitting tension.

The real problem of evil lies in its cosmic aspect. Those who treat evil as a subjective experience and explain it in terms of moral failure or associate it with the corruptibility of life can fall back upon a philosophy that overlooks its radical nature. On the moral side evil can be explained as a failure of human responsibility in the full exercise of freedom; on the creaturely side evil retains a purely subjective aspect: death and dissolution of the individual in no sense affect the continuance of the universe. In fact death may be viewed as a good either because such is the will of God or because it offers release from suffering.[20] The problem only becomes acute when evil acquires a cosmic connotation.

That such is the case in the Bible, at least in the New Testament, there can be little doubt. The question we have to face is whether the New Testament view of cosmic evil

---

[17] *Ibid.*, p. 75, in his essay: "The Gift of Freedom."

[18] Cf. Novatius, *De Trinitate*, IV, 22: ex quo omne malum facessat a deo nec enim potest fieri; Tertullian, arguing against Marcion, exonerates God for creating the Devil (*Adv. Marc.*, II, 10). For Tertullian evil is mainly disciplinary and a means of grace. God is not the author of *culpae* but of *poenae* (cf. *ibid.*, II, 14). Cf. also Irenaeus' argument against Marcion, *Adv. Haer.*, III, 25, 3f. Origen argues in a similar strain (*De Principiis*, II, 5), as does also Hippolytus in his *Refutation against All Heresies* (VII, 19).

[19] Cf. B. Russell, *op. cit.*, pp. 612f.

[20] Barth is able to see death as a *bonum* inasmuch as it expresses man's radical dependence upon God. Cf. *CD*, III/2, 608ff. For Schopenhauer death means freedom. Cf. "Über den Tod und sein Verhältnis zur Unzerstörbarkeit unsers Wesens an sich," *Die Welt als Wille u. Vorstellung*, Leipzig, 1847, IV, 41 (especially the end of the chapter). Cf. Jung's essay, "The Soul and Death," *The Meaning of Death*, ed. H. Feifel, 1959.

has to be treated seriously or can be dismissed as primitive mythology. The Christian concept of salvation, especially in the Pauline and Johannine literature, and in the letter to the Ephesians, hinges upon the question of cosmic evil. Ragnar Leivestad, who has examined in detail the ideas of conflict and victory in the New Testament, has shown how the contest between cosmic evil and Jesus Christ dominates the New Testament theme: *"Jesus is fighting the same hostile power both when exposing and overcoming temptations, and when delivering possessed persons, and . . . when healing the sick."*[21] The battle is fought in the cosmic arena and is in no way confined to the immediate situation. Leivestad says of John in relation to Paul: "The Johannine idea of cosmic trial is simply the Pauline idea of a cosmic triumph translated into forensic terms."[22]

It would appear that the drama of the Cross, according to the New Testament perspective, though taking place at a given moment in history, had suprahistorical significance. The "power of darkness" suffered defeat while to all appearances it was Jesus who was being conquered. In this context sin ceases to be moral deficiency and acquires an other-worldly, sinister aspect. It becomes a mystery. Bultmann's definition of sin as *Eigenmächtigkeit*[23] would appear to be inadequate to convey the link with the beyondness of evil. Tillich's use of "the demonic" to express the structural, and therefore inescapable power of evil,[24] has at least a New Testament ring.

Leslie Hunt in an unpublished thesis dealing with the subject of "Cosmic Spirit Powers in Pauline Thought" finds "that Paul's treatment of the subject of sin is largely governed by his conception of it as something external and objective. It is for him a mysterious power and not native

---

[21] Ragnar Leivestad, *Christ the Conqueror*, 1954, p. 42 (Leivestad's italics).

[22] *Ibid.*, p. 260.

[23] In *Kerygma und Mythos*, 1948, p. 41. Cf. also Bultmann's *Theologie d. Neuen Testaments*, 1948, pp. 237ff.

[24] Paul Tillich, *The Protestant Era*, 1951, XXXV. Tillich observes that "religious self-determination is the negation of religion" (p. 151). "Eigenmächtigkeit" and "self-determination" mean the same; the difference between the two writers is that while Bultmann "demythologizes," Tillich "psychologizes," while the N.T. literally assumes cosmic intrusion of evil into the human sphere. For the demonic aspect of freedom, see P. Tillich, *Courage To Be*, pp. 151f.

to man or to the material world, but intruding into human nature on its lower side."[25] This would suggest a fatalistic concept of human life in which man finds himself the playball of capricious and mischievous spirits. But oddly enough, there is nothing fatalistic about Pauline theology or New Testament theology in general. The reason for it is that evil is not another god; there can be no anti-god as opposed to the Father of Jesus Christ. Tertullian's argument against Marcion turns on this issue. But on the other hand evil cannot be rationalized; it is more than *privatio boni,* it is a cosmic fact which God allows but did not create. There can be no simple escape from the paradox. To "demythologize" evil destroys the cosmic meaning of salvation, to psychologize it makes salvation a purely subjective experience.[26]

The second reason why there is no trace of fatalism in the New Testament, as in the rest of the Bible, has something to do with the biblical view of man. It belongs to his dignity to make a moral choice: "sin is couching at the door, its desire is for you, but you must master it" (Gen. 4:7). Berkouwer rightly stresses that freedom is a God-given endowment but it is the peculiar freedom tied to creaturely existence: not freedom from God but freedom for God. "Speaking biblically," he observes, "we can only say that sin enslaves man, just as it originally robbed him of his freedom and made him a man bound in the fetters of sin."[27] Man is therefore, and paradoxically so, both free and bound: bound, because empirically he is always a sinner; and free, because God's gift of freedom is never denied.

The contradiction is inherent in the human situation that derives from man's creaturely position. He cannot so be free as to exceed his limitations. Because God made him for Himself, he can only be free in his freedom *for* God. Whenever he makes himself free for evil, he becomes a slave.

Another approach to our problem lies in the area of Hegelian dialectic: good cannot be a reality unless evil is

[25] Leslie Hunt, *Principalities & Powers,* MS at Wycliffe College Library, Toronto, n.d., p. 379.

[26] Prof. Donald McKinnon: "It is sheer nonsense to speak of the Christian religion as offering a solution of the problem of evil. There is no solution offered in the gospels" (*The Listener,* April 4, 1963, p. 587).

[27] G. C. Berkouwer, *Man: The Image of God,* 1962, p. 321.

also real. Tillich's concept of nonbeing[28] and Barth's doctrine of the *nihil*[29] can only serve as possible hypotheses in order to satisfy man's natural need for an answer. The fact of evil itself is beyond rationalization not only because it appears to contradict the goodness of God, but because by its very nature it is irrational. Man knows about evil as a contradiction of reason and can only express it in terms of the absurd.[30] But he experiences it as a fact both in the arena of history and in his own private life. The demonic aspect of history is classically expressed in Jean-Paul Sartre's play, *The Devil and the Good Lord.* Götz von Berlichingen has the best of intentions, but no matter how he may try, it all comes to naught and only results in misery to others. Nonsense is the result of man's best efforts and evil always triumphs. For a modern description of personal evil deliberately chosen as a "good," the life-story of Jean Genet is perhaps the best example.[31] A numinous description of an intuitive encounter with evil is provided by Sir Ralph Richardson. He tells how during a stay in a hotel in Corsica he suddenly awoke about 3 o'clock in the morning and was overcome by a sense of the presence of a malevolent power: "It was in fact, like a great dynamo of power, to me something super-human." The nearness became so intolerable that he had to leave the room and walk into the street. This is how he concludes his story: "I have never seen anything supernatural, but since my visit to Vizzavona, I have never lightly dismissed the possibility of a power of evil."[32] We cannot build a theory on the subjective experience of a man half-awake, though Sir Ralph assures us that there was no

[28] Paul Tillich, *Courage To Be*, 1952, pp. 32ff.

[29] For a discussion of Barth's concept of the *nihil* see G. C. Berkouwer, *The Triumph of Grace in the Theology of K. Barth*, 1956, pp. 60ff.

[30] The irrational nature of evil is forcefully portrayed in the writings of French existentialists who conceive of life itself as an evil because devoid of meaning. For a study of the literature see Hazel E. Barnes, *The Literature of Possibility*, 1961. For a discussion of the nature of the absurd in the American novel see Richard Kostelanetz, *The Listener*, May 13, 1965, pp. 705ff. Also: Angus Wilson, "Evil in the English Novel," *The Listener*, Dec. 27, 1962, pp. 1079f.

[31] Sartre, *Saint Genet, Martyr-Comedian;* cf. Hazel E. Barnes, *op. cit.*, pp. 29f, 324f, 340ff, etc.

[32] *The Listener*, July 19, 1962, pp. 89f. For the demonic aspect of evil and as a force in the "great economy of history," see Jacob Burckhart, *Force & Freedom*, Meridian Books, 1955, pp. 64, 164, 320f.

trace of sleep left in him. But the accumulative evidence of human experience through the ages provides sufficient ground for a more serious view of the demonic. The tendency in our day is to explain evil psychologically as the projection of the human subconsciousness, as is done by Jung with great persuasiveness.[33] But there may be more to the Devil than we moderns are prepared to allow. Goethe once said: *"macht mir den Teufel nicht zu klein, einen Kerl den alle Menschen hassen der muss was sein."*[34]

We have again dwelt on the subject of evil because it lies at the heart of the doctrine of salvation. We freely admit that there is no logical answer to the problem. To break the vicious circle we have to give up the idea that the "plan" of salvation is God's answer to man's Fall. Here Barth has seen with great clarity: God's purpose with man in Christ is from all eternity. Jesus Christ is the Man who not only follows but also precedes Adam. In Him is constituted the interior history of humanity: "This history between God and man in the person of Christ is, *as such*, God's history with mankind." In these few words Robert W. Jenson has managed to define Barth's view regarding the relationship between God and man.[35] From this position the story of the Fall and the fact of sin appear in quite a different light. The Devil, evil, sin, man's fallenness, cannot be taken more seriously than God and His purpose with man.

On the one hand, we have to take evil seriously in all its cosmic significance, but on the other hand we must not make of evil *another* god, a rival to the Holy Trinity. The Devil is not an anti-God, though he is anti-Christ. Sin, in the last resort, is, as Barth puts it, an "ontological impossibility." God has said "no" to sin in Christ from all eternity, and God's "no" is an eternal No. Sin, therefore, though a terrifying reality in history, cannot and must not carry ultimate ontological significance. Grace outweighs sin: this is the message of the Bible. Berkouwer has summarized Barth's position in the following sentence: "Sin is horrible reality but it *cannot* break through the limits set by the boundary

[33] Cf. C. G. Jung, *Psychology and Religion: West & East*, pp. 168, 197, etc. Cf. also H. L. Philp, *Jung and the Problem of Evil*, 1958, p. 42.

[34] Don't tell *me* the Devil is small:
a chap whom all hate must be tall (free translation).

[35] R. W. Jenson, *op. cit.*, p. 131.

of grace."[36] To Berkouwer this appears as a subtle way of demythologizing evil. He asserts that the struggle against sin is a real struggle and evil must not be pre-empted in such a way that the Cross appears as a dramatic gesture of an already predetermined result. Such an "*a priori* triumph" would reduce the passion and the death of the Son of God to a mere symbol.

Barth's answer to Berkouwer's criticism is illuminating: whereas Berkouwer treats grace as a theological principle which is supposed to dominate Barth's thinking, Barth himself proceeds on different lines. Not impersonal "grace" as a principle, but the living presence of Jesus Christ is the decisive factor: "We are concerned with the living person of Jesus Christ. Strictly, it is not grace, but He Himself as its Bearer, Bringer and Revealer, who is the Victory, the light which is not overwhelmed by darkness, but before which darkness must yield until it is itself overwhelmed. He Himself is present as the Victor from the very outset."[37] Once this priority of Jesus Christ is grasped in all its ramifications the sting of evil is broken and God is seen as sole Victor.[38]

Because Jesus Christ is seen as the object of God's eternal election, evil as opposition to God is already "in time and in all eternity negated, rejected, condemned and excluded" by His eternal decree. This does not deny the reality of sin; on the contrary, when it is seen in the light of Christ's victory, it is seen "in its concrete opposition to the will of God active and revealed in Jesus Christ." In fact it is here that we see it in all its stark reality. The fact that we cannot explain it only adds to its starkness: "If we could explain how it may have reality it would not be evil."[39] In Jesus Christ God is for and on behalf of man in spite of sin and death. The covenant in Jesus Christ extends to all mankind. This covenant is not annulled by Adam's fall; as Barth puts it: "Adam excludes Christ, but Christ does not exclude Adam." In view of God's eternal purpose in Jesus Christ, the "plan" of salvation cannot be understood as an emergency decision. Salvation does not begin with the Fall and

---

[36] *Op. cit.*, p. 88.
[37] *CD*, IV/3/1, 173.
[38] *Christus ist Sieger* was Blumhardt's motto.
[39] *CD*, IV/3/1, 177.

with sin; it begins with election. In Christ, Adam was chosen to be man before he fell from grace, and because God is God Adam is still God's chosen one in spite of sin and evil.[40]

2. THE MEANING OF SALVATION

"Salvation" is a peculiarly Old Testament expression: *yasha'* etymologically denotes "width," "spaciousness," "freedom from constraint," and in a wider sense, "deliverance." Darwell Stone, the author of the article "Salvation" in Hasting's *Dictionary of the Apostolic Church,* takes care to distinguish between "external deliverance" and "spiritual deliverance."[41] But such a distinction would be utterly foreign to the Old Testament writers. In the Old Testament salvation is concretely understood as deliverance from danger or trouble.[42] Such deliverance is wrought by God Himself: "in the thought of the Old Testament salvation is affected by no human act, but by God alone."[43] That God acts as Savior on behalf of man is basic to the whole Bible. The peculiar emphasis upon "spiritual" salvation in later theology is a departure from the holistic view of the Bible. The Gospels portray Jesus as the Savior who heals body and mind at the same time. By the same token, the Old Testament, against all appearances to the contrary, lays stress upon the inwardness of salvation, as does the New Testament. Here is H. H. Rowley's considered opinion: "There are passages in the O.T. which think of salvation from physical and political subjection. . . . But such salvation was never thought of as the deepest and most fundamental need of man. Salvation from sin that separated him from God, and that cursed him by its corrupting touch, and restoration to the favour and fellowship of God were of greater significance and importance."[44]

It would appear that in both Testaments, though the emphasis will vary from book to book, salvation extends to the whole man and society in all physical and spiritual aspects. The great lexical variety employed in the Old Testa-

---

[40] For a good discussion of the problem of evil, see Alasdair C. MacIntyre, *Difficulties in Christian Belief,* SCM Book Club, 1959, especially pp. 28, 32f, 43.

[41] Cf. Hasting's *Dict. of the Apostolic Church,* II, 445.

[42] Cf. Hasting's *Dict. of the Bible,* 1903, IV, 358b.

[43] H. H. Rowley, *The Rediscovery of the O.T.,* 1945, p. 156.

[44] *Ibid.,* p. 156.

ment to describe salvation is matched by Greek equivalents in the New Testament.[45] *Apolutrōsis* as a basic New Testament concept has Old Testament roots and a long history behind it. In the New Testament λύω carries the connotation of being *freed* on the one hand, and forgiven and reconciled on the other. The Hebrew equivalent for λύτρον is *kopher*, "covering" of sin, with the connotation of expiation and the price of redemption at one and the same time. The same applies to *go'ēl*, redeemer: the one who acts on behalf of him who is in need of redemption and also pays the price. The *go'ēl* is usually a next-of-kin to whom falls the duty of redemption as the head of the family. Proksch tells us: "When applied to God, *go'ēl* means that He assumes the legal responsibility of the family to act as next-of-kin and to pay the ransom money for his chosen one whether it be on behalf of the forebear Jacob (Gen. 48:16) or the people of Israel."[46]

The Old Testament vocabulary with its cultic background and tribal custom was carried over into the New Testament. The question we have to face is whether the sacrificial terminology associated with the concept of salvation is to be treated literally or only carries metaphorical significance when used in the New Testament.

Alan Richardson treats the sacrificial nomenclature in the New Testament as "redemption-metaphors." He discounts the idea of a transaction, or "actual payment" of the ransom price in the New Testament: "the suggestion of a ransom-payment has virtually disappeared from the conception of ἀπολύτρωσις."[47] Alan Richardson's position may be difficult to defend in view of passages like I Corinthians 6:20; 7:23; Acts 20:28; Ephesians 1:7; I Timothy 2:6, where salvation is paid for with the life-blood of the Savior. Furthermore, the New Testament sometimes uses expiatory expressions in reference to the Cross (cf. John 1:29; I Peter 1:18f). These and other passages could be explained as metaphors only on the assumption that salvation is a purely subjective experience. The moment we give objective significance to the story of redemption, the position changes.

---

[45] *TWNT* lists 13 derivations in addition to λύω.

[46] *Ibid.*, IV, 331. The structure of the German sentence is somewhat complicated.

[47] Alan Richardson, *An Introduction to the Theol. of the N.T.*, 1958, pp. 218, 220f.

Paul Tillich has tried to circumvent the old antithesis between the objective and subjective approach in theology but it is doubtful whether this can be successfully accomplished.[48] Richardson seems to evade the problem by identifying atonement with the "fact of salvation," but this only creates a tautology and thus results in a circular argument.

On the other hand, if there is an objective aspect to salvation, then the New Testament "metaphors" acquire a meaning closely related to Old Testament concepts. The whole issue hinges on the answer to the simple question: how and in what sense does Christ's death benefit me? The *forensic* answer, which relates forgiveness to divine justice, appears artificial if it is meant that God the Son pays the debt to God the Father. It is only when the story of redemption is placed in the context of the covenant that the perspective changes. Within the covenant relationship atonement on the Cross ceases to be a *special* act because nothing else proved sufficient; it becomes the supreme sign of God's eternal faithfulness. Because the covenant keeps the relationship on God's side open, the Cross becomes the token that God is for sinners all the time whether the sinner accepts Him or not.

The covenant also safeguards the objectivity of Christ's sacrifice. It is not merely an appeal to my conscience to repent but a manifestation of God's love *before* I repented. Christ died, not in order to preserve a principle of law, but in order to reveal the extent of God's love. The Cross is not a parable nor is it a dramatic gesture but a *real* sacrifice — Jesus truly died. But man's salvation is not in the fact that Jesus died — but that He died for us. The sacrifice of the Cross is God's sacrifice. Unless we associate Jesus of Nazareth with God the father in a unique and unheard of way, He becomes a martyr and the gospel makes no sense. It is only when the Cross is seen as a sacrifice of God that its radical nature becomes evident.

Seen in this light, atonement is a real and historic act. But it is not man's act, and does not depend upon man's experience. It is an act of God on our behalf: He atones for the sins of the world. But why should the Son die so that the Father might forgive?

---

[48] Cf. Otto Wolff, "Paul Tillich's Christologie des 'Neuen Seins,'" *NZST*, Heft i, 1961, pp. 140.

Here there are two necessary corrections which must be kept in mind: (1) the unity of will and purpose between Son and Father. It is not so that the Father watches the Son die for the sake of a principle. If the mind of Jesus is at all a reflection of the mind of God, then in the Son's death the Father participates. Within the Christian context we may legitimately speak of the death of God for the sake of mankind, though this may appear sheer blasphemy to non-Christians. (2) Forgiveness without atonement is essentially an immoral act. It becomes a display of arbitrary sovereignty and makes a mockery of the distinction between right and wrong. A god who forgives by decree or *fiat* is not the kind of God we know from the Bible.

The *skandalon* of the Christian faith is that God in the person of Jesus Christ identifies Himself with sinners and dies in their stead. This is no cheap victory, nor is it a mythological dramatization of an inner-psychological process, whereby the suffering of the victim becomes a cathartic experience to the onlooker.[49] Salvation, i.e. atonement, forgiveness, and rehabilitation, requires more than a psychological subjective experience in order to be effective. It requires an "objectivity" quite apart from the subjective experience of the believer. This is to say that the death of the Son of God radically affects God's attitude toward sinners. But we cannot accept Anselm's concept of "satisfaction" in the sense that Christ's endless worth makes amends for God's offended honor. Such an approach is out of keeping with the nature of God as we know Him in Jesus Christ.

Johann Christian Konrad von Hofmann (1810-77) like every other theologian struggled with the problem of the Atonement. In spite of criticism by Hübner[50] and others[51] there is an aspect in his theology that commands attention. For him the *telos* of the world is to bring to completion God's loving purpose with man. Barth observes that von Hofmann was led to evolve a Christian philosophy of history by reason of his linking predestination with providence.

---

[49] Compare the anonymous article by "A Barrister," "Society & the Criminal," *The Listener*, Dec. 27, 1962, p. 1072.

[50] Cf. E. Hübner's article in *RGG*, 3rd ed., III, 420f.

[51] For Barth's assessment of v. Hofmann see *Die protestantische Theologie im 19. Jahrhundert*, 1952, pp. 553ff, especially in relation to Schleiermacher.

Biblical revelation, as von Hofmann sees it, is nothing else but the historic realization of God's eternally predetermined purpose to overcome sin and so to restore fellowship with sinners. "This leads him," says Hirsch, "to the concept that there is an eternally posited relationship in God towards man which breaks forth and overcomes all opposing disruptions which dominate temporal-terrestrial life."[52] We can see that for Hofmann salvation is not an emergency measure undertaken to overcome the obstacle of sin but part of God's eternal purpose. But von Hofmann still operates with the "recapitulation" concept originating with a passage in Irenaeus.[53] This is understood to signify that the humanity that suffered defeat in Adam triumphed in Jesus Christ: "For if man's conqueror had not been man," explains Rashdall, "the enemy would not have been conquered justly."[54] Behind the recapitulation concept is the ἀνακεφαλαίωσις theory, which operates on the basis that "humanity" stands for "nature" shared by both Adam and Christ. But such abstractions as "humanity" and "nature" are ill fitting to the concrete biblical singularity of the Man Jesus. It is a New Testament premise that the Messiah precedes Adam and that the Second Adam is First. St. Paul's "Man of heaven" (I Cor. 15:48) is the prototype of Adam, the latter bearing the image of the first. It is the believer's destiny to be conformed to the image of God's Son (Rom. 8:29). The curious passage in the Lucan genealogy where the son of Adam and the Son of God are placed in juxtaposition (Luke 3:38) means exactly this: Christ is before Adam (cf. also John 8:58; 17:5, 24). In Pauline thinking, predestination, foreknowledge, election, are all connected concepts relating to God's eternal purpose with man. Reconciliation (καταλλαγή) literally means "exchange": the Son of God becomes man, so that man becomes God's son — this is the free gift of God's grace (Rom. 5:15) whereby rebellious man is restored to the covenant.

The question, therefore, how is man "saved" by Christ, is patient of a very simple answer: man is saved by God's

---

[52] E. Hirsch, *Geschichte der neuern evangelischen Theologie*, 1960, V, 425.

[53] Cf. Irenaeus, *Adv. Haer.*, III, 18, 1. The Latin reads: in seipso recapitulavit. Cf. Hastings Rashdall, *The Idea of Atonement in Christian Theology*, 1919, pp. 237ff.

[54] *Op. cit.*, p. 239.

condescending Presence in Jesus Christ. That God deigns to be present in *this* way is the objective aspect of Atonement. This is a thoroughly biblical answer in complete conformity with Old and New Testaments: God saves by His Presence.

The thrice-holy God, before whom no sinner can survive, stoops to the point of man's greatest need and unreservedly offers Himself at the risk of rejection. This is God's sacrifice: His dignity, His honor, His majesty, He places on the altar for the sake of sinners. The Cross can be rightly described as an act of "propitiation" if we care to use cultic terms, but it is propitiation in the reverse order: it is God who propitiates. He is the acting agent: He sacrifices, He dies,[55] he initiates an act of At-one-ment in which all mankind becomes involved.

It is in relation to the Cross that the depth of the *skandalon* embedded in the gospel becomes apparent. That God relinquishes His glory and becomes a Servant for the sake of sinners is near blasphemy. Such a statement cuts at the very meaning associated with the universal concept of God. It is a frightening statement to make that God dies so that man should live; only pagans could hold such a view.[56] The God of Israel is from eternity to eternity. It is monstrous to speak of the birth and the death of God.[57] But in the last resort, this is exactly what the gospel seems to imply: God becomes man and dies upon a cross.

When Moses asked to see God's glory (Gen. 33:18f), we are told that He let all His goodness pass before him. This remarkable insight that God's glory is His goodness and not His majesty is a foreshadowing of the statement by Jesus that to be a servant is greater than to be served (Luke

---

[55] The death of God in Christ Jesus constitutes a theological problem that is paralogical. It does not mean that when Christ died upon the Cross, for three days the Godhead was minus the Second Person of the Holy Trinity. Barth insists that the humiliation and death of the Son of God in no sense alter His Godhead; cf. *CD*, IV/1, 179, 185. Cf. also D. M. Baillie, *God Was in Christ*, 1948, pp. 96f.

[56] A. Toynbee in *The Study of History*, VI, 1939, Appendix, discusses the "correspondences between the story of Jesus and the stories of certain Hellenistic saviours." Cf. also T. W. Doane, *Bible Myths & Their Parallels in Other Religions*, 1882, pp. 216ff.

[57] The protracted controversy regarding the Virgin Mary as *theotokos* relates to the sense of the inappropriateness of reducing God to human frailty.

22:27). The task of the Son of Man is to give His life a ransom for many (Matt. 20:27). The New Testament applies the logic of these statements literally. It sees in Jesus the Son of God who stoops down to the level of sinners. This stooping down spells salvation. The crude literalness of the Incarnation, namely that God makes His abode with man, is softened by the dimension of faith. This is especially the case in the Johannine writings.

Outside the dimension of faith Jesus remains the carpenter's son, the man of Nazareth, a prophetic figure full of charm. But within the category of faith, He is the Son of God, the Sin-bearer of the world, the Savior of sinners, the Representative of God the Father. These two aspects run parallel and constitute an inner tension in the story of the Gospels. As a prophet, Jesus of Nazareth appears as a preacher of righteousness. In this context "salvation" carries a moral connotation and makes an appeal to man's conscience: "repent," return, and be healed. But at a deeper level Jesus of Nazareth is the Son of God, the Harbinger of God's reign, the Executor of His Father's will. He pronounces forgiveness and acts with extraordinary authority. He is God's unique plenipotentiary among men.

Because man lives at one and the same time within and without the category of faith the two presentations go together. The way to God is from the outside toward the inner circle: from Jesus the prophet to the Son of God. There is a straight line from the Sermon on the Mount to the story of the Resurrection, from the message of the Kingdom to the Presence of the King. Not everyone is able to enter the inner circle: some will only hear the Sermon and listen to the parables and admire the preacher. For them forgiveness, at-one-ment, sonship, participation in the covenant promises, are as much available as for those who believe. But they lack the penetration, the ability to see beyond the merely visible, and so they remain unaffected. The fact that some believe and others do not, we cannot explain, for it touches upon the mystery of human freedom and divine grace.[58] We can, however, say that there is here a moral element involved: inability "to see beyond the merely visible" is not a lack of a mystical sense or of the gift of special perception, but moral

[58] Cf. the author's article in *Cap and Gown*, Wycliffe College, 1965: "The Gift of Faith," p. 20.

failure. There is a sense in which man refuses to see and respond: he prefers darkness to light (cf. John 3:19f). This raises the question: in what manner is Jesus Christ present to sinners?

The answer is that He is present to them by total identification: He is the Man utterly for others.[59] It means that Jesus Christ places Himself at their side and stands with them. He pronounces no judgment, for He came not to condemn the world but that the world might be saved (John 3:17). But according to the New Testament He does more than identify Himself with sinners: He takes upon Himself the judgment and punishment that follow upon godlessness. The meaning of this can only be understood if we allow a moral universe, so constructed that evil, sin, godlessness carry consequences from which there can be no escape. A fortuitous universe indifferent to right or wrong would imply that God Himself is both Creator and Destroyer, Judge and Executioner. This goes contrary to the meaning of the gospel.

The burden of man's godlessness the Son of Man willingly takes upon Himself. The Resurrection is a mighty act of God vindicating the principle of right over wrong and love over hate. Since Jesus died and rose again no man stands alone: the Son of God is with him even at the gate of hell. Here the Old Testament concept of *ḥesed* as covenant love celebrates its greatest triumph. The covenant in Christian terms means God's solidarity with sinners. Salvation therefore carries a double connotation: God's freedom for man and man's freedom for God.

There remains to be said something about the "substitutionary" theory. The Methodist bishop G. Bromley Oxnam, like many others, here registered his objection to this theory on the grounds that it is utterly unmoral. He asks: "If Jesus paid it all, or if He is the substitute for me, or if He is the sacrifice for the sins of the world, then why discuss forgiveness?" His rejection of the theory is uncompromising: "I cannot see forgiveness as predicated upon

---

[59] Cf. K. Barth's chapter: "Jesus, Man for Other Men," *CD*, III/2, 45, 1 (pp. 203ff). Cf. D. Bonhoeffer, *Christology*, 1966 trans., pp. 114f: "*Christus pro nobis*"; also Ulrich E. Simon, *A Theology of Auschwitz*, 1967, pp. 107ff, where he writes of Christ's presence in the concentration camp.

the act of someone else. It is my sin. I must atone."[60] Similar criticism has been voiced by Jewish writers. It must be granted that some Christian theologians present the "substitutionary" theory of the Atonement in terms that suggest a legal fiction. But at a deeper level the substitutionary theory goes to the heart of the gospel. It is only when interpreted in personal terms — the involvement of Jesus Christ in the life of sinners — that the theory expresses the depth of divine love. Here forgiveness precedes repentance: while we were yet sinners, Christ died *for us* (Rom. 5:8). The *pro nobis* (ὑπὲρ ἡμῶν) carries an echo of the temple cult and is reminiscent of Isaiah 53: "he was wounded for our transgressions, he was bruised for our iniquities." But there is also a profound difference between the principle of equity as expressed in the sacrificial cult[61] and the Atonement by the Cross. In the sacrificial cult it is man who propitiates God; the Cross stands for the opposite: God, the offended party, takes the initiative and pays the penalty. For the writer of the letter to the Hebrews the temple cult was only a "shadow" of better things to come (Heb. 9). He did not think that the blood of bulls and goats could take away sins (Heb. 10:4). By contrast to temple worship the Messiah rendered the sacrifice of obedience, even to the point of His own death. This total surrender on behalf of others is a new kind of sacrifice: here is personal, willing, obedient commitment prompted by measureless love. Christ becomes sin for us so that we should in Him be made the righteousness of God (II Cor. 5:21). This strange "exchange" is the real meaning of the substitutionary theory.[62]

The Cross cannot be viewed from a position of formal ethics, neither can it be understood as an impersonal principle. If it were a matter of juridical justice Paul's concept of grace would contradict all norms of equity. But the gospel does not uphold an impersonal principle — the righteousness of God is utterly different from what man calls

---

[60] G. Bromley Oxnam, *A Testament of Faith*, 1958, p. 144.

[61] The moral question: Why should the life of an innocent animal take the place of the life of a guilty man?, is not easily answered except by the psychological process of projection. For a theory of the origin of sacrifices cf. George Every, *Lamb to the Slaughter*, 1957. Cf. also H. Ringgren, *Sacrifice in the Bible*, 1962, pp. 30ff.

[62] On καταλλάσσειν, see K. Barth, *CD*, IV/1, 75.

righteousness. God's righteousness is the righteousness of the "One who loves in freedom."[63] The Cross stands for the incredible statement that God chooses to exchange places with sinners. The bitter cry of dereliction (Mark 15:34) the church interprets as Christ's determination to share man's godforsakenness to the very end of the road. He chooses to endure the consequences of sin to the last drop: for the sake of sinners He goes to hell.

Once again we come face to face with the doctrine concerning the Holy Trinity. It is only on the assumption that God acts personally and uniquely in Jesus Christ that the Christian doctrine of the Atonement makes sense. If God merely accepted the vicarious death of a third party He could not be the Father of Jesus Christ. The Christian faith stands and falls with the premise that in Christ God Himself acts on man's behalf, not by proxy and not by a divine fiat but by sacrifice.

In the light of biblical revelation we may thus arrive at a few principles that can serve as a guide to the meaning of salvation:

(1) Salvation in biblical terms implies an I-Thou relationship. God does not offer *something,* but Himself. He treats man as a person in his own right and addresses Himself to him. The Word of God, the Voice of God, the messenger of God, presuppose a personal encounter. There is here dialogue between God and man. This fact is of great significance for the Christian doctrine of salvation. When we say that God acts in Christ on our behalf we do not mean that He acts by proxy but that He Himself acts. Because God is not a thing but a Person[64] we must assume that the relationship between God and man is essentially personal. Salvation by fiat does violence to the moral order and contradicts man's status as a person. God does not impose salvation, He offers it. "It," though a grammatical necessity, is here a theological misnomer: Salvation is not a "something," God offers Himself. God in His humility allows man the choice. He lets him say No and allows Himself to be rejected.

Strictly speaking, salvation is not a noun but a verb; it is not a concept but an act; it is God's action on behalf

---

[63] *CD,* IV/I, 187.
[64] Cf. Edgar Sheffield Brightman, *Is God a Person?,* 1932.

of man. It is best described as a verbal noun: "God acts as Savior."

He acts as Savior not from the height of His majesty and the security of heaven. He acts as Savior from below, by taking man's position and carrying his cross. He would not be the Father of our Lord Jesus Christ if God offered less than Himself. Certain aspects of Patripassianist theology are not entirely devoid of truth. The suffering of the Son involves the Father in suffering: "the Son suffers, the Father, however, shares in the suffering,"[65] is theologically well justified. An impassible God may suit philosophy but ill accords with Christian theology. St. Thomas Aquinas' position that "God is altogether impassible and immovable" (*Summa Contra Gentiles,* ch. XIII) is motivated by philosophical and not theological suppositions.

As far as man is concerned salvation means accepting God in the person of Jesus Christ. We are told that to know the love of Christ is to "be filled with all the fullness of God" (Eph. 3:19). "Fullness" is here a metaphor and must not be taken literally. No creature can contain the fullness of God but he can experience His boundless love in Jesus Christ. That love is expressed in the fact that the Son of God takes the sinner's place; there is an exchange of positions: God humbles Himself so that we may be exalted in Christ Jesus.[66] Love is impossible in impersonal terms; if it means anything, it must mean a relationship between persons. Salvation therefore cannot mean the legal promulgation of a decree, or the fiat of a god who acts as he likes. Salvation carries a moral connotation: God gives Himself away and acts on behalf of sinners.

(2) This raises the question of equity. Salvation in the Christian context violates the law of justice: I incur the penalty and someone else pays the price. This constitutes an outrage to man's established values.

Unless we distinguish between God's righteousness and human justice there is no answer to this problem. *Tsedāqāh* in relation to God cannot be translated into legal language. The righteousness of God of which St. Paul speaks (Rom. 3:

[65] J. F. Bethune-Baker, *An Introd. to the Early Hist. of Christian Doctrine,* 1949, p. 104. For the subject of Patripassianism see J. K. Mozley, *The Doctrine of the Incarnation,* 1936, pp. 148ff; also Bertrand R. Brasnett, *The Suffering of the Impassible God,* 1928.

[66] Cf. *CD,* IV/1, 131f.

21f) is not legal justice; it means clemency, compassion, pity. This is already so in Deutero-Isaiah where it frequently carries the connotation of salvation and redemption.[67]

St. Paul uses the expression δικαιοσύνη τοῦ θεοῦ always in connection with the atoning sacrifice accomplished by the Messiah. It stands for God's free and sovereign will to justify sinners. Jesus Christ is the token of God's χάρισμα as a personal and free gift (Rom. 5:15, 16). That Christ should die for the ungodly (Rom. 5:6) is an odd "righteousness," for it upsets all our moral values, which are mainly based upon the principle of *lex talionis:* tit for tat.

This constitutes a major revolution in the moral order: it not only violates the concept of equity, it abolishes it. No wonder that theologians have strained to interpret Christ's Atonement on the Cross in legal terms. Every legal interpretation of the Cross is an effort to save the toppling structure of our own moral values. But God's righteousness as we discover it in the gospel not only exceeds, but contradicts legal justice. This is not only a moral revolution but a profound theological upheaval: God ceases to be the guarantor of legal justice — He is seen as the Father who loves to the uttermost.

(3) Salvation carries a moral and inward connotation. The saving act, though objectively demonstrated in history when Jesus died upon a Cross, becomes a subjective experience to all who in faith accept God's gift. This is an experience of renewal followed by forgiveness, reconciliation, and justification. As such it can never be a legal pronouncement impersonally performed, but rather a personal relationship between God and sinners. Salvation is here an involvement, a relatedness between persons. The extent of man's involvement in the saving act of Christ is best illustrated in the sacrament of baptism where the believer becomes caught up in Christ's death and resurrection (cf. Rom. 6). It is not so that Christ dies while the believer remains a passive onlooker. He dies with Christ in order to be raised with Him to newness of life: "For if we have been united with him in a death like his, we shall certainly be united with him in a resurrection like his" (Rom. 6:5).

This complete identification of disciple and Master in

---

[67] Cf. N. H. Snaith, *A Theol. Word Book*, ed. A. Richardson, 1950, p. 203.

death and resurrection has a double aspect. It takes place as it were on a twofold plane: here and now in the process of history, but also in the *eschaton* when ultimate salvation will become the experience of God's saints.

The metamorphosis within the believer would carry no moral significance if it were accomplished by a divine fiat in which the believer has no personal part to play: he must accept salvation; he must want to be saved. God graciously withdraws His sovereignty out of respect for the human person. Salvation imposed, or mechanically processed, is not salvation in the biblical sense and carries no moral value.

The result of salvation is man's openness for God. Enclosed, self-centered man, entirely sufficient in himself, in constant vigil of his autonomy, is now open to hear and to obey.

These few remarks in no sense exhaust the mystery of the Cross. In the last resort we do not understand why it was necessary for the Son of God to die so that we might be reinstated as sons. It is significant that the church was never able to work out a dogma of Atonement as it did in the case of the Holy Trinity.[68] There is no ultimate answer for the reason of God's love for man nor the unusual form He took to express it. All we can say is that the Cross is God's way of saving man. Before the Cross we must refrain from rationalizing; it will not do to reduce Christ's sacrifice to a theological formula. God's ways are past finding out. We will return to the subject when we come to speak of the Cross.

But one thing we must say and say with every emphasis, namely that salvation cannot be discussed at all outside the covenant. It is only in the context of the covenant that God reveals Himself as *Deus pro nobis*. Salvation is just this: God is for us and was so from the beginning, though we did not know it. The covenant is the pledge and token of this fact. Barth rightly regards "the Covenant as the presupposition of reconciliation."[69] For without the background of the covenant, reconciliation, redemption, salvation, sonship, etc., remain mere theological concepts devoid of the historical background that warrants

[68] Cf. Eric L. Mascall, *Words & Images*, 1957, p. 96.
[69] Cf. *CD*, IV/1, 22-66. This is the title of a whole chapter.

the assumption of God's condescension toward mankind. Within the covenant salvation is grounded in God's predetermined council to act in all eternity as the God *for us.* Seen in this light, New Testament salvation is the manifestation of His faithfulness as the covenant-keeping God. Here *ḥesed* assumes dimensions of depth that by far exceed man's sin and rebellion.

3. THE TIME OF SALVATION

Time must primarily be conceived as a dimension within space.[70] Because God is not confined to space He is outside time. But He is the author of time. Time began when God created heaven and earth. Aristotle's definition of time as "the measure of motion and rest" relates to the fact of change in the physical realm. Here time has meaning only in a world of constant change. In this context there is no correlation between time and eternity.

But for man time has yet another aspect. Time is primarily a subjective experience, time "is essentially man's time."[71] As such it is experienced in a double context: in reference to nature and in reference to history. These two aspects do not necessarily coincide. Time in relation to nature is described by the cycle of birth and death. In this respect man participates in the constant change of the physical world. But time also relates to history; on this level time acquires a totally different quality. It becomes the bearer of moral values where it is determined not by change but by acts and decisions. In this case time and eternity correlate.

In the historical perspective of time, past, present, and future relate differently than in the case of the cosmic cycle.

---

[70] Whether time can be conceived as an entity is a complex philosophical problem. Leibniz in controversy with Samuel Clarke, Newton's disciple, contradicted the idea that time exists by itself. It only represents an "order of succession" and is formed by relation to bodies. This is in contradiction to Newton, who treats time as a "something," irrespective of external things. Cf. Ralph B. Winn, "Our Pre-Copernican Notion of Time," *The Journal of Philosophy,* Vol. XL, No. 15 (July 22, 1943), 409f. For the concept of time in modern physics, see Lincoln Barnett, *The Universe and Dr. Einstein* (Mentor ed.), 1962, pp. 46ff, etc.

[71] Ralph B. Winn, *op. cit.,* p. 404.

a. The two aspects of time

Because man lives in these two perspectives of time, the cyclic (physical) and the historical (moral), he frequently confuses the one with the other. Sidereal time relates to the rhythmic flow of nature and prescribes the duration of our pilgrimage here upon earth. But historic time takes us out of the realm of cyclic existence and places us in a different realm. In the moral realm where historic time operates, man exercises his will in contradiction to physical law. Here he affirms his humanity in terms of personal and corporate existence. On this level, past, present, and future are not related chronologically but morally, so that Bultmann can say with justification, "In your present lies the meaning of History."[72]

In order to understand the difference between time historically conceived and chronological time we must bear in mind that past, present, and future only relate to events but not to experiences. Ralph Winn has shown that human experience moves in the opposite direction from events: the subject moves to the future while events remain in the past. Thus subjects move "forward" while events move "backward." He therefore contradicts Bergson's concept of the Now that is made to depend upon chronological time. Winn contends that only subjective time has the Now as its basis: the objective Now always passes, the subjective Now is always present.[73] The fact that we experience objective events as receding into the past is only an illusion. In themselves they are timeless, but they become present to us in the Now of subjective experience.

This is important to us in order to understand biblical time, especially with reference to salvation. Biblical time is not to be conceived chronologically but historically in the sense of divine and human actions. Especially when the decisions and actions are God's, biblical time carries the connotation of salvation-history (*Heilsgeschichte*). In this special context an unusual reversion takes place: events are not any more measured by time, but time by events.

---

[72] R. Bultmann in an address on the Third Program of the BBC; cf. *The Listener*, Sept. 1, 1955, p. 330: "The Quest for the Meaning of History."

[73] *Op. cit.*, p. 408.

Paul S. Minear puts it this way: "In the Bible God's activity is not defined by time; on the contrary, his activity is the basis for the only genuine measurement of time."[74] It is obvious that the reference is not to chronological time, but to historical time, i.e. time that can only be defined in terms of decision and action. It means that the circular flow of time in which human life is caught up is impinged upon in such a way that it suddenly assumes direction moving toward a goal.

It would therefore seem that human life that takes place both on the physical and historical planes is determined by a double motion: the cycle of birth and death, and the goal set by history. These two aspects of time are determined by the will of Almighty God, who is both Creator and Savior. Within the realm of creation we depend upon sidereal time; within the realm of salvation we depend upon historical time. This leaves us with a dichotomy, an existence broken in two parts: physical and spiritual. But oddly enough the Bible refuses to accept such a dualism. It cannot do so for the reason that the same God who is Creator, is also Savior. The answer to our problem is the eschatological hope: the redemption of our bodies (cf. Rom. 8:23). It means that man is redeemed in his totality, both body and soul. It is for this reason that we referred to the breaking asunder of our cyclic existence.

But redemption in history can never be a completed experience as far as man is concerned. While exposed to chronological time he can only be a pilgrim on the move to his ultimate goal (Heb. 11:10, 14-16). Here he can only have a "taste" of salvation (Heb. 6:4), awaiting in patience God's faithful promises.

Biblical time is thus futuristically orientated: the *eschaton* is not "timelessness" as Cullmann rightly insists but the coming Age (αἰὼν μέλλων) when God's gracious purpose will find ultimate completion.[75] History must not be con-

---

[74] P. S. Minear, *Eyes of Faith*, 1946, p. 99.

[75] Cf. O. Cullmann, *Christ & Time*, 1951, p. 50. Prof. Cullmann deplores the Gnostic tendency in theology toward the "timeless Beyond." He refuses to oppose time to eternity, for the reason that eternity is anchored in time. "Timeless metaphysics," he says, is foreign to the N.T. It is, however, a question whether Cullmann is not going too far in his insistence upon the coincidence of time and

ceived as time endlessly extended so that it assumes a cyclic character but rather as limited in both directions: in the backward direction it begins with Creation and the covenant; in the forward direction it ends with the eschatological hope realized.[76]

b. THE CONNECTION BETWEEN χρόνος AND καιρός

We have seen that the distinction between chronological time and historic time creates a rift in the human situation which seems to be contradicted by the Bible. We therefore have to investigate the nature of the relation between χρόνος and καιρός.

Theologians understand under χρόνος "measured time," describing duration, whereas καιρός they interpret to mean time in the sense of "opportunity and fulfillment."[77] It therefore appears that in the New Testament καιρός acquires the specific significance of redemptive time or *Heilsgeschichte*. At what point, if at all, do the two aspects of time coincide?

So far we have related these two aspects of time only eschatologically. It means that in God's good time His purpose will ultimately extend to the whole of creation and the totality of human life, soul and body. But this overlooks the important fact that salvation touches man not only eschatologically but in his temporal existence. Does this mean that "redemptive time" (καιρός) touches man sporadically, from time to time, while chronological time continues without a break? The same question can be differently formulated when approached from another angle: how is general history related to *Heilsgeschichte?* Or else: what is the connection between the history of the nations and the history of Israel? Or, we can put the same question in more general terms: how does the history of revelation relate to world history?

All these questions touch upon the problem of biblical particularity. What concerns us here is to demonstrate the uniqueness of biblical revelation within the repetitious circularity of chronological time. In other words, if there are two kinds of time, at what point do they converge?

---

eternity. His concept of eternity as extended time gives it a spatial aspect.

[76] Cullmann, *op. cit.*, p. 47.

[77] John Marsh, in *A Theological Word Book*, p. 258.

The importance of this question becomes clearer when we ask ourselves why certain events within the area of biblical revelation should become endowed with special significance while similar events outside that area carry no such significance. To give a concrete example: the death of Jesus of Nazareth is endowed with unique importance and carries revelatory significance of the first order. But the death of Socrates, which is equally impressive from a human point of view, carries no revelatory significance.

If the birth and death of Jesus Christ is of such importance that it decides about the salvation of the human race, what will happen to the millions who have lived before His time or who have never yet heard of Him?

Such questions were already raised by pagan objectors to the exclusive claims of the early church, and Christian apologists were hard pressed for an answer. Justin in his *First Apology* refers to the objection by pagan critics that those born before Christ are left outside salvation and must be declared "irresponsible." Justin falls back upon his doctrine of the *logos* whereby Christ was already present, though not in visible form, to mankind prior to the Incarnation; and all those who lived according to reason (κατὰ λόγου) were Christians without knowing it.[78]

Another answer, already suggested in the New Testament, is in reference to the forebearance and patience of God: because of divine forebearance God "had passed over former sins" (Rom. 3:26). A similar statement we find in Paul's sermon on the Areopagus: "the times of ignorance God overlooked, but now He commands all men everywhere to repent..." (Acts 17:30).[79]

The question of time was brought up by that severe critic of Christianity, Celsus. For Celsus time is essentially circular: "the appointed cycles recur in the past, present and future." There is a sameness about events in nature; and though things go and return, in essence they remain unchanged. Under such conditions neither contingency nor particularity is possible, which makes the Christian claims futile.[80]

---

[78] Justin, *First Apology*, ch. 46; cf. *Second Apology*, ch. 13.

[79] Cf. Justin's *Monarchia* where he speaks of the longsuffering of God, who allowed a time of forgetfulness (ch. 1).

[80] Cf. Origen, *Contra Celsum*, IV, 60, 65.

Origen's answer is most illuminating. First, he points to the consequences of Celsus' position with regard to free will: if Celsus is right then "our free will is annihilated."[81] Next, he shows that his opponent's argument would lead to the extraordinary conclusion that there is no movement in history at all and thus Socrates as well as his accusers will return and do as they did before. This is an absurdity that needs no refutation. Origen proceeds then to give a biblical construction to history as against the static and circular concept. He points out that God disrupts the flow of time and intervenes in history. The acts of God are not reducible to general principle but occur whenever God chooses to exercise His "healing power upon those who were labouring under the disease of wickedness." Origen therefore allows for *special* times as and when determined by a sovereign God: "I am of the opinion that it is at periods which are precisely determined beforehand that He sweeps wickedness away, so as to contribute to the good of the whole world."

Events in history take place according to plan and order, as nothing is ever neglected by God: "for He does at each particular juncture what it becomes Him to do in a perverted and changed world."

Origen compares God's acts in history to those of the farmer who acts "according to the various seasons of the year." Like the husbandman whose actions depend upon the soil and the season "so God administers entire ages of time, as if they were, so to speak, so many individual years, performing during each one of them what is requisite with a reasonable regard to the care of the world; and this, as it is truly understood by God alone, so also it is accomplished by Him."[82]

Origen understands *Heilsgeschichte* as sovereign acts of God that intervene in the flow of time and so impinge upon world history. But we must not so divide history as if biblical events were God's acts and all other events that make up the history of the nations were outside His providence.

---

[81] *Ibid.*, IV, 67.

[82] *Ibid.*, IV, 69. Hanson has shown Origen's deficiency in historical perception. For Origen, history is mainly a parable. Cf. R. P. C. Hanson, *Allegory and Event*, 1959, pp. 276f, 278f, 283, 286.

Prof. Cullmann, in order to relate world history to the history of revelation, draws two concentric circles: with Christ in the center, the inner circle represents the church, the outer circle represents the world. Because Cullmann regards eternity as the extension of time in the direction of infinitude, he has no difficulty in attaching to revelation a horizontal dimension. For this there is a legitimate reason in view of the Incarnation as the "mid-point" of history.[83] Cullmann criticizes Barth for his hesitancy to discard the nontemporal aspect of eternity.[84] He protests that primitive man knew nothing of a timeless God. But such emphasis upon time robs revelation of its vertical dimension and so tends to blur the difference between καιρός and χρόνος.

Admittedly, timelessness in the Platonic sense of eternal ideas is totally foreign to both Testaments. But at the same time we must not lose sight of the fact that for the Bible, though God is the Lord of history, He Himself stands outside the flow of history. He is thus beyond and above time. John Marsh regards Psalm 90:2 as the classical example where *'ôlām* ceases to be a quantitative entity and assumes qualitative proportions: "Before the mountains were brought forth, from everlasting to everlasting thou art God."[85] Barth's view seems to be more accurate when he says that "eternity does not cease when time begins, but time begins and continues in the lap of eternity."[86]

We suspect that Cullmann's insistence upon the confluence of time and eternity may have something to do with the modern prejudice toward any form of dualism. But where no such prejudice exists, as for instance in the Fourth Gospel, time and eternity are held apart. John sharply distinguishes between τὰ ἄνω and τὰ κάτω: those who are

---

[83] Cf. *Christ and Time*, pp. 82ff. Cf. also *Salvation in History*, 1967 trans., pp. 176, 270f, 285.

[84] *Ibid.*, pp. 62f. On Cullmann's quarrel with Barth, see *Salvation in History*, pp. 16, 62, 176.

[85] *Theological Word Book*, p. 265b. Marsh observes that though the O.T. "never quite breaks clear" of the temporal aspect of "everlastingness," Ps. 90 suggests the "beginning of a qualitative differentiation" (*ibid.*, p. 266a).

[86] *CD*, II/1, 593. In the later edition of *Christ & Time* (1962) Cullmann explains that his concern is not with *time* but with promise and fulfillment. Cullmann's more recent views in *Salvation in History* seem to be nearer the Barthian position.

born "from above" move within a different dimension. Christ Himself came "from above" and is returning thither. Flesh and spirit are here two separate realms; the first belongs to earth, the second to heaven. Prof. Dodd has no doubt that in John we meet an assumed dichotomy which cannot be expressed in any other way than in terms of this-worldly and other-worldly: "This pre-temporal (or more properly non-temporal) existence of the Son is affirmed with emphasis and assumed all through the Gospel."[87]

A similar division exists in St. Paul's letters. As in John, so here, there is a sharp distinction between flesh and spirit, Kingdom of God and world, earth and heaven. For Cullmann to deny that there is such a dialectic in the New Testament is simply to fly in the face of textual evidence.[88]

It would thus appear that in terms of time, eternity is "nontime," or to use the more technical New Testament expression, ζωὴ αἰώνιος. Eternal life is qualitatively different from "this world" (cf. John 12:31). But such a radical separation would make encounter impossible. If revelation is to be a real encounter between God and man it must take place upon the plane of this world and within the contingency of history. Within the category of revelation the two times, καιρός and χρόνος, must somehow coincide. The Christian faith rests on the premise that the coincidence of time and eternity takes place in the person of Jesus Christ. This is both the Pauline and Johannine view. As far as history is concerned Jesus' life takes place within the category of χρόνος. He is exposed to all the contingencies of history: born at the time of Caesar Augustus . . . died under Pontius Pilate. As far as eternity is concerned: "He reflects the glory of God and bears the very stamp of His nature" (Heb. 1:3). He is both, an act of God (καιρός) and a historical phenomenon (χρόνος). As history, Jesus belongs to the past; as revelation He is present to the world. In Him time and eternity converge and impinge.

From Jesus Christ, the "midpoint" of history, we can

[87] C. H. Dodd, *The Fourth Gospel*, 1953, p. 260; cf. p. 304.

[88] Cf. Cullmann, *op. cit.*, p. 146. Cullmann's insistence upon alignment "with the horizontal process" (*Salvation in History*, p. 176) lessens the tension which he tries to maintain between the "already" and the "not yet."

approach the problem of the particularity of biblical revelation. If χρόνος is conceived not in terms of circular movement but horizontally, then it carries with it the characteristics of history such as particularity, contingency, and limitation. The writer of Ecclesiastes was not presenting the biblical position when he said that there is nothing new under the sun (Eccl. 1:9). History as movement implies newness, eventfulness, and surprise. Origen's answer to Celsus is well taken: history that constantly repeats itself makes no sense. God creates new things (Isa. 48:6f).

But because God impinges upon history the old is not abandoned, but recreated. He renews the face of the earth (Ps. 104:30); He renews man into His own image (II Cor. 4:16). He renews the covenant with His people (Jer. 31: 31). He makes all things new (II Cor. 5:17). The connection therefore between καιρός and χρόνος is not concurrent on the horizontal line like two contiguous movements, but rather like the convergence of two lines moving in different directions. καιρός impinges upon χρόνος so that history achieves a purpose.

c. Continuity and discontinuity

This still leaves us with the problem of the *continuum* of time in relation to the spontaneity of revelation. It centers on the question why God waits and bides His time.

D. M. Baillie discusses this problem in respect to the doctrine of Atonement.

Unless atonement has both an eternal and a historical aspect, it becomes meaningless. If we confine it to a moment of time in history we rob it of its eternal significance; if we see it in terms of eternity we take away the concrete aspect of historical event and reduce it to a general principle. Baillie rightly remarks that this would "obscure the reality of evil" and "reduce the historical episode of the Cross to a merely accidental symbol of a timeless truth."[89] Bonhoeffer touches upon the same problem in a different connection.

As a believing Christian, Bonhoeffer discusses the question of the continuity of being which is disrupted by the discontinuity of acts. He has at least two answers to give: First, "faith as an act knows itself as the mode of being

---

[89] D. M. Baillie, *God Was in Christ*, 1948, p. 190.

of its being in the Church"; which means that the believer participates already in Christian action by association with the community of believers. Though he may not be involved at a given moment in acts of faith personally, he is involved corporately by reason of belonging to the church. Second, discontinuity does not inhibit "the continuity of divine activity at work upon man." [90]

It is the second answer that helps us in our query regarding the spontaneity of revelation. Baillie rightly observes: "We cannot say that God was unforgiving until Christ came and died on Calvary."[91] But such an answer only makes sense if we posit a covenantal relationship at the beginning of history. What God is toward us, He was already to our fathers, because He pledged Himself to be our God from the very beginning. At no time was man outside God's providence. *Sub specie aeternitatis,* revelation is a continuous act, but within the contingencies of history it carries the character of spontaneity. The discontinuous acts of revelation derive from the nature of history and not the whimsicality of God. Within the flow of time life consists of sequences. Time is divisible and progressive, there is a before and an after. Only thus do events take place; they intersect the continuum of time and fill it with significance. Biblical particularism is anchored in this fact.

Universal principles are not timebound. They apply to every age and under all circumstances. But because of this they are impersonal and therefore lack the concreteness of historical event. Biblical history, by reason of its particularity, is tied to a certain age, culture, geography, ethnic group, etc. This constitutes a stumbling block to those who deal with principles and not with concrete events.

Origen feels most apologetic about biblical particularism. His problem is how to relate Israel's national history to the rest of humanity. Celsus asks, Why of all people the Jews? Origen's answer is most unconvincing: when the nations were scattered as a result of the confusion of tongues, the Jews were the only people who remained in the East. Not only so, but they retained the primeval

---

[90] Dietrich Bonhoeffer, *Act & Being*, 1956, pp. 128f. For continuity and discontinuity as a theological principle, see S. T. Such, *Justification,* A Reaffirmation and a Reinterpretation (MS at Knox College Library), Toronto, 1965.

[91] *Op. cit.,* p. 191.

language, loyalty to God and to His ordained constitution. Moreover, though this people became guilty of sin and suffered punishment, their sins were not of a nature that could not be pardoned.[92] Origen thus falls back upon merit in answer to Celsus' questioning; he maintains that the Jewish way of life and Jewish wisdom were far superior to that of other nations, even to "those who have the appearance of philosophers."[93] There is thus good reason why they were called a "chosen generation," "the portion of God," and "a holy nation." But all this belongs to the past. Since the Jews rejected their Messiah, "this economy of things and this divine favour" is now transferred to Christians who have received from Jesus the power that was formerly manifested among the Jews.[94]

From a theological point of view Origen's answer is less than satisfactory for several reasons, but mainly because election is here explained in terms of merit and not of grace.[95] Once election becomes a matter of merit God's covenant loyalty is by-passed and the covenant itself is pushed into the background.

The offense of particularism, which is a basic feature of historic revelation, remains a stumbling block to this day. But at no time was it felt more keenly to be contrary to the canons of reason than at the time of the Enlightenment in the eighteenth century. One of the most representative figures of that age was undoubtedly Gotthold Ephraim Lessing (1727-81). Lessing lays down the principle that divine truth by its very nature must be timeless and a-historical. Because "historical truths" are uncertain and therefore accidental these can never serve as a substitute for the necessary truths of reason. In this regard Lessing only voices a common view. Henry Chadwick has shown that both philosophers and theologians of the period were all agreed on this point. Leibniz, Fichte, Kant, Schleiermacher, D. F. Straus, and even Newman, all give preference to the universal idea, as against the particular-

---

[92] Cf. *Contra Celsum*, V, chapters 31-32.
[93] *Ibid.*, chs. 42-43.
[94] *Ibid.*, ch. 50.
[95] For the patristic deviation from the biblical concept of grace see T. F. Torrance, *The Doctrine of Grace in the Apostolic Fathers*, 1948.

ism of history.[96] Chadwick's observation on the subject is well taken: "A certain devaluation of the process of history is a perennial characteristic of all idealism, whether in Plato, Clement and Origen, Leibniz and Lessing, Bernard Bosanquet and W. R. Inge."[97] As an example, Chadwick quotes Lord Herbert of Cherbury (1583-1648), who is regarded to be the forerunner of English Deism, as saying: "My belief in God . . . is not derived from history, but from the teaching of the Common Notions."[98] The appeal to Common Notions is the perennial appeal of the philosophy that in the Middle Ages found its expression in scholastic Realism. We can now see why a man like Martin Luther, who took biblical revelation seriously, had to side with the Nominalist school as against the Realists.

Karl Jaspers of Basel in an article on "The History of Mankind as seen by the Philosophers" still speaks within the tradition of Realism when he says: "God does not show himself in history in any single, unique manner."[99] The Bible takes the exactly opposite view: here each event is unique, unrepeatable, and carries a personal connotation. It cannot be subsumed under any general rule. Here lies the radical difference between καιρός and χρόνος: χρόνος is the continuous flow of time circumscribed by the laws of nature, whereas καιρός takes place in the Now of decision on the moral and personal plane.[100]

Only what is continuous can be reduced to Common Notions and defined as a law of nature. The discontinuous is unpredictable, undefinable, and outside the flow of time. Though it takes place in time it moves on the historical plane and not the chronological. The Now of decision disrupts the cycle of continuity and introduces a moral element: in this context things do not just happen, they are *willed*.

---

[96] Cf. Henry Chadwick, *Lessing's Theological Writings*, 1956, pp. 31ff.

[97] *Ibid.*, p. 41 note.

[98] *Ibid.*, p. 33. The quotation is from Lord Herbert's *De Veritate*, published in Paris, 1624.

[99] *Universitas*, Vol. 6, No. 3, 1964, p. 218.

[100] Cf. E. Brunner, *The Mediator*, 1947, p. 303: "All study of nature is directed toward overcoming the idea of uniqueness; our whole aim is to be able to discover and apprehend the laws of nature. In nature anything that is unique can safely be ignored; it is non-essential."

The urgency of the gospel message stems from the biblical concept of time as καιρός. Hence the emphasis upon the Now of opportunity and decision: Behold, now is the acceptable time; behold, now is the day of salvation (II Cor. 6:2). The whole emphasis in the letter to the Hebrews is upon the importance of "Today": today, when you hear his voice, do not harden your hearts (Heb. 4: 7; cf. 3:7, 13, 15). In the Fourth Gospel the now –νύν– is a more concentrated form of the Old Testament *hayyom*. According to C. H. Dodd, John has transformed the whole perspective of the original *kerygma* by placing all possible emphasis upon messianic time as fulfilled eschatology: the hour has come and *now* is (cf. John 4:23; 5:25; 12:23; 13:1; 16:21; 17:1).[101] St. Paul's attitude is not very different. Although for him eschatological fulfillment belongs to the future, the messianic future begins Now.

d. Salvation and the Kingdom of God

The crisis of messianic time derives its seriousness from the message of the presence of God's Kingdom. The Now of salvation is the Now of opportunity and grace. This was the message that Jesus preached. It is summarized in the short sentence: Return, the Kingdom of God is at hand! The Here and Now of God's reign has become visible in the person and witness of the Messiah. He represents God's presence in the midst of His people. Jesus thus says to Zacchaeus the tax-collector: "Today salvation has come to this house" (Luke 19:9). Israel's tragedy is precisely in this, that he did not know the time of his visitation (Luke 19:44).

Man cannot say: "I still have time." "How could one speak," asks Brunner, "of the Kingdom of God otherwise, than in terms of the most urgent decision?"[102] Man's time is never his own. In the presence of Jesus Christ history is placed at the brink of eternity: in Him the End becomes visible. The End is both a day of judgment and a day of salvation. The *yom YHVH* always carries this double connotation.[103] Man is invited to place himself under the grace

---

[101] C. H. Dodd, *op. cit.*, p. 7. On the subject of promise and fulfillment, see Walther Zimmerli, *Interp*, July 1961, pp. 330ff. For criticism of Dodd's view see Cullmann, *op. cit.*, 1967, pp. 32ff, etc.

[102] *The Mediator*, p. 421.

[103] Cullmann quotes Markus Barth, who holds that the O. T. *yom*

of God. The invitation extends to the ends of the earth: Come unto me, all who labour and are heavy laden, and I will give you rest (Matt. 11:28). [104] Those who refuse to come place themselves under judgment in that they love darkness rather than light (John 3:19).

This raises once again the vexed question regarding those who lived before the time of the Messiah.

We have already seen how early Christian apologists have tried to cope with this problem. The New Testament answer that in the times of ignorance God "winked" at man's folly (Acts 17:30) is only a preliminary answer. Justin's effort to fall back upon the concept of *logos* in the broad Greek sense is even less satisfactory. Even Brunner's answer does not quite meet the problem. He holds that "before Christ there was no final decision, because the ultimate had not yet been presented to man; all that faced him was the historical element." With the coming of Christ "an alien element" entered history.[105] This does not completely answer the problem why those before Christ should be denied the privilege of knowing Him whom to know is life eternal (cf. John 17:3). There is no way out of the difficulty unless we fall back upon the covenant once again.

From the Christian point of view Jesus Christ breaks history asunder: there is a difference between *ante et post Christum natum*. He constitutes the "midpoint" in the story of man's sojourn here upon earth.[106] But those who lived before Christ were not outside the covenant. Naturally, God does not demand what He does not give. No one who lived before Christ could have been expected to know Him as we do, namely in the historical context. But by reason of the covenant man already moved within the area of God's promises, God's grace, and God's Kingdom. The covenant is the area of God's providence over history. It means that though knowledge is historically conditioned, salvation is not. Those who walked in God's ways before Christ are

Yahweh is carried over in the N.T. as "the day of our Lord Jesus Christ" (cf. I Cor. 1:7f, etc.). In this case the aspect of judgment is even more obvious.

[104] There is a direct connection between Matt. 11:28 and Isa. 45:22.

[105] *The Mediator*, p. 306.

[106] Cf. Hegel's dictum: "All history goes back to Christ and originates in Him. The appearance of the Son of God is the axis of world history" (*Die Germanische Welt*, Leipzig, 1920, IX, 331).

caught up in the great act of salvation so that together we rejoice in God's infinite grace. This is what the writer to the Hebrews meant when he said of the Old Testament saints who were kept in suspense — that "apart from us they should not be made perfect" (Heb. 11:40).

God was as near to the patriarchs as He was to the apostles; He was as present to the prophets as He was to the early church. The signs and tokens of His grace may vary but His grace remains eternally the same. *Immanu-El* — God with us — is both a promise and an experience within the covenant.

This, however, does not solve the problem regarding those who are ignorant of the covenant and live as men without hope. This refers not only to the ignorance of the nations before Christ's coming but to the majority of the human race in our days.

If salvation spells out God's reign upon earth, then salvation has not yet reached to the nations. We still face a situation in many ways similar to that at the time of the Apostle Paul. But the Kingdom of God is governed by *καιρός* and not *χρόνος*. It is not an evolutionary process within history but the impingement of God's presence in Christ upon history. Salvation is Now but is never completed on this side of eternity. Biblical time points to an ultimate future. The Kingdom of God is here and not yet.[107] The church lives between the two Advents and the world is kept in suspense.

Salvation on the historical plane can never be an absolute, unless history be halted. Within the flow of time there can be no finality. At the point where *καιρός* and *χρόνος* meet there is tension, and man is exposed to it on every side. Though the Kingdom of God is made visible in the Person of Jesus Christ, Christ Himself is invisible except to the eyes of faith.

Here we must say a word about the world religions.

The unique and exclusive claims the church makes on behalf of Jesus Christ are contradicted by the fact that there are other ways that seem to lead in the same direction. Especially at times when syncretism is rife, as it is today, it is difficult to maintain the uniqueness of the gospel message. There seem to be only two attitudes possible:

---

[107] Cf. J. Jocz, *The Spiritual History of Israel*, p. 219.

either the cults of the nations are demonic aberrations of the truth, which seems to be the New Testament position; or else, all religions express an intuitive knowledge of God though marred by many accretions. There are Christian protagonists for both views.

Prof. Hendrik Kraemer, who spent years of study of world religions in relation to the Christian faith and who has lived in non-Christian countries, is able to avoid both alternatives without surrendering the exclusiveness of the gospel message. He readily acknowledges the positive values in the non-Christian religions but at the same time maintains that they are *erroneous* when viewed from the perspective of the Christian faith. The radical difference between the religions and Christianity is the fact of Jesus Christ: "Jesus Christ presents us with an entirely new world of facts and norms."[108]

J. H. Bavinck's view is somewhat similar. He rejects Barth's radical negation of all religion as unbelief and prefers to see in every religion a modicum of truth. This he does by distinguishing between the individual and the system. He contends that we must not underestimate the power of God's mercy, though he readily admits that "God's word which He is speaking to the individual Gentile is always thwarted and frustrated." At the same time we must not take the view that God cannot break man's resistance and stir his heart.[109]

There is, however, a difficulty that we must not evade: if God is no respecter of persons then He could not have confined His revelation to one particular people and leave the nations in utter ignorance.[110]

There are several answers to this question; the best known is by the Apostle Paul: what can be known about God, namely His eternal Power and Deity, can be clearly perceived in the things of creation. But the nations have misused that knowledge and have perverted it into idol-

[108] Hendrik Kraemer, *Why Christianity of All Religions?* 1962, p. 96.

[109] Cf. J. H. Bavinck, *The Impact of Christianity on the Non-Christian World*, 1949, p. 108.

[110] This is exactly Arnold Toynbee's contention: If God is love, He must in some measure and form have revealed Himself to other civilizations as well; cf. *Christianity Among the Religions of the World*, 1957, p. 96.

worship (cf. Rom. 1:18-23). This passage has given rise to the theory of universal revelation as distinct from the special revelation vouchsafed to Israel. Whether the elaborate structure of natural theology can be borne by this slender text has been questioned by theologians under Barthian influence. Johannes Witte has examined the text as to its inner meaning and related it to other texts that bear on the subject. The result is negative: the nations have a presentiment of God (*Ahnung*) but He remains to them the "unknown God." There is no such thing as universal revelation.[111] Not that God has left Himself without a witness, but His witness has been perverted and misunderstood: "therefore they are without excuse" (Rom. 1:20).

It would therefore seem that St. Paul's answer is largely negative: the nations do not know God in spite of their religions (cf. Gal. 4:8; Eph. 2:12).

In classical federal theology of the seventeenth century, the difficulty was overcome at least in part by making a distinction between two Greek expressions: before Christ's coming God "overlooked" the former sins (*paresis*) but now since Christ died upon the Cross only *aphesis* applies, i.e. man is forgiven in virtue of expiation by His blood (Rom. 3:25).[112] Though the philological distinction is somewhat artificial the theological insight cannot easily be contradicted. An important passage in Barth's *Church Dogmatics* helps us out of the difficulty. Paul, according to Barth, admits that the heathen know God by revelation through the natural order, but inasmuch as "in religion man bolts and bars himself against revelation by providing a substitute," that revelation is contradicted by man's religious autonomy. They therefore are unable to assess their real condition until confronted with the proclamation of the grace of God in Jesus Christ. That they have no excuse they only know subsequently when offered forgiveness through the Cross of Christ.[113]

This answer, which is thoroughly biblical, would appear

---

[111] Cf. Johannes Witte, *Die Christus Botschaft und die Religionen*, 1936, pp. 36-45. For Barth's exposition of Rom. 1:20 see *CD*, I/II, 306f.

[112] Cf. Gottlob Schrenk, *Gottesreich und Bund im älteren Protestantismus*, 1923, p. 81.

[113] Cf. *CD*, I/2, 303ff.

harsh and unloving except for the fact that here historic "Christianity" must be included insofar as it is religion and not gospel.[114]

In one sense, because God is the God of history, He is also the God of the religions. But this general statement must not blind us to the fact that man also is the maker of history and therefore the maker of his religion. It is only when we take seriously man's sinful nature, his rebellion and his self-sufficiency, that we can assess properly the demonic character of the religious instinct. Idolatry is prompted by the demonic desire to reduce God to man's own size so that He becomes manageable and can be exploited to advantage. What good is a god who cannot be thus used? This fact must be taken into full account when dealing with the phenomenon of religion.

As far as the Christian faith is concerned, it stands and falls with the uniqueness of Jesus Christ. Visser 't Hooft has shown the weakness of syncretism and how it annuls the essential meaning of the gospel. Syncretism, he notes, has no use for revelation in the decisive sense, has no center and no point of reference.[115] Because the church stands upon the premise of the covenant as God's gracious calling in Jesus Christ it can never truly be syncretistic. It may have acquired foreign elements in the course of time, but these are never central to its faith. The center of the Christian faith is Jesus Christ. Inasmuch as the religions of the world refute the exclusive claims Christ makes upon man, they are aberrations of the truth and therefore falsehoods.

---

[114] H. Kraemer, *op. cit.*, p. 91.

[115] W. A. Visser 't Hooft, *No Other Name*, 1963, p. 89. Cf also J. Jocz, "Syncretism or Faith?" *Cap & Gown*, Wycliffe College, Toronto, 1967.

CHAPTER FIVE:

THE MEANS OF SALVATION

The whole structure of Christian theology rests upon the biblical supposition that man cannot live without God and fulfill his destiny. His dependence upon God is already implied in his creaturehood: his life depends upon his Creator. Salvation, therefore, unless it spells out God's availability for man and man's freedom for God, is not salvation in the biblical sense. The gospel is Good News because it proclaims that in Jesus Christ God stoops down to man's level and becomes the Servant of sinners. This is so radical a statement that it outrages all concepts of religious propriety.

Religion is the guardian of God's honor. Its appeal is to man's nobility. Religion rests upon the assumption that man is able to respond to the moral challenge and work out his own salvation if he only tries hard enough. The offense of the gospel lies in the implication of man's religious bankruptcy, his utter inability to live up to the moral law. The gospel thus exposes the religious man on several counts: (1) it points to his helplessness and his need of reconciliation with God and man; (2) it suggests that all man's efforts are under judgment, his religion included; (3) it throws a shadow upon his religious effort in that it questions his self-righteous autonomy *vis-à-vis* a holy God; (4) it calls for a radical return *(teshūbāh=* μετανοία); (5) it points to God's radical grace in view of man's radical need (the

Cross); (6) it relates God's grace to the person of Jesus Christ, His life, passion, death, and resurrection; (7) it stresses the personal aspect of grace, namely that grace is not a "something" that man receives but a personal relationship or friendship between Master and disciple; and lastly, (8) that God does not give "something," He gives Himself.

These aspects of the gospel require an existential situation and do not easily fit into the rarefied atmosphere of religious sentiment. This goes some way to explain the reason for the resistance put up by religious men wherever the gospel is preached. The biblical drama of salvation creates a situation of tension chiefly in the area of religion: it questions every effort of self-salvation on the part of the religious man.[1] Whenever an effort is made to annul or even reduce the tension it results in a falsification of the human condition by overlooking man's estrangement from God. The "means" of salvation derive their complexity from the fact of the strained relationship that exists between man and God. Autonomous man is at enmity with God. The gospel therefore opens up the whole predicament of man who lives in tension between judgment and grace.

1. THE HUMAN PREDICAMENT

A monistic view of the universe requires a purely evolutionary view of man: man is an animal in process of development. The strains and stresses of his psychic life bear evidence of an inner struggle toward adulthood. What measure of perfection man will ultimately reach we cannot tell, but we know that he has behind him a long and weary journey. Scientists tells us that *homo sapiens* still carries about his body the many evidences of his humble origin.[2] This lowly assessment of man met with violent resistance on the part of the church and for good reason.

The Christian doctrine of salvation requires for man a special position in creation. In the Bible man, though related physically to the animal world, is singled out by the fact that he is regarded as the bearer of the image of God. In addition to his material existence he has a spiritual life

---

[1] Cf. Hendrik Kraemer, *World Cultures & World Religions*, 1960, p. 367.

[2] Joseph McCabe calls it a "museum of useless antiquities" and "the old curiosity shop." Cf. *Evolution* — A General Sketch from Nebula to Man, n.d., p. 86.

which singles him out from the animal kingdom. Man is a composite creature of body *and* soul. It would appear that the Bible never separates body from soul and soul from body. Man is one and indivisible: an organism in which soul and body are intertwined.[3]

Traditionally the church emphasized the importance of the soul as the imperishable part of man and paid scant attention to the body. This attitude she inherited from nonbiblical sources, mainly from neo-Platonism. It is only under extreme pressure that she is gradually giving way to a new orientation.

The most violent attack upon traditional Christian anthropology comes from the school of evolutionism. Though the evolutionary theory regarding man has undergone many modifications since Darwin's *The Descent of Man* (1871), the principle upon which it rests is now regarded as an incontestable fact of science.

Here we must point out that in some respects both the Bible and later Christian writers have anticipated the evolutionary theory by maintaining a definite biological link between man and the animal world. St. Augustine tells us that man is in nothing separated from the cattle except that he has a rational mind.[4] Amandus Polanus (1561-1610) holds a similar view: *homo est animal ratione praeditum.*[5] William Paley, the Archdeacon of Carlisle best known for his *Natural Theology* (1801), anticipates Darwin by more than half a century. He simply writes of man as "the human animal" without any further qualifications. But no Christian writer means to suggest that man's biological existence exhausts his significance. An interesting example is Marcus Dods. Prof. Dods wholeheartedly endorsed the evolutionary theory without in any way diminishing the importance of man. According to Dods the material universe "would have been dark and unintelligible, mechanical and without sufficient purpose" had there been no man.[6] By contrast we mention the name of Weston La Barre, who arrives at

[3] Cf. Robert Laurin, "The Concept of Man as a Soul," *ET*, Feb. 1961, pp. 131ff.

[4] *De fide et symbolo*, IV, 8.

[5] Quoted by K. Barth, *CD*, III/2, 76. Cf. also Augustine, *De Civitas Dei*, V, 77.

[6] Marcus Dods, *The Book of Genesis*, 1888, p. 13 (The Expositor's Bible Series).

opposite conclusions from the fact that man is physically related to the animal world.[7] This is the difference between the Christian and the monistic perspective: while the first sees meaning to the universe because God has created it, the latter reduces it to an immanental law that carries no meaning because it is fortuitous.

We can see why Christian writers so vehemently opposed the evolutionary theory by reason of the implications suggested by professional anthropologists.[8] Ever since Bishop Wilberforce of Oxford raised his voice against evolutionism, Christian opposition in one form or another has never ceased. There is to this day an extreme conservative wing in Anglo-Saxon countries dedicated to anti-evolutionism under the name of The Evolution Protest Movement. The subject remains a perennial theme with Church apologists. But however much Christians may try to disprove the theory, the accumulation of data seems to favor the infidels. Prof. Thomas Leith in his review of a more recent book on the subject edited by Paul Zimmerman has pointed to the futility of the effort.[9] For the theologian the question of man's origin touches upon the most fundamental issue: is this a closed universe bent upon itself or is it an open universe in which God not only intrudes but determines man's ultimate destiny?[10]

The ingenious attempt by Fr. Pierre Teilhard de Chardin to resolve the impasse between science and theology has met with little success thus far. Though Julian Huxley wrote the Preface for the English edition of the *Phenomenon of Man* he confesses his inability to follow the author's "gallant attempt to reconcile the supernatural elements in Christianity with the facts and implications of evolution." Huxley admits that certain aspects in Teilhard's exposition would

---

[7] Cf. Weston La Barre, *The Human Animal*, 1955, pp. 279ff.

[8] Not a few liberal theologians have hailed the evolutionary theory as a liberating concept. An outstanding example is the erstwhile President of Oberlin College, Henry Churchill King; cf. his *The Moral & Religious Challenge of Our Times*, 1911, pp. 125ff. But such theologians usually tend to gloss over the difficulties arising for the Christian faith once the theory is accepted without qualifications.

[9] *Darwin, Evolution & Creation*, ed. Paul A. Zimmerman, 1959; *Christianity Today*, Aug. 29, 1960.

[10] Cf. George Gaylord Simpson's verdict: evolution has no goal; man was not planned; the operation is wholly planless (*The Meaning of Evolution*, Mentor series, 1951, p. 143).

seem to point toward evolutionary transcendence from individuality to personality but this is not enough to outweigh the naturalistic suppositions of the scientific view.

What Huxley calls the "supernatural element" is the very point where the naturalist and the Christian part company. Huxley's "naturalistic general approach" allows no interference from the outside of the material world. Teilhard's "directed evolution" therefore contradicts the canons of Huxley's monistic faith.[11] The teleological supposition behind Teilhard's theory assumes an Intelligence over and above the forces of nature, which co-ördinates the "radial and tangential energies of the world" with the result that cerebralization and consciousness make their appearance in the course of evolution.[12] This is an assumption a materialist must deny in order to maintain a closed universe.

It seems that as far as theology is concerned the difficulty is not so much with evolution as a principle but with the inference behind the theory that rests upon a monistic presupposition. Theology would find no difficulty in accepting the natural pattern of evolution if this were sufficiently supported by evidence, as long as it is kept within the design of God's purpose. What it cannot accept is a universe from which God is excluded and which evolves by an immanental law. It is precisely Père Teilhard's latent monism that makes his approach difficult for the Christian believer. Teilhard is straining "to avoid a fundamental dualism" which in his view is "impossible" and "anti-scientific."[13] This brings him perilously close to a pantheistic position, though he tries hard to guard against it. It is interesting to note that Huxley's objections arise precisely at the point where Teilhard's monism begins to waver.

The subject of evolution concerns us because the Christian concept of salvation stands and falls with the biblical understanding of man. If man is not a responsible being but only "an ape fallen from arborial grace,"[14] then the Christian doctrines of Atonement, Reconciliation, and Salvation rest upon a misunderstanding and make no sense. Apes cannot be held morally responsible for their deeds and

[11] Pierre Teilhard de Chardin, *The Phenomenon of Man*, 1959, p. 19.
[12] Cf. *ibid.*, pp. 141ff.
[13] *Ibid.*, p. 64.
[14] Weston La Barre, *op. cit.*, p. 69.

are therefore unable to commit sin. The Christian concept of man presupposes responsibility on the part of rational creatures. Judgment and grace can have no meaning in the case of innocent animals prompted by instinctual impulses. Only if man is truly a sinner can there be any relevance to the Christian concept of salvation: those who are whole need no salvation but only those who are sick (Matt. 9:12).

The question of man's sickness is not a matter of theological quibbling. It is clearly spelled out in blood and tears upon the pages of history. The seriousness of the human condition finds full confirmation in clinical psychology.[15] Man is shown to be a strangely divided creature whose neurotic state is always the symptom of an "inner cleavage."[16] The facts of life belie David E. Roberts' optimism that "granted the establishment of favourable conditions, there is nothing in man himself which prevents him from reaching emotional stability and a satisfying use of his capacities."[17] Man as we know him has never achieved "favourable conditions" but has certainly excelled in the opposite direction. Man's greatest need is "meaningful" existence, and this distinguishes him from the animal. Jung readily concedes that much of the mental anguish leading to neurosis is related to the problem of meaning.[18] Victor E. Frankl rests his whole structure of logotherapy upon the essential human need of meaningful existence.[19] Meaningful living, according to Jung, has nothing to do with "ordinary reasonableness, sound judgment, science as a compendium of common sense." These, Jung admits, may "help a good part of the road, but never take us beyond the frontiers of life's most commonplace realities, beyond the merely average and

---

[15] Cf. C. G. Jung, *Psychology & Religion*, 1958, p. 15. We would especially draw attention to Jung's realistic assessment of the human condition: "we are constantly living on the edge of a volcano..." (cf. p. 18); also Alfred Adler, *Understanding Human Nature*, 1949, pp. 165ff; also Edith Weigert, *The Nature of Man*, ed. by Simon Doniger, 1962, pp. 17f.

[16] Jung, *op. cit.*, p. 340.

[17] David E. Roberts, *Psychotherapy & a Christian View of Man*, 1950, pp. 9f.

[18] Jung, *op. cit.*, pp. 330f.

[19] Cf. Victor E. Frankl, *Man's Search of Meaning*, 1964. Cf. also Donald F. Tweedie, *Logotherapy & the Christian Faith*, 1961, pp. 130ff. For Prof. Frankl's personal story, see Earl A. Grollman, *Judaism*, Winter, 1965.

normal." Apparently man needs more than an answer to his immediate questions. In order to meet his deeper needs he has to transcend his mundane *milieu* and ask ultimate questions. What makes Jung such a fascinating writer is the fact that he constantly moves on the periphery of theology. Jung is not satisfied with epiphenomenal explanations by Freud and Adler regarding the strains and stresses of the inner life. He is strangely conscious of the human burden placed upon the slender shoulders of the psychoanalyst as he faces the great enigma of the soul. A moving passage in his essay on "Psychotherapist or Clergy" carries an interesting personal confession: "Anyone who uses modern psychology to look behind the scene not only of his patients' lives but more specially of his own life — and the modern psychotherapist must do this if he is not to be merely an unconscious fraud — will admit that to accept himself in all his wretchedness is the hardest of tasks, and one which is almost impossible to fulfill."[20]

Jung suggests that most psychologists prefer to remain in blessed ignorance for fear lest they themselves succumb to neurosis. His honest questioning brings him remarkably close to a biblical position and therefore within the domain of Christian salvation: "How can I help those if I myself am a fugitive?"

The discovery that man is a fugitive is essentially a biblical discovery. But the answer Jung proffers is a Promethean answer prompted either by despair or rebellion: man must come to terms with himself and accept himself for what he is. It is odd that Jung should point to Jesus Christ as an example of such acceptance of oneself. Jesus, Jung avers, "sacrificed his historical bias to the god within him, and lived his individual life to the bitter end without regard for conventions or for the moral standards of the Pharisees." This is such an oversimplification of the inner life of the Master of Nazareth and of His teaching that it comes as a surprise. When, we would ask, did Jesus advocate self-forgiveness and self-reconciliation? Jung's stratagem aims solely at mental health as if this were possible without paying full attention to the moral side of the problem.

In Jungian psychology we thus face the human con-

[20] Jung, *op. cit.*, pp. 339f.

dition in an acute form: man's sickness on the one hand, and his helplessness on the other. There is here an inner contradiction from which we cannot extricate ourselves: the evolutionary theory presupposes a progressive development from animal to *homo sapiens;* psychoanalysis points to a different conclusion: man upon a volcano, constantly threatened by destructive forces within him that drive him to animal existence. The dichotomy that every man carries in his own bosom constitutes a puzzle to all students of human nature. The theologian has a right to ask: What is the cause of man's restlessness? Why is he at variance with himself? Is the guilt complex about which psychologists have so much to say the result of a sick imagination and only "real" in a subjective sense, as Jung maintains, or is there an objective side to it?

A Christian answer to these questions is founded upon at least two basic presuppositions:

(1) that there is an objective scale of values independent of subjective attitudes and cultural conditioning;

(2) that man's sense of guilt is somehow related to objective standards of right and wrong, good and evil.

Animals have no moral problems. Sin can only have meaning when the above suppositions are granted. Implied in the concept of sin is a moral universe coexistent with and as real as the physical universe. Kant's moral law within is therefore not as farfetched as is sometimes made out.[21] The dividing line between man and animal is not physical but moral. This is the basis of biblical anthropology. If the moral distinction be lost theology is left with nothing more definite than pious sentiment and wishful thinking. But if our assumption is correct the evolutionary theory proves inadequate to explain man's *humanitas* in that it by-passes an essential aspect of his being.

Man's predicament derives from his difficulty to balance his moral and physical life so that he maintains an inner unity without contradiction.

---

[21] Cf. Immanuel Kant, *The Metaphysics of Ethics*, II, 7, etc. Max Scheler's affirmation of "objective values" is essentially Kantian. The objective aspect of values is defended by F. Brentano, G. E. Moore, and W. Köhler; cf. Hans Meyerhoff's introduction to Scheler's *Man's Place in Nature*, 1961, p. XVII. Cf. also Hegel, *Philosophy of History*, 1901 trans., p. 81.

2. THE FALL

The Fall is essentially a theological concept. There is no place for it within the theory of biological evolution. It has meaning only on the assumption that man carries moral responsibility before God and acts in freedom. It is for this reason that the Bible places the Fall at the beginning of history. After the Fall man is no more a free creature, for he is weighted by the sense of guilt. The Fall, however, must not be so radically conceived as to imply a total loss of man's *humanitas*. This would mean that God's purpose was totally thwarted, which cannot be. Man cannot rid himself of his calling to be man no matter how much he may try, for man is man not by his own choice but by the will of God who created him. It is for this reason that neither Barth nor Berkouwer is prepared to allow a radical Fall. Because man cannot fall out of the hands of God, his calling remains irrevocable.[22]

There is, however, a radical difference between true Man as we meet him in the person of Jesus Christ, and fallen man whom we know both from history and experience. It would appear that the animal origin of man does not completely explain human depravity. In the animal world aggression, especially toward members of the same species, is unusual. Prof. Harry Harlow and his wife have studied monkeys in their natural habitat and have found their individual and social life governed by the principle of affection as a primary mechanism.[23] Robert Eisler in a lecture delivered to the Royal Society of Medicine defended the thesis that primitive man while still frugivorous was not a war-making animal. He quotes a considerable literature on the subject of "The Peaceable Habits of Primitive Communities."[24] But at the same time fallen man is not exempt from his responsibility before God.[25] Barth warns against the modern tendency to depreciate the significance of man and to reduce him to the animal level: "To try to deny man his humanity and to understand him as the expression of a universal dynamic,

---

[22] Cf. *CD*, III/2, 43-50, 54f; Berkouwer, *Man: The Image of God*, 1962, ch. V: "Corruption and Humanness."

[23] Cf. *The Listener*, Feb. 11, 1965, pp. 215ff; Feb. 18, 1965, pp. 255ff.

[24] Cf. R. Eisler, *Man into Wolf*, An Anthropological Interpretation of Sadism, Masochism & Lycanthropy, 1951, pp. 27, 29, 33, 51, 86 n. 33.

[25] Cf. *CD*, II/2, 641ff.

was to do something which could avenge itself, and has done so, and will probably do so further."[26] The argument is not wholly convincing as the negative effect upon society cannot determine man's quest of the truth. Barth himself writes cautiously about evolution and is quick to admit that no "layman" is qualified to assess the data gathered by experts.[27]

The difficulty about the Fall lies in the fact that it requires a dualist interpretation of human nature. Here man belongs to two worlds: the world of the spirit which is the world of freedom, and the world of matter which is the world of determinism. It is because of our modern fear of dualism that we are constantly threatened by a "diffuse monism"[28] which separates God from His creation. This does not mean that we need fall back upon the neo-Platonist principle of an immortal soul.[29] Biblical dualism differs radically from the Gnostic kind. It does not separate spirit and matter, for both belong to the order of creation. But it does make a radical distinction between Creator and creature. This, in biblical terms, is a fundamental distinction which allows of no compromise. Much of New Testament dualism derives from the Creator-creature principle. This is especially so in the Fourth Gospel. In appearance σάρξ and πνεῦμα — *caro* and *spiritus* — are sharply divided in the Johannine Gospel. But B. F. Westcott has already noticed that these expressions convey not *a priori* concepts but modes of being that make up the complexity of human nature.[30] *Sarx* therefore does not stand under the contempt of Gnostic spirituality but only emphasizes the other side of man's make-up.

The Johannine world, Dodd tells us, is two-directional: it consists of "two orders of being, τὰ ἄνω and τὰ κάτω."[31] This is the difference between Creator and creature: God is "above" and man is "below." Man's creatureliness is determined by the fact that he is earthbound. It is only in

[26] *CD*, III/2, 84.
[27] *Ibid.*, p. 88.
[28] Cf. Berkouwer, *op. cit.*, p. 222.
[29] We have purposely avoided reference to Platonism as P. Tillich sees fit to question whether it ever taught the immortality of the soul in the neo-Platonic sense; cf. *Courage To Be*, 1952, p. 110.
[30] Cf. B. F. Westcott, *The Gospel according to St. John*, 1908, I, 110.
[31] C. H. Dodd, *op. cit.*, pp. 258, 305.

his encounter with God that man is lifted to a new dimension. His existence *coram Deo,* in the presence of the Son of God, relates him to the spiritual realm.

Neither the materialistic nor the psychological explanations are sufficient to account for man's humanity. Man is a mystery and remains inexplicable apart from God. The very fact that he is capable of sinning differentiates him from the rest of creation. The Fall therefore expresses not a theological theory but an existential fact: man who was made for partnership with God[32] became a stranger and a fugitive.

It is Barth's main contention in his controversy with Brunner that man is not in a state of neutrality ("neutral capacity") but in active rebellion against his Maker.[33] In theological language the Fall expresses this fact in radical terms: all men, everywhere, at all times, are in a state of war with their Creator. This fact can be overlooked only by a falsification of man's condition. It is sheer shortsightedness to define man in only biological or psychological terms. In this respect Jung has seen more clearly than did Freud or even Adler: no "one-sided" interpretation can do justice to the human condition. Jung adds that "all attempts to explain the psychic factor in terms of merely elementary physical factors were doomed to failure."[34] But Jung is too committed to a monistic world-view to escape the trap of pantheism: "God is in everything already," the incarnation is therefore superfluous.[35] The differentiation within nature itself, he regards sufficient to account for the human psyche.

The biblical position is more primitive: man consists of matter *and* spirit. The secret of his personality depends upon the balanced combination of these two factors. Man's spirit depends for its life upon the Spirit of God. There are therefore three contexts to human life: the material world, the inner life of the psyche, the Presence of the Holy Spirit of God. Man's freedom, his dignity, and his meaningful existence require an integration of these three dimensions. The Fall expresses the imbalance that is the experience of every human life. The bias toward material

32 Cf. *CD*, III/2, 30f, etc.; also Berkouwer, *op. cit.*, p. 309.
33 For Barth's controversy with Brunner, see *CD*, III/2, 128ff.
34 Jung, *op. cit.*, p. 328.
35 *Ibid.*, p. 401.

existence demands autonomy and severance of spiritual ties. Man declares himself an independent creature and stretches out his hand to usurp ultimate authority. He thus breaks the bond of fellowship with his Maker and finds himself a fugitive (cf. Gen. 4:2).

Theology has no need to contradict the data gathered by biological science. The evolutionary theory as such in no way interferes with the biblical doctrine of man. The Bible never held that biological man is man in the spiritual sense. *Humanitas* is not defined by efficient physiology. Even Weston La Barre, who is an atheist, has to admit that man is an unusual phenomenon.[36] He goes so far as to say that "with man, genetic evolution and organic experiments have come to an end." It is his view that "nothing like it has ever happened before in evolution." La Barre admits to a sense of awe as he contemplates the revolutionary aspect of the human phenomenon.[37] In regard to the inner life of man there is a wide gap between him and the animal world: "No wild animal can have a psychosis arising from a confusion of cues and symbolisms and appropriate reaction patterns."[38] The very fact that man is able "to make mental illness" singles him out from all other creatures. His distinctive mark is the *logos* in the literal sense, i.e. the *word* that gives meaning to human life.[39] Karl Stern, who has the advantage over La Barre in that he is able to see the human condition from a Christian perspective, makes the following observation: "In dealing with neurosis, one always encounters something which lies beyond the purely psychological order. It just cannot be avoided: the human psyche is a metaphysical meeting-place."[40] It is this dimension of "beyondness" that lies at the heart of human existence. Man's humanity, therefore, is a built-in fact of which he cannot rid himself. Man "is the only 'animal,'" says David E. Roberts, "for whom acceptance or rejection of his status can arise as a problem."[41] The Fall expresses the acuteness

[36] "Man is not only a new species but also an entirely new kind of animal" (*op. cit.*, p. 149).

[37] Cf. *ibid.*, pp. 89f.

[38] *Ibid.*, p. 257.

[39] *Ibid.*, p. 212.

[40] Karl Stern, *The Third Revolution*, 1955, p. 215.

[41] For a discussion of a historic Fall see G. V. Jones, "Was There a Historic Fall?" *The Listener*, Aug. 5, 1965; also John Hick, "The

of man's problem at the point where the question of his status is in jeopardy.[42]

a. The broken fellowship

We have already said that only man is capable of sin. This is his peculiar characteristic. In this he differs from all the other creatures. We will now look at the result of sin in relation to the covenant.

It is misleading to speak of sin as if it were a noun. Sin is primarily a verb: it is an inward attitude before it expresses itself outwardly. Sin has been defined as inward rebellion against man's creaturely limitations. The result of this inward condition is the disruption of fellowship between man and God. God is felt to be a limiting factor circumscribing man's freedom and inhibiting his life. The broken fellowship is thus the result of man's No to God. Whether this No is philosophically, morally, or existentially expressed makes little difference.

Because creaturely rebellion is a denial of the very foundation of man's being it is always accompanied by a sense of guilt. Traditionally guilt is regarded as a concomitant of sin and is treated as a subject in the discipline of moral theology.[43] But modern psychology has removed guilt from the domain of ethics and understands it as a pathological phenomenon. Psychologists regard guilt as a morbid strain connected with the desire for self-punishment. In this view there is no objective aspect to guilt and the moral side of the problem is treated as incidental.

It must be admitted that there is a neurotic aspect to the guilt complex but this need not obscure the fact that a genuine sense of guilt is usually the result of moral failure. Quite ordinary and reasonably healthy people are troubled by a sense of guilt which is best put down not to morbid introspection but to a built-in sense of justice. The psychiatrist Karl Stern tells us that "true guilt is related to debt."[44] He differentiates between the conscience and the

---

Purpose of Evil," *The Listener*, Aug. 12, 1965. For the meaning of being human see Rabbi Abraham J. Heschel, *Who is Man?*, 1966.

[42] David E. Roberts, *Psychotherapy & a Christian View of Man*, 1950, p. 89.

[43] Cf. John J. Elmendorf, *Elements of Moral Theology*, 1892, pp. 299ff.

[44] K. Stern, *op. cit.*, p. 168.

primitive super-ego: whereas conscience transcends psychological data and carries the marks of reason, the super-ego is prompted by primitive libidinal drives. Guilt, though frequently rationalized in order to turn it into pure subjectivity, has yet an "objective" side to it. It stands for more than mere neurotic introspection.

The fact that man somehow *knows* right from wrong must not be treated lightly. Paul Tillich's definition of guilt is too psychologically conceived: he defines guilt as man's estrangement from himself which leaves him with a feeling of ambiguity.[45] There is an objective aspect to guilt that transcends man's conscience.[46] A classical description of the inward struggle with the sense of guilt is provided by Albert Camus in his monologue, *The Fall.* Here rationalization, defiance, and contrition make up the complexity of man's inner life.[47] The fact that it is possible for man to know himself guilty and yet "to be perfectly relaxed about it,"[48] speaks for an objective side to guilt.

We argue for a scale of values independent of social custom and which stands over against man's instinctual drives and circumscribes his humanity. This is in contradiction of Montaigne's cynical view that the "laws of conscience," which some say are born of Nature, are in fact born of custom.[49] In this respect Niebuhr provides us with a better answer when he relates conscience to the "dependent character" that is the mark of all human life.[50]

Guilt, conscience, and sin are related phenomena. They are different aspects of man's rebellion against his creatureliness, which delimit his freedom to act as he wills. His drive toward autonomous existence bears evidence to the demonic character of evil. In the last resort autonomy leads to the "abyss of meaninglessness" (Niebuhr), for it denies the very nature of the created order. It thus stands in direct

---

[45] P. Tillich, *Courage To Be*, 1952, p. 52.

[46] Whether conscience has universal application is a matter of dispute. Tillich points to the Stoics, who do not seem to experience the despair of personal guilt; cf. *ibid.*, p. 17.

[47] Cf. Albert Camus, *The Fall*, 1957. For a more recent description of guilt see Winston Graham, *After the Act*, 1965.

[48] K. Stern, *op. cit.*, p. 174.

[49] *The Essays of Montaigne*, trans. E. J. Trechmann, 1927, p. 111.

[50] Cf. Reinhold Niebuhr, *The Nature & Destiny of Man*, I, 1941, p. 181.

contradiction to the covenantal promise that God the Creator wills to be man's Father and Friend.

The broken relationship with God results in a need to create a fictitious world, a mental subterfuge for the world of reality. Because of the discrepancy between reality and fiction man finds himself in a state of anxiety, which Niebuhr regards as the precondition of sin.[51] The Christian psychologist has no need to deny the subjective and psychological aspect of guilt, but he knows of the connection between subjective guilt and the objective reference outside man: the disorder with oneself has an outside reference to man's question in respect to his ultimate destiny.[52] That question cannot be answered philosophically or psychologically but only existentially, namely by a positive relationship to God both as Creator and Father. The means of salvation refer to the restoration of the broken relationship. "Salvation" thus stands for the creature-Creator relationship under a positive sign: the covenantal partnership between man and God.

b. Sin and grace

Theologically conceived, sin is always in reference to God. The psychological analysis of guilt as the conflict between the libidinal instincts of the id and man's conscious dignity fails to touch the core of our problem. Once we relate sin to man's highest aspirations the psychological disorder can only be seen as a symptom of a more fundamental conflict. At this point psychology must yield to theology. In the theological perspective man appears as the opponent of God. Sin therefore is not in reference to man's lowest but his highest nature. It is the demonic dimension, which reveals man in his Mephistophelian role. James I. McCord uncovered something of the Promethean aspect of man when he noted that sin is the misuse of man's "highest endowment."[53] It is not the animal in man that sins but the fallen angel who in his pride defies his Creator.[54] The driving force behind man's pride is his lust for power. He needs unlimited power in order to escape his creaturely destiny.

---

[51] *Ibid.*, p. 183.

[52] Cf. Paul Tournier, *Guilt and Grace*, 1962.

[53] *The Nature of Man in Theological & Psychological Perspective*, ed. Simon Doniger, 1962, p. 24.

[54] Cf. Niebuhr, *op. cit.*, pp. 186ff: "Sin as Pride."

Niebuhr has rightly noted that man's mortality is the greatest offense to his pride: "the greater (man's) power and glory, the more the common mortality of mankind appears to him in the guise of an incongruous fate."[55] Behind man's craving for power is the hidden desire to overcome his finitude. This can only be achieved by wresting ultimate authority from the hands of God. Sin is therefore that overweening attitude whereby we manage to disregard our creaturely limitations and try to usurp what belongs to God alone.[56]

In this regard the religious man is in a more precarious position than the godless, for under the cloak of piety he frequently hides the desire to cheat God of His power in order to use it for his own ends. By comparison, the open defiance of atheism is mere childish stubbornness.

A characteristic of sin is that it blinds man to his true position. It makes it impossible for us to see ourselves as we truly are. "Nothing is more difficult," writes Dr. Edith Weigert, "than to be honest with oneself."[57] Sin not only deceives us but so distorts our perspective that the inflated ego comes to occupy the whole of our horizon.[58] Such infatuation with self takes the form of idolatry and becomes man's chief occupation. For this reason the "Socratic injunction 'know thyself' " is a sheer impossibility.[59] To see himself man needs the grace of God as it comes to us through His Word (cf. Jas. 1:25).

It is only *extra nos,* from the outside, that man can make the twofold discovery: the discovery of his need and the discovery of God's grace.

The grace of God, i.e. His covenant loyalty, cannot be annulled by man's rebellion. This is the fundamental biblical principle and our whole theology hangs on it. Once it is proved to be unfounded the gospel ceases to be Good News. For this reason there is no need to create the artificial distinction between the *imago essentialis* and the *imago exis-*

---

[55] *Ibid.,* p. 193.

[56] The outstanding example is Nietzsche's superman. Zarathustra plainly admits that he wants to be God. Niebuhr quotes Bertrand Russell to the effect that man desires to be God (cf. *op. cit.,* p. 189n.).

[57] Edith Weigert, *The Nature of Man,* p. 17.

[58] Dr. McCord quotes Luther as saying that sinful man becomes *incurvatus in se* — bent upon himself; *op. cit.,* p. 28.

[59] Cf. J. I. McCord, *op. cit.,* p. 33.

tentialis in order to save man's dignity.[60] His *humanitas* is anchored not in the vestigial relic of his original state of innocence but in God's sovereign will that man should be man. For this reason Barth's refusal to make the "contradiction" resulting from sin a "basic principle" is theologically well founded.[61]

Here not man's sin but God's grace forms the motive behind the means of salvation. Human history takes place in the tension between sin and grace.

3. THE CROSS

At the risk of repetition we once again revert to the subject of salvation.

Central to the means of salvation is the Cross of Jesus Christ. The Cross symbolizes the paradox of the Christian concept of salvation: an instrument of torture becomes the means of redemption. The efficacy of the redemptive act does not reside in the Cross but in Him who died upon it. It thus stands as the eternal sign of the atoning death of the Son of God for the sins of the world.

Here a number of questions immediately arise: Why did the Messiah have to die to accomplish salvation? How does His death benefit sinners? What is meant by atonement?

Oddly enough, none of these, nor similar questions relating to the Cross, has ever received a final answer no matter how theologians have tried.

We have already referred to Eric Mascall's observation that there is no definitive doctrine of the Atonement in Christian theology. While we have an orthodox definition regarding the Holy Trinity and the Incarnation, there is no such "clear-cut" definition in respect to the Atonement.[62] There is, however, a vast literature dealing with the subject and there are a number of "theories" that purport to explain its efficacy and meaning. But none of these efforts has proved sufficient to provide satisfactory answers. This fact must be borne in mind as we deal with the subject.

The problems relating to the Cross of Jesus Christ resolve themselves into three questions: (1) Why is salva-

---

[60] Cf. Paul Tillich's article in *The Nature of Man*, pp. 42ff. For a fuller discussion of these concepts see Berkouwer, *op. cit.*, pp. 39ff.

[61] Cf. *CD*, III/2, 205.

[62] E. L. Mascall, *Words & Images*, 1957, p. 96. *Supra*, p. 127.

tion related to suffering? (2) How can the suffering of the innocent benefit the guilty? and (3) How can God's suffering benefit man?

In view of the difficulties inherent in the doctrine of the Atonement it would be nothing short of presumption to attempt more than a few tentative remarks:

a. Salvation in relation to suffering

The first question was already raised in the primitive church as can be seen from the letter to the Hebrews. The writer of this letter suggests several answers: the Messiah suffered in order to attain unto perfection (Heb. 2:10); He suffered to destroy the Devil's hold over death (2:14); He suffered so that He would be made like His brethren (2:17); He suffered and was tempted so as to be able to help those who undergo similar experiences (2:18); He suffered so that He might learn obedience (5:8); He suffered death so that "He might taste death for every one" (2:9).

It will be noticed that none of these answers provides a reason as to the why of suffering, if salvation is an act of God. Surely, God ought to be able to save in more obvious and less complicated a manner. In the letter to the Hebrews several important suppositions are discernible: suffering is the result of sin (cf. 12:4-7); suffering is man's inevitable lot; the Messiah in order to enter into the human situation submitted to suffering. In addition, the writer shares the basic Christian assumption with the rest of the New Testament: Jesus Christ suffered death for the sake of others. The last assumption becomes even more complicated when we discover that in the New Testament the death of the Messiah is not accidental but within the eternal purpose of God. It is not something that need not have happened and could have been prevented. On the contrary, Herod, Pontius Pilate, Gentiles and Jews, have all acted according to the predetermined council of God (cf. Acts 4:27f). We are told that the Son of Man *must* suffer many things and be rejected (Mark 8:31; 9:12). This δεῖ expresses the inevitability of the Messiah's fate, as can be seen from our Lord's rebuke to Peter, who tried to prevent it.[63] Austin Farrer suggests that this "must" has something to do with the Messiah's determination to identify himself with man's

[63] Cf. Austin Farrer, *A Study in Mark*, 1951, pp. 230, 280.

destiny.[64] He takes Adam's lot upon himself and undergoes Adam's trials. This accounts for the designation Son of Man in the Marcan Gospel.

But it is a curious fact that what Mark predicates of the Son of Man, Luke ascribes to the Christ (Luke 24:26) and Paul to the Son of God (Gal. 2:20). These distinctions go back to different local traditions but in the end amount to the same conviction, namely that in the person of Jesus of Nazareth God Himself acted on man's behalf. We cannot properly assess the meaning of salvation in the New Testament sense without taking into full account both sides of the gospel emphasis: in Jesus the Messiah, the Son of Man and the Son of God coincide. What is said of the one is equally true of the other. Any emphasis of one side to the neglect of the other inevitably results in a soteriological impasse.

The offense of the Cross lies in the affirmation that in the Man Jesus, God suffers and dies. This is so sacrilegious a statement that no Jew could even as much as hear it without complicity in blasphemy. No wonder the preaching of the gospel met with such fierce opposition on the part of pious Jews. But at the same time, a god who saves by proxy, or by the magician's wave of a wand, or by some other impersonal means, is not the Father of Jesus Christ. It means that in the act of salvation God is personally involved. The ancient heresy of Patripassianism, though wrong in one sense, was right in another sense, namely that God the Father participates in the suffering of His Son.[65] If the gospel story is true at all, it cannot be otherwise. It is an unbearable thought that God looked on unaffected while the Messiah died upon the Cross. The "fellowship of His suffering" of which St. Paul speaks (Phil. 3:10) is a bond that extends from man to God and from God to man. Not only does the disciple enter into the suffering of the Master, but God the Father participates in it. In view of the Cross it is difficult to understand how Christian theology could accept the dogma of the impassibility of God.[66] Barth has no hesitation

---

[64] "The destiny of the Messiah is the destiny of man," *ibid.*, p. 287; cf. pp. 279ff.

[65] Barth says, "There is a *particula veri* in the teaching of the early Patripassians" (*CD*, IV/2, 257). Cf. *supra*, p. 125.

[66] Cf. Thomas Aquinas, *Summa Contra Gentiles*, ch. XIII; also the

to ascribe suffering to God the Father and regards it as "the mystery, the basis, of the humiliation of His Son."[67] That God is afflicted in the afflictions of His people is already recognized in the book of Isaiah (Isa. 63:9).[68]

Sin, suffering, and death are interrelated causes. The real nature of sin remains hidden from us until we see it in the light of the Cross of the Son of God. Viewed within the context of the Cross it assumes terrifying proportions. The Cross, therefore, reveals man for what he is, namely a godless rebel.[69] But the Cross also reveals God for what He is: the eternal Lover. God's answer to sin is judgment: not judgment of the sinner, but judgment that He takes upon Himself. He Himself in the Second Person of the Holy Trinity submits to indignity, punishment, and death so that the godless rebels should be justified (cf. Rom. 4:5). In the Person of the Christ, the Son of God and the Son of Man, God Himself stands with, by, and for sinners in an act of humble identification. He takes their place not as a sympathetic onlooker but as a fellow-sufferer.[70]

The Cross is God's answer to sin not by an omnipotent fiat but by a personal, loving, and patient involvement in the life of sinners. There seems to be no other way to pre-

---

article "That in God there is no passive potentiality": "now God is altogether impassible and immovable. . . ." Article II of the Anglican Church echoes the traditional doctrine when it says that God is without "passions" *(impassibilis)*. Griffith Thomas interprets it to mean that God is "incapable of being subjected with anything by an agent stronger than Himself." This would deny "impotence and imperfection" to God but not deny His ability to suffer by reason of man's unrequited love. We question, however, whether this was the original meaning of *impassibilis* (cf. W. H. Griffith Thomas, *The Principles of Theology*, 1930, p. 15). Cf. Cosslett Quin, *The Ten Commandments*, 1951, pp. 21f.

[67] *CD*, IV/2, 357.

[68] There is an alternative reading of the text: "in all their afflictions, he did not afflict" (cf. RSV margin). But this appears less genuine and was probably prompted by the desire to avoid ascribing passibility to God.

[69] Luther defined sin as *superbia et amor sui*. Cf. the whole section by Anders Nygren, *Agape and Eros*, 1939 trans., pp. 491ff.

[70] Paul Tillich, in a penetrating analysis of the psychologist's difficulty to guard against reducing his patient to the status of a subject without destroying his own and the other man's humanity, has pointed to an insuperable problem (*The Nature of Man*, pp. 51f). But in the fellowship of suffering created by the Cross the difficulty is overcome by a love-relationship.

serve man's dignity and to redeem his humanity than to suffer with him and on his behalf. This is ultimate love, for it is love to the extreme. Beyond it no one can go (cf. Rom. 5:6-8; John 13:1; Matt. 20:28).

b. THE SUFFERING OF THE INNOCENT ON BEHALF OF THE GUILTY

The connection between sin and suffering is not difficult to establish once we assume a moral universe. In this case sin would be related to suffering as cause to effect. The difficulty arises when the Messiah's suffering is understood as substitutionary. That it is so understood in the New Testament there can be no doubt. Substitutionary suffering creates problems both theological and moral.

From a theological point of view the substitutionary suffering of the Messiah reflects upon the nature of God. How can God the Father not only allow but accept the death of His Son for the sin of others? The righteousness of God of which St. Paul speaks (Rom. 3:21-26) seems to be contradicted by God's insistence upon legal satisfaction before He is ready to forgive.

On the moral side the situation is no less difficult, for substitutionary suffering seems to do away with all standards of equity. How the guilty can be benefited by the suffering of the innocent party is from a moral point of view beyond comprehension.

It is therefore no wonder that the Christian doctrine of Atonement is beset by many ambiguities.

Every theory suggested in connection with the doctrine of Atonement breaks down at the crucial point where the dialectic of objective and subjective reality comes into play. There seems to be no possible escape from the dilemma: either the Cross operates subjectively by an appeal to the conscience or else it is an objective sacrifice offered to an angry God. In the first case, Christian atonement becomes a purely subjective experience limited to those who believe. This would mean that Jesus Christ is not the Savior of the world but only of the pious. In the second case, God refuses to forgive without a sacrifice equal to the weight of human sin.[71] In either case there is no straightforward answer, nor is there a satisfactory solution when the subjective-objective

[71] Cf. Anselm, *Cur Deus Homo?*, XXI.

aspects are combined.[72] The question always arises: why the necessity of a sacrifice?

Tillich speaks of an atoning "process" that becomes manifest in history when Christ dies upon the Cross. But in the New Testament, atonement upon the Cross is not a process but an act, a decisive, once-and-for-all act, which carries objective significance apart from the subjective experience of the believer. The objective aspect of the Atonement is essential for an answer to our problem. In spite of Tillich's objection to a theology that postulates a conflict between God's "reconciling love and his retributive justice" we cannot possibly resolve the antithesis without destroying the meaning of the sacrifice. Christian atonement is not a legal act, nor is it a pious phrase, but an act of love on the part of God expressed in terms of suffering and death.[73] Tillich has rightly seen that there is here a dialectic between God as Father and God as Lord. It is only in terms of sacrifice that the conflict is resolved: God Himself takes the consequences of sin upon Himself in order to overcome the barrier that divides the estranged parties.

But if forgiveness were treated as an impersonal principle or a mere expression of sovereign power, salvation would assume the character of a "legal mechanism," to use a Tillichian expression. To avoid this we must speak of atonement, forgiveness, salvation, always in the context of *ḥesed,* i.e. the covenant relationship which binds God to sinners. "The grace-character of justification," writes Hans Küng, "in which precisely the *un*just person is acquitted and declared just, shows that God's justification can be conceived only analogically as a legal act."[74] The reference to "analogy" is of a metaphorical nature, for all theological speech is derived from human situations. As far as God is

---

[72] P. Tillich has attempted a synthesis between the two antithetical theories of atonement: the subjective-objective. Cf. his *Systematic Theology,* 1957, II, 175f. For a discussion of Tillich's position see Otto Wolff, "Paul Tillich's Christologie des 'Neuen Seins,'" *NZST,* Heft I, 1961.

[73] In another passage Tillich himself admits that "man can believe in forgiveness only if justice is maintained and guilt is confirmed. God must remain Lord and Judge in spite of the reuniting power of his love" (*op. cit.,* I, 288); cf. also P. Tillich, *Love, Power & Justice,* 1954, pp. 113f.

[74] Hans Küng, "Justification in the N.T.," *Christianity Divided,* 1962, p. 315.

concerned, forgiveness is without analogy; it is a divine verdict expressed in a singular, historic act. But it is not a verdict apart from God's suffering but in the context of it. It is here that the covenant relationship becomes fully visible in that God in the Person of His Son accepts the verdict of justice upon Himself on behalf of sinners.

Such interposition on behalf of others can only make sense on the assumption of three coherent principles: (1) the close interrelatedness between Father and Son in the Holy Trinity; (2) the interrelatedness between the Son of God and the Son of Man in the person of Jesus the Messiah in the sense that in Him both God and man meet in an indissoluble union; (3) the inherent connection between Jesus and the human race.[75] It would appear therefore that without the concept of covenant, substitutionary suffering is an impossible doctrine. But within the covenant relationship, where there is close fellowship between Father, Son and man, the covenant-partner, there is nothing immoral about it. In fact, it lifts morality to a higher plane in that it exemplifies the meaning of love as the supreme reason for God's concern with man.

Forgiveness in Christ is an act of love that takes precedence over every other principle. In a sense God violates the principle of equity in order to practice mercy — and takes upon Himself the consequences in terms of suffering. The passion of the Son of God is therefore not a mere "demonstration" of the extent of God's love but the real and painful act of loving.

That man finds it offensive to accept forgiveness on such terms is a sign of his pride. As long as he thinks himself adequate to cope with the situation in his own strength he is still blinded to the meaning of sin. "That man does accept and bow to this verdict is the work of the Holy Spirit which makes him a Christian";[76] this we call the miracle of faith.

c. THE PRINCIPLE OF IDENTIFICATION

The inner spring in the Christian doctrine of Atone-

[75] Cf. Irenaeus, *Contra Haer.*, III, 18, 1: *in seipso recapitulavit* — "He summed up in Himself the long line of human beings. . . ." At the beginning of the paragraph Irenaeus had already said that the Word was never really separated from the human race: *qui est semper aderat generi humani. . . .*

[76] *CD*, IV/I, 93.

ment is the principle of *ḥesed,* namely God's gracious condescension toward sinners. "Condescension" is inadequate to express the humility of God as revealed in the Cross, for in the Cross of Jesus Christ God *identifies* Himself with sinners. This is the ultimate meaning of vicarious suffering: not that Christ acts as a substitute in order to placate a wrathful God so as to satisfy an impersonal principle of justice, but rather that in Christ God Himself goes the way of sinners to suffer with them. This is the meaning of the credal statement: "He went down to hell."

The identification of God with sinners is rooted in the doctrine of the Incarnation. Without the Christological definition of the church, atonement has no foundation. Only if Jesus Christ is both *vere homo et vere Deus* is it possible to keep the structure of the Christian doctrine of salvation intact. He is the connecting link between God and man. No one has seen this more clearly than has Karl Barth, who never tires in his emphasis upon the two aspects in the person of Jesus the Messiah.

On the one hand we meet in Jesus of Nazareth the faithful servant of God who dies upon the Cross and so proves His faithfulness in an act of unreserved identification with godless men. The whole weight of God's judgment He humbly accepts for the sake of others. In Him sinful humanity dies once and for all. But on the other hand, we meet with the triumphant and risen Christ, who lives by the power of God. In Him humanity makes a new start in the power of the Holy Spirit.

If Jesus was only man the Cross at best is a Promethean act: *per ardua ad astra.* Only if He is also the Second Person of the Holy Trinity is His death upon the Cross not merely an act of heroic self-sacrifice, but a divine act of identification with sinners. The Christian doctrine of salvation hinges upon these two aspects: the humanity and divinity of Jesus the Messiah.

As there are two aspects to the Man Jesus, so there are two aspects to the Cross: the humiliation of the Son of God and the exaltation of the Son of Man. It means that God's identification with sinners results in the restoration of man to the covenant relationship. In the risen Christ humanity is exalted and restored to sonship. In this way God has vindicated Himself and redeemed His promise. But it is a strange victory, for it is achieved at the price of the

Messiah's humiliation and death. This paradox is at the very heart of the gospel message: the Cross is Christ's throne and the wreath of thorns His crown; the Son of God becomes the servant of sinners for their salvation. The offense of the Cross is rooted in the principle of identification: God so identifies Himself with sinners that He dies for them.[77]

4. THE SACRAMENTS

We cannot understand the meaning of sacrament apart from the concept of grace. But we have already said that grace in terms of *ḥesed* means covenant loyalty on the part of God. Because sacrament is meant to unite the visible sign to invisible grace, the sign stands as an effective symbol of the covenant. It is in Augustine's words: *signum efficax gratiae.* This grace is none other than God's gracious condescension toward sinners. But the efficacy of the sign transcends the symbol. To the believer the sacrament is God's pledge to be present with His people. It is for this reason that *signum* and *res* cannot be separated. In this sense we must accept St. Thomas' principle: *sacramenta causant quod figurant.* But this happens not by the human act but by reason of God's promise. Behind the sacrament is therefore the living Word of the triune God. This was clearly understood by St. Augustine, who laid down the rule that it is only by the power of God that His invisible Word becomes visible in the physical sign.[78] It means that in the sacraments God's Word acquires a visible form,[79] so that the *sacra signa* by the power of the Holy Spirit become effective means (*virtus*) in the life of the believer (*Joann.* 26.11). All this is to emphasize the givenness of salvation, the *dant salutem.* It is, however, the awesomeness of the Christian concept of salvation that in Jesus Christ God does not give us a "something," but Himself.

Salvation, in the Christian sense, is nothing other than our Lord's gracious promise to abide with us (Matt. 28:20). The sacrament is the pledge and token of His presence.

---

[77] To speak of the death of God, except in a parabolic sense, is both a contradiction and an offense. But within the context of Christian theology this is inevitable. Cf. *CD*, IV/2, 357.

[78] "accedit verbum ad elementum, et fit sacramentum, itiam ipsum tanquam visibile verbum" (*Joann.* 80.3). For Thomas, see *Summa Theol.*, pt. III, art. 5, reply 1-3.

[79] *De Catechizandis Rudibus*, 26.50.

That God is present to His people, the church has never called in question. The long, drawn-out disputes regarding the sacraments only concern the *mode* of His Presence, but never the Presence as such.

The center of the dispute turns on the question of the *opus operatum* principle. On the Catholic side the efficacy of the sacrament is made to depend upon priestly ordination. On the Protestant side the emphasis is upon the Word of promise and the efficacy of grace. This apparently slight difference of theological opinion is fraught with grave consequences. The issue hangs on man's part in the act of salvation. For the Protestant grace is entirely God's gift; for the Roman Catholic, it is God's gift by means of the church. But once the church becomes the dispenser of grace man's salvation is made to depend upon the right function of an ecclesiastical system. At the same time Protestants realize that God uses the church as a means of grace and that salvation is not outside the church. This is our dilemma.

In order to obtain a balanced perspective we must place the sacraments in their proper context.

The sacraments relate to two historical acts — the baptism of our Lord in the river Jordan and the Institution of the Holy Communion at the Last Supper. These acts are inseparable from the messianic purpose of the gospel, namely the translation of sinful men into God's Kingdom. The sacraments therefore are a dramatized form of the Christian *kerygma:* God's saving purpose with man. For this reason, neither the solemnity of the rite nor the expressive nature of the symbols constitutes a sacrament. What turns the symbols into Christian sacraments is the context into which these symbols are placed, namely God's saving acts in Jesus Christ. Once placed in this context they acquire an efficacy that derives from God's original purpose to save sinners. In this sense we may safely speak of an *ex opere operato* principle as Oberman has shown.[80] According to Luther even nonbelievers are confronted by God's saving acts each time these rites are performed, though they may fail to respond in faith.[81] It means that

---

[80] Cf. Heiko A. Oberman in *Christianity Divided*, p. 232.

[81] Cf. Ernst Kinder, "Zur Sakramentslehre," *NZST*, Heft 2, 1962, p. 163.

the effective power of the sacraments does not depend upon the subjective experience of the recipient or the worthiness of the one who administers, but solely upon God's gracious will to save.[82] The *virtus* of the rite is grounded in God's promise to be our God. It is for this reason that not even Protestants can do away entirely with the principle of *opus operatum*. Otherwise the *ordo salutis* becomes completely dependent upon subjective faith.

By the sacraments the church is made free from the subjectivity of faith and rests upon grace alone. But at the same time the subjective aspect of faith must not be overlooked. Man's response to God's offer is necessary for the completion of the rite. There can be no giving without willing acceptance of God's Gift. This aspect of the sacraments requires a personal confrontation between the recipient and the risen Christ. Any talk about impersonal grace administered by the church rests upon a fatal misunderstanding.[83] Such confrontation results in faith, i.e. in a personal and intimate relationship. The sacraments are the visible signs of the καταλλαγή — the exchange — between Master and disciple: He takes my place and offers me His. Jesus Christ puts Himself willingly under God's judgment so that I should become a son. This may look like a compensatory device on the part of man's guilty conscience in search of a scapegoat, except for the covenant. The covenant extends over the history of the whole human race and does not depend upon the experience of the individual. This, at least in part, removes it from the Freudian suspicion that man invented a gracious God because he needs one.[84]

We will now proceed to discuss the two sacraments.[85]

---

[82] According to Oberman, *ex opere operato* for Protestants can only mean the "availability" of Jesus Christ; *op. cit.*, p. 232.

[83] Roman Catholic writers frequently speak of grace as if it were a "something" that the church dispenses: "the sacraments of the Church give grace because the Church herself is visibly and perceptibly full of grace" (*Christianity Divided*, p. 265). Schillebeeckx argues for the *ex opere operato* principle on the grounds that "the grace of Christ operates by itself" (*ibid.*, p. 268).

[84] Cf. Freud, *The Future of an Illusion*, 1949, pp. 39, 58.

[85] In limiting the sacraments to two we follow a Reformation principle, though the contention that a sacrament must be a rite instituted by Christ Himself carries only a limited validity. In the case of baptism the dominical character of the rite is not so evident as in the case of the Eucharist. There is, however, the fact that it was

a. Baptism

On the assumption that there is a vital connection between the two Testaments, baptism has to be considered in relation to circumcision.

The importance of circumcision in Judaism can be gauged from the fact that it takes precedence over the Sabbath.[86] There is recorded a saying of Rabbi Judah ha-Nassi (*ca.* 135—*ca.* 220): "So great is circumcision that despite all religious duties which Abraham, our father, fulfilled, he was not accounted perfect, until he was circumcised" (*Nedarim,* 3:11). The reason for the emphasis upon the importance of circumcision lies in the fact that it is the sign *par excellence* of the covenant. By this outward sign the Jew is meant to express his utter commitment to God's law.[87] In the case of male proselytes circumcision was the *conditio sine qua non* of full membership in the synagogue, while women were accepted on the basis of baptism and sacrifice alone.[88] According to Prof. D. Daube Christian baptism derives from proselyte baptism in the synagogue. Such baptism was regarded as more than a purely purificatory rite: "a convert — even a female one, received by baptism alone — had a status of a new-born child." So much so that such a person could marry any of his own relatives, even within the Jewish faith, for the relationship was completely changed. Prof. Daube comes close to an *opus operatum* principle when he declares that for the Rabbis "the new birth was effected by baptism alone."[89]

There can be little doubt that originally the church practiced both rites simultaneously.[90] The question why

---

practiced from the very beginning and even before the appearance of the Christian church, in the synagogue. Cf. D. Daube, *The New Testament & Rabbinic Judaism,* 1956, p. 112.

[86] Cf. *Shabb.* 18.3; also John 7:22f.

[87] The secularization of Jewish life has turned the sign of circumcision into a purely ethnic characteristic though not among orthodox Jews.

[88] Cf. Werner Foerster, *From Exile to Christ,* 1964 trans., pp. 132, 142.

[89] *Op. cit.,* p. 112.

[90] The Rabbis worked on the principle that Gentiles are received into the covenant on the same basis as were the Israelites at Mount Sinai, i.e. by circumcision, baptism, and sacrifice; cf. Daube, *op. cit.,* p. 121 and notes.

the church ultimately dropped the rite of circumcision is therefore of considerable theological importance.

From the New Testament evidence we know that in some Jewish Christian circles there was an insistence that Gentiles can only be received upon circumcision (cf. Acts 15:1; Gal. 6:12). Paul was the chief spokesman for the opposite view. The reasons behind his opposition are important, for they bear upon a theological assessment of the baptismal rite.

For Saul of Tarsus the key to the messianic *kerygma* is grace and grace alone. Such insistence upon grace derives from the recognition of the utter insufficiency of man to justify himself before God by keeping the law.[91] Circumcision in the case of proselytes was a declaration of willing acceptance of the minutiae of rabbinic law as far as the Pharisees were concerned. Such submission to the precepts of the law was acknowledged to be the means of man's justification before God. This stood in direct contradiction to Paul's deepest conviction that man is not justified by his pious deeds. The pretence that man is able to comply with the demands of the law he regarded as sheer hypocrisy (cf. Rom. 2:17ff). For anyone to attempt to justify himself before God is to make void the death of Christ (cf. Gal. 2:21). A piety that was built upon the assumption of man's ability to keep the commandments ultimately ended in a merely external compliance with the letter of the law.[92] In such a situation the personal aspect of grace is completely overlooked and legalistic rectitude takes its place. It is for this reason that the Old Testament balances the outward rite with the demand of a circumcised heart (cf. Jer. 4:4; Deut. 10:16; cf. Rom. 2:29).[93] For the early church such change of heart as foretold by the prophets (cf. Jer. 31:33f; Ezek. 11:19; 18:31; 36:26) was the very sign of messianic fulfillment (cf. II Cor. 3:3). The outward

[91] For the problem of the law in the early church see Walther Schmithals, *Paul & James*, 1965, pp. 25f, 44ff, 48f. Unfortunately, Schmithals finds it necessary to throw doubt upon Acts in order to establish his theory that there prevailed a laxity toward the law in the early church; cf. pp. 57, 79ff, 108.

[92] Cf. Foerster, *op. cit.*, p. 5.

[93] Cf. also *Manual of Discipline*, 5.5; and *Commentary on Habakkuk*, 11.13.

sign of circumcision was therefore only a type of the inward experience of grace.

In addition, circumcision was the mark of segregation between Jew and Greek. But Christ removed the wall of partition (Eph. 2:14) and brought about a unity not on the basis of the law but on the basis of grace. In the messianic Kingdom there can therefore be no difference between man and man (cf. Gal. 3:28; Rom. 10:12). The universality of the gospel presupposes the universality of the human need without distinction (Rom. 3:9ff). This is the way Paul reasoned: "since all men have sinned and fallen short of the glory of God" (Rom. 3:22f), there can be no real difference between a Jew and a Gentile. Circumcision, therefore, created an illusionary situation in that it implied that by obedience to the letter of the law man achieved a privileged position before God.

The logic of Paul's reasoning led him to the inevitable conclusion that Gentiles need not be circumcised in order to enter the covenant. Through faith in Christ men are already grafted into the community of believers whether they be circumcised or not. But if this is so in the case of circumcision, why does it not apply to baptism as well?

This is an important question, which has received all too little attention. Christian writers err when they associate the change of the sign with the change of the covenant. Justin Martyr goes as far as to suggest that the rite of circumcision was given to the Jews so that they could the easier be singled out for punishment.[94] This is an unusual case of misrepresentation, but we must not overlook the theological reasons behind his view. Justin's main concern is to deny that man is saved because he is circumcised. If that were the case, he says, then women were most unfortunate, for the rite cannot be applied to them.[95] Tertullian argues in the same vein: he points to Adam, who was created uncircumcised, and from this he deduces that circumcision is only a "sign" and not a title to salvation.[96]

There is here, however, a remarkable inconsistency. While Christian writers argue that in the case of circum-

---

[94] Cf. *Dial.*, 16; cf. also 19.
[95] *Ibid.*, 23.
[96] *Adversus Judaeos*, 2f.

cision the outward sign does not warrant salvation, they do not draw the same conclusion in the case of baptism. Tertullian's argument against Marcion turns on this point: he chides Marcion for failing to attach sufficient importance to the outward sign.[97] But, we would ask, if the rite in itself is efficacious, on what grounds is baptism to be preferred over circumcision?

The traditional answer to our question is that Christ abolished one rite and established the other.[98] But this is an utterly unfounded view. We have nothing to show that Christ abolished circumcision; in fact He was Himself circumcised. The church still commemorates this event on January 1st each year. By the same token, St. Paul himself, who so vehemently argues for the freedom of the Gentiles, does not underestimate the value of circumcision as long as one keeps the law (cf. Rom. 2:25). What he questions is not the rite itself but the feeling of sufficiency that goes with it, providing a false security. What matters to the Apostle is not circumcision or uncircumcision but the keeping of the commandments (I Cor. 7:19). This, he holds, no man can accomplish in his own strength, but by the grace of God.

The same logic that questions the efficacy of the outward sign in the case of circumcision must equally apply to baptism as well.[99] There can be no reason why one sign should be regarded as more efficacious than the other. In both cases the reason for the rite is grounded in God's promise: circumcision refers to the "everlasting covenant" (Gen. 17:7) and baptism confirms that covenant by the death and resurrection of the Messiah (cf. Gal. 3:27). The efficacy therefore does not rest in the magic of the act, whatever the rite, but in the decision of God that precedes it. Circumcision could take place in the name of the Holy Trinity as does baptism. The fact is that it is not the rite

---

[97] Cf. *Adversus Marcionem*, I, 28.

[98] Cf. *Barnabas*, IX. *The Belgic Confession* reads: "He (i.e. Christ) having abolished circumcision, which was done with blood, has instituted the sacrament of baptism" (art. 39). But since when is water better than blood?

[99] Zwingli in his treatise on *Baptism* observes: "We must not allow the letter to kill us, for the letter of the Gospel kills no less surely than the letter of the Law" (English trans. by G. W. Bromiley, *Zwingli and Bullinger*, 1953, p. 142).

that matters but what it stands for. The significance of baptism derives from its Christological center: the death and resurrection of Jesus Christ. Baptism is therefore preferred, not because it is more efficacious but because it is more fitting. It expresses more precisely the drama of salvation, namely dying and rising with Christ.

The Christian concept of sacrament requires an *ex opere operato* principle but only after very careful definition. It is not the priestly act when "rightly" performed that makes the sacrament efficacious, but the efficacy entirely rests in God's promise of which the covenant is the token and pledge. Neither priest by his action nor recipient by his faith can effect grace. Grace is already promised and assured by the givenness of the covenant. In the sacramental act the church and the individual believer appeal to God's promise and place themselves at His disposal.

We thus hold that there is a correspondence between circumcision and baptism. Once this premise is granted, we will have to say that God acts in both rites and that only the signs are different. If this is the case we will have to assess circumcision in a more positive light than heretofore. Our approach to circumcision must be determined by our approach to the law as a whole. Because Christ did not come to abolish the law but to fulfill it (Matt. 5:17ff), circumcision is not "abolished" but fulfilled in the rite of baptism. This is important to us in our decision regarding infant baptism.

As in the case of circumcision, baptism carries profound social implications: by it the individual is received into the community of believers and becomes an integral part of it. But there is here also a difference: while circumcision has come to connote a biological and ethnic distinction, baptism is meant to transcend the physical bond. It therefore testifies to the new order of messianic society based upon spiritual regeneration. It means that the individual's participation in the life of the community is not biologically but spiritually determined. But under the principle of federal theology the individual's spiritual awakening is not, and cannot be, the determining factor. He already belongs to the people of God by reason of the covenant, though he may not know it.

The Reformers, in their opposition to the Anabaptists,

argued for infant baptism from the rite of circumcision.[100] In view of their insistence upon the unity of the covenant their position is unassailable. Calvin goes so far as to say that both these rites reside in Christ, inasmuch as He is the foundation of circumcision as well as of baptism, for both rites express the same promise of God's paternal favor.[101] The issue for which the Reformers fought in their controversy with Anabaptism is of central importance, for it turned on the basic question of grace and merit. "According to the Anabaptists," says Luther, "baptism is nothing unless a person is a believer." But this, in Luther's view, does away with God's work and puts man's work instead.[102] Similarly, Zwingli chides them for making perfection a condition for baptism.[103] We can see why the Reformers fell back upon the rite of circumcision in their defense of baptism: it expresses to them the utter gratuity of grace.[104] Barth, who is most critical of infant baptism as now practiced in the church, readily admits that it demonstrates the meaning of grace as no other rite.[105] Our difficulty with infant baptism lies in the fact that it assumes more than is legitimately warranted.

Baptism in the New Testament is described as "the circumcision of Christ," which is made without hands and comes about through faith "in the working of God," who in His grace causes sinners to die and rise with Jesus Christ to newness of life (cf. Col. 2:10-12). Such a process of transformation requires willing and conscious participation, which cannot be said of an infant. This is Barth's main contention and it is justified. By a misapplication of the principle *ex opere operato* the church was tempted to apply to the rite a power that can only be ascribed to God. But God respects the human person and refuses to

---

[100] Cf. George H. Williams, *The Radical Reformation*, 1962, p. 302; cf. also XXIV.

[101] Cf. *Institutes*, IV, 16, 3f.

[102] Cf. Luther's *Commentary on Galatians*, 1953, pp. 18f.

[103] Zwingli, *op. cit.*, pp. 139f.

[104] More recently Prof. R. F. Aldwinckle, arguing the Baptist point of view, denies the importance of circumcision to the argument of infant baptism, but he does so on the assumption of a radical break in the covenant (cf. *Of Water and the Spirit*, The Baptist Federation of Canada, 1964, p. 12).

[105] Cf. Karl Barth, *The Teaching of the Church Regarding Baptism*, 1948, p. 27.

use magic. Luther, who is so insistent on the importance of baptism, is the first to admit that, as a rite, baptism "justifies nobody, and gives advantage to nobody." What justifies is not the human action but "faith in the word of promise to which baptism is conjoined." It is not the ritual that counts but the faith behind it.[106] But Luther also knows that infants cannot be expected to have faith. He therefore falls back upon "infused faith," i.e. the vicarious faith exercised by the godparents.[107] Such a device entirely overlooks the personal aspect of faith, and Zwingli's objections to such a position are only too justified.[108] We must hold to the principle that faith requires personal involvement, and for this reason no sacramental act can serve as a substitute. In this respect Barth's insistence that baptism is not the *causa* but only the *cognitio salutis* must be taken seriously. The *causa salutis* can only be Jesus Christ Himself. But Jesus Christ deals with adults and not infants.[109]

The concept of baptismal regeneration when applied to infants is full of ambiguity. Traditionally, infant baptism was justified on the grounds of original sin. This was Origen's argument in the later years of his life,[110] but especially Augustine's argument in his controversy with Pelagianism.[111] But with all the emphasis upon the efficacy of the rite, Augustine still knows that water as such is only the external sign of the sacrament, and that it is only by the Spirit of God that the inward effect of grace becomes evident.[112] Augustine is explicit on this point: those who believe in Christ are regenerate by the Holy Spirit; it is not water but the Spirit who makes us children of God.[113] Yet Augustine is anything but consistent. He so ties grace to the outward sign that he does not hesitate

---

[106] Cf. *Reformation Writings of Martin Luther*, trans. by Bertram Lee Woolf, 1952, pp. 263f. Cf. p. 255: "Unless faith is present, or comes to life in baptism, the ceremony is of no avail."

[107] Cf. *ibid.*, p. 271.

[108] Zwingli, *op. cit.*, p. 139; cf. also Aldwinckle, *op. cit.*, pp. 20f.

[109] The traditional appeal to Mark 10:13ff is without justification, as if these infants were brought to Jesus to be baptized.

[110] Cf. N. P. Williams, *op. cit.*, pp. 220ff.

[111] Cf. Gerald Bonner, *op. cit.*, pp. 319ff.

[112] Cf. W. J. Sparrow-Simpson, *The Letters of Augustine*, 1919, p. 290.

[113] Cf. *Enchiridion*, 39, 49, 119.

to regard unbaptized infants under judgment though mitigated to the point of allotting to them *minima poena*.[114] This is so superstitious a position as to be indefensible. It only shows that the *opus operatum* principle unless applied with caution leads to magic. This principle can only be safely used when counterbalanced by the rule that God's hand can never be forced, not even by a priest or a bishop. The *opus operatum* principle must be so interpreted that the theological axiom, *Deus non alligatur sacramentis* is never violated.

This was the issue in the controversy between Gorham and the Bishop of Exeter. At no point did Gorham deny the efficacy of the sacrament; what he denied was the assertion that regeneration is a condition upon baptism. His position was that regeneration may occur "*in* baptism, *before* baptism, or *after* baptism." This the Bishop refused to accept, pointing to the language of the baptismal office in the Prayer Book.[115] It is peculiar to the Anglican position that both contenders could prove their right from the same sources. The language of the Prayer Book is certainly not without ambiguity.[116] Such ambiguity has prevailed in the church since Augustine. This is plainly evident in his evasive answer to the question put to him by Bishop Boniface: How can sponsors possibly affirm that this child believes in God?[117] He cannot have it both ways: either grace is "suspended" or "effective"; it cannot be both at the same time.[118]

---

[114] Cf. Bonner, *op. cit.*, pp. 155, 295.

[115] Cf. J. C. S. Nias, *Gorham and the Bishop of Exeter*, 1951, p. 46.

[116] The circular argument for the efficacy of infant baptism is plainly demonstrated in the Catechism:

> Q. What is required of a person to be baptized?
> A. Repentance and faith.
> Q. Why are infants baptized?
> A. Because they promise both repentance and faith by their Sureties [Sponsors].

But how can infants promise repentance and faith when they do not even know what is happening? The revised *Canadian Book of Common Prayer* has done nothing to remove this *petitio principii* (cf. p. 551).

[117] Cf. Sparrow-Simpson, *op. cit.*, p. 292; also Augustine, *De Peccatorum Meritis et Remissione*, 1.38.

[118] Sometimes theologians make the artificial distinction between "regeneration" and "conversion" (so Griffith Thomas, *The Principles of Theology*, 1930, p. 385), but this is only a play with words.

In some Anglican quarters the suggestion has been made that infant baptism be replaced by a Service of Dedication to avoid the ambiguities.[119] But this is a drastic departure from ancient Christian practice.[120] There is no valid reason why baptism should not be administered to children of Christian parents as a sign of their covenant relationship within the family of God. In the Christian home the *whole* family belongs to the church of God, not by reason of the "blood nexus" but by reason of election. Barth's opposition to infant baptism stems from his conviction that it contradicts a vital principle in the church, namely that her existence must not depend upon biological increase but upon the Holy Spirit of God.[121] This is a legitimate concern, and there is no doubt that baptism has frequently degenerated into a cultural and national institution. It thus acquired the same characteristic as has circumcision in Jewry. But misuse can never be a justification for abandoning the rite altogether.

There are good reasons for retaining infant baptism, but it must not become a substitute for personal faith. To be born in a Christian family is a privilege and must be understood as an expression of God's special providence and grace. Here baptism stands as the supreme mark of the covenant. The infant's incorporation into the life of the church is demonstrated by the rite of baptism. The church administers the rite as a "sign" of regeneration and does so in prayerful hope. Barth rightly calls it a "sign of hope." Infant baptism also testifies to the sanctity of the Christian family and constitutes a link between succeeding generations.[122] It means that there is a historical continuity within the covenant relationship. For these reasons we must not discontinue infant baptism but give it a more precise theological definition.

There is a basic difference between adult baptism and infant baptism. Our difficulties derive from the fact that

---

119 Cf. George Saunders, "A Service of Dedication of a Child," *Theology*, Dec. 1962, pp. 501ff.

120 Cf. Joachim Jeremias, *Infant Baptism in the First Four Centuries*, 1960.

121 Cf. *CD*, III/2, 586.

122 There is here a parallel situation with being born a Jew; cf. J. Jocz, "The 'Advantage' of the Jew," in *Jews and Christians*, ed. G. A. F. Knight, 1965, pp. 79ff.

this difference is completely overlooked in the formularies of the church.

In the case of infants the only basis for baptism is the covenant. For this reason children of nonbelieving parents ought not to be baptized until they reach years of discretion.[123] But the case with children of believing parents is different. Here election is the basis of church membership. Not that the others are not elect; but because they disregard, or else do not yet know of God's grace in Jesus Christ, baptism would be meaningless to them. Such children are deprived of a Christian home and the influence of the church but are not under condemnation in any way, not even under *minima poena*. That children can be received into the covenant there can be no doubt. Referring to Genesis 17:14 Hooker rightly observes "that infants may contract a covenant with God, the law is plain."[124] But that children cannot believe and repent is common sense. For this reason infant baptism is different from adult baptism and no theological quibbling can alter this fact. In fact the church acknowledges this by providing for the baptismal promises to be affirmed at Confirmation.[125] The personal aspect of faith cannot be treated lightly. In this respect Baptists have a true and legitimate concern, which the historic churches cannot afford to neglect. The givenness of salvation and man's willingness to accept it are not contradictory. That man who bears the image of Adam and is called to bear the image of Christ in order to attain to full manhood is the most profound messianic understanding of the covenant. Augustine in his homilies on I John dwells on this characteristically Christian insight: "There are two births for your understanding, my brothers, of Adam and of Christ: two men, but of them one man is man, the other is God."[126] The second birth,

[123] Cf. Tertullian, *De Anima*, p. 39. In *De Baptismo* Tertullian seems to favor delay in baptizing the young (cf. ch. 18), but according to Jeremias this does not apply to children of Christian parents (cf. *op. cit.*, p. 85). Hooker argues in favor of infant baptism even in the case of unbelieving parents but he bases his views on the authority of St. Augustine; cf. *The Laws of Eccl. Polity*, V, 64, 5.

[124] *Op. cit.*, V, 64, 4.

[125] Calvin rightly says: "Children are baptized for future repentance and faith" (*Institutes*, IV, 16, 20).

[126] For a summary of the homilies, see *A Compendium to the Study of Augustine*, ed. Roy W. Battenhouse, 1955, pp. 212ff.

however, is not achieved by magic but by a willing and personal response to the grace of God. For this reason baptism of adults moves in a different dimension. Here faith is not achieved by proxy but by a personal and conscious response.[127] Here the conditions for baptism as laid down by the Catechism are fully met. The baptismal liturgy of the church fits adults to perfection but only creates confusion in the case of infants.

We thus conclude that we need two baptismal offices and two theologies, one applicable to infants and the other to adults. The sacrament remains one and the same but the circumstances are different; for this reason the application is different. In both cases baptism dramatizes in a unique manner the Christian *kerygma.* It proclaims that the way to life is death to the old man. Each baptism, says Mentz, is a demonstration of God's gracious renewal of the church. For this very reason, he insists that the church must refrain from acting *quasi altera persona Christi.* There can be no identification between the acts of God and the acts of the church. Baptism must remain a constant reminder of the free grace of God. It points to the ever-present need of the Holy Spirit of God in the church. It stands as a sign that God has already called us into His family and has welded us into a brotherhood. In this sense baptism carries the meaning of "salvation-assurance" (*heilsame Sicherung*), in that it points to the covenantal promises.[128] It does not "convey" grace, but points to Him who is eternally gracious. But this infants can only know later, whereas adults can know it now; this is the difference.

This does not mean that there are two baptisms, one for infants and the other for adults. It only means that the application of the same rite varies with the circumstances. We do not deny grace to the infant because of

[127] Adults therefore require no sponsors, only witnesses; cf. D. S. Bailey, *Sponsors at Baptism & Confirmation,* 1952, p. 113. It is difficult to see the meaning of confirmation for those baptized in adulthood, unless it only means official reception into the church by a bishop.

[128] Cf. Hermann Mentz, *Taufe und Kirche, in ihrem ursprünglichen Zusammenhang,* 1960, pp. 70ff. Mentz concludes his study with a short discussion as to the advisability of infant baptism. Of his five points the last one is the most telling: in a church in which the original meaning of baptism is lost, namely that of true fraternity (*Brüderlichkeit*), infant baptism misses the point and is therefore best left in abeyance.

his inability to respond to it personally; we only say that God is present to the infant in a different way than He is to an adult who is able to respond and make a personal decision.

By the same token, we deny the argument of the Anabaptists, for under no circumstances can human fitness be the ground for baptism. As there is one Lord, one faith, so there is only one baptism (Eph. 4:5). The rite of baptism requires no repetition, for man is not saved by baptism but by grace. This is the meaning of I Peter 3:21 — "the outward act signifies a spiritual transformation — the end of the old life and the inauguration of the new."[129] In this passage baptism is described as ἀντίτυπον. This antitype, Dr. Beare tells us, is here used "inversely of the symbol which points to a higher reality." There can be no identification between the sign and the thing signified; the repetition of the sign cannot alter this fact.

b. Holy Communion

For a theological interpretation of the Holy Communion the circumstances of the Institution are of special importance. The context within which the rite was initiated bears considerably upon its meaning and symbolism.

If the Last Supper took place in the atmosphere of the paschal meal we will have to give more careful attention to the theological interplay between the Old Testament and the New Testament than would otherwise be the case. Furthermore, in the context of Passover the Holy Communion adds to the importance of federal theology.

The discussion regarding the connection between the Last Supper and the Holy Communion is to a large degree a matter of conflicting historical data. The Synoptic Gospels present the Last Supper as a Passover meal; if this is the case, then Jesus died on the first day of Passover. The Fourth Gospel tells us that Jesus died on the eve of Passover; in this case the Last Supper could not have been a Passover meal. There is a large literature dealing with this problem and a great variety of views. Just to mention a few: Marxsen proposes that the meal was nothing else but a dramatized and symbolic act in the tradition of the ancient prophets; Lohmeyer thinks that it was an ordinary table fellowship

---

[129] Cf. F. W. Beare, *The First Epistle of Peter*, 1957, pp. 148f.

as practiced in some pious circles; Kuhn connects the meal with the Essene custom of eating in community; Bultmann makes allusions to the mystery cults; Lietzmann, Arnold, and Jungmann connect it with later liturgical developments; Cullmann finds its origin in the postresurrection fellowship of the early disciples.[130] Again, G. H. Box connects the Last Supper with the Sabbath *kiddush;* W. O. E. Oesterley prefers the Passover *kiddush;* Dom Gregory Dix opts for the *ḥaburah;*[131] Ernst Fuchs sees in it an eschatological meal.[132] We have thus a large variety of opinion to choose from. It is noticeable, however, that till recently the Passover background tended to be neglected. This situation is now changing rapidly. It seems that, whatever the date of the Crucifixion, the paschal aspect cannot be overlooked.

We will now take another look at the Gospel evidence.

If the Synoptics are right then Jesus was crucified on the first day of Passover, 15 Nisan, at the height of the Feast. Joachim Jeremias accepts this as a plausible possibility and dismisses the difficulties that arise from such a view.[133] But other scholars feel that Jewish participation in the Crucifixion on such a day, a Sabbath and a high festival, casts doubt upon the veracity of the whole story. It raises more problems than it answers.[134] On the other hand, the Johannine dating raises no such problems; but if John is right and Jesus died on Passover eve then the Last Supper could not have been a paschal meal in the proper sense.

In Christian tradition the Institution of the Last Supper is closely associated with Passover. This goes back to the most primitive times. The Quartodeciman position upheld by Melito of Sardis, Apollinarius of Hierapolis, and above all by St. Polycarp, the Bishop of Smyrna, represents the most ancient tradition in the church. It is on these grounds

---

[130] For references see Albrecht Peters, *Realpräsenz*, Luthers Zeugnis von Christi Gegenwart im Abendmahl, 1960, p. 174.

[131] For references see A. Gilmore, "The Date & Significance of the Last Supper," *SJT*, Sept. 1961, pp. 257f.

[132] Ernst Fuchs, *Studies in the Historical Jesus*, 1964, p. 24.

[133] J. Jeremias, *The Eucharistic Words of Jesus*, 1955, pp. 49ff.

[134] Cf. George Ogg, "The Chronology of the Last Supper," in *Historicity & Chronology in the N.T.*, 1965, pp. 86f; cf. also V. Taylor, *The Gospel according to St. Mark*, 1952, pp. 666f; D. Daube, *The N.T. and Rabbinic Judaism*, 1956, p. 312; J. B. Segal, *The Hebrew Passover*, 1963, p. 244 n. 8.

that Polycarp argues with Anicetus, the Bishop of Rome, to accept the custom.[135] Recent studies in Quartodecimanism have established its close connection with the primitive church, though this in itself does not warrant the conclusion that the Last Supper was a Passover meal.[136] There is some doubt whether the Quartodecimans followed the Jewish custom of beginning the new day at sunset the night before, but their insistence upon the 14th of Nisan reveals the ancient connection between Passover and Easter (cf. I Cor. 5:7). Quartodecimanism was not only practiced in the East but took deep roots in the British Isles to the consternation of the Venerable Bede, who never tires to plead for the "orthodox" date of Easter.[137]

For more questionable evidence we may point to the suggestion by F. L. Cross that I Peter is a paschal liturgy. If this is the case we have here yet another link with Passover in the early church.[138] Prof. A. Guilding's contention that the Supper Discourses are patterned after the Passover lectionary, also deserves attention.[139] Leon Morris questions Prof. Guilding's method of proof but he does not question the importance of the Passover motif for John.[140] There is

---

[135] Fragments from the lost writings of Irenaeus, *Ante-Nicene Library*, Edinburgh, IX, 161; Eusebius, *Eccl. Hist.*, IV, 14, 1.

[136] Cf. George Ogg, *op. cit.*, p. 91. Cf. the fragment found from a lost work "On the Passover"; 13 Nisan is described as the day when "both the consecration of the unleavened bread and the preparation for the feast took place." But it was "on the following day our Saviour suffered, He was the Passover propitiously sacrificed by the Jews" (*Ante-Nicene Christian Library*, XXIV, 167). That this is an ancient document closely linked to Jewish tradition can be seen from the following remark, namely that the resurrection occurred "on the first day of the weeks of harvest, on which the law prescribes that the priest should offer up the sheaf" (*ibid.*, p. 168). The counting of the *'omer* would take place on Sunday, i.e. the day after the Sabbath (cf. Lev. 23:11, 15).

[137] Cf. Bede, *A Hist. of the English Church & People*, pp. 101, 104, 133, 182f, 185, etc., 310ff (Penguin ed.). There is reason to suspect that the mixing of the cup, like the use of unleavened bread, was taken over from the Jewish *seder* (cf. Jeremias, *op. cit.*, p. 143). There is early evidence for the mixing of the cup in the Eucharist; cf. Justin, I *Apology*, 65, 67; also Cyprian, *Epistle* 62, 2). The same will hold for the ablution of hands, which is a feature of the Passover *haggadah.*

[138] Cf. F. L. Cross, *I Peter*, 1954, pp. 13ff.

[139] Cf. Aileen Guilding, *The Fourth Gospel & Jewish Worship*, 1960, pp. 154ff.

[140] Cf. Leon Morris, *The N.T. and the Jewish Lectionaries*, 1964, pp. 50, 64f. Though Prof. Guilding may have overstated her case, we must

therefore no doubt that the Passover tradition is more than a theological concept and that it goes back to a definite historical situation. This, however, does not warrant the conclusion that the Last Supper was a Passover meal.

Jeremias has tried to show in detail that the meal described by the Synoptics was in fact a *seder*. The fourteen points he makes in support of his argument carry considerable weight. At the same time the Johannine date for the Crucifixion is increasingly recognized as the only possible date.[141] Apart from the direct evidence in John, there is circumstantial evidence in favor of the Fourth Gospel: it is better informed regarding Jewish custom than are the Synoptics, Matthew included; scholars increasingly tend to concede an Aramaic, even precanonical base for it;[142] the whole passion narrative has a "clear and consistent" chronology and appears to have the support of astronomical calculations.[143]

To complete the discussion we will briefly mention the matter of the calendar differences in ancient Jewry and the possibility of a misunderstanding of Jewish custom among Gentiles.

(1). The calendar dispute

One device to reconcile the double tradition in the Gospels regarding the date of the Crucifixion is to point to the sectarian difference regarding calendaric calculations. That there were such differences has been recently confirmed by the Dead Sea scrolls. The Qumran sect, it appears, made the matter of fixing the calendar a major issue.[144] Long before the discovery of these documents, Prof. D. Chwolson of the Imperial University at St. Petersburg, already mooted a difference of opinion regarding the fixing of dates among

---

not dismiss her argument too lightly. Anyone familiar with traditional Judaism will know the importance of the *sedra* for a pious Jew. The weekly reading of the O.T. colors his thinking for the rest of the week. St. John Thackery has rightly drawn attention to the importance of the synagogue's lectionary for N.T. exegesis (cf. *The Septuagint and Jewish Worship*, 1923, pp. 40ff).

[141] Cf. Ogg, *op. cit.*, pp. 87, 89, 92, 94.

[142] Cf. C. H. Dodd, *Historical Tradition in the Fourth Gospel*, 1963, pp. 424ff.

[143] Ogg, *op. cit.*, pp. 87, 94f.

[144] Cf. Matthew Black, *The Scrolls & Christian Origins*, 1961, pp. 199ff.

Pharisees and Sadducees.[145] The dispute concerned the "counting of the *'omer*" according to Leviticus 23:11, 15. The Sadducees, being literalists, insisted that "the morrow of the Sabbath" is to be taken to mean the first day of the week, so that the counting of the sheaf-offering always began on Sunday. The Pharisees, however, understood "Sabbath" in a metaphorical sense as the first day after Passover no matter what day of the week it was, as long as it fell on 16 Nisan.[146] The result was that the Sadducean date for Passover was calculated so as to fall always upon the Sabbath day, whereas the Pharisees would allow any day of the week to be the 15th of Nisan. It is therefore suggested by some scholars that the discrepancy between the Synoptics and John rests upon a misunderstanding of the original dispute. But such a compromise is not without difficulties.

To start with, there is no evidence that at our Lord's time Passover was celebrated at two separate dates to suit the contending parties. Furthermore, we would have to allow that Jesus sided with the Pharisees on a trivial matter and celebrated Passover on an "illegal" date. From what we know of Sadducean jealousy regarding jurisdiction over Temple matters it is not likely that they would give way on so important an issue. We therefore conclude that the dispute over the calendar in no way solves the discrepancy between John and the other Gospels.

(2). Misunderstanding regarding Jewish custom

From Josephus we know that preparations for Passover began early and that crowds were already arriving in the capital by the 8th of Nisan.[147] Some scholars therefore suggest that the chronological inaccuracy in the Gospels stems from a confusion whereby the preparation for the festival was later identified with the festival itself. Segal holds that

---

[145] Cf. D. Chwolson, *Das letzte Passamahl Christi und der Tag seines Todes*, 1892; revised ed., 1908.

[146] Cf. Matthew Black, "The Arrest & Trial of Jesus and the Date of the Last Supper," *N.T. Essays in Memory of T. W. Manson*, 1959, p. 31; for a more detailed discussion see Segal, *op. cit.*, pp. 249f. The difference of opinion regarding the fixing of the calendar was recently brought out by Mlle A. Jaubert. She is able to distinguish between an "official" calendar and an ancient sacerdotal calendar; cf. Ogg, *op. cit.*, p. 80; and A. Jaubert, *La Date de la Céne*, 1957.

[147] Josephus, *Wars*, VI, 5, 3.

this was a mistake easily made since the preliminary period of purification lasted full seven days.[148] This perhaps may throw some light on Mlle Jaubert's thesis, which allows several days for the trial leading to the Crucifixion.[149] There is yet another possibility sometimes proposed by scholars, namely that the eves of festivals were regarded as days of special observance equal to the festivals themselves.[150] But even this would not allow for the paschal lamb a day before Passover. There is even the less likely suggestion that because of the throngs the Temple sacrifices for Passover had to be begun a day earlier.[151] But none of these speculations carries sufficient weight.

The likelihood that the Synoptic account is the result of a fusion of two ancient traditions is not impossible, namely that Jesus celebrated a solemn meal the night before He was betrayed and that His death occurred at the time of Passover. Schlatter in reference to John 13:2 cautiously describes it as a *festliches Mahl*.[152] Our contention is that it was more than a solemn meal, for it had all the overtones of a *seder*, and yet it was not a complete paschal meal, for the lamb was missing.

There is good reason to give John's dating preference.[153] There may even be a trace of the Johannine tradition left in the Synoptic record, namely that Jesus died in the ninth hour. This is precisely the time when the slaughter of the paschal lambs would begin in the Temple.[154] The Sabbath did not interfere with the Passover ritual, for according to rabbinic law "the Passover-offering overrides the Sabbath" (*Pes.* 6.1). Our problem arises from the fact that the Johannine tradition explicitly contradicts the Synoptics when it states that the day of the trial and crucifixion was:

---

[148] Cf. J. B. Segal, *The Hebrew Passover*, 1963, p. 139.

[149] See the chart in Ogg, *op. cit.*, p. 80; for a criticism of her position, see *ibid.*, pp. 81ff.

[150] Cf. Segal, *op. cit.*, p. 245.

[151] Cf. M.-J. Lagrange, *The Gospel of Jesus Christ*, 1938 trans., II, 193f.

[152] Adolph Schlatter, *Der Evangelist Johannes*, 1930, p. 279.

[153] Cf. W. F. Howard, *The Fourth Gospel in Recent Criticism and Interpretation*, rev. C. K. Barrett, 1955, pp. 137ff.

[154] Cf. Segal, *op. cit.*, pp. 30, 34, 39, 262. According to the *Mishnah* whenever Passover falls on the eve of the Sabbath the paschal sacrifices are advanced by one hour (cf. *Pes.* 5.1).

παρασκευὴ τοῦ πάσχα (John 19:14).[155] We have already given reasons why his dating is to be preferred.

(3). A theological solution

All are agreed that the Last Supper took place in the atmosphere of the paschal preparations if not on the very night of the feast. There is also general agreement that the Last Supper is strongly suggestive of the Passover *seder*. The Qumran documents have shown that it was possible for at least one group to follow its own calendar in respect to festivals.[156] Some scholars put forth the suggestion that originally Jesus fully intended to celebrate the Passover as stated in the Synoptics, but when events took an unexpected turn and time ran short He decided to anticipate the feast by one day. In view of the general festive atmosphere, the nearness of the feast, and the message that it carried, He gave to the Last Supper a paschal meaning. This is not an impossible suggestion and has the advantage of reconciling the two traditions.

(1) From a strictly technical point of view the Last Supper was not a paschal meal for the lamb was missing, as the eve of Passover was a day later.[157] There is therefore good reason why John does not refer to the Last Supper as a Passover though he knows all about the meal (cf. John 13:2f). Not only was the lamb missing but Jesus purposely refrained from completing the ritual part of the meal. In Jewish tradition the fourth cup drunk on Passover night is associated with the celebration of the Kingdom of God. The cup of blessing is the third cup drunk after the meal. It was at this point that the Institution took place. The

---

[155] Edersheim puts down the discrepancy between the two traditions to a difference in reckoning the time of the day; John is supposed to be following the Roman custom from midnight to midnight, hence the difference (cf. A. Edersheim, *The Life & Times of Jesus the Messiah*, 1907, I, 408 note 1). The longer and shorter version in Luke in respect to the Institution goes back to a similar misunderstanding of Jewish custom. Kenyon and Legg have given reasons why the longer version is to be preferred; cf. *The Ministry & the Sacraments*, ed. Roderic Dunkerley, 1937, p. 285.

[156] Cf. Segal, *op. cit.*, pp. 248f.

[157] Edersheim, who accepts the notion that the Last Supper was a full paschal meal and that Jesus was crucified on Friday, the first day of Passover, contradicts the contention that on so great a day participation on the part of the Jews would have been impossible. Cf. *op. cit.*, II, 508.

fourth cup was never drunk, for the Kingdom of God was not yet inaugurated.[158] Jesus was still to face the ultimate trial and pay the price of salvation. In His case, the fourth cup would be the cup of sorrow and death (cf. Luke 22:42; John 18:11). The Son of Man had first to suffer and die (Mark 8:31) before the victory could be celebrated (Mark 14:25).

The absence of the lamb adds theological significance to our Lord's own sacrifice on the eve of Passover. Edersheim, who takes it for granted that the paschal lamb was not missing and that in fact this Passover was the only time ever when Jesus Himself offered a sacrifice,[159] leaves one peculiar feature completely unexplained: why the reference to the bread and not to the lamb? For Jesus, who was a master of metaphor, to pair "bread" with "body" while all the time the lamb was on the table, strikes one as unnatural. There is also the fact that there is no direct mention in the Gospels of the lamb while there is mention of the bread, the wine, and the sop; and yet the lamb is the most important part of the festival. Segal, who is well versed in Jewish tradition, is rightly puzzled by this circumstance. He says: "The very fact that the most important component of the *Pesaḥ* meal is not mentioned by the Synoptic Gospels is a clear indication that the identification of the Last Supper as a *Pesaḥ* meal is an artificial device."[160] His insistence that while the Temple stood in Jerusalem, a Passover celebration without the lamb would be meaningless, is well justified.[161] This sentiment on the part of a Jewish scholar would have been shared by the writer of the Fourth Gospel. Segal solves the difficulty by suggesting that it was a "symbolic meal." This meets our own position, except that the symbolism was entirely paschal.[162] The absence of the paschal lamb heightens the sym-

---

[158] For the significance of the omission of the fourth cup see Daube, *op. cit.*, pp. 330f.

[159] Cf. Edersheim, *op. cit.*, II, 490f.

[160] Segal, *op. cit.*, p. 245.

[161] Cf. *ibid.*, p. 246. Jeremias sees in Luke 22:15 a direct reference to the paschal lamb (cf. *op. cit.*, p. 42). Unfortunately the transmission of the text is uncertain and there is a variant reading. Assuming that Jeremias is right, why the metaphor, "bread and body," and not lamb and body, or flesh and body? This Jeremiah cannot explain (cf. *ibid.*, p. 144).

[162] Cf. J. Jocz, *A Theology of Election*, 1958, pp. 37f.

bolic significance of the Messiah's own sacrifice for the redemption of the world (cf. John 1:36, 42; Heb. 7:27). Celebrating Passover without the lamb was not entirely without precedent as this must have been the custom among Jews in the diaspora, who would observe the Feast of Unleavened Bread though they could not participate in the paschal offering.[163]

We thus have good reason to conclude that the Last Supper, though not a complete paschal meal, was celebrated in the context of Passover, followed the theme of Passover, and gave to the festival of Passover a messianic and eschatological conclusion.

(2) We will now try to establish the theological significance of the Holy Communion in relation to the meaning of Passover.

Passover is first and foremost a season of remembrance. The *seder* ritual is so ordered as to create the most vivid impression of the story of God's redemption from the land of Egypt. Passover is essentially a home festival, and the liturgy has remained almost unaltered from the time of Jesus. At the paschal table the story is dramatized by word and action and the various ingredients of the meal are symbolic representations of the plight in Egypt, the hasty departure, and the ultimate victory. The accent at the meal is upon "remembrance" (*lezikkārôn*); this is in accordance with the precept of the *torah*, "this shall be for you a day of remembrance" (cf. Exod. 12:14f; 13:9; Deut. 16:3).[164]

This act of "remembering" is more than looking back to the past. By reason of the Hebrew sense of the cohesion of history, every generation experiences afresh the miracle of redemption from Egypt. The Rabbis are very insistent on the fact that every Israelite of every age participates personally in the flight from Egypt. The *Mishnah* lays down the rule: "In every generation a man must so regard himself as if he came forth himself out of Egypt, for it is written, 'And thou shalt tell thy son in that day, saying, it is because of that what the Lord did for me when I came forth out of Egypt'" (Exod. 13:8).[165] To the question asked by the son: "Why is this night different

---

[163] Cf. Gabriel Hebert, *When Israel Came out of Egypt*, 1961, p. 26.
[164] Cf. Jeremias, *op. cit.*, p. 161.
[165] *Pes.* 10.5 (Danby's trans.).

from all other nights?" the *pater familias* gives the following answer: "We were slaves unto Pharaoh in Egypt, and the Lord our God brought us forth from thence, with a mighty hand and an outstretched arm. . . ."[166] The personal pronouns "we" and "us" are not in the mode of rhetorical sentimentality but are meant literally. Every Jew personally relives the past on Passover night. The Rabbis stress the importance of the first person singular in the text of Exodus 13:8: "What God has done for *me*, when *I* came out of Egypt."[167] This principle of personal involvement in the nation's past applies also to the covenant at Sinai and to every other experience of God's dealing with His people.[168] By this rule every living Israelite is brought under God's providence and participates in all His benefits. *Lezikaron* means all this.

The next thing we must notice is the message associated with Passover.

Traditionally Passover is called *zeman herutenu*, the season of our freedom — this is the underlying theme of the festival. This, again, is not a pious phrase but a deeply experienced fact in history. Passover carries the message of Israel's *renaissance* and the offer of franchise by an act of God. Having been *manumitted* by God no Jew can ever be a slave again. Passover is therefore a festival of national rejoicing. This note of joy and praise finds magnificent expression in the liturgy: "Therefore we are bound to give thanks, to praise, to glorify, to honour, to exalt, to bless Him who wrought all these wonders for our fathers and for us. He brought us out from bondage to freedom, from sorrow to gladness, and from mourning to a Festival-day, and from darkness to great light, and from servitude to redemption; so let us say before Him the Hallelujah."[169]

For the Jewish people Passover is *the* Festival of redemption in the national sense. But because of the strange vicissitudes of Jewish history the theme of joy always carries a note of sadness. Together with the great act of deliverance Israel remembers the long trek through the wilderness, the bitter wars of liberation, the suffer-

---

[166] Cf. *Haggadah of Passover*, trans. Maurice Samuel, 1942, pp. 8f.

[167] Cf. G. F. Moore, *Judaism*, 1927, II, 41 and note 7.

[168] Cf. J. Jocz, *A Theology of Election*, pp. 49f.

[169] *Pes*. 10.5 (Danby); cf. *Haggadah*, pp. 27f. The "Hallelujah" is the Greal Hallel, i.e. Pss. 113 to 118.

ings and the hardships down the centuries to this very day. The cup of joy is tempered by the presence of the bread of affliction[170] and the bitter herbs. All these serve to convey the undeniable fact about human life: salvation entails suffering.

The year when Jesus was celebrating the Last Supper with His disciples was a year of tension and oppression not unlike the time under Pharaoh in Egypt. Once again Israel was in bondage, though this time upon its own soil. A ruthless pagan overlord kept God's people in utter subjection. The very House of God was under constant surveillance by a Roman garrison (cf. Acts 21:30ff). The office of the highpriesthood was in the gift of the Roman governor. Even the Temple treasure was at his disposal.[171] Israel's life and fortune, it would appear, was dependent upon the whim of a cruel pagan emperor.

Under such circumstances it was only to be expected that the Passover season would provide the opportunity to fanatical nationalists to promote the cause of insurrection. Passover engendered an explosive atmosphere in those days and became notorious for abortive rebellions.[172] It was therefore natural to associate the Festival of Freedom with messianic hopes. To this day the *seder* liturgy connects the hope of salvation with the coming of the Messiah, the Son of David. Together with the patriarchs and the Holy City, God is asked to remember His Servant, the Messiah. For the God of Israel is "the One who enacts salvation and consolation."[173]

It is in this historic context that the cup of salvation and the bread of affliction are placed upon the same table, side by side. This paradox of Passover symbolizes not only Israel's condition but the condition of humanity at large: man is born to freedom but never quite reaches the promised land.[174]

---

170 *leḥem 'ani* (Deut. 16:3). For the bread of affliction see Jeremias, *op. cit.*, pp. 33ff.

171 Cf. Josephus, *Antiq.*, XV, 11, 4. The High Priest's vestments were held in Roman custody, though this humiliation was later mitigated; cf. XVIII, 11, 4 and XX, 1, 1.

172 Cf. *ibid.*, XVIII, 9, 3.

173 The Hebrew wording is even more expressive and cannot be rendered without paraphrase; cf. *Haggadah*, p. 37.

174 Cf. *Haggadah*, p. 8: "This year finds us here, may the year to

It is a puzzling fact that Jewish aspirations to national freedom are completely by-passed in the New Testament. There are only incidental references to the political situation, like the question of tribute to Caesar (Luke 20:22), the arrest of Barabbas and his companions for insurrection (Mark 15:7), the political fears of the priestly hierarchy (John 11:47f). But the subject itself is never discussed directly. What is more, the Fourth Gospel obviously intends to contradict the nationalist understanding of freedom: "he who commits sin, is a slave to sin — only if the Son makes you free, you will be free indeed" (John 8:34ff). Joseph Klausner finds this attitude intolerable and complains of Jesus' total lack of national sentiment. He paraphrases with obvious irony: "What does it matter if you *do* pay tribute to Caesar, if only you are at peace with the Lord your God!"[175] Klausner tells us that in this respect Jesus differed fundamentally from the ancient prophets, for he completely lacked "a wider political perspective." It is for this reason that he feels justified to chide the Master of Nazareth for his extreme ethical idealism which led to a disregard of Israel's political plight. Judaism, Klausner tells us, is only interested in a messianic kingdom that is of *this* world. It can only accept a messianism in national culture and serving the survival of Jewish nationhood. Some scholars have felt that this lack of national interest is a later development and have even proposed that Jesus originally was at the head of a political movement.[176] But there is little support for such a a view. The whole trend of the Gospels, as of the rest of the New Testament, is to reinterpret Passover in new and universal terms.

It is against the background of frustrated political aspiration that the Last Supper acquires a paschal meaning specifically its own. Here messianism is being enacted

---

come find us in the land of Israel; this year Jews are enslaved, may next year see them free."

[175] Joseph Klausner, *Jesus of Nazareth*, 1926, p. 373.

[176] Cf. Robert Eisler, ΙΗΣΟΥΣ ΒΑΣΙΛΕΥΣ ΟΥ ΒΑΣΙΛΕΥΣΑΣ, 2 vols., Heidelberg, 1929f. Also *The Enigma of the Fourth Gospel*, 1938, pp. 175f. For the opposite view see Martin Hengel, *Die Zeloten*, 1961, pp. 306f. Hengel concludes that the Fourth Gospel is the end result of the antipolitical tendency in the early church; p. 386.

in different terms and on a different level from that of popular national hope.

(a). *The memorial meal*

In keeping with the traditional intention of Passover the Last Supper is also a memorial meal — *lezikaron:* "this do in remembrance of me" (I Cor. 11:24f). There is here, however, a conscious and deliberate transition from the paschal lamb to the person of the Messiah. This is in perfect harmony with the prophetic vision of the true servant of God who like a lamb is led to the slaughter without protest (Isa. 53:7). Hence the reference to the broken body and poured-out blood. There is here a fusion of two basic concepts: the paschal concept of redemption and the cultic concept of the sin-offering. The Messiah is both: the true paschal lamb (cf. I Cor. 5:7), and also the sin-sacrifice that used to be burned outside Israel's camp (cf. Heb. 13:11f).

Jeremias has shown how the words uttered at the Institution of the Holy Communion easily fit into the context of the *pesaḥ haggadah.* It is therefore obvious that Jesus as the Messiah looked upon Himself as the substitute for the paschal lamb.[177] But together with this allusion to the paschal lamb there is the other allusion to the Suffering Servant who willingly and vicariously bears the sins of many. The πολλοί in the words of the Institution is obviously an echo of Deutero-Isaiah's *rabbim* as rendered in the Septuagint (cf. Isa. 52:14; 53:11f). [178] "This is the blood of the covenant poured out for *many*" (Mark 14:24).

A. Richardson is therefore right in arguing against an exclusively paschal interpretation of the Eucharist on the grounds that the expiatory aspect is included. He points to Exodus 24:8 where the "sprinkling of the blood" for the ratification of the covenant with Israel serves as a means of expiation. The Suffering Servant, by the shedding of His blood on the Cross, assumes the function of the Lamb of God who bears the sins of the world.[179]

---

[177] Cf. Jeremias, *op. cit.*, p. 145.

[178] *Ibid.*, p. 142.

[179] Cf. A. Richardson, *An Introduction to the Theology of the N.T.*, 1958, p. 371.

(b). *The sign*

Rengstorf in his learned article on σημεῖον connects the word with the Hebrew אוֹת as it occurs in the Old Testament. Here *'ôth* and *mōphēth* (wonder) are related terms. There is therefore a similar relationship between σημεῖα and τέρατα in the New Testament.[180] This, however, will depend upon the context. In the case of the Last Supper the more removed meaning of τέρας in the sense of portent, omen, wonder, miracle, remains in the background. The same applies to the paschal meal: the unleavened bread, the cup of wine, the whole ceremony point to the miracle of redemption.

In the forefront, however, is the sign itself with its appeal to the eye: *'ôth,* says Rengstorf, is primarily an object of sense perception. But as such the sign always points beyond itself to the giver who appointed it. Behind the sign is the hidden authority that makes the sign effectual. In the Old Testament a sign is a token and reminder of God's mighty acts. The unfortunate preoccupation with the sign itself as a vehicle of grace so characteristic for Eucharistic theology both in the Middle Ages and at the time of the Reformation rests upon a misunderstanding. Richardson rightly scorns the mystical and metaphysical attempt to define the *esse* of the wine in the cup.[181] Identification of the sign with the thing signified abolishes the whole meaning of the sign and creates a situation where direct confrontation between the beholder and the thing signified takes place. This is exactly what happened in the doctrine of transubstantiation. The cruder aspects of consubstantiation usually associated with the name of Luther[182] make a similar mistake. Such coalescence of sign with thing signified loses the typological aspect of the sign, which plays an important part in the New Testament, especially in John.[183] Richardson's remark that the

---

180 *TWNT*, VII, 209.

181 *Op. cit.*, pp. 230f.

182 For a denial that Luther taught a straightforward doctrine of consubstantiation, see Otto W. Heick, "Consubstantiation in Luther's Theology," *CJT*, Jan. 1966, pp. 3ff. But at the same time there is in Luther a stress of identity between element and the Presence of Christ which cannot be explained away; see Albrecht Peters, *Realpräsenz, Luthers Zeugnis von Christi Gegenwart im Abendmahl,* 1960, p. 89.

183 Cf. Rengstorf, *op. cit.*, pp. 256f.

Eucharist is not a re-enacting of Christ's dying, "but a parable of the significance of his death,"[184] must be taken seriously, if we are to pay attention to the meaning of a "sign" in the New Testament.

On the principle of an analogy between the Passover and the Last Supper we may proceed to interpret the Eucharistic bread and wine as signs of God's redeeming acts. The Last Supper thus dramatizes as if by parable the paschal theme and carries it to an ultimate conclusion. It begins with the theme of redemption as demonstrated by the flight from Egypt and ends with the messianic triumph in the death and resurrection of Jesus. The Last Supper is a proleptic enactment performed with a view to the Cross. On the basis of the paschal analogy the Eucharistic elements serve as reminders and visible signs of God's gracious dealing with sinners.

But in accordance with biblical semantics the sign also carries the meaning of pledge: it sets the seal (σφραγίς) that God is faithful (John 3:33). Paul plainly identifies the sign with the seal or pledge in the case of circumcision (cf. Rom. 4:11). All God's signs carry such an assurance. It is for this reason that we allowed the principle of *ex opere operato* in the sacraments, though in a modified form. The emphasis is here upon the promise of God's Word as vouchsafed in the covenant, and not upon the sign as such. The Greek Fathers were therefore justified in their use of the synonyms for the biblical sign, like σύμβολον, ἀντίτυπον, or ὁμοιότης. Even μυστήριον meets the case as long as it is understood in the Hebrew sense of *sôd* (סוֹד) as God's purpose or plan of salvation disclosed in His revelation."[185] It is only when it becomes associated with the current concepts derived from the mystery religions that it acquires the meaning of rite, ritual, and magic.[186]

This in no sense affects the presence of the risen Christ at the Eucharist. It only differentiates between the elements as signs and the Presence of Christ as the inward experience. The idea that at the consecration of the elements the miracle of the Incarnation is repeated

---

[184] Richardson, *op. cit.*, p. 370.

[185] *A Theol. Word Book of the Bible*, ed. A. Richardson, 1950, *sub voce.*

[186] Cf. *HDCG, sub voce.*

or extended in time is an idolatrous notion. The idea that man eats his God bodily is even worse. Wyclif felt outraged at the thought that "any priest can daily make or consecrate the body of the Lord by saying Mass." To him the consecration of the host is not the Lord's body but only "an efficacious sign." But this does not mean that for Wyclif Christ was absent and all that was left was the sign. All he does is to deny "that bread which we consecrate is identical with the body of Christ, although it is the efficacious sign thereof."[187] Wyclif finds it too terrible to contemplate that we should "eat the flesh carnally and drink the blood carnally of a man loved so dearly."[188] In spite of Luther's insistence upon the incarnate Presence of Christ in the Eucharist, this Presence was never to him a mechanical process. The Presence of Christ in the Eucharist was the *beneficium spiritus sancti* and was in answer to faith.[189] Though Luther believed in the coincidence between the *mundicatio oralis* and the spiritual *mundicatio* he made it quite clear that what really matters is the *mundicatio cordalis*.[190] Otto W. Heick has tried to show that for Luther the sacrament is not a static concept physically extended in time but rather a "dynamic force" by which Christ is personally present and uses the elements "instrumentally."[191] This is what we mean by an efficacious sign: it is a sign in the sense that it points beyond itself to the One who, by His promise to be with His people, uses it as a token of that promise.

(c). *The Messiah's victory*

The two notes that blend in the Passover theme, namely suffering and redemption, recur in the Holy Communion. But in the case of the Holy Communion emphasis is differently placed: suffering is still the result of sin, and salvation is still an act of God, but the experience of Israel at large is now concentrated upon one single person. The Messiah is the Sufferer *par excellence* and in Him God wins His greatest victory, namely the victory over sin and death. In the Eucharist, therefore, suffering and the

---

[187] Wyclif, *On the Eucharist*, Library of Christian Classics, XIV, 1953, p. 87.
[188] *Ibid.*, p. 65.
[189] Cf. Peters, *op. cit.*, p. 67 n. 97.
[190] *Ibid.*, p. 53.
[191] *Op. cit.*, p. 8.

Sufferer, the victim and the Victor, are inseparable. In the center of the drama stands the risen Christ. As sufferer He represents mankind; as Victor He is God incarnate.

The Messiah's suffering points to the fact that man's salvation depends upon reconciliation with God and that there is no reconciliation without forgiveness. The Messiah's death is the ground of God's forgiveness. But the note of victory goes beyond Good Friday and derives from the Easter message: by raising Jesus from the dead God has defeated all evil powers and has thus freed man from the slavery of sin. This note of victory is already anticipated in the story of the Last Supper though the Cross looms large on the horizon. The Last Supper is not a funereal meal in any sense: the fourth cup will yet be drunk at the triumph of God's Kingdom (Mark 14:25).

Such assurance of victory is the highest expression of faith. Faith means exactly this: unconditional trust in God. For this reason Good Friday is not the end of the messianic drama, but only the penultimate act. The last word belongs to God and was uttered on Easter Sunday.

Jeremias has noticed an interesting deviation from accepted custom on the part of Jesus at the Last Supper. The words of the Institution apparently were uttered at the moment of distributing the bread and the wine and not while handling them. Jeremias thinks that this slight alteration of the Passover *haggadah* was deliberately done in order to give greater emphasis to the fact that both forgiveness and salvation depend upon the Messiah's self-sacrifice.[192] All that is left for his followers to do is to accept it: "take and eat," i.e. the Messiah's sacrifice is God's gift to man.[193]

The defeat the Messiah suffers is only an apparent one. In terms of worldly success Jesus has failed. The Cross is man's No to God and His purpose for man. Had it been the end of the drama, the Last Supper would have been a funerary rite. The *euangellion,* the Good News, is exactly this, that the last word is not with man but with

[192] Cf. Jeremias, *op. cit.,* pp. 142, 153.

[193] There is a similar expression of the *dant salutem* in the case of the washing of the disciples' feet, especially our Lord's words to Simon Peter (John 13:6ff).

God. The Holy Communion is thus a victory celebration, and in this respect too it resembles the Passover.

(d). *The messianic fellowship*

Table-fellowship is the most intimate expression of community in the tradition of the East. The Last Supper was a table-fellowship between Master and disciples at a critical moment in their lives. The Eucharistic meal is a re-enactment of the original scene, except that the Master is not present in the physical sense. But by prayer and invocation of the Holy Spirit the messianic community believes that Christ is present spiritually. The basis of the Holy Communion service is the assumption that Jesus Christ acts as the invisible Host and that we are His guests. By participation in this table-fellowship, the individual believer affirms his relationship with the Master and the brotherhood. The messianic community derives its family character from the eating of the same loaf and sharing of the same cup at their Lord's table. Such participation in the Eucharistic meal carries covenantal significance: it is not only a reminder of God's covenant with His people but also an expression of loyalty to the covenant on the part of the messianic community. It is for this reason that the church attaches such importance to the rite.

Käsemann has shown that for Paul, and probably for the early church, participation in a gift conveyed something of the character of the giver.[194] Thus the host at a sacred meal offers something of his own graces to those who share in it. To share in the Lord's Supper is therefore tantamount to sharing in His grace. This gracious fellowship with the Master extends to all participants and becomes a fellowship in the grace of the Lord Jesus Christ.

The Eucharistic fellowship moves along the lines of two dimensions: in time and space it is the visible fellowship of believers; in the realm of the Spirit it comprises the *communio sanctorum* of all ages. Here the visible and the invisible church, or the church militant and the church triumphant, meet at the center, namely around their risen Lord.

But such a "mystical" interpretation of the Holy Communion would tend to relieve the Christian community

---

[194] Cf. Ernst Käsemann, *Essays on N.T. Themes,* 1964, pp. 113, 118, 131.

from its historic obligation and provide a means of escape from the concrete demands of life. Whenever the eschatological aspect of the Eucharist was neglected, this in fact took place. It is only under the sign of eschatology that the Holy Communion retains the character of tension between "already" and "not yet."[195] Salvation is here, because Jesus Christ has not only come, but is present with His people; yet in history salvation is never complete. Here we can only walk by faith and not by sight. The messianic community is a pilgrim community on the way to man's ultimate destiny.

Apart from the covenant, humanity remains divided between believers and nonbelievers, between those who enjoy their fellowship in the Messiah and those who remain outside. The Eucharist would thus become the gateway to eternity for those who know themselves "saved." The others are left to perish. But under the sign of eschatology the division becomes more ambiguous. Here the situation may be reversed: not those who say, Lord, Lord, shall enter into the Kingdom of heaven, but those who do the will of God (Matt. 7:21). Some will plead, "We ate and drank in your presence, and you taught in our streets"; but the answer will be: "I do not know where you come from; depart from me, all you workers of iniquity!" (Luke 13:26f). It means that history provides an inconclusive answer. The covenant goes beyond historic contingency and leaves God to pronounce the last verdict about life and death.

The eschatological note in the Eucharist derives from the covenant perspective. The covenant points beyond history: God remains our God even beyond the grave. This is the meaning of our Lord's answer to the question regarding the resurrection (Matt. 22:32). The Eucharist does not translate us into eternity but is limited to time: till He comes (I Cor. 11:26).[196] There is yet an encounter to take place with the Son of Man who will judge the quick and the dead. The parousia is necessary to complete the drama of salvation.

---

[195] Cf. J. Jocz, *The Spiritual History of Israel*, 1961, pp. 228ff.

[196] According to Ignatius the Eucharist is φάρμακον ἀθανασίας: *To the Ephesians* 20.2. But such an understanding of the Eucharist takes us beyond the realm of the personal into the sphere of magic. It is likely that Ignatius never meant it in that sense.

In the discussion regarding the Second Advent the covenant is hardly ever taken into account. John A. T. Robinson thinks that the New Testament idea of a Second Coming rests upon a misunderstanding of what Jesus meant by the coming of the Son of Man. But in our view the parousia is the concomitant to the covenantal relationship as far as history is concerned. It may well be that the idea of a Second Coming has its roots in the Old Testament and that it grew into a definite Christian doctrine as the result of unfulfilled hopes,[197] but the deeper reason lies in the covenant concept.

The covenant in the Old Testament context is primarily a this-worldly arrangement. God binds Himself to be man's God at the very beginning of history. This is already implied by man's creation: he is God's creature *par excellence*. The early church, because it was rooted in the Old Testament, never entirely surrendered the earthly hope of God's reign. The parousia expresses as nothing else the concrete messianic hope for palingenesis (cf. Matt. 19:28) within history. Behind this apocalyptic hope is the conviction of God's unswerving loyalty to His promise. This too belongs to the paschal context: the Passover *haggadah* carries a definite eschatological note: "May He who is the Merciful One make us worthy for the days of the Messiah and for life in the world to come. He bestows great salvation to His king and shows mercy to His anointed: to David and his seed for ever."[198] Here is expressed the twofold aspect of the messianic hope: this world and the world to come are here inextricably intertwined. For the church the *this*-worldly aspect of the Kingdom is linked to the hope of the Second Coming.

We may therefore speak of the Messiah's Presence in a threefold sense: the historic Jesus of Nazareth, the risen Christ of Easter Sunday, and the Christ of the Second Advent.[199] The Eucharist is meant to convey these

---

[197] Cf. J. A. T. Robinson, *Jesus & His Coming*, 1957, pp. 141ff. Cf. also Stephen Neill, *The Church of England Newspaper*, March 21, 1958, p. 7.

[198] *Haggadah*, *op. cit.*, pp. 39f.

[199] Cf. the interesting formula: "who is and who was and who is to come" (Rev. 1:8). Dr. Robinson's insistence upon the one single historic parousia (cf. *op. cit.*, p. 185), unduly spiritualizes history and suspends the covenant.

three dimensions: it looks back to the Cross; it expresses the joy of Christ's Presence; it looks forward to the consummation of history.

That Jesus the Messiah is present to His people is not a Pauline invention but goes back to the most primitive tradition of the church.[200] It is His Presence that constitutes the messianic fellowship of believers in the intimacy of the Eucharistic meal.

(e). *The universal meal*

Käsemann, in his essay on "The Pauline Doctrine of the Lord's Supper," tries to show how the Apostle's approach to the Eucharist is grounded in the concept of the new *diatheke*. It is by means of this concept that believer and Master achieve an intimacy that amounts to identification: "whoever cleaves to the Lord is one spirit with Him" (I Cor. 6:17). According to Käsemann, this sacramental incorporation into the body of Christ does not come about by a magical, metaphysical, or mystical device. St. Paul guards himself against such misconceptions. In the Pauline view, the Lord Himself encounters man by laying hold on his will and laying claim to his obedience: "By claiming our bodies sacramentally for service in his body, Christ emerges as the Cosmocrator, who in our bodies takes possession of the present world as its Lord and in his own body inaugurates the new world."[201] This sacramental relationship is established by way of the covenant, whereby an "identity between past and present saving events" takes place. It is important to note that Käsemann refers back to "primitive Christian eucharistic theology," which Paul has taken up and used for his own purpose.[202]

The reason why St. Paul lays such stress upon the *diatheke* in connection with the Eucharist is not far to seek: it expresses as no other rite the atoning act upon the Cross.

Sinful man cannot associate with the holy God except by an act of propitiation. This act the Messiah performs by His willing and obedient sacrifice. His broken body thus becomes "the new and living way" to God the Father (Heb. 10:20). The solidarity between sacrificer

---

[200] Cf. Käsemann, *op. cit.*, p. 114.
[201] *Ibid.*, pp. 134f.
[202] Cf. *ibid.*, p. 114.

and victim is here reversed: the Messiah who is the Victim identifies Himself with sinners. καταλλαγή conveys the meaning of atonement as no other word: Jesus exchanges places with sinners (Rom. 5:10f). It is important to note that for St. Paul this act of atonement is the highest expression of God's love for man (Rom. 5:8). The love of Christ and the love of God are here identical. It is not a cruel God who is pacified by the death of His own Son, but a loving Father who gives His greatest treasure for the sake of man's salvation.

Jeremias notices that in later Jewish thinking death was ascribed atoning efficacy, especially in the case of those who died innocently. He deduces from this that our Lord will have regarded His own death as of atoning significance.[203] The reference to the "many" in the words of the Institution (Mark 10:45) carries catholic meaning in the widest sense: "all" are included to share in the benefit of the Messiah's sacrifice (cf. II Cor. 5:14f).[204] This striking extension from Israel to mankind is here understood as the very mark of messianic fulfillment. Jesus is not Messiah unless He is Messiah for all. Here the national boundary of Judaism is broken and God's promise to Abraham is fulfilled: "and in thy seed shall all the nations of the earth be blessed" (Gen. 22:18).

The all-inclusiveness of the messianic sacrifice requires a catholic approach to the table-fellowship: here no one is left out; even Judas participates. It is questionable whether the restrictions the church imposes are theologically justified. According to Gregory Dix the exclusion from the Lord's table of the unbaptized goes back to the Jewish restrictions regarding table-fellowship with non-Israelites.[205] This is, however, anything but a theological explanation. It would seem to contradict all that Paul stood for in his struggle for the universality of the gospel.

The *Didache* has somehow preserved a double tradition regarding participation in the Holy Communion: "let no one eat or drink of your Eucharist, except those bap-

---

[203] Jeremias, *op. cit.*, p. 152.

[204] ὑπὲρ πάντων is the characteristic Christian interpretation of *rabbim* in Isa. 52:14; 53:11f.

[205] Cf. Dom Gregory Dix, *The Shape of the Liturgy*, 1945, p. 46 n., p. 83.

tized into the name of the Lord." The reason given for the restriction is the dominical logion: "Give not that which is holy to the dogs" (Matt. 7:6).[206] But at the same time there follows the invitation: "Whoever is holy, let him come; whoever is not, let him repent."[207] This is an open invitation to all present and may go back to a more primitive tradition. The liturgical formula: "Holy things unto the holy"[208] is reminiscent of a cultic attitude that contradicts the spirit of the gospel.[209]

The Passover *haggadah* prescribes that the *pater familias* on elevating the tray with the paschal ingredients is to say: "Let all those who are hungry enter and eat; all who are in need, come and celebrate (the Passover)."[210] But this open invitation, possibly echoed by the *Didache,* would only apply to Israelites, as no stranger was allowed to eat of the Passover (cf. Exod. 12:43-45).[211] The text in Numbers 9:14, which is less restrictive, the Rabbis applied exclusively to proselytes.[212] In contradistinction to the Passover, the Holy Communion must be an open meal, for as no other rite it expresses the innermost meaning of the gospel: God's undeserved grace to the unworthy. The parable about the prodigal son (Luke 15:11ff), the parable about the great banquet (Luke 14:15f), but above all the Matthean version of the marriage feast is of decisive importance to us (Matt. 22:1ff): "and the servants went out into the streets and gathered whom they found, both *bad* and *good;* so the wedding hall was filled with guests" (v. 10).

There can be therefore no theological restriction upon participation in the Holy Communion but only a practical one connected with church order and discipline. The *correptio* of the church demanded that catechumens do not

---

206 *Didache,* 9.11f.

207 *Ibid.,* 10.9.

208 Cf. Dix, *op. cit.,* p. 514.

209 For the restrictions practiced in the early church with respect to the Eucharist, cf. Justin, I *Apology,* 66; *Apostolic Constitutions,* VIII, 12; Gregory Dix, *op. cit.,* pp. 41f, 82f, 437f, etc.

210 *Haggadah, op. cit.,* p. 8. פסח is here in the verbal form *yiphsaḥ,* "to partake of the paschal lamb."

211 Maurice Samuel in his English translation of the text fails to convey the spirit of the invitation by omitting to translate the word "all."

212 Cf. Daube, *op. cit.,* pp. 107f.

participate before baptism. Penitents would naturally be expected to refrain until received back into full communion.[213] Outsiders would not understand the significance of the meal until instructed. The Eucharistic service, however, must never lose the kerygmatic character and the universal appeal: for as often as you eat this bread and drink this cup, you proclaim the Lord's death until He comes (I Cor. 11:26). This aspect of the Eucharist is beautifully expressed in an ancient liturgy: "Brethren, receive the body of the Son, cries the Church, and drink ye His chalice with faith in the house of His Kingdom."[214]

Because the Holy Communion is the most characteristic rite of the Christian church it must always be open to outsiders. Eduard Schweizer has shown that in the New Testament the church is conceived as an open community, a *corpus mixtum*, and this even at the danger of "cheap grace."[215] The Eucharist is certainly a family gathering, but it is not an exclusive family of privileged status that gathers at the Lord's table. The messianic community is by definition an open community into which everyone is welcome. In this sense it transcends the Hebrew Passover. Passover celebrates the birth of a nation. Although any Gentile can choose to become a Jew, he can never fully overcome the handicaps of his foreign origin.[216] To the end of his life he remains a proselyte. But in the messianic community, everyone is a newcomer. This fact has been specially emphasized by the Jewish philosopher-theologian, Franz Rosenzweig: the Christian church is always in the state of beginning.[217] For this reason, no one is here a born native. Every man of every age and clime is expected to make his own decision to come to the supper (cf. Luke 14:16ff). The church invites him in the name of Christ, and when he accepts the invitation he comes as an equal, for everyone else is also a guest.

c. The church

Under the "means of grace" we have to include, together with baptism and Holy Communion, the church

---

[213] Cf. Dix, *op. cit.*, p. 478.
[214] *Liturgy of the Holy Apostles*, Ante-Nicene Lib., XXIV, 90.
[215] Cf. E. Schweizer, *Church Order in the N.T.*, 1961, p. 56.
[216] Cf. Wm. G. Braude, *Jewish Proselyting*, 1940, pp. 100ff.
[217] Franz Rosenzweig, *Der Stern der Erlösung*, 1954, III, 146ff.

as God's gift to man. By doing so we lay emphasis upon the fact that the church is not a human decision but a divine gift. If the church were merely the result of man's decision, church order would have had to depend upon the cultural changes in society. Each age would evolve its own structure of church to suit its needs. But because the church is a gift, it comes to us under definite shape and form. This ordering of the church is connected with the fact that Jesus Christ precedes the church as its Lord. For this reason Barth's criticism of Sohm and Brunner is well justified.[218] We must not so define the church in anthropocentric terms as if her main task were to serve our needs. The opposite is true: the church exists to serve her Lord.

The church is primarily the decision of Jesus Christ. It means that the *raison d'être* of the church is not to be sought in sociological circumstances but in the will of God. Barth insists that this is the only reason why we can speak of church order and church constitution as the framework of church life. Such order and constitution is God's gift to His people as a token of His grace. The ordering principle within the church which Barth calls *Grundrecht* derives from the disposition, command, and arrangement of Him who is the Head.

(1). The church as a gift

We have said that a sacrament is a sign that points beyond itself to God who is the Giver. Because the church is the sign of God's Presence with His people it therefore carries sacramental meaning: it points beyond itself to Him who is its Foundation (cf. Eph. 2:20). What differentiates the church from the world is not that the one is religious and the other secular, but rather that the one is open to receive salvation at the hands of God, whereas the other seeks to save itself as best it can. The church therefore is not a building but an attitude peculiar to those who place themselves under the obedience of Jesus Christ. Any place where Christ is preached and obeyed the church becomes manifest. But because such preaching and such obedience can only take place under the sign of the covenant, the church can never be divorced from the past. An ahistorical church can only be a human decision; as

---

[218] Cf. *CD*, IV/2, 67.

such it is not the church of Jesus Christ because it is not the church of the covenant. Here the historic coherence with the past acquires fundamental importance. The reason for this is not far to seek: unless God is the God of the past, He cannot be the God of the present. A newly discovered God can only be an invention. The God the Bible testifies to is not discovered by man; He graciously reveals Himself as man's God by word and deed. The covenant is the historic basis of biblical revelation, and the quintessence of the covenant finds symbolic expression in the Holy Communion rite.

The givenness of the church as part and parcel of the *dant salutem* is safeguarded in the Eucharistic meal. In the context of the Holy Communion we are reminded that this is not our church but the church of Jesus Christ. Karl Barth describes the church as a "table fellowship" over which Christ presides and at which His followers enjoy His hospitality.[219] This serves to emphasize that the church is under the sign of God's grace and exists by His will and decision. It is only thus that the gates of hell (or the powers of death, RSV) shall not prevail against her (Matt. 16:18). There is thus a real sense in which there is no salvation outside the church of Jesus Christ.[220] Not so that the church disposes of salvation; on the contrary, she is at the receiving end. Salvation is only *within* the church insofar as Jesus Christ is its Head.

The soteriological aspect of the church must not be interpreted as if grace were tied to a human institution. In this regard, Roman theology is sorely remiss by failing to make a radical distinction between church as a gift and church as a human decision.

As in the case of baptism and Holy Communion, so in the case of the church; the human decision must not be discounted. No one may be pressed into the church against his will. The *communio sanctorum* is a fellowship of free men and women who belong together by reason of their loyalty and love toward the Master and to each other. A church that depends upon duress is not the church

---

[219] Barth uses such expressions as *Gastgenossenschaft*, *Abendmahlsgenossenschaft*, etc. to describe the church; cf. *CD*, IV/2, 67.

[220] Cf. Cyprian, *Epistles*, 44; 62.18: *extra ecclesiam nulla salus;* Augustine, *Sermons*, No. 131 §10: *extra ecclesiam catholicam totum potest praeter salutem.*

of Jesus Christ. In history it happened that the church became the servant of the state and was used for other than Christ's purposes. In such a situation the Lordship of Jesus Christ is challenged and the boundary between church and nonchurch becomes obscured. Such a church ceases to be a gift and becomes the property of a particular group or nation. The question arises whether in such a case there are still vestiges of the church left to identify her as the church of Jesus Christ.

This has been the problem in history from the very beginning. The Donatist schism was prompted by a desire to safeguard the church from all ambiguity. The many Christian sects are similarly motivated; they all press toward a perfect church. But even such noble motivation does not make a pious gathering of religious people into the church of Jesus Christ. The church of Christ even in her captivity and submission to the world is still His church, not by reason of her achievement but only by reason of His calling. It is here that the covenant assumes its proper proportions: the church of God exists not by man's decision but by God's decree, who is pleased to call sinners into the fellowship of His Son (cf. John 6:44, 65; 15:16).

In the context of the covenant, election ceases to be a private affair between the individual and his God. The covenant places the individual in a historic situation in which the witness and experience of the past bear in upon his relationship to God. It is only within the community of believers that the personal relationship to God assumes concrete form. The church as a gift helps to stress the freedom of God and man's utter dependence upon Him. Here it is not that man in his quest for God organizes a religious society which he calls the church, but it is God who takes the initiative and stretches out saving hands in the person of the Messiah. In this context election goes beyond the election of the individual and carries universal implications.

The church as a gift is thus the area where grace assumes historic proportions and extends beyond the individual or the local congregation to the world at large. Those who desire to restrict grace to an institution and place it in the competence of man utterly mistake the meaning of grace. It is only when we treat grace as a "something" or a "fluid" that we can speak of the church as the depository of grace. There is a radical distinction between the historic church and Jesus Christ. He graciously identifies Himself with the church, but it is nothing less than *hybris* for the church to identify herself with her Lord. For this reason Schillebeeckx badly overstates his case when he affirms that to worship Christ is to "worship the Church herself," for, as he puts it, "the Church is visibly and perceptibly full of grace."[221]

At no point can the church be so identified with her Lord that she takes His place. In history, the church can only be the pilgrim church, never complete and always in a state of becoming the church of Jesus Christ. Like the sacraments, the church is always a gift whereby God's gracious Presence becomes the experience of the believing community under the covenant.

(2). The church as decision

There is a sense in which the church is not only a gift but also man's decision, though this contingent aspect of church is secondary. It derives from the fact that Christ's Presence is never imposed: He stands at the door and knocks; only when the Voice is recognized and the door is opened does He come in (Rev. 3:20). There is, however, a vast difference between a religious society and the Christian church. The difference lies in the place Jesus Christ occupies in the community. Whenever He is removed from the center and allotted a peripheral position only, the nature of the church becomes adulterated. It still exhibits the traditional emblems, and continues the historical structure; it shows all the outward signs of church. But by displacing the center of gravity its character is changed and it is both church and nonchurch at the same time. Like historic Israel it becomes church in suspense: here *'ammi* and *lo'-'ammi* — my-people and not-my-people — remain dialectically in tension as long as history lasts.[222] By promise and election the church is the church of God, but to be what she is called to be she can only achieve by faith and repentance. The church can never afford to take herself for granted as a historic phenomenon or an accomplished fact. It means that what we receive from the past we have to appropriate and make our own.

---

[221] *Christianity Divided,* p. 266.
[222] Cf. J. Jocz, *A Theology of Election,* pp. 4, 128, 133, 192.

That there is a hiatus between the ideal church without spot and wrinkle (Eph. 5:27) and the church of our experience in her lowly state, does not mean that Jesus failed in His mission. This is the very nature of history: that here nothing is ultimate, that life is a process, that man is in motion, that the church is in a state of suspense. It is only because we think of the church as an institution and not as a living organism that we speak of her in the abstract. As an objective reality in history we must speak of the church concretely, i.e. as man's failing response to God's offer of grace. In this sense, the church is only a frail human effort to become the church of Jesus Christ. Whatever positive aspect we may attach to the church in history, Brunner exhorts us not to obscure the fact that it "has again and again stood revealed as one of the major obstacles to the creation and preservation of the true Ecclesia."[223] He therefore regards the church as the *externum subsidium* of Christian fellowship; the true church is beyond the institution and can only be described in eschatological terms, as the church that is to be.[224]

We thus hit once again at the parallel between the historic Israel and the historic church: Israel's election cannot be explained empirically; the same applies to the church. Election can never be the result of cultural or moral achievement. The familiar *notes* of the church — unity, holiness, catholicity, apostolicity — are not the obvious marks for everyone to see. If we were to judge the church by the credal "notes," we could never identify her in history, not even in New Testament times. Both Israel and church can only be explained in terms of election, which is only another word for grace. Because God's purpose is never frustrated the church *is,* in spite of herself.

According to the New Testament Jesus is not the "founder" of the church but her Cornerstone (Eph. 2:20). In the strictest sense He is the church,[225] as He is the representative Israelite *par excellence.*[226] Nygren's contention therefore, that the church must be interpreted in

---

[223] E. Brunner, *The Misunderstanding of the Church,* 1952, p. 117.

[224] *Ibid.,* p. 56.

[225] Cf. Anders Nygren, *This is the Church,* 1952, p. 10: "Christ's body is Christ himself"; cf. also Ignatius, *To the Smyrnaeans,* 8: ". . . Where Jesus may be, there is the universal Church."

[226] Cf. J. Jocz, *op. cit.,* pp. 104f.

Christological terms, is well taken: we must not start with the "familiar ecclesiastical society," but rather with Jesus Christ, for in Him the church is already a fact that goes beyond our immediate observation.[227] It is only when we take Jesus Christ seriously that we can take the church seriously, for as Nygren rightly puts it, "the Church is the work of Jesus."[228] It is for this reason that we connect salvation with church.[229]

Jesus Christ's redemptive mission was to call men and women into a renewed fellowship with God. Such a new and vital relationship to God naturally results in a new and vital relationship to other people. The dynamic of messianic society is the discovery of the depth of God's love in the Messiah. This love was the magnet that drew crowds to the Master of Nazareth. But the response to his challenge was a varied one: some listened and went their way, others hesitated, some entered the most intimate circle of His friends. The parable about the sower graphically describes the situation in Jesus' own experience as He preached the Kingdom of God (Matt. 13:1-23). In the course of history the same situation persisted throughout: some remained on the periphery, others came close to the center where Jesus stood. But in human life, periphery and center are never a fixed condition. The relationship between believer and Master is a dialectical one and always fluid; it varies from day to day. Election therefore must mean more than to know oneself elected.[230] At the point where the horizontal and the vertical meet there is always tension: grace is never without judgment and judgment without grace.[231] The fixity of election we meet in Augustine and Calvin[232] fails to take account of this vital fact. The tension must not be resolved by a divine fiat once and for all but must be kept alive as an indispensable element of faith.

Without discounting the doctrine of the invisible church

---

[227] Cf. Nygren, *op. cit.*, p. 6.

[228] *Ibid.*, p. 37.

[229] Nygren chides Protestant theology for failing to lay sufficient stress upon the importance of the church in Christ's work of redemption (cf. *ibid.*, p. 4).

[230] To know oneself "saved" and to be saved are not the same.

[231] Cf. J. Jocz, *The Spiritual Hist. of Israel*, pp. 129ff.

[232] Cf. Augustine, *Enchiridion*, 98f; Calvin, *Institutes*, III, 21, 5.

we must pay every attention to the empirical church as a historic fact. As there can be no substance without form, so there can be no *ecclesia* without the concrete and visible community. The dialectic therefore created by the church in history in relation to the true church of God cannot be resolved, except eschatologically. The ultimate boundary of the church is known only to God. On this side of history we can only walk by faith and not by sight. It is a persistent weakness of Christian theology to generalize "truth" and so to lose sight of historic particularity, which is a prime ingredient of life. The Old Testament helps us to rediscover the uniqueness of each historic situation as challenge both to the individual believer and to the believing community. In this context the church is man's decision to claim God's grace, to walk in His ways and to do His will.

(3). The church as promise

The transient aspect of history points to the impermanence of all human institutions. The church as an institution will always remain *corpus permixtum*. The *corpus verum* can only be beyond history. It is for this reason that the church in her fullness as the body of Jesus Christ must remain an eschatological hope. Only in the parousia, when He will come to judge the quick and the dead, will the true church be revealed. While history lasts there can be no separation between the good and the bad, the true and the false. All we can do is hold on to God's promise, vouchsafed by the covenant, to be our God.

Over against the impermanence of history there stands the eternal and unchangeable God (cf. Mal. 3:6; Jas. 1:17). He is a God whose faithfulness endures to all generations (Ps. 100:5 RSV). This and this only is the basis for the unity of the covenant and the catholicity of the church. The Bible witnesses to the fact that the God who deals with man is always the same in His purpose and in His love. The church exists by God's creative act: He chose us in Him (i.e. in Christ) before the foundation of the world, that we should be holy and blameless before Him (Eph. 1:4). We therefore must take seriously the promise that He who began a good work in us will complete it to the end (Phil. 1:6). For this reason the church goes beyond our subjective experience in history, though we know her only in her lowliness and degradation.

Whereas the church in history is geographically defined, the church of promise extends to the whole of the human race: "behold a great multitude which no man could number, from every nation, from all tribes, and peoples, and tongues, standing before the throne and before the Lamb . . ." (Rev. 7:9), all with one voice praising God, for "The kingdom of the world has become the Kingdom of our Lord and of his Christ" (Rev. 11:15). Here the periphery becomes the center and the rejected become God's elect. This goes beyond St. Gregory's vision, which is limited to the *sancti ante legem, sancti sub lege, sancti sub gratia, omnes hi perficientes corpus Domini in membris sunt ecclesia constituti.*[233] Our hope must go beyond the *sancti* and enfold the *reprobi,* for Jesus died for sinners and not saints. Irenaeus tells us that "the apostles did not change God, but preached to the people that Christ was Jesus the Crucified One, whom the same God that sent the prophets . . . raised up, and gave in Him salvation to men."[234] Cyril of Jerusalem explains why the church is called καθολική: because she has spread to the extremes of the earth teaching without fail to the enlightenment of mankind profitable doctrine concerning things visible and invisible . . . so that all mankind may attain to εὐσέβεια.[235] This sense of catholicity, which stretches over the whole of history and enfolds humanity, more accurately expresses the meaning of covenant than a more restrictive interpretation of grace.

This does not mean a latitudinarian attitude to sin. God's wrath is as real as His mercy: "It is a fearful thing to fall into the hands of the living God" (Heb. 10:31). It certainly matters most vitally how man lives here upon earth: God is not to be mocked, man always reaps what he sows; it is a deception to think otherwise (Gal. 6:7). Universalism, as it is called in theology, is always in danger of overlooking the stern side of the gospel: "unless you repent you will all likewise perish" (Luke 13:3); and: "He who believes in the Son has eternal life; he who does not obey the Son shall not see life, but the wrath of

---

[233] St. Gregory the Great (540-604) in *Joanni Episc.* (5) 18. Compare what Barth says about Calvin's "grim doctrine," *CD,* IV/1, 57ff.

[234] Irenaeus, *Adversus Haereses,* III, 12.4.

[235] Cyril (*ca.* 315-386), *Catechesis,* 18.23.

God rests upon him" (John 3:36). Berkouwer rightly contends that we must not explain away this aspect of the gospel by connecting it merely with the hortatory nature of the *kerygma,* for the consequences of unbelief are too serious to be trifled with.[236] Man's rejection of grace is a serious matter fraught with fatal consequences. We thus are faced with an insoluble situation: in Christ all men are elected to salvation — this is the meaning of the sovereignty of grace — but unbelief, rejection of Jesus Christ, the spurning of God's grace, is an empirical fact that cannot be denied. Thus Barth's "ontological impossibility of unbelief" is unfortunately not only a possibility but a fact. At the same time we must not fall into the trap of treating sin more seriously than God's grace. Though we cannot understand the enigma of evil over against God's good creation, we cannot allow the Devil to be a second god. Barth therefore understands sin as a contradictory fact that has no basis in creation and as such is *contra voluntatem Dei.* Its only "existence" is negative existence in that it derives its peculiar form from God's wrathful No. Its only reality is that of chaos and nonbeing, and is best described as an enigmatic absurdity.[237] At the same time evil, though Barth calls it *das Nichtige* (*nihil*), is not a "nothing" but a "real dimension" which exercises an irrational and destructive force over human life. We are thus faced with an impossible situation: the almighty and all-merciful God who gives Himself to man in Jesus Christ, on the one hand, and evil, sin and unbelief on the other which seem to mar and triumph over God's purpose in history. There would seem to be no way out of the dilemma except by a "logical inconsistency."[238]

The question that concerns us in this context is whether evil, sin, and death are beyond God's power and merciful will to save. The problem of universal salvation and the ancient teaching of *apocatastasis* associated with the name of Origen hangs on this question.[239] "Origenism" was con-

---

[236] Cf. G. C. Berkouwer, *The Triumph of Grace in the Theology of K. Barth,* 1956, pp. 279ff; cf. Barth's answer to this book, *CD,* IV/3/1, 173-180.

[237] Cf. *CD,* III/3, 349ff.

[238] Cf. Berkouwer, *op. cit.,* p. 63 n. 49.

[239] Origen, *De Principiis,* I, 6.2f; III, 6.1-9; cf. also II, 3.5; 10.8 (this latter passage is somewhat obscure).

demned by the fifth ecumenical Council at Constantinople in 543. Origen found the destruction of the wicked inconsistent with his concept of soul, which he regards as containing "certain seeds of restoration and renewal."[240] He therefore allows even sinful souls the possibility of ultimate reconciliation with God that would lead to a state of happiness. The recovery of the soul takes place by slow degrees by means of amendment and correction, but in the end God wins. For this view Origen goes back to the New Testament where he finds the promise of ultimate consummation when God will be "all and in all."

Origen in his argument with Celsus at the end of the book comes back to the subject of the restoration of all things: Christians believe, he tells his opponent, "that the Word shall prevail over the entire rational creation, and change every soul into His own perfection." He explains that "the consummation of all things is the destruction of evil" and that "there is no evil so strong that cannot be overcome by the Supreme Word and God."[241] There is an undeniable logic behind this view: if God is truly God, then His will must triumph in the end. *Apocatastasis* must mean more than making amends; it must carry the connotation of complete restoration: "to restore to an earlier condition" is the proper rendering of the word.[242] Though the noun does not occur in the New Testament and the verb carries a variety of meanings (even Acts 1:6 is remote from the later connotation given to the term), the idea of ultimate renewal is built into the whole meaning of biblical salvation.[243] Augustine may poke fun at the "tender hearts" who, pleading God's goodness, believe that even those justly condemned will be delivered from hell-fire, but his arguments against this view carry little conviction. He asks, Why limit God's mercy to mankind only and not also include the Devil? He taunts the "tender hearts" for not daring to extend their pity to the

---

[240] *De Prin.*, IV, 1, 36.

[241] *Contra Celsum*, VIII, 72. In a previous chapter Origen refuses to enter into a detailed discussion with Celsus on the question of punishment as a process of purification on the grounds that even fear of eternal punishment does not seem to deter those who are "plunging into any degree of wickedness." Cf. VI, 26.

[242] Cf. *TDNT*, I, 391f.

[243] Cf. J. Jocz, *The Spiritual History of Israel*, pp. 216f, 226ff.

Devil.[244] But does he realize that an eternal devil is another god? The difficulties that are raised by the concept of eternal punishment are too many to contemplate. The idea of a vengeful God runs dead against the message of the gospel. John Baillie has shown how retributive justice "can hardly be held adequate to the truth of Christianity."[245] To make evil an eternal element in the universe smacks of Manichean dualism. The God who created the world and declared it good can hardly be credited with an eternal chamber of horrors built into it. Baillie therefore rejects this alien idea, though he realizes that if we decide for universalism it must be of a kind that will in no way reduce the urgency of repentance and the need for decision here and now.[246]

Johannes Scotus Erigena (ninth century), influenced by Gregory of Nyssa, belongs to the few medieval writers who refused to be reconciled to the perpetuity of evil. Using Gregory's "magnificent metaphor"[247] of the rays of the sun dispersing the darkness of night, so Erigena believes, the eternal goodness of God will disperse and overcome all evil. He refuses to accept corporal punishment in a literal sense. Retribution to him is not something meted out by God but takes the form of a perverse and evil will, a corrupt conscience, and fruitless remorse. He locates evil in the perverse motion of the will and opposes it with the *donum* of God's grace. But it is mainly on Christological grounds that Erigena bases his doctrine of universal restoration: because the humanity of Jesus Christ is now translated into divinity as a result of His resurrection all mankind is caught up in the process of restoration (*adunatio*) that has now begun. Because light is stronger than darkness hell will be vanquished and God will be all in all.[248]

Bett notices Erigena's valiant struggle to remain within the accepted orthodox views, which resulted in inconsistent

---

244 *De Civ.*, XXI, 17.

245 John Baillie, *And the Life Everlasting*, 1934, pp. 243f.

246 Cf. *ibid.*, p. 245.

247 Henry Bett, *Johannes Scotus Erigena*, 1964, p. 71. We are indebted to Mr. Bett's excellent summary of Erigena's theology in the remarks that follow.

248 Cf. *ibid.*, pp. 68-82.

statements.[249] But it is in the nature of the case that inconsistency is here inevitable. A similar inconsistency we already find in St. Paul, who speaks of the wrath of God coming upon the sons of disobedience (Col. 3:6) and that the impenitent store up wrath for themselves for the day of wrath when God's righteous judgment will be revealed (Rom. 2:5). But at the same time he knows that through Christ all things are reconciled (Col. 1:20), that Christ's righteous act leads to acquittal and life for all men (Rom. 5:18), and that when all things become subjected unto Christ, God will become all to all (I Cor. 15:28).[250] Paul Althaus notices that no attempt is made to reconcile the two views. The tension that is thus created he lays down to the fact that man meets God in a twofold manner: law and gospel, judgment and grace. Though grace carries the victory, Althaus feels that theology must refrain from an ultimate solution. It must not affirm nor deny *apocatastasis,* for it is a question that does not belong to theory but to the realm of practice and faith.[251]

This counsel of caution may, however, mar our understanding of the gratuity of grace in Jesus Christ and dim the Christian hope of ultimate victory. Althaus rightly reminds us that a Christian must desire for others what he hopes for himself. Reformation theology has shied away from the great hope of ultimate restoration and has left it in the hands of the radical groups.[252] Barth does not like the concept of *apocatastasis* and for interesting reasons: it spells out beforehand what must always remain God's prerogative and freedom of grace;[253] it leads to an optimistic assessment of the human situation that takes an ultimate solution for granted;[254] it by-passes the personal and loving relationship with God, and it attempts to answer a question that is meant to remain open to leave room for the situation created by preaching.[255] Barth contends that this "burning question" must remain unanswered; it should

---

[249] Cf. *ibid.,* pp. 77, 147.

[250] RSV reads "everything to every one," but this misses the cosmic aspect of *apocatastasis.*

[251] Cf. *RGG,* 1962, VI, 1694.

[252] Cf. George H. Williams, *The Radical Reformation,* 1962, *passim,* especially p. 389.

[253] *CD,* II/2, 462 (German ed.).

[254] *Ibid.,* p. 325.

[255] *Ibid.,* pp. 528f.

suffice us to know that it is God's almighty mercy (*allmächtige Barmherzigkeit*) that makes each time a renewed decision on behalf of sinners.[256] But with all the caution Barth has shown he has not managed to avoid the consequences of the meaning of grace. Berkouwer has shown that his rejection of *apocatastasis* has in nò sense lessened Barth's tendency toward a universal hope.[257] As in the case with Erigena so with Barth, it is at the point of Christology that the vista of a universal hope becomes apparent: because of Jesus Christ "the Yes of God, which cannot be disputed by any conceivable No, has been pronounced and has to be received ... it was and is the Yes of His faithfulness to Himself. But as such it was and is His Yes to the human race whom from all eternity He has elected and loved in His Son ... without involving or leaving the way open for any possible objections or doubts or questions."[258]

The church as promise means that man as an individual and man collectively will accomplish the purpose for which he was created. The church in history is a token and pledge of that promise. As historic Israel is representative of the human race, so is messianic society, in spite of all failure, the bearer of the larger Hope for the rest of humanity. That eternal punishment cannot be man's ultimate destiny is vouchsafed by the miracle of God's grace. Even James Orr, who warns against such a conclusion, finds it "difficult to see the utility of keeping a being in existence merely to sin and suffer."[259] In spite of his warning he ends his discourse on sin with a note of hope for the unsaved,[260] and no Christian who believes in the mercy of God can do otherwise. The moving passage by F. D. Maurice, the great protagonist of universal redemption, may serve as a fitting example of the only possible Christian attitude: "I ask no one to pronounce, for I dare not pronounce myself what are the possibilities of resistance

---

[256] *Ibid.*, p. 467.

[257] Berkouwer, *The Triumph of Grace*, pp. 188ff, 295.

[258] *CD*, IV/1, 356f (Eng. trans.). The English text reads "human people," which is an odd expression.

[259] James Orr, *The Christian View of God and the World*, 1897, p. 341.

[260] James Orr, *Sin as a Problem of Today*, n.d., pp. 315ff.

in a human will to the loving will of God. There are times when they seem to me — thinking of myself more than of others — almost infinite. But I know that there is something which must be infinite. I am obliged to believe in an abyss of love which is deeper than the abyss of death: I dare not lose faith in love. I sink into death, eternal death, if I do. I must feel that this love is compassing the universe. More about it I cannot know. But God knows. I leave myself and all to Him."[261]

The church as promise is a sign and a token of the eschatological hope of ultimate redemption when hell will be no more and death will be swallowed up in victory (Isa. 25:8; I Cor. 15:54-57). For, as Farrar so valiantly contended: "All souls are His. He has mercy upon all, for He can do all things and is long-suffering that men should repent, and He abhors nothing that He has made or He would not have made it."[262]

Church as promise points beyond the historic plane to the living God who is the Lord of history. He has in store for His children "an eternal weight of glory beyond all comparison" (II Cor. 4:17). Whereas the Vincentian formula with its strong appeal to tradition — *quod ubique, quod semper, quod ab omnibus creditum est*[263] — operating on the horizontal plane forms the historic core of the Catholic Church, the beyondness of the church transcends doctrinal definition. Vincent of Lerins provides us with too static a concept, useful as it is. The personal aspect of God's relationship to man goes beyond formal orthodoxy and is best described by the ancient concept of the *visio Dei:* No eye has seen, nor ear heard, nor the heart of man conceived what God has prepared for those who love Him (I Cor. 2:9; cf. Isa. 64:4).

This is not the mystical achievement on the part of the specially enlightened few, but the ultimate hope held out to man: *quod nunquam, quod nusquam, quod nemine*

---

[261] F. D. Maurice, *Theological Essays*, 1853, p. 476.

[262] F. W. Farrar, *Sermons and Addresses delivered in America*, 1886, p. 127. Farrar's masterful exposition of Dante's concept of hell (cf. pp. 307ff) deserves special mention.

[263] Cf. *Vincentii Lirinensis Commonitorium*, editio altera, Oxford, 1851, p. 9.

is yet to be ours "if God in whom we trust is the living God."[264]

---

[264] W. Manson, *Evangelical Quarterly*, XVII, 1945, p. 28. Manson's remarks may seem to belong to a somewhat different context as he discusses Presbyterianism and Episcopacy, but in essence they bear upon the same subject.

CHAPTER SIX:

THE COVENANT AS A THEOLOGICAL CATEGORY

We have made frequent reference to the covenant and have tried to see it in a variety of perspectives. We have now reached the stage where we have to consider it in strictly theological terms.

Our purpose in this investigation is to recognize the covenant as a fundamental principle or presupposition at the core of all Christian theology. In this effort we can choose one of two possible methods: the strictly exegetical method whereby each text is evaluated in accordance with the insights, religious concepts, and cultural values of a given age; or the synthetic method whereby we overlook the nuances of meaning attaching to each text and try to see the covenant as an overall concept. Biblical scholars usually tend to adhere to the first method with the result that we have a large variety of conflicting opinion. The second method though less precise has the advantage of reducing the different views to one common denominator. In this way the covenantal relationship can be stated in one single sentence: *God's condescension to man.* This simple formula is sufficient to cover every biblical situation bearing upon the divine-human encounter. But it applies with equal relevance to every theological utterance in which revelation is assumed.

It is our purpose to show that the covenantal relationship is the basic presupposition of all theological endeavor.

1. DEFINITION OF CATEGORY

In our effort to elucidate the theological aspect of the covenant we shall try to define our terms with some precision. We shall begin with an explanation of what is meant by *category* in this particular context.

Kant in his *Critique of Practical Reason* makes use of the term in a strictly defined sense: for him *categories* are concepts of pure understanding, which he explains as *a priori* forms of intuition independent of time and space.[1] Heidegger uses the term in quite a different sense: *categories* define the being of things as distinct from the being of man.[2] When we go back to Aristotle who is the originator of this philosophical concept we find that his ten categories are predicates attaching to being in order to help us grasp noetically the manifold forms of existence.[3] But this mental effort to translate facts into concepts carries a danger in that it tends to falsify the existential situation by reducing the flow of life to static rigidity. This was Henri Bergson's main concern, namely to show the inadequacy of concepts to grasp reality.[4] We shall therefore be well advised to avoid assigning to the concept of category a purely logical connotation, as in the case of Aristotle. At the same time Kant's psychological approach by way of intuition is too subjective to suit a theology that depends upon objective revelation. Heidegger's *category,* which derives from a metaphysical analysis of being, is even less appropriate. But on the other hand we cannot entirely escape the circularity of reasoning that inevitably inheres in every epistemological effort.

It is for this reason that we have chosen the term *category* to express the concept of covenant as an ultimate principle. By this we mean a theological axiom beyond which we cannot go.

But a theological axiom is different from a geometrical

---

[1] Kant, *Critique of Practical Reason,* trans. T. K. Abbott, 1901, pp. 233f.

[2] Cf. Magda King, *Heidegger's Philosophy,* 1964, p. 60.

[3] Cf. Windelband-Heimsoeth, *Lehrbuch d. Geschichte d. Philosophie,* 1948, p. 118.

[4] Cf. Henri Bergson, *Creative Evolution,* trans. A. Mitchell, 1922, pp. 332ff.

axiom in that it is not self-evident. Here axiom is a supposition that can only be accepted existentially but not proved. It is not a self-evident truth that can be inferred outside the realm of faith. The covenant as a theological category cannot be presented as a general principle to explain the universe. It is also not a principle confined to religious awareness, but is strictly related to historic revelation. Historic revelation is grounded in the fact that God turns His face toward man and addresses him. That God speaks to man is a strictly theological statement, hence the theology of the Word of God as a basic supposition.

What theology means is not that God *can* speak. This would have been a metaphysical statement derived from the assumption that there is a God. Theology does not discuss the existence or nonexistence of God. This is not within the terms of reference within theological endeavor. Theology derives its task from the fact that God speaks *to* man and man is called to listen.

We may ask the question: Why does God speak to man? Is it to impart information? Is it to unveil the secret of His Being? Is it to pronounce judgment?

When we probe deeper into these questions we soon find that they refer back to something more fundamental than the satisfaction of man's curiosity or his sense of guilt. The reason why God speaks to man can only be answered from within the principle of the covenantal relationship: God chooses man as His partner.[5]

Covenantal partnership is here not a pact of equals but the condescension of the Creator to His creature. God addresses man as a person. But the covenant expresses more than an interpersonal relationship: God reassures man, He claims him for Himself; He gives Himself to man; He holds on to him as a Father to an unruly child.

The covenant as a theological *category* opens up the whole aspect of human destiny and puts man and creation in a new perspective. This is so fundamental to theological reasoning that we may describe it as the axiom of biblical faith.

By the term *category* we mean to define the axiomatic assumption of biblical revelation, namely that God binds Himself to man as His covenant partner.

---

[5] Cf. *CD*, III/2, 14, 30f, 40, 202ff, etc.

2. THE COVENANT AS CREATION

In the Bible God is described as Creator of heaven and earth. To modern man this looks like a primitive statement going back to a prescientific age which was trying to answer the question of existence. Though science has as yet no better answer to the same puzzle it regards the "religious" explanation as too naive to be considered seriously.

None of the time-honored arguments for the existence of God is acceptable to modern man, both for scientific and philosophical reasons. The famous cosmological argument, which infers from the existence of contingent beings the logical proof of necessary being, has been shown to be fallacious. It posits a relationship between these two forms of being that is implied but not proved.[6] Paley's argument from the clock and the watchmaker to the universe and God as chief designer, carried conviction when matter was conceived as essentially in a state of inertia and the question of *primum mobile* constituted a puzzle.[7] But in our days when the natural state of matter is understood in terms of motion the physicist concerns himself with the opposite question, namely the cause of inertia. But this requires no supernatural agency, only a mathematical formula to define the relation between mass and gravity.[8]

Theologians have tried hard to undergird the old arguments of the existence of God with additional proofs from psychology, mysticism, and even spiritism, but with little success. Only reluctantly are they discovering that no argument is beyond contradiction. It is as a last resort that theologians fall back upon "faith," but here too the same rule applies: "whatever can be believed can be doubted."[9] We have to admit that every argument carries a hidden *petitio principii* somewhere, for there cannot be an argument for the existence of God that is not circular. That such is the case has been shown with great clarity

[6] Cf. Alasdair MacIntyre, *Difficulties in Christian Belief*, 1959, p. 82.

[7] Cf. Wm. Paley, *Natural Theology*, ch. 1 (*Works*, 1847, pp. 435f).

[8] Cf. Prof. Hermann Bondi, "Gravitation the Universal Force," *The Listener*, Jan. 20, 1966, pp. 89ff.

[9] MacIntyre, *op. cit.*, p. 57.

by Alasdair MacIntyre.[10] Because traditional theology was largely dependent upon argumentation it is forced to retreat each time an argument becomes untenable. This, however, can be camouflaged and treated as a virtue by making "uncertainty" into a "principle." Ninian Smart, who has applied Heisenberg's "Principle of Uncertainty" to the discipline of theology does not feel very happy about it: "It looks bad for theology to keep changing its principles in the face of adverse criticism. It looks as though Christians are saying: 'We are going to stick to our faith even if it means changing the container — and even the contents — from time to time.' And again this appears to be downright cheating."[11] It is only when we recognize the fact that there is an important difference between the correctness of our reasoning and truth itself that we will hesitate to depend upon formal logic for a grasp of what is primarily an ontological situation.[12] We come here upon an epistemological impasse that defies every attempt at a breakthrough: man cannot understand himself and the world without an outside reference, but at the same time he cannot prove that there is such a reference. All he knows is that without such a reference he is left in the void. Nihilism, in this case, is the only possible philosophy that makes sense; but it is a negative sense, which is senseless.

An autonomous, self-contained world with an "immanent theology" reduces existence to futility, for at the end of it is the *nihil.* Heidegger's concept of "care" (*Sorge*) derives from the fact of man's finitude: in a fortuitous world man is "thrown" into being without an explanation. The dread that attaches to human life is the result of the foreknowledge of death. This "uncanny not-at-homeness" cannot be rationalized, try as we may.[13] All that we can

---

[10] Cf. *ibid.*, pp. 78f, 116f.

[11] Ninian Smart, "The Uncertainty Principle in Religion," *The Listener*, Aug. 17, 1961, pp. 244f.

[12] Cf. Sir Almroth E. Wright, *Prolegomena to the Logic Which Searches for Truth*, 1941, pp. 13ff. We meet a similar impasse in modern physics in connection with the quantum theory. Cf. Lincoln Barnett, *The Universe & Dr. Einstein*, 1957, pp. 33ff; cf. also *Determinism & Freedom*, ed. Sidney Hook, 1958, p. 61: "It is an essentially new insight for the physicist that the act of acquiring knowledge itself disturbs the object of knowledge."

[13] Cf. Magda King, *op. cit.*, pp. 129ff.

do is to reconcile ourselves to a hopeless situation and face it with courage.[14] Thielicke wisely observes that "Nothingness cannot be overcome by setting one's face against it. . . . Anybody who attempts to hypnotize Nothingness will himself be caught in its spell."[15] This is the major existential problem of our day, in the words of Graham Greene put into the mouth of one of his heroes: "a vacant universe and a cooling world."[16]

Some scientists evolved the hypothesis of a universe that is self-perpetuating and self-renewing. It is suggested that matter is still being formed from cosmic dust and that the universe itself is in a process of expansion. Such a self-perpetuating universe would thus present a perfect example of a *perpetuum mobile,* the dream of every engineer. Unfortunately, the Second Law of Thermodynamics, which in spite of the great changes in physics is still regarded as unassailable, stands in direct opposition to such a view. It rather points in the opposite direction, spelling out the fact that the processes of nature are irreversible and only move in one direction, namely toward decay. This specter of "maximum entropy" as the last chapter in the story of the universe throws a shadow over every form of scientific optimism. In the words of Lincoln Barnett: "Entropy is the measure of randomness."[17]

The biblical doctrine of Creation, which posits a Creator, is by itself no solution to man's problem. The creation of the universe may have been an impulsive or capricious act. The emergence of human consciousness in an impersonal and hostile world may be regarded as a mockery on the part of man's Creator. YHVH may have had the same intentions as Zeus, who sends all miseries upon humanity in Pandora's famous box in retaliation for being

[14] Paul Tillich provides an outstanding example of such courage born of despair. His concept of "absolute faith" he defines as "the accepting of the acceptance without somebody or something that accepts." This utter pessimism is in no way dispelled by the explanation that "it is the power of being itself that accepts and gives courage to be" (*Courage To Be*, 1952, p. 185). No "it," no matter how profoundly conceived, can fill the void.

[15] Helmut Thielicke, *Nihilism,* trans. J. W. Doberstein, 1961, p. 175.

[16] Graham Greene, *The Power & the Glory.* An analysis of existential despair as far as the French school is concerned will be found in Hazel E. Barnes' book, *The Literature of Possibility,* 1959, pp. 41ff, etc.

[17] Barnett, *op. cit.,* p. 103.

cheated by Prometheus.[18] Schopenhauer may be right after all: man is something that ought not to have been.[19] The concept of Creation by itself is insufficient to answer man's question as to the meaning of his existence. It is also insufficient to answer the question that goes with it: what kind of God is the Creator of the universe? Much pessimistic philosophy derives from a realistic approach to nature where the law of the jungle rules supreme. This is Hume's main contention: we cannot deduce from the "jarring" and "discordant" facts of life that God is both powerful and good.[20] In a gloss to his manuscript *Concerning Natural Religion,* Hume observes that it would have been better had the power of the author of nature been more limited so that there would have been fewer animals but "with more faculties for their happiness and preservation."[21]

It seems an overstatement to maintain that the doctrine of Creation as such "provides that primary definition of God which gives meaning and significance to all else that is said about God."[22] We cannot and we must not overlook the stark and cruel aspects of creation for the sake of a theodicy. Leibniz' effort to explain evil as a deficiency that derives from the "essential and original limitation" adhering to created things[23] does not answer our problem. His very concept of justice as "goodness in conformity with wisdom" makes it difficult to see how "justice" is the overruling principle in life. Hume's description seems to ring more true: "The first entrance into life gives anguish to the new-born infant and to its wretched parent: weakness, impotence, distress, attend each stage of that life: And it is at last finished in agony and horror."[24] There is no escaping the fact that on the ordinary physical level suffering is built into the very essence of life and that death makes it meaningless. In a world where chance reigns supreme and where *accident* is the only rule,

---

18 Cf. J. J. I. Döllinger, *The Gentile & the Jew,* 1862, I, 296f.

19 Arthur Schopenhauer, *Die Welt als Wille und Vorstellung,* II, 4, 51: "Wir sind im Grunde etwas, das nicht sein sollte, darum hören wir auf zu sein."

20 Cf. David Hume, *Dialogues Concerning Natural Religion,* part X.

21 Cf. Norman Kemp Smith's edition, 1947, p. 208.

22 Langdon Gilkey, *Maker of Heaven & Earth,* 1959, pp. 15f.

23 Gottfried Wilhelm Leibniz, *Principles of Nature & Grace, Founded on Reason,* 1714 (Everyman's Library), p. 26.

24 *Op. cit.,* p. 194.

there can be no room for purposeful intelligence behind creation.[25] We are left in a vacuum.

It is only when the doctrine of Creation is linked to the covenant that the perspective changes. Emil Brunner has a definite advantage over Barth by starting not with the first chapter in Genesis but with the Fourth Gospel and the Epistles in order to formulate a biblical doctrine of Creation.[26] Not that Genesis 1 contradicts such a doctrine; on the contrary, it magnificently expresses the very meaning of creation, namely that God is Lord in the most absolute sense. But when treated in isolation this chapter conveys the awesome concept of *creatio ex nihilo* but omits the motive behind creation, namely God's eternal love for His creation. It means that creation outside the covenant confronts us with God's eternal power and glory but the purpose is still hidden from our eyes: "I am thy God— thou art my property."[27]

a. COVENANT: GOD WITH HIS CREATION

Pantheism, the most primitive and the most pervasive form of idolatry, depersonalizes God and deifies matter. Oddly enough, the mystical form of pantheism resulting from the discovery that man is a spiritual creature is peculiar to the higher forms of culture. We thus meet pantheism at both ends of human society: in the primitive and in the civilized context. Pantheism, which is the most subtle expression of the monistic principle, refuses to distinguish between Creator and creature. God and the world exist alongside each other and interpenetrate. God and world are two different aspects of the same fact. It is true, as Tillich points out, pantheism does not necessarily mean that God is the sum total of all that is, but rather "the essence of all essences."[28] This, however, is only a distinction within the created order, for as long as we speak of God in impersonal terms He is something other than Himself. This has been the Tillichian problem, that

[25] It is a matter of surprise to discover that in the field of materialist philosophy Lucretius has already said all there is to be said; cf. his chapter on "Matter & Space," *De Rerum Natura*.

[26] E. Brunner, *Dogmatics*, II, 1952 trans., pp. 6f, 52.

[27] *Ibid.*, p. 9. Though Brunner fails to stress the covenant in this connection, he implies it by his constant reference to Jesus Christ in whom God gives Himself to man (cf. pp. 55ff).

[28] P. Tillich, *Systematic Theology*, I, 233.

the "ground of being" could only be conceived impersonally as the principle underlying existence. We now understand why Tillich is able to speak of "the process of divine life"[29] because there is an equation between Being and "everything that participates in Being."[30] Unless we are prepared to make a radical distinction between Creator and creature, pantheism in one form or another is the inevitable result.

The radical biblical distinction between Creator and creature is a necessary absolute if God's true Lordship is to be maintained. This is the only dualism we meet in the Bible and it serves to emphasize the ontological difference between God and His creation.[31] But this leaves us with a God exterior to the world and over against it. There is no doubt that in some instances biblical writers conceived God in exactly such terms: God was *above* and man was *beneath;* it is difficult to devise a language that would avoid the spatial concepts and yet express the otherness of God.[32] This, however, is not the biblical position; here the God exterior to the world is at the same time the God *with* the world. Not only is this God's world because He made it; it is His world because He sustains it, directs it, and cares for it. Hence the biblical preoccupation with history. The providence manifested in history was to the Hebrew the tangible expression of God's Presence within the created order. God's Presence in the world and *with* His people cannot theologically be justified, except as His gracious condescension toward sinners. This is meant by the covenant relationship: God, who is both Creator and Judge, deigns to be our Savior and our King.

God as Creator is *above* this world as the totally Other One; God as Judge is over against this world as the absolutely Holy One. In either case, His Presence can only constitute a threat to His creation. But though the Bible knows God to be both Creator and Judge, it also knows Him to be a merciful God "abounding in *ḥesed* and faithfulness" (Exod. 34:6). That His Presence is not a threat but a bless-

---

29 P. Tillich, *Courage To Be*, 1952, p. 34.

30 P. Tillich, *The Protestant Era,* 1951, p. 70. For a critique of Paul Tillich, see Kenneth Hamilton, *The System & the Gospel*, 1963.

31 Cf. J. Jocz, "A Theology of Tension Resulting from the Juxtaposition of Church & Synagogue," *Judaica*, June 1963, pp. 75ff.

32 Cf. Kenneth Hamilton, *Revolt Against Heaven,* 1965, pp. 50ff.

ing is entirely due to His covenant love. We can now see why the Ark, the Tent of Meeting, and later the Temple, which were symbols of God's Presence, were associated with the covenant. It is only on the basis of the covenant, which is the expression of God's Presence *with* His creation, that a divine-human relationship is at all possible. Outside the covenant God remains the stern Judge and man the sinner banned from His Presence.

b. Covenant: God for His creation

The covenant prevents the attempt to remove God from His creation; or else, so to identify Him with His creation as to make Him part of it. The Bible insists that God is present *to* His creation but vertically and not horizontally. It therefore speaks of an "up" and a "down," however much we may dislike spatial expressions when applied to the dimension of the spiritual.

The covenant also prevents us from a wrong spirituality whereby an eternal rift is created between spirit and matter. This Manichaean attitude, which ascribes to matter a maleficent quality,[33] is a form of Gnosticism that has survived in theology to this day. It is only when the covenant is taken seriously that the ancient dualism of spirit and matter is overcome without infringement of God's sovereignty and without reduction of matter to nothingness. The covenant stands for the fact that this is God's world and belongs to Him in the double sense: He created it and He redeemed it. Though the Johannine σωτὴρ τοῦ κόσμου (John 4:42; I John 4:14) does not occur elsewhere in the New Testament literature, the conviction that salvation carries cosmic meaning is by no means foreign to the Apostle Paul (cf. 8:22f). The "thraldom of decay" so evident in nature the Apostle associates with the moral fall of man. Nature itself expresses a deep longing for "something," which St. Paul identifies as a "longing" for the revelation of the sons of God.[34] The

---

[33] Cf. Augustine, *Contra Faustum*, XI, 1. On the connection between Manichaeism & Gnosticism, see R. McL. Wilson, *The Gnostic Problem*, 1958, p. 70; also Floyd V. Filson, "Studies in Gnosticism, Gnosticism in the N.T.," *McCormick Quarterly*, May 1965; also Geo. Widengren, *Mani and Manichaeism*, trans. Chas. Kessler, 1961, p. 65.

[34] Cf. C. H. Dodd, *The Epistle of Paul to the Romans*, 1932, pp. 133f; cf. Ragnar Leivestad, *Christ the Conqueror*, 1954, p. 260: "The Johannine idea of a cosmic trial is simply the Pauline idea of a cosmic triumph translated into forensic terms."

very meaning of the resurrection as a conquest over sin and death carries cosmic overtones. Paul understands Psalm 8:6 — "All things are put in subjection under his feet" — to apply to the Messiah, whose task it is to bring all things back to God, so that He may be all in all (I Cor. 15:26ff). That this is the implication can be seen from the text in Colossians: in Christ God reconciles "to himself all things, whether on earth or in heaven, making peace by the blood of his cross" (Col. 1:20). It would therefore appear that *κόσμος* in II Corinthians 5:19 carries a much wider connotation. Sasse allows that *κόσμος*, which ordinarily would connote the inhabited world, or humanity (*Menschenwelt, Menschheit*), in the context of Pauline theology assumes much wider proportions. It becomes the theater of redemptive history reaching far beyond the story of mankind: the whole universe (*πᾶσα ἡ κτίσις*) in the sense of Romans 8:22 and Colossians 1:16 becomes drawn into the drama of salvation. At the same time *Heilsgeschichte* never ceases to remain primarily true human history. God's reconciliation of the world to Himself in Jesus Christ includes the whole of creation, things visible and invisible; whether thrones or dominions or principalities or powers, they all stand under the authority of the Son of God.[35]

Salvation in cosmic terms expresses the fact that human life is not only dependent upon fellowship with others but moves within the wider circle of creation at large. The new order initiated by the Messiah affects not only human relationships but every other relationship in which man is involved. It is only when God is truly our Father that the cosmos becomes, in spite of its immensity, an ally and not a crushing weight. Human life takes place in a double context: within history and within the cosmos; both history and creation stand under the providence of God's covenant with man.[36]

We touch here upon the deepest meaning of providence. The covenant forms "the internal basis of creation" and gives meaning both to the cosmos and to history. It stands for the fact that God is with us: *immanu - El.* Jesus Christ,

---

[35] Cf. Hermann Sasse, *TDNT*, III, 893. K. Barth holds that the question whether the Word is also addressed to the cosmos at large, we can neither deny nor affirm, though "we dare not reject the possibility" (cf. *CD*, III/4, 332).

[36] Cf. *CD*, III/4, 575.

the Son of God, is the token and pledge that God acts toward His creation as Father both in history and the cosmos.

This God-with-us is in spite of man's rebellion and refusal to act as a child of God. In the Bible judgment is taken seriously: God is not our "natural" Father, in the sense that we are spiritually related to Him as a matter of course. Prof. Dodd warns against the confusion of the popular notion of the "Fatherhood of God": "The biblical doctrine all through is that God *created* man in His image, so that the natural, universal, and permanent relation of man to God is one of creaturely dependence. The New Testament knows only one Son of God in the absolute sense."[37] Yet God wants us as His children and seeks to win us back from rebellion to obedience. The whole biblical message is geared to express this fact. Prof. Dodd points to the paradox that is here implied: God is Father of all men, yet not all men are His sons. But this does not mean that He has left us to ourselves to perish. His providence extends to the whole of His creation both in history and in the cosmos. This is not an impersonal kind of arrangement: YHVH is *with* His people. He hears the cry of an infant (Gen. 21:17) and the groaning of an enslaved nation (Exod. 3:7); He is the protector of the fatherless and the widow and extends His love to the stranger (Deut. 10:18); He is the helper and upholder of those who trust in Him (Ps. 54:4) and is especially close to those who are falling and are bowed down (Ps. 145:14). The eyes of all look to Him and He gives them their food in due season, He opens His hand and satisfies the desire of every living thing (vv. 15f). He never ceases to care "for the existence and welfare of all His creatures."[38] The God of the covenant is everlastingly active to prove His faithfulness. This covenant loyalty on the part of God is expressed in the words of the Messiah: "My Father is working still, and I am working" (John 5:17). God's love is active love, redeeming love, self-sacrificing love, and at no point does this appear more clearly than at the point of the Incarnation when the Son of God enters bodily into history. The eternal Son of God who becomes man's humble servant demonstrates the depth of God's commitment to His creation. In the Person of the Messiah the covenant reaches

---

[37] C. H. Dodd, *Epistles of Paul to the Romans*, 1949, pp. 130f.
[38] *CD*, III/4, 517.

the utmost limit of commitment: the Son of God is *for* man to the point of self-abandonment (cf. Phil. 2:5ff).

In several Old Testament passages we meet the frightening sentence: "I am against you, says the Lord God" (Ezek. 13:8; cf. 5:8; Jer. 21:10, 13). But this announcement of judgment has a parainetic motive; the prophet's intention is to call to repentance while there is yet time. His enunciation of judgment carries a hidden message of hope:[39] His judgment is man's salvation. God wills that man should live and be saved (Ezek. 18:23). This is the meaning of the covenant: that God is *for* us; He is on our side and *with* us.[40] Hence the Good News: He who did not spare His own Son and gave Him up for us all, will He not also give us all things with Him? asks the Apostle (Rom. 8:32).

That God is for sinners is St. Paul's greatest discovery. As a Jew he knew that God loves the righteous and those who keep His commandments. But that God is *for* sinners, for those who do not deserve His love, he had to learn at the foot of the Cross. Everyone in Israel knew that the wages of sin is death,[41] but that the free gift of God was eternal life in Jesus Christ our Lord (Rom. 6:23), was direct denial of Jewish piety. In the Epistle to the Romans the Apostle introduces a concept of grace whereby *ḥesed* as covenant love reaches its climax: it is grace to overflowing and is offered as a free gift. This is especially so in Romans 5:15-17: "the grace of God and the free gift which comes by the grace of the one man Jesus Christ overflowed far more richly upon the rest of men." Here χάρισμα and δώρημα can only be translated as the "free gift of grace" with all the emphasis upon the utter gratuity of God's offer. The reason for this is that the offer is made not to saints but sinners. Paul admits that under certain circumstances somebody may venture to die for a righteous man, though more likely one may choose to die for a good man. But God's love for us is such that Christ died for sinners (Rom. 5:8). This

---

[39] J. Jocz, *The Spiritual History of Israel*, pp. 116f.

[40] Edmond Jacob, *Theology of the O.T.*, 1958 trans., pp. 137f: "To the question: Why had God created the world? the O.T. would answer: He has created it for the covenant, that is to say because of his plan of love and salvation for humanity by means of Israel; in creating the world God already had the covenant in view, and it is this motive which gave to the idea of creation its specific orientation."

[41] Cf. Dodd's translation, *op. cit.*, p. 78.

is so amazing a discovery to the former Pharisee Saul of Tarsus, that it made the profoundest revolution in his life. From henceforth he was a man dedicated to preaching the Good News that God justifies the ungodly (Rom. 4:5) gratis to all who will receive the Messiah as God's gift to man.

The extravagance of God's covenant love as expressed in the gospel that Paul preached constitutes an offense to the religious man and to his moral sensibilities. It hurts his pride and contradicts his values. He is left with no merit of his own and is made equal to sinners who have been squandering their inheritance while he was laboring in the sweat of his brow to find favor with God. No wonder that Jewish piety was outraged by Paul's message. The religious man, both in church and synagogue, stands aghast at Pauline "antinomianism." He refuses to accept the verdict that "there is no distinction" between the sinner and the righteous before God (Rom. 3:22f), for all are guilty. He knows himself better than his neighbor. This is the deception common to those who seek their freedom from God and so deny their creatureliness. Such autarchy whereby man is able to assert himself before his Creator, is the most subtle form of *hybris*. In terms of covenant, autonomy carries an inner contradiction, for it distances the creature from his Creator and leads him to a self-centered existence. That God is *for* us means that we are for Him — in the words of the psalmist: "He has made us and we are His" (Ps. 100:3).

c. The "new" covenant

To understand the New Testament meaning of the "new" covenant we must place the concept in the Old Testament cycle of ideas, especially in the prophets. We have argued elsewhere that "new" in this context is inseparate from the prophetic hope of messianic renewal.[42] The *locus classicus* is Jeremiah 31:31. The sound rules of exegesis would demand that we treat this text not in isolation but in conjunction with the rest of the passage. Once this is done it becomes obvious that the "new" covenant refers to a change of method or procedure: the "old" covenant was written upon the tables of the law: the "new" covenant is to be written on the hearts of God's people. St. Paul alludes to this passage in II Corinthians 3:2f. That this is the case

---

[42] Cf. J. Jocz, *A Theology of Election*, pp. 114ff.

can be seen from what follows: "God has qualified us," says the Apostle, "to be ministers of the new covenant, not in a written code but in the Spirit" (v. 6).[43] The allusion to Jeremiah 31:31-34 is obvious. To decide therefore what is meant by "new" we have first of all to go back to Jeremiah. Does the prophet visualize a *berîth* with no reference to the past whatsoever?

The answer is somewhat complicated by the fact that commentators are inclined to regard the text as an interpolation. The suggestion is made that it was written by someone "familiar with Jeremiah's manner but not wholly imbued with his spirit" and at a somewhat later date.[44] Happily, the question of authorship does not affect our contention. Whoever the author, this is a prophetic utterance in the profoundest sense and is with good reason regarded as a "climax" of the book.[45] We hesitate to concur with Cunliffe-Jones that this passage is "alien to his (i.e. Jeremiah's) mind and not in his idiom."[46] Both Blank and Cunliffe-Jones fail to pay due attention to the main purpose of prophetic utterance, namely the call to repentance. There are two reasons why no prophet of YHVH could afford to despair because of the lack of response to his message: God's *ḥesed* and His sovereignty. The new covenant spells out God's ultimate triumph in history.[47]

Whoever the author of Jeremiah 31:31ff, it is abundantly clear that no Hebrew writer could possibly speak of Israel's past as if it were of no account. To do so would have meant to deny God's providence over His people and to declare His mighty acts null and void.

Although the following passage (Jer. 31:35-57) differs stylistically there is nevertheless an inner connection that links the two. The concept of an "everlasting covenant" that we meet in Jeremiah 31:40 epitomizes the prophetic attitude throughout. In spite of the scruples on the part of commentators in respect to Jeremiah 33:20, 25 because of

---

[43] The Greek text reads καινῆς διαθήκης without the article; for this reason it is usually translated "a" new covenant (cf. RV, RSV), but in view of the obvious allusion to Jer. 31:31 the definite article is correct as in AV.

[44] Sheldon H. Blank, *Jeremiah, Man & Prophet*, 1961, p. 209.

[45] Cf. *IB*, V, 1037.

[46] *The Book of Jeremiah*, 1960, p. 203.

[47] Cf. J. Jocz, *The Spiritual History of Israel*, pp. 118ff.

the "nationalistic" overtones[48] and the differences of style, we argue for a logical cohesion no matter who the authors of the texts are. The "new" covenant, the "everlasting covenant," and Israel's endurance as long as the fixed order of nature continues are all of one piece. These passages, odd as they may seem to us, are in no sense expressions of a chauvinistic attitude, but an affirmation of the faithfulness of God. In this context the "new" covenant can only mean the renewed covenant, for the God of Israel is the God of renewal.[49]

Once we have taken a firm hold on the prophets' insight into the character of God, that He is not like man (Hos. 11:9), that His mercy exceeds His anger, and that YHVH wills Israel's salvation (Jer. 3:12, 23), then and only then will the concept of the "new" covenant fit into the general scheme of the prophetic message.

The new covenant therefore stands for God's ultimate triumph in history: His purpose with His people as a nation of priests and a holy people will ultimately be achieved. This eschatological hope held out to Israel is inseparable from the messianic expectation. Edmond Jacob suspects that the passage in Jeremiah 31:31 became the source of inspiration to the other prophetic writers who now speak of the *b^erîth 'ôlam* (Jer. 32:40; Ezek. 16:60; Isa. 55:3; 61:8), or the *b^erîth shālôm* (Ezek. 34:25; 37:26), as a messianic hope.[50] Once we admit that to the writers of the New Testament Jesus is the fulfillment of the messianic expectation we will interpret the "new" covenant in closest connection with the "old."

It is easy to misunderstand the situation if we take the concept of covenant in the legal sense to mean a juridical contract whereby God binds Himself constitutionally. Kennett's protest against such a narrow and legalistic approach is well justified: "That God should bind Himself by a covenant to do that which He would not do of His own eternal unchanging righteousness is unthinkable."[51] We agree that this is not the prophetic understanding of the covenant and is certainly not in the spirit of the New Testament.

---

[48] Cf. *IB*, V, 1040.
[49] Cf. J. Jocz, *A Theology of Election*, pp. 114ff.
[50] Cf. Edmond Jacob, *Theology of the O.T.*, 1958 trans., p. 216n.
[51] Robert Hatch Kennett, *The Church & Israel*, 1933, p. 145.

The covenant is not a legal document by which God finds Himself committed against His better judgment. The covenant is the highest expression of His determination to be our God. It is for this reason that we cannot properly speak of the "old" covenant as null and void.[52] If we give to "covenant" the wider meaning as advocated by Kennett, i.e. to denote "God's friendly treatment of Israel in delivering them from Egypt,"[53] the "new" covenant simply means another gesture of outgoing friendship on the part of the merciful and long-suffering God. In this case, the "new" covenant indicates "the beginning of a new relationship" in the Messiah, "between the Lord and Israel."[54]

In the words of the Institution according to the Synoptic Gospels, ἡ καινὴ διαθήκη occurs only in Luke (22:20).[55] But the identical phrase occurs in Paul's account (I Cor. 11:25), and it is held that Luke is dependent upon this source.[56] In view of Paul's insistence that he is transmitting a tradition he himself received there is no doubt that καινη is genuine. Kenyon and Legg after comparing the two texts conclude that the Lucan account both in the shorter and longer version in no sense differs from the Pauline text, except that Luke records the distribution of the first cup[57] in addition to the cup of the Institution. But if we credit Paul with any measure of consistency the καινὴ διαθήκη in his theology never means an abrogation of the "old." If it were otherwise he could not have possibly written the opening verses of Romans 9: "They are Israelites, and to them belong the sonship, the glory, the covenants, the giving of the law, the worship and the promises, to them belong the patriarchs, and of their race, according to the flesh, is the Christ." On the contrary, the fact that the Messiah appeared in the midst of Israel is evidence

---

[52] Cf. Jacob, *op. cit.*, p. 274: "by announcing a 'new covenant' Jeremiah and Ezekiel naturally understood that the old one was to be annulled."

[53] *Op. cit.*, p. 144.

[54] *Ibid.*, p. 229.

[55] The Marcan account (14:24) is uncertain as some MSS omit καινη from the text; cf. Westcott & Hort.

[56] Cf. Sir Frederick G. Kenyon & S. C. E. Legg on the Textual Data of the Eucharist in *The Ministry & the Sacraments*, ed. Roderic Dunkerley, 1937, p. 286.

[57] The shorter version they put down to a misunderstanding of the Passover ritual, which began with the *kiddush* cup (cf. *ibid.*, p. 285).

to him that God has not cast off His people whom He foreknew (Rom. 11:1f). By contrast the Fathers of the church held quite a different view, but it was based upon a fateful misunderstanding. Lactantius speaks for most of them when, alluding to Jeremiah 31:31, he tells us that the prophets warned that God "would change His covenant" and bestow the inheritance upon an alien people, unless Israel repented.[58] What he really means is that God has already changed the covenant, rejected the Jews, and given their patrimony to outsiders.[59] Once we take the covenant as a legal transaction by which the contracting parties bind themselves to reciprocal obligations, we can argue, as the Fathers did, that the "contract" is annulled because of unfulfilled conditions. But such an argument is inadmissible on moral grounds, for it presupposes that the Gentiles have succeeded where Israel has failed.[60] To understand the biblical meaning of covenant we have to allow for two irreconcilable facts: human failure and God's grace. It is with a view of this odd situation that we cannot accede to a suspension of God's grace, which is only another aspect of covenant love.[61]

Before we leave the subject we still have to deal with the letter to the Hebrews, which like no other New Testament document has contributed to the notion of an absolute breach between the two covenants.

At first sight it would appear that the anonymous writer takes an extremely radical view: the first covenant was faulty (Heb. 8:7f); it has become obsolete (8:13); the former commandments are set aside by reason of their weakness and uselessness (7:18). In parenthesis he explains that the law was unable to make anything perfect. For this reason God has abolished His first disposition and has established a second one (10:9).

---

[58] Lactantius, *Divinae Institutiones*, IV, 11.

[59] "Now that the Jews were disinherited, because they rejected Christ, and that we, who are the Gentiles, were adopted into their place, is proved by the Scriptures" (*Epitome Div. Inst.*, 48). Lactantius reiterates the same in the following chapter.

[60] Cf. J. Jocz, *A Theology of Election*, pp. 149f.

[61] Mr. H. L. Ellison sees fit to contradict our view that *de jure* the covenant was never abolished (cf. *A Theol. of Election*, p. 117). But his own view is in essence no different: "The covenant vanished, but the love and the loyalty remained" (*The New Covenant*, Hebrew Christian Alliance of Gr. Britain, 1966, pp. 6f).

Such radical statements would suggest a complete disparagement of what went before. But there is another side to the story which must not be overlooked. First, the writer appeals again and again to Old Testament history: the letter is full of quotations from the *torah,* the Psalms, and the Prophets. In fact the whole book is a messianic exposition based upon the Old Testament. For proofs of Jesus' messiahship he goes back to the Hebrew Bible.

Second, the "cloud of witnesses," consisting of Old Testament heroes and Maccabean martyrs,[62] the writer regards as signal examples of unwavering faith and endurance. Moses, the chief representative of the old covenant, is described as the faithful servant of God (cf. Num. 12:7) and is placed next to the Messiah (Heb. 3:1-3).

Third, and most important of all, the preincarnate Christ, both as Wisdom and Logos, is the One who reveals Himself in the saving acts of Old Testament history.[63] The late Prof. Manson's scholarly opinion deserves attention. He tells us that in the view of the writer to the Hebrews "the Christ, the preincarnate son of God, was actually, though invisibly, an agent and participant in the redemption effected for Israel at the Exodus and Moses by his decision of faith was sharing in the Saviour's passion. He was already identified with the Christian people of God."[64] Prof. Manson warns against the idea that the Old Testament types of faith depicted in chapter 11 were sub-Christian in any sense. This he refutes on two grounds: (1) for Hebrews the eschatological calling takes place on the same principle in both Testaments; and (2) for Hebrews "the Christ of God is veritably active in the history of Israel."

Once we accept these points as valid, points well supported by evidence in the text, and add the fact that the crucial passage, Jeremiah 31:31ff, is built into the argument of Hebrews and is quoted *in extenso* (Heb. 8:8-11), the situation is greatly altered.[65]

It is obvious that to Hebrews the "new" covenant is primarily a messianic concept. It signifies the new order

---

[62] Cf. W. Manson, *The Epistle to the Hebrews,* 1951, p. 80.

[63] *Ibid.,* pp. 92, 96.

[64] *Ibid.,* p. 185.

[65] The importance the writer of Hebrews attaches to Jer. 31:31ff can be seen from the fact that it is quoted in two different instances (8:8-11 and 10:16-18).

introduced by Jesus the Messiah and carries eschatological overtones. It exposes the climax of history, the end of the age (Heb. 9:26) which is marked by the new approach to God through Jesus the Messiah (12:18-24). Both E. F. Scott and W. Manson acknowledge that the "ritual institutions," though only earthly shadows of the heavenly things, are yet not deceptive or misleading, "only imperfect and incomplete."[66] The difference between the "old" and the "new" is in degree and not in kind: τελείωσις is the dominating principle associated with messianic fulfillment. Even if we accept the abrogation of the law — the writer is only concerned with the ceremonial law — this does not abrogate the covenant.

There is one more point that must be made: διαθήκη is not always used in the same sense. In at least one passage it obviously means will or testament (Heb. 9:17 RSV): by reason of the Messiah's death the new will has become operative, spelling out the renovation of the covenant relationship with God.[67]

It would therefore appear that Hebrews does not warrant a radical break between the "old" and the "new"; the two covenants are interlocked and interdependent. The Old Testament saints already participate in the New Age in anticipation though in time they still belong to the old order. The new covenant is the "better" covenant because it is based upon "better promises" (Heb. 8:6), namely that God will write the law upon the heart of His people. We therefore hold that Dalman's equation of *berîth* with *qeyām*[68] fits remarkably well into the scheme of the letter to the Hebrews: new covenant means here the completion of God's promises in the Messiah and the *establishment* of *the* New Age. The "new" is only different from the old in the sense of completion: the old order hinted at what has now become a fact in the messianic age.

It seems to us that this is the only possible theological basis for the unity of the Canon, the continuity of historic revelation, and the eternal consistency of God's purpose with mankind. Biblical exegesis that only pays attention to a

---

[66] Mason, *op. cit.*, p. 125. Cf. E. F. Scott, *The Epistle to the Hebrews*, 1922, pp. 82ff.
[67] Cf. Manson, *op. cit.*, p. 127.
[68] Cf. J. Jocz, *A Theology of Election*, p. 117.

given text without any consideration for the wider context, limits our vision and perverts our purpose. Cohesion is a basic theological principle; there can be no cohesion as long as there is a rift in revelation.

3. THE COVENANT AS REVELATION

Biblical theology and therefore Christian theology is tied to the concept of revelation. By revelation is meant that God takes the initiative and addresses Himself to man. The concept of revelation therefore carries the meaning of God's condescension to the human level. Revelation in biblical terms contradicts popular assumption that man is a seeker of God[69] while God forever remains an illusive ideal. In the Bible the opposite view predominates: man is the fugitive while God is in pursuit.[70]

Revelation in the biblical context is never a direct occurrence; God does not reveal Himself in direct encounter, but veils Himself at the same time. At all times He remains the Invisible One; this distinguishes Him from idols. The barrier between God and man is never broken, so that God be exposed to human sight. There is always a gap between the Holy One of Israel and sinful man. The approach to the thrice-holy God is by mediation, propitiation, and forgiveness. At-one-ment with God is not mystically but cultically and morally achieved. God reveals His will, His law, His purpose, but not Himself. Deutero-Isaiah gave classic expression to the biblical concept of revelation when he described God as the One-who-hides-Himself (Isa. 45:15).

---

[69] That man is the God-seeker is the prevailing view with theological writers. Here is a quotation taken at random: "Man seeks his God, as the sunflower the sun, the hart the waterbrooks, and the infant the mother's breast" (J. J. van Oosterzee, *Christian Dogmatics*, 1873 trans., p. 5).

[70] Abraham Heschel is unique among Jewish writers in stressing that revelation is primarily God's initiative: "Unless God asks the question, all our inquiries are in vain" (*God in Search of Man*, 1956, p. 137). The title of his book, *God in Search of Man*, is not a traditional Jewish formulation. The Jewish way to God begins with man. Heschel does not exclude the human effort, though assisted by God man is meant to exert himself (cf. *ibid.*, pp. 28, 153); but the real quest is God's (cf. *ibid.*, p. 198). For Heschel's theology with particular reference to his concept of revelation, see Jacob J. Petuchowski, "Faith as the Leap of Action," *Commentary*, May 1958, pp. 390ff; E. LaB. Cherbonnier, "A. J. Heschel and the Philosophy of the Bible," *Commentary*, Jan. 1959, pp. 23ff.

Revelation therefore is a dialectical process and cannot be described otherwise than in paradoxical terms. This, of course, constitutes a difficulty both for the philosopher and the theologian. Each has tried to explain the inherent difficulty in his own way. But most of the time the theologian is tempted to provide a philosophical answer, which means that he has so to formulate the concept of revelation as to make it a human quest after eternal truth.

The whole theological effort revolves on the question of revelation; in fact it constitutes the central problem of theology. Seen historically, revelation was understood by theological writers under roughly four headings:

(1) God reveals truth, doctrine, moral teaching.
(2) God reveals His character, attributes, essence.
(3) God reveals Himself in acts: He overrules, protects, guides, judges, and forgives.
(4) God reveals Himself to the soul inwardly, mystically, in religious experience.

In theological thinking only a matter of emphasis determines which of these concepts predominates, for they are usually held in combination as none excludes the other aspects. It is only on closer examination that we discover their deficiency when measured against the biblical situation. We will now attempt a brief discussion of each of these aspects.

a. Revelation as "truth"

Truth is a wide, illusive term. Judged from a theological perspective it lacks several essential elements to bear the full weight of biblical revelation. The main difficulty lies in the fact that it lacks the strictly personal aspect so important to the Bible. Furthermore, it is devoid of existential urgency and conveys an air of academic detachment. In addition, there is linguistic difficulty which compacts the situation: our reaction to "truth" is determined by the Greek concept of ἀλήθεια rather than the Hebrew אמת. There is here an important difference which must not be lost.

'emeth always carries an existential connotation: it refers to personal involvement in a given situation in relation to moral action. *'emeth* describes trustworthiness of character in the testing of moral commitment. *'emeth* is primarily descriptive of personal relationships. The opposite of *'emeth* is not error but rather falsehood in the moral

sense. ἀλήθεια, on the other hand, is in reference to intellectual cognition and is a term describing "the real state of affairs" of a given fact.[71] Admittedly, in the New Testament Hebrew and Greek meanings are interchangeable, and Quell has shown that even the Old Testament shows a "multiple" use of the term allowing sometimes for the Greek meaning of truth. But even he admits that "the rational element in the concept of *'emeth* is not the essential feature" in the Old Testament; the essential feature is the "strong moral feeling" that this term evokes.[72] The same may be said of the New Testament, where ἀλήθεια frequently carries the meaning of personal and moral commitment.

Outside the Canon, however, the situation changes. Here the predominant Greek background determined the meaning of truth in the direction of detached philosophical statement. Truth now becomes an impersonal noun of universal application independent of the existential context. Truth now defines "true and genuine reality" outside the area of personal involvement in the test of moral challenge. This is of course a legitimate approach to truth in philosophical terms, though even here it constitutes an infraction of the classical position.[73] But in the area of theology, where truth always carries personal and moral overtones, revelation interpreted in terms of impersonal and universally applicable truths, is bound to play havoc with the particularity of the historic content derived from the Bible.

The transition from the Hebrew *'emeth* via the New Testament use of ἀλήθεια to the Greek concept of ἐπιστήμη meaning the intellectual grasp of "correct doctrine"[74] describes the development from Hebrew existential faith to Christian orthodoxy in Greek terms. This is in keeping with the classical Platonic position according to which *doxa* as "right opinion" is the precondition for the mind to achieve a state of truth. The opposite is *false* opinion because it "fails to connect with the realities of life."[75] Prof. Lodge has shown that for Plato the philosopher's commitment is

---

[71] Cf. Bultmann, *TDNT*, I, 243.

[72] *TDNT*, I, 235f.

[73] Cf. R. C. Lodge, *Plato's Theory of Ethics*, 1928, p. 33: "It is especially in regard to ethical convictions that Plato emphasizes the importance and absolute fundamental value of right opinion."

[74] Cf. *TDNT*, I, 239.

[75] Lodge, *op. cit.*, p. 32.

more to the overriding principle of consistency demanding a condition of mind for grasping the wholeness of truth, than it is to the achievement of the moral ideal.[76]

Truth, then, in Platonic terms means the ability to transcend the prescribed limits of the various sciences in order to attain to a unified, single, "purely intelligible system of ideas."[77] This helps us to appreciate the important difference between the philosophical and the biblical concern in respect to truth. The discrepancy derives from the difference of purpose: the philosopher pursues knowledge, the believer pursues righteousness, which corresponds to the Presence of a holy God. There is here a radical difference in attitude: the philosopher enjoys self-sufficiency (αὐτάρκεια) which allows him to repose in himself, whereas the believer's *'emunāh* spells utter dependence upon a God who demands righteousness.

It is our contention that there is no synthesis possible between the biblical and the philosophical approach to truth. The semantic assimilation of the term must not blind us as to the utter difference of content. For this reason *orthodoxa,* right opinion, can never serve as a substitute for the biblical concept of truth for the simple reason that *'emeth* in the context of historic revelation is never truth in the abstract sense. Biblical *truth* is inseparable from the covenantal context and the existential situation in which man finds himself. Like the term *ḥesed,* so *'emeth* spells out the fact of God's active Presence in human history; while *doxa,* even though *right doxa,* is a detached statement of impersonal verities in general terms. Such "truths" have universal application and therefore can be abstracted from the existential situation. *Doxa* engages the intellect and presses for consistency while *'emeth* presses for *'emunāh* and demands total commitment.

The prodigious effort of medieval scholasticism was bent toward the achievement of a unified intellectual perspective. This is essentially a philosophical effort and deserves respect. But it failed to pay sufficient attention to truth conceived in biblical terms, which demands not just an intellectual grasp of doctrine but rather a personal response to the Presence of a holy God. The result was a

---

[76] *Ibid.*, pp. 73ff.
[77] *Ibid.*, p. 132.

division within the discipline of theology into two parts: dogmatic and moral. Hence St. Thomas' division of his *Summa:* the doctrine of God and the doctrine of man.[78] "The subject matter of dogmatic theology," we are told, "is those doctrines which serve to enrich the knowledge necessary or convenient for man, whose destination is supernatural"; while moral theology, we are given to understand, "is limited to those doctrines which discuss the relations of man and his free actions to God. . . ." Though these two parts are "closely related" and comprise "universal theology"[79] the emphasis lies upon the first part, "which treats of the theoretical truths of faith concerning God and His works."[80] We could argue that such a division is a matter of convenience and organization rather than theological orientation had not the traditional concept of truth in relation to faith demanded such an approach. The very tidiness of the dogmatic effort pressing for intellectual consistency bypasses the biblical meaning of *'emeth,* which is primarily a total and personal response to the covenant-keeping God.

This in no way denies the validity of dogmata as the doctrinal deposit of Christian truth. The intellectual effort to formulate doctrine is a legitimate and necessary task on the part of theology. What we deny is the perception of Christian truth in purely intellectual terms that abstract from the personal commitment and the existential situation, so that Christian truth becomes general truths to inform the mind.

That knowing the truth has saving quality is a purely Gnostic idea.[81] The origin of the idea stems from the Greek principle that identifies truth with nature: what is natural is true.[82] It is of interest to note how Albertus Magnus and Thomas Aquinas are agreed on this typically Greek definition of truth: *veritas est adaequatio rei et intellectus.*[83] This coincidence of truth and being makes for an integrated

[78] This is in reference to parts I & I-II; the rest of the *Summa* deals with Christology, salvation, church, etc.

[79] Cf. *Catholic Encycl.,* 1912, XIV, 60 i b.

[80] *Ibid.,* 580a.

[81] In this respect there is little difference between Gnosticism and neo-Platonism. For Plotinus διά-νοια is the Intellectual Principle whereby the soul knows God by knowing itself (cf. *The Enneads,* trans. Stephen MacKenna, 1956, pp. 385ff).

[82] Cf. *RGG* (3rd ed.), VI, 1519b.

[83] *Summa Theol.,* pt. I, Q. 21, a. 2.

universe that can be both ordered and grasped intellectually. But when the same principle is applied to God a strange falsification takes place: either God is not truth or truth cannot be grasped. The way out of the difficulty is to relate intellect to God so that a connaturality is established between Creator and creature. This is the basic principle of Thomist theology.

St. Thomas places truth primarily in the intellect, and being primarily in things; but these are only two aspects of the same reality and are indivisible in essence.[84] Because reason is always one and the same whether applied to the world or to God, and because faith and reason are only two different modes of apprehending the same truth, there can be no essential difference between believing and knowing. Though St. Thomas differentiates between speculative reason and practical reason, the difference is only formal, for it is only a difference in respect to method and not in respect to conclusions. Speculative reason is not something reserved for philosophers but is available to all, is known by all, and is the same for all.[85] It is on these grounds that the church expected everyone to hold the right views and regarded heresy as a form of perverse obstinacy deserving punishment.

Once truth is conceived in universal terms revelation ceases to be a personal encounter and of necessity becomes a mental exercise. All truth becomes revelation whether it spells out man's relationship to God or to the world. St. Thomas tells us that "every knowledge of truth is a kind of reflection and participation of the eternal law, which is the unchangeable truth." He goes on to explain that because all men partake of some knowledge of the truth, they are therefore "more or less cognizant of the eternal law."[86] The principle of rationality so profoundly pervades the Thomist system that he feels compelled to endow even the animals with Eternal Reason, though in many ways they appear to be irrational.[87] In this scheme of things *ratio* constitutes the invisible link between God and His creation. This monistic approach, which refuses to differentiate between faith

---

[84] Cf. *ibid.*, Q. 16, reply to obj. 1-3; cf. also art. 1.
[85] *Op. cit.*, I-II, Q. 94, a. 4.
[86] *Ibid.*, Q. 93, a. 2.
[87] Cf. *ibid.*, Q. 91, a. 2, reply to obj. 3.

and reason, is founded upon the premise that faith is only another way of knowing: "imperfect knowledge belongs to the very nature of faith." By this he means to say that faith is only a temporary substitute for the *visio Dei*, which will be granted to the blessed when they have finished their pilgrimage and arrive *in patria*. The passage is a clear reference to I Corinthians 13:10ff: "Now we know in part. . . ." But there is a difference between St. Paul's meaning and St. Thomas' meaning. To walk by faith and not by sight (II Cor. 5:7) is to the Apostle an expression of utter trust and commitment; to the Angelic doctor, it is an intellectual process of cognition whereby progress is achieved from lesser to greater knowledge. On the basis of intellectual apprehension revelation is never absent but only a matter of degree: truth is always available and reason apprehends it. Thus the bond between Creator and creature is never broken, for there is an underlying unity encompassing the universe. We can now see the close connection between Gnosticism and scholastic theology, especially in its neo-Platonist form.

From the enchanted circle of Gnostic metaphysics the schoolmen never managed to free themselves. Duns Scotus (*ca.* 1264-1308), who in many respects represents a rival position to that of St. Thomas and frequently contradicts him on matters of epistemology, can serve as an example of the persistence of neo-Platonism.

In place of St. Thomas' knowledge and reason, Duns Scotus substitutes love and will. He also stresses the importance of revelation as the only possible basis for man's knowledge of God. It is God's free and sovereign decision to make Himself known to man. Because man in his present state is unable to know God by reason of his fall (and not by reason of his entanglement with material things) supernatural revelation becomes a necessity. Finkenzeller explains the difference between Thomas and Duns Scotus in this way: the former proceeds from below upward, while the latter proceeds from above downward.[88] This is an important difference, for it puts the meaning of covenant in its proper perspective. Duns Scotus is therefore more closely related to biblical categories than is St. Thomas. But when

---

[88] Cf. Josef Finkenzeller, *Offenbarung und Theologie nach der Lehre des Johannes Duns Skotus*, 1961, p. 17.

we come to matters of epistemology the difference between these two rivals becomes merely a difference of nomenclature. For both of them reason is an adequate faculty wherewith knowledge is achieved not only of things visible but also of things invisible. Duns Scotus tends to emphasize intuition in the process of acquiring knowledge and endows the soul with greater supernatural qualities than is the case with St. Thomas. In fact, Duns Scotus is more closely aligned with neo-Platonism, especially in respect to the soul, for which he claims perfection even while it is still in the body. Once this is accepted as an epistemological principle revelation ceases to be a special act of grace and becomes an endowment peculiar to the human race. In principle, man already knows God before He has spoken.

Duns Scotus readily admits that God is greater than the human experience of Him. But this does not deter him from a positive evaluation of man's cognition of God, which becomes possible by reason of his ability to proceed by means of abstraction. Man arrives at a valid knowledge of God in terms of general statements *(in universali)*, though not concretely (*ut haec natura*). But in spite of this limitation the human intellect has the capacity to achieve the highest form of natural cognition of God, even to the extent of the *visio Dei.*[89]

In essence, man is a God-seeking creature who is in possession of an *a priori* and natural desire for God — *appetitus naturalis* — which he seeks to satisfy and which is his ultimate and last goal. Duns Scotus inherited this God-seeking instinct from Augustine, but it was and still is the unchallenged premise of most theologians. Given the principle of an *a priori* God-seeking instinct and the perfection of the human soul, the whole idea of revelation becomes redundant, except to confirm what man already knows in his innermost self.

Duns Scotus, like Thomas Aquinas, is not unaware that his epistemology does not easily fit into the biblical scheme of revelation. He frequently goes out of his way to make room for the Other Voice, which reaches us from the authority of Scripture. He allows that "speculative verities" derived from reason are insufficient to carry the full weight of revelation. In the last resort, authoritative knowledge of

---

[89] Finkenzeller, *ibid.*, p. 24.

God is a matter of the heart, which responds to the love of God.[90] But even this concession carries definite mystical overtones and in no way interferes with his epistemological assumptions.

We can see, therefore, that on the important problem of epistemology the difference between Thomas and Duns Scotus is only a formal one. Basically, their assumptions are similar: man is naturally endowed with the capacity to reach God and he does so by the use of reason. In essence, both these two great medieval schoolmen pursued the same goal and moved in the same direction. C. R. S. Harris has a passage that well illustrates the point we are trying to make. Comparing St. Thomas with Duns Scotus, he says: "Both laboured to express the nature of the divine personality and its relation to the human spirit in terms of dry and abstract conception of substance, essence, idea, actuality, and so forth and so desiccate and condense into exact and precise formulae the whole rich content of the spiritual experience of mankind as it is reflected in the light of the living Church. And both were alike doomed to failure."[91] Harris rightly attributes the failure to the impossibility of their task rather than to the abstractness of their terminology. He holds that Greek philosophy cannot be wedded to biblical faith, for the assumptions are totally different.[92]

It is a noteworthy fact that in the tremendous intellectual structure underlying the *Summa* the covenant plays no recognizable part. The same applies to scholastic theology in general. It was only during the theological unheaval at the time of the Reformation that the biblical concept of covenant was rediscovered.[93]

The significance of the covenant lies in the restrictions it imposes: God's condescension is the only legitimate basis for man's knowledge of God. Here the order is radically reversed: the quest is God's; it is He who seeks man, who

---

[90] *Ibid.*, p. 30.

[91] C. R. S. Harris, *Duns Scotus*, 1959, II, 180.

[92] St. Thomas is bold to affirm, "Our faith is the same as that of the Fathers of old" (*Summa*, pt. III, Q. 70, a. 1), but his suppositions are certainly not the same.

[93] Characteristically enough the *Catholic Encyclopedia* carries no major article on the covenant and has only one single reference, buried in the text, to the covenant with Abraham. This does not apply to the *New Catholic Encyclopedia*, 1967. But even here the concept is not given the theological weight it deserves.

accosts man, who offers Himself to man. The initiative is entirely His.

Under such conditions revelation ceases to be man's quest for the Ultimate. It becomes an encounter with a Person rather than intellectual perception of verities. From the perspective of the covenant every metaphysical effort to define God and every unitive effort on the part of mysticism falls under the condemnation of idolatry. Unless God relates Himself to man all man's questioning is futile. Within the finitude of creaturely existence the circle remains hermetically closed. The distinction between Creator and creature is inviolate and can never be abolished. There can be no way from man to God once we take man's creatureliness seriously. It is only when we overlook the distinction between God and man, Creator and creature, that the barrier is broken down and the difference is minimized.

It is a strange fact that within Jewish tradition with all its emphasis upon the covenant, the personal aspect of revelation has been lost. This is mainly the result of its opposition to the incarnational theology of Christianity. But it is also the result of a narrow interpretation of the meaning of covenant. The restricted concept of covenant confined to the biological descendants of Abraham and associated with the rite of circumcision has reduced the personal aspect of God's condescension in two ways: revelation has become commandment and election affects only the Jewish people. A Jewish writer who has described the essence of Jewish theology as *Jewishology* has unconsciously given expression to the innate restriction that hampers Jewish thought.[94] An interesting case is Abraham Heschel. His concept of revelation reduces itself to God's Presence to the extent that he speaks in almost Christian terms of *the effulgence of the living Presence* of God, an expression reminiscent of the letter to the Hebrews (Heb. 1:3).[95] But in order to forestall any Christian associations he has to depersonalize by confining God's Presence to the "outwardness of the world" which "communicates something of the indwelling greatness of God." With all the emphasis there-

[94] Cf. Monford Harris, "Interim Theology," *Judaism*, 1958, p. 305; cf. also E. B. Borowitz, "The Jewish Need for Theology," *Commentary*, Aug. 1962, pp. 138ff. Borowitz discusses the problem of faith and ethnicity in modern Judaism.

[95] The italics are Heschel's; cf. *op. cit.*, p. 83.

fore on a personal God, encounter is reduced to "sensing the presence of God in the world, in things . . . in the Bible, . . . in sacred deeds."[96] Thus the impersonal aspect of revelation intrudes here and puts man in a dominant position: "Judaism," we are told, "is based upon a minimum of revelation and a maximum of interpretation," so much so that the original text given by God is left to Israel to "refine and complete."[97] Heschel lacks a deeper insight into the meaning of covenant; to him it either expresses God's need of man,[98] or Israel's willing partnership.[99] We thus find the problem of understanding biblical revelation is as acute to Judaism as it is to Christianity. It is seldom realized how pervasive was Greek influence upon Jewish thinking.[100] Measured against the concreteness of biblical revelation, Jewish theology is as pale as is Christian theology: "How can mortal man, bound by his five senses, be in communication with an abstract God, of whom we may posit only His existence, and then forbid ourselves any attempts to grasp His essence."[101] Solomon Simon, the author of the above quotation, senses the difference of the abstract God in theology from the God of the prophets, whose Presence is acknowledged in all concreteness. In the view of the prophets, "God Himself comes down to man, and teaches him how to walk in His ways."[102]

The Christological assumptions of the Christian faith are inseparable from the concrete personal revelation of Almighty God not in terms of truth but in terms of encounter: God meets man within time and space, exactly where man is to be found, in the dimension of history. But such a supposition can only be justified on the basis of the covenant, for otherwise it is left to accident or caprice whether God wills to reveal Himself or not.

b. Revelation in terms of divine attributes

Once we accept the covenant as the ground of theological reasoning the personal aspect of revelation becomes a logical necessity. It means that theological under-

---

[96] *Ibid.*, p. 30.
[97] *Ibid.*, p. 274.
[98] *Ibid.*, p. 68.
[99] *Ibid.*, p. 214.
[100] Cf. *Commentary*, Aug. 1962, pp. 108f.
[101] Solomon Simon, "Illusion or Wish?" *Judaism*, Winter, 1960, p. 33.
[102] *Ibid.*, p. 33.

standing does not precede but only follows from the fact of revelation. We do not begin with the assumption of God's existence and then proceed to verify the validity of the assumption. Theology is only a legitimate enterprise when it follows upon man's encounter with God in the concreteness of history. In this existential situation it is not man but God who does the questioning. It is He who initiates the dialogue by asking Adam: "Where are you?" Naturally, Adam wants to puzzle out who the Questioner is and what the meaning of His question is. He tries to formulate an opinion; he has an urge to give Him a name; he has a need to reduce Him to manageable proportions.

All these efforts on the part of Adam are evasive attempts to respond in all honesty to the original question: Where are you? Instead, he tries to name God, analyze His character and formulate a thesis. In this endeavor, Adam is bound to forget the disparity between the Questioner and himself and is likely to take his *vis-à-vis* with the Other One as his due. Covenantal theology guards against this fatal misunderstanding. In the context of the covenant God's Presence means His condescension by grace. It is not man who names God, but it is God who names Himself before man. All that man knows about Him is by God's self-revelation: He gives Himself a Name and in so doing reveals His intention. There is therefore a legitimate place for the divine "attributes" within the history of revelation. It is only when these "attributes" become detached from the concreteness of revelation and are treated as impersonal concepts of divinity that the falsification occurs.

The Bible makes definite statements *about* God. The source for the doctrine of attributes is Exodus 34:6f, but this text cannot be detached from the wider context of redemptive action to which it belongs. Here God acts on behalf of His people and in so doing reveals His character and intention. He reveals Himself as the God of the Fathers, which is a direct reference to the covenant. The proclamation that goes with His redemptive action describes Him as the God of Love and the God of Judgment. He is always both: faithful to His promises and impartial in His judgments. But these two attributes are in no sense detachable from the given situation and cannot be used as impersonal statements of divine "essence." Unfortunately, church and synagogue have frequently abstracted the proclamation from the existential situation and treated the text as a source of information of God's innermost Being. A metaphysical science of attributes was developed which gave rise to esoteric speculations and cabalistic formulae.

The tradition regarding the Names of God is somehow connected with the doctrine of attributes. Because of the sanctity attached to the *Tetragrammaton* the synagogue evolved a whole catena of substitutes for God's holy Name, which gradually acquired hypostatic significance of their own.[103] The *Midrash* is able to account for as many as seventy Names, presumably all derived from biblical texts.[104] The traditional number of Names is usually seven. These Names are meant to describe, define, and express God's nature as revealed to man. In this regard there are two definite trends discernible in rabbinic tradition: on the one hand there is a persistent effort being made to explicate the nature of God and to define its essence; on the other hand, the reverse attitude is maintained, that God must not be named, for no name can adequately describe Him.[105] But seen from a biblical perspective, naming God or refraining to name Him are both inappropriate attitudes. In the first case, man attempts to pry into God's ultimate secret and make Him an object of uncurbed curiosity; in the second case, man avoids the personal encounter by refusing to take historic revelation seriously. Instead of a confrontation with the living God, man prefers a philosophical system of ideas to serve as a substitute.

The transition from the Bible to metaphysics is a long and complicated process. The syncretic bent of the human mind makes it next to impossible to keep out foreign, even contradictory, ideas. No theologian has ever managed to maintain an uncompromising position. It is more a matter of emphasis than of absolute purity: in theology

---

[103] For the cabalistic use of the 42-lettered Name, see *JE*, IX, 163a.

[104] Cf. *Num. R.* to 7:78. Israel, the *torah*, and Jerusalem also have seventy names each.

[105] Cf. Rabbi Samuel S. Cohon, "The Nature of God, A Study in Rabbinic Theology," *HUCA*, XXIII, pt. I, 581.

biblical insights and metaphysical inventiveness go hand in hand. But historically a line can be drawn at the point of contact between biblical faith and Greek philosophy. It is the preponderance of the latter that changes the balance.

The ancient synagogue by exegetical methods arrived at thirteen attributes and called them "the thirteen modes of compassion."[106] Rashi,[107] the great Jewish exegete, follows the ancient tradition in his understanding of Exodus 34:6f by putting all the emphasis upon God's compassion as His chief attribute. He even works out a scale of comparison between God's mercy and His judgment: "the measure of good is greater than the measure of punishment in proportion of one to five hundred." But this is an imbalance that runs contrary to the traditional rabbinic views of equity. The Rabbis were concerned that an overemphasis upon *ḥesed* might diminish meaning of *mishpat* and thus upset the equilibrium. They therefore employed exegetical ingenuity to maintain a reasonable balance between mercy and judgment.[108] We are here still moving within the area of biblical exegesis.

But the synagogue, like the church, was exposed to Greek philosophy and speculative thought. As the process continued, "the attributes of mercy" acquired philosophical status and became detached from the biblical context. Philo already injected elements in his theology "not altogether in accordance with antecedent Jewish thought."[109] Later when the synagogue came in more direct contact with Greek philosophy via Arab writers, the biblical "attributes" acquired a more speculative character. It now becomes a problem how to relate the active God of biblical revelation to the god of philosophy who, *ex hypothesi,* is a simple changeless substance, utterly devoid of properties.

It became the main concern of Moses Maimonides (Ben Maimon, 1135-1204) so to interpret the anthropomorphic statements about God we meet in the Old Testament as

---

[106] R. Yohanan (d. 279): thirteen kinds of mercy are written in the Scriptures about God (*Pes. K.* 57a).

[107] Rashi=Rabbi Solomon ben Isaac of Troyes, 1040-1105.

[108] Cf. the learned note by H. Loewe in Montefiore's *Rabbinic Anthology,* 44.

[109] *JE,* VI, 5a.

to bring them in line with the philosophical suppositions regarding divine essence. He holds fast to the main philosophical premises that the substance of God must not be differentiated, for this would contradict His immutability.[110] In his view, not even existence can properly be ascribed to God since this is a predicate that applies primarily to created beings. All that we can legitimately say about Him is that He is, and nothing more. Maimonides deals with the subject extensively in his *Moreh Nebukhim* where he employs every possible argument to show the utter inappropriateness of ascribing attributive distinctions to the Godhead.[111]

Maimonides' philosophical reasoning is interesting, for it illustrates the extent of his departure from the biblical position. Here are his main reasons why attributes of any kind must not be ascribed to God:

(1) God cannot and must not be defined, as any definition is inappropriate for it is bound to use human standards.

(2) God being incorporeal is a "simple" nature and therefore has no parts.

(3) God being immutable is unaffected by psychological change.

(4) No actions can properly be ascribed to God for this would contradict His changelessness.

This kind of reasoning was already adopted by the Head of the Talmudic Academy at Sura in Babylon, Saadya (892-942),[112] and constitutes a major departure from the biblical position.

In spite of Maimonides' insistence upon creation as a beginning in time and the difference between Creator and creature, there is an inner logic that leads from an attributeless God of pure and undifferentiated Being, to the god of pantheism. Once God is conceived in abstract and impersonal terms as eternal essence without predicates, the differentiation between Creator and creature becomes difficult to maintain. Logically speaking, creation becomes

110 For this reason Philo already held to the view: God is without qualities; cf. *De Allegoriis Legum*, 13.

111 Cf. Moses Maimonides, *Guide for the Perplexed*, 1947 trans., I, 21; cf. also chs. 10, 25, 28, 64.

112 Cf. *JE*, art. "God"; cf. also Alexander Altmann, *Judaism*, Winter, 1966, pp. 44f.

part of His Being and *Deus sive natura* is the only possible result.

Spinoza drew the last consequences from Maimonides' position though his reasoning moved in the opposite direction. Unlike Maimonides, he endowed God with an infinite number of attributes, which made Him coeternal to His creation. Oddly enough, there is no substantial difference between an attributeless god, utterly undifferentiated, and a god of unlimited attributes. Spinoza's reasoning is not far removed from that of Maimonides once we are prepared to press for logical conclusions. Here are Spinoza's premises: beside God no substance can be granted or conceived; substance is absolute infinity and therefore indivisible; God or substance consists of infinite attributes — hence God is all in all.[113] All we have to do is to exchange Spinoza's *substance* with Maimonides' *pure Being* and we arrive at the same conclusions.

The distance between the living God of biblical revelation and the pale existence of cosmic *substance* acting as a kind of *élan vital* in the universe is too great for comparison.

Behind the question of the divine "attributes" as treated philosophically is the perennial problem of the relation of unity to multiplicity.[114] This unresolved puzzle, which has divided the schoolmen into Realists and Nominalists, makes its appearance whenever we try to establish a monistic principle for the universe. The God of the Bible does not easily fit into any philosophical system without losing His essential character. Whenever He becomes a concept or a principle He ceases to be the living God and becomes an idol. In place of a true and existential encounter we are left with abstract concepts.

To show the corrosive influence of philosophy upon biblical theology we will use another Jewish example. The reason we turn to the Rabbis is to contradict the opinion frequently held that the synagogue escaped the fate of the church in its resistance to syncretism. Abraham ibn Daud (1110-1180), a contemporary of Maimonides, is credited to be the first Jewish Rabbi to have employed Aristotelian premises in his writings. It is therefore interesting to see the transformation of the traditional "thirteen modes

---

113 Cf. B. Spinoza, *Ethics,* I, Propositions XIV, XIII, XI.
114 Cf. Ludwig Stein, *JE,* VI, 12a.

of mercy" constituting the divine attributes as these same attributes appear in their new formulation at the hands of ibn Daud. He allows only eight attributes describing the divine nature: unity, existence, immutability, truth, life, knowledge, power, and will.[115] We have here a combination of personal and impersonal aspects with the impersonal predominating. It is obvious that behind these definitions are two heterogeneous sources that do not easily combine, the Bible and Aristotle's *Metaphysica*.[116]

The names of God and the "attributes" are treated as synonyms in Jewish theology. Rabbi Marmorstein is able to provide proof from rabbinic sources to establish eight basic attributes that define the nature of God: (1) omnipresence, (2) omniscience, (3) omnipotence, (4) eternity, (5) truth, (6) justice, (7) goodness, (8) purity and holiness. In themselves, these definitions constitute no offense to biblical revelation. It is only when these are treated as impersonal nouns that the contradiction arises. The very phrasing of these nouns strongly contrasts with a similar number of attributes as provided by the *Midrash:* (1) beneficence, (2) lovingkindness, (3) mercy, (4) righteousness, (5) faithfulness, (6) redemption, (7) blessing, (8) peace.[117] There is a decided difference between the homiletic warmth of the *Midrash* and the abstract treatment of the subject by Rabbi Marmorstein.[118] In the detached atmosphere of the philosophical formulation the personal and active God of salvation-history dissolves into a bundle of metaphysical concepts.[119]

It is a strange fact that incarnational theology, which presupposes concrete historical and personal categories as the characteristics of the Christian faith, has not managed to resist the metaphysical attempts upon the God of Israel. In fact, Christians appear to be even more vulnerable to the disruptive influence of Greek philosophy than are Jews.

---

[115] Cf. *'Emunah ramah,* pp. 54ff.

[116] Cf. Joseph Owens, *The Doctrine of Being in the Aristotelian Metaphysics,* 1957, pp. 280f.

[117] Cf. *Esther R.,* X, 15 (to 8:15).

[118] Cf. A. Marmorstein, *The Old Rabbinic Doctrine of God,* 1927, pt. II.

[119] It is in keeping with Greek tradition to speak of God as a "predicative" and not as a person; cf. W. Jaeger, *The Theology of Early Greek Philosophers,* 1947, p. 173.

We put it down to the difficulty the church has with the Old Testament. She has never managed to treat it seriously as the only and legitimate background for the New Testament. The result is a spiritualized concept of "holy" history that robs it of all concreteness. With this goes hand in hand a conceptualization of God devoid of the redemptive Presence we find in the Bible, a God "passionately and actively interfering in all earthly affairs."[120]

After quoting Jewish sources so extensively it is only right that we turn our attention to Christian writers. Proceeding chronologically we will select Gregory of Nazianzus (330-389) as a useful example.

In Gregory, one of the three famed Cappadocian Fathers, we have a learned Greek with a thorough philosophical background and under strong neo-Platonic influence. But he is also a devout Christian, committed to incarnational theology and biblical revelation. The result is an unresolved tension between his metaphysical suppositions and his biblical knowledge.

Gregory is sometimes tempted to compromise by indulging in abstract philosophical speculation regarding the "attributes." He tells us: "We sketch him (i.e. God) by his attributes and so obtain a certain faint and feeble and partial idea concerning him."[121] In this effort he is even prepared to countenance an etymological suggestion to explain the meaning of θεός.[122] On one occasion he seriously considers the *via negationis* as a possible method for defining the divine essence.[123] But these stray attempts are only incidental. In principle he remains true to the central premise of the Christian faith: Christ's condescension is the only warrant for "embodied creatures" to arrive at a valid knowledge of God. There can be no other way of compre-

[120] Max Wiener, *Die lehren des Judentums*, ed. Fritz Bamberger, pt. IV, "...leidenschaftlich wirksam in alle irdischen Dinge eingreifend." For a contemporary discussion of the doctrine of attributes in Jewish theology, see Alexander Altmann, "The Divine Attributes," *Judaism*, Winter, 1966, pp. 40ff.

[121] Cf. *The Theological Orations*, IV, 17 (Library of Christian Classics, III, 189).

[122] *Ibid.*, §18.

[123] *Ibid.*, III, 11.

hending the otherwise incomprehensible and unknowable God.[124]

Gregory never tires of telling us that God is beyond and above every human attempt to describe Him. He tries hard to resist the allurements offered by metaphysical speculation. He gallantly adheres to biblical revelation and refuses to accept any analogy of God's otherness as adequate. Outside biblical revelation man may know God only by His benefits.[125] But even he comes perilously close to a speculative concept of God when dealing with the attributes.

Other Fathers of the church are equally tempted. Arnobius (d. *ca.* 330) does not hesitate to define God as cause, place, and space of all creation: *prima causa, locus et spatium rerum.*[126] Augustine (354-540), for whom the authority of Scripture is an overriding principle and who is well aware of the limitations of reason,[127] so much so that he refuses to enter into an argument with those who deny God's existence,[128] is not beyond philosophical definitions and arguments for God's existence. He occasionally refers to God as "truth" in an impersonal sense,[129] and describes Him as immutable and simple.[130] Though Ludwig Schopp contradicts Schulten's statement that Augustine calls God alone *vere esse,*[131] we have the authority of Etienne Gilson that his frequent references to God as *substantia* mean in effect *essence.* Gilson provides the reason why this must be so: "otherwise God would appear to be a subject

---

[124] Cf. *ibid.,* IV, 21; cf. also §6.

[125] *Ibid.,* II, 26. H. F. Cherniss describes Gregory of Nyssa as an unmitigated Platonist who "merely applied Christian names to Plato's doctrine and called it Christian" (cf. *The Platonism of Gregory of Nyssa,* 1930, pp. 63f). But the same cannot be said of his namesake, Gregory of Nazianzus, who all his life strove toward Christian orthodoxy, though Greek philosophy was the only medium in which to express it.

[126] "Thou art the first cause, in Thee created things exist, and thou art the space in which rests the foundation of all things..." (Arnobius, *Adversus Gentes,* I, 31). We have in this text the *Urquelle* for Tillich's "ground of being"!

[127] *De Moribus Ecclesiae Catholicae,* 11.

[128] Cf. *ibid.,* 10.

[129] *De Immortalitate Animae,* 7.12.

[130] *De Utilitate Credendi,* 36.

[131] *The Fathers of the Church,* Writings of Augustine, 2, 35 n.l.

whose attributes are accidents."[132] Augustine's elaborate proofs of God's existence in *De Libero Arbitrium* and in *De Vera Religione* are evidence enough of his lapse from biblical revelation into philosophical rationalism. At the same time, Augustine knows only too well that God is unknowable, but only because as pure Being He is removed from every kind of determination. Yet man is not entirely unaware of God's existence and may even discern, if he only looks well enough, that He is a Trinity. The triune nature of God he sees already reflected in the very constitution of man, and Augustine suggests a number of analogies to this effect: soul, mind, spirit; mind, cognition, love; memory, intelligence, will; etc.[133] In the act of knowing God, *mens* plays a most important part but not without the cooperation of the soul, which, as Gilson explains, constitutes "the metaphysical background" for Augustine's epistemology.[134]

Ultimately it is not revelation but the immortal soul that constitutes the link between time and eternity. Once the principle of the immortal soul enters theology the whole significance of biblical revelation is inevitably shifted from God to man. It is now man who is seen as the seeker and discerner of God. He is called upon to investigate, prove, define, and analyze the divine principle. In this case revelation at best can only mean supplementary and confirmative information of what man already *knows* by reason of his origin. With philosophy as the tool God ceases to be a Person and becomes an intellectual proposition.

It happened to Augustine, as it happens to all philosophers who engage in theology. The personal qualities of the living God of revelation, to be grasped by reason, have to be reduced to impersonal concepts. Augustine's God is sometimes the God of the Bible, but more often he is the god of philosophers: an attributeless god, absolute Being, impersonal Strength, Justice, Wisdom — these qualities constitute His very essence.[135] There is good reason for this change; on logical grounds God cannot be both the

---

[132] Etienne Gilson, *The Christian Philosophy of St. Augustine*, 1960 trans., p. 353 n. 6; cf. Augustine's phrase: *aeternitas, ipsa Dei substantia*, quoted by Gilson, p. 22.

[133] Cf. *De Trinitate*, 1963 trans., pp. 277f; 310ff; 323ff.

[134] Cf. Gilson, *op. cit.*, p. 103.

[135] *Ibid.*, p. 217.

source of creation and the sum of it. Attributes cannot be properly ascribed to Him, since He Himself is the cause of all values. The Arab philosopher al-Nizzam (d. *ca.* 845) gives the reason for this undifferentiated god: "He is living not by virtue of life but by virtue of Himself." This sentence is echoed by the Jewish philosopher-poet Gabirol (Avicebron, 11th cent.): "Thou art alive but not by virtue of a living soul; Thou art wise . . . without having acquired knowledge from elsewhere."[136] Augustine in his discussion of the Trinity has put it in precise terms: God is what He has: "Thus, when He is said to be living, we mean that He has life and is the very life He has."[137]

This then is the problem of theology: we either speak of God anthropomorphically as the Bible does, or else we speak of Him conceptually.[138] If we do the latter He falls under the rules of syllogistic reasoning and becomes the object of logical analysis. At this point He ceases to be a Person. As a nonperson God can have no attributes and remains undifferentiated. It is difficult to see how Augustine managed to maintain a distinction within the Trinity except by a *petitio principii.*

At this point no compromise is possible: either God is a Person to whom attributes may be ascribed, which means that we may say something *about* Him; or else He is pure Being and as such beyond language altogether. In the latter case, God is a notion, a concept, an idea, and can be used for metaphysical purposes. From the metaphysical position revelation is an unnecessary encumbrance and is best overlooked and not taken seriously.

Charles Hartshorne has tried to solve the difficulty created by metaphysical reasoning by a compromise: he posits a personal God who has social relations and is therefore definable. But at the same time he proceeds on the principle of *via eminentiae* in order to preserve His maj-

---

[136] Cf. Augustine's remark: *Deum nihil aliud dicam esse, nisi idipsum esse.* The English translation does not quite convey the precision of this sentence: "this (i.e. God) cannot be called anything other than Being itself" (*The Fathers of the Church,* 1965, 56, 21; *De Moribus Ecclesiae Catholicae,* 14.24).

[137] *Quae habet haec et est, et ea omnia unus est* (*De Civitate Dei,* XI, 10.3).

[138] Cf. Fred Sommers, "What we can say about God," *Judaism,* Winter, 1966, p. 72.

esty so as to keep Him free "from all anthropomorphic crudities."[139] But Hartshorne's concept of panentheism can hardly stand up to the test of consistency. There is a logical contradiction in a god who is all-inclusive in the universe and at the same time independent of it. The premise that God exists and that He is one with His essence Hartshorne posits as an analytical truth.[140] By this he means that it is derivative from logical analysis. But prior to this he has already decided to lay down the premise that God is the *"one individual conceivable a priori."*[141] This creates a circular argument from which there is no way out. To conceive of an *a priori* god is a metaphysical assumption hardly patient of analytical verification. To ascribe to such a god personal qualities, as Hartshorne does, would require an anthropomorphic approach, which he emphatically rejects. His "surrelativist" system at the very outset refuses any revelational assumptions. He is determined to proceed on purely logical reasoning.

Hartshorne's concern is a legitimate one. He rejects the idea of an impassive god who is utterly unrelated to his creation. His criticism of the sterility of traditional theology is only too justified. But the remedy, to our mind, is not a reshuffle of metaphysical argumentation but a more serious consideration of revelation in history. The fact is that there can be no valid correlation between God and man except on Christological grounds, and this presupposes the covenant. The covenant means that God freely relates Himself to His creation from the very beginning. Creation in time is therefore essential to covenantal theology. Hartshorne's problem arises exactly at this point: he rejects a "first moment of creation."[142] In this case creation is either coexistent with God or God and creation are undifferentiated. In either case He cannot be a personal God but merely impersonal Essence — the very idea that Hartshorne sets out to refute.

---

[139] Charles Hartshorne, *The Divine Relativity, A Social Concept of God*, 1948, p. 77.

[140] *Ibid.*, p. 87.

[141] *Ibid.*, p. 38; Hartshorne's italics.

[142] Hartshorne prefers Whitehead's concept of a god who as an all-sensitive passive Nature suffers in and through mankind (cf. *ibid.*, p. 153).

c. The Covenant as Epistemological Premise

There seems to be no solution to the dilemma except by way of the covenant, which posits the condescension of God to the level of creation. This has been recognized on the Jewish side by Oskar Goldberg[143] and his disciple Erich Ungar,[144] who reckon with an extramundane God who assumes concrete historic form and enters creation without destroying it.[145] It is a curious fact that traditional theology preferred the Greek method by constituting the immortal soul as the link between God and man, rather than the covenant. Christian theology mainly depended upon the mystical experience of the soul for man's knowledge of God.[146] Hence the attraction of neo-Platonist metaphysics. St. Thomas justifies his position by falling back upon the tradition of the past: "All the ancient philosophers attribute infinitude to the first principle . . . for they considered that things flow forth infinitely from the first principle." This, of course, he could not accept without qualification, for it would imply infinitude of matter.[147] But the qualification is only a minor one: grace renders God present to things, not as part of their essence but as *added* to it.[148]

As far as Thomas is concerned the *addition* of grace, which is meant to qualify God's Presence to His creation, ill befits the metaphysical context. Thomas has already affirmed that God is everywhere present by Essence; the introduction of grace is thus an added qualification. That this is an artificial device can be seen from the fact that there is yet a "special mode" of God's existence in man, namely by *union*. Grace therefore appears to be some additional preservative sustaining creation; as an added favor there is the mystical union that is reached by the process of cognition. Basically Creator and creation are correlated by participation in Being. The whole structure of *analogia entis* depends upon this principle. It is only on this as-

143 Cf. Oskar Goldberg, *Die Wirklichkeit der Hebräer*, Berlin, 1925.

144 Erich Ungar, *Das Problem der Mythischen Realität*, Berlin, 1926.

145 Schalom Ben-Chorin, "Jüdische Aspekte der Entmythologisierung des Neuen Testamentes," *Judaica*, März, 1956, p. 30; see also *Judaica*, März, 1954, pp. 41ff.

146 Cf. Gilson, *op. cit.*, p. 104.

147 F. C. Copleston has shown that for St. Thomas eternity of creation is not an impossibility; cf. *Aquinas*, Pelican ed., pp. 54, 138.

148 *Summa Theol.*, I, Q. 8, art. 3, reply to obj. 4.

sumption that a "scientific definition" of God's nature can be attempted.[149] Analogical reasoning can only be justified on the assumption of a possible comparison between Creator and creature. Once the radical difference is affirmed metaphysical reasoning ceases to make sense.[150]

Analogical reasoning inevitably leads to an impersonal doctrine of God. The *Deus pater* we know from revelation and the *Primum ens* we obtain from metaphysical reasoning do not easily relate except by a *tour de force*. Once the covenant is missing grace can only be introduced as an *addition* to what man already possesses by reason of his creatureliness. From this follows the *infusio gratiae* as *added* sacramental grace. Thomas Bonhoeffer has raised the question in respect to the connection between revelation as creation (*Schöpfungsoffenbarung*) and revelation as grace (*Gnadenoffenbarung*), but fails to provide a straightforward answer.[151] Without serious attention to the covenant there is no connection except by a divine fiat: God creates and as an afterthought decides to reveal Himself as an additional act of grace.

We have dwelt on the subject of the divine attributes, for it discloses the epistemological difficulty that besets our knowledge of God. He is either the Unknowable One before whom we can only keep silence, as suggested by Arnobius[152] and by Augustine,[153] or else He is the impersonal "ground of being" as defined by philosophers. In the first case He is incommunicable and all man can do is follow the example of Nicholas of Cusa (*ca.* 1400-1464), who employed

---

149 Cf. William D. Bruckmann's *Glossary* appended to the English trans. of the *Summa Theologica,* III, 3558f.

150 For a limited usefulness of metaphysics as a stepping-stone to revelation, see Edward Farley, *The Transcendence of God,* 1960. For the *analogia entis* principle in favor of St. Thomas, see George P. Klubertanz, *St. Thomas Aquinas on Analogy,* 1960.

151 Cf. Thomas Bonhoeffer, *Die Gotteslehre von Aquin,* 1961, pp. 62, 68, 103, 107. For a modified analogical approach see E. R. Fairweather, "Christianity and the Supernatural," *CJT,* Jan. 1963, pp. 12ff; and April 1963, pp. 95ff.

152 Arnobius, *Adversus Gentes,* I, 31: "concerning whom nothing can be clearly expressed by the significance of man's words. That Thou mayest be understood we must keep silent."

153 Augustine, *De Doctrina Christiana,* I, 6: "God should not be spoken of as ineffable, because when we say this word, we are saying something about Him . . . a thing is not ineffable which can be called ineffable. We should guard this contradiction in terms of silence. . . ."

mathematical analogies as the only possible way of expressing something meaningful about Him.[154] In the second case He has nothing to communicate, for He is only a concept.[155]

The only way out of this logical impasse is to allow God to speak for Himself. This *third* possibility is behind the theological assumption of revelation. But in this case it cannot be allegorical revelation as suggested by Origen;[156] as if God suddenly decided to break His silence and then withdraw again into obscurity. Only if revelation is the underlying principle behind creation can it be taken seriously. The fact of revelation is thus inseparable from the fact of the covenant. This is the unbroken witness of the Bible. The covenant is thus the key to the epistemological question regarding God. There is a passage in Philo which indicates that in spite of his predilection for Platonism he remained a Jew on this vital issue. In his treatise *Quod Deus immutabilis est* he comes to speak about the gratuity of grace: "But God remembering His perfect and universal goodness, even though the whole vast body of mankind should through its exceeding sinfulness accomplish its own ruin, stretches forth the right hand of salvation, to them under His protection and raises them up, and suffers not the race to be brought to utter destruction and annihilation."[157] This passage might have come out of Barth's *Church Dogmatics* for its emphasis upon covenantal grace. Christian writers, in spite of their philosophical loyalties, have found themselves in a similar situation, and no one more so than St. Thomas. He is never purely a philosopher.[158] In the last resort, God is not just Divine Essence but the Heavenly Father upon whom every creature depends, "so that not for a moment could it subsist, but would fall into nothingness were it not kept in being by

---

[154] Cf. Gordon Leff, *The Listener*, Feb. 10, 1966, p. 204.

[155] Fred Sommers points to the inadequacy of silence in order to escape incoherence, *Judaism*, Winter, 1966, p. 69.

[156] Cf. R. P. C. Hanson, *Allegory and Event*, 1959, pp. 276ff; cf also *Origen's Doctrine of Tradition*, 1954, pp. 73ff. T. Such understands continuity and discontinuity as a "noetic principle," kept in polar tension between the infinite and the finite (cf. *op. cit.*, p. 8).

[157] Philo, *The Unchangeableness of God*, XV, 73 (Loeb trans.). This passage is the more noteworthy as elsewhere Philo extends God's grace under the covenant only to those who are worthy (cf. *On the Change of Names*, VI, 52).

[158] On this point cf. F. C. Copleston's remarks, *op. cit.*, pp. 53ff.

the Divine power, as Gregory says."[159] Not only did God create entirely by a free decision but He "continually pours out existence" into His creation.[160] This is exactly what is meant by the covenant, though Thomas never consciously builds his theology upon it.

Fr. Joseph Owens, who writes in the Thomas tradition, readily admits that "no reasoning in the order of essence can reach anything that of itself is necessarily identical with the God of Christian worship."[161] He is quite aware of the danger of conceptualization, which inevitably leads to "the loss of what is proper" to the Christian concept of God.[162] It is our contention that revelation unless structured in the covenant is without anchorage and becomes a matter of speculation. Within the covenant context the biblical attributes cease to be philosophical concepts but become descriptions of God's saving acts within history. It is only in the covenant that we know Him, that He is for us and on behalf of us. In the last resort covenantal knowledge of God is Christologically conditioned. That God is truly for us and that the covenant still stands we can only know through Jesus Christ.[163]

---

[159] *Summa Theol.*, pt. I, Q. 104, art. 1.

[160] *Ibid.*, art. 3.

[161] Joseph Owens, *An Elementary Christian Metaphysics*, 1963, p. 351.

[162] *Ibid.*, pp. 353f.

[163] God *for us* in Christ must not be reduced to an existentialist position of "meaningfulness." G. C. Berkouwer contends that Bultmann has misinterpreted Melanchthon's famous sentence: *Christus cognoscere est beneficia eius cognoscere* (cf. *Christianity Today*, March 18, 1966, p. 47). For the danger of reducing the gospel to "meaningfulness" see Kenneth Hamilton, *Revolt Against Heaven*, 1965, pp. 13ff. The gospel always exceeds our state of consciousness.

CHAPTER SEVEN:

THE COVENANT AS A HISTORICAL CATEGORY

The discovery that God is *for* us, means that He is for us *here* and *now,* i.e. in the *chronos* of history. The Presence of God turns *chronos* into *kairos* so that the mere flow of time becomes a transcendent experience of eternity. God's Presence in history is for us a covenantal act and not a metaphysical conclusion.

From a metaphysical point of view God's immanence relates to the concept of Being. Because God is the source of all Being, all that exists has a share in His Being. In this way an *a priori* connection is established between creation and Creator. On this supposition revelation and creation remain undifferentiated, so much so that creation itself becomes the bearer of revelation: we deduce about the Maker from His handiwork. But we have already seen the danger inherent in this view: it depersonalizes God and robs Him of His freedom, while at the same time it divinizes the creature.[1] On the other view, God's Presence

[1] The Eastern church, both ancient and modern, does not hesitate to draw the full consequences of the logos theology and unhesitatingly speaks of the "deification of man." For the modern expressions of the Greek Orthodox tradition, see Isaac C. Rottenberg, *Redemption and Historical Reality,* 1964, pp. 122ff. The divinization of the church in Roman theology is another aspect of the same trend and for the same reasons; cf. *ibid.,* pp. 102f, 104, 120. On the relation of being to Being

to His creation by way of the covenant is His free and sovereign choice: He graciously bends toward His creation as Father and Protector. In this case the emanation theory is inapplicable, for God is supremely a Person and relates Himself personally to His creatures.

These two different perspectives yield two diverse theologies: on the premise of Being, God and creation exist alongside each other and move horizontally; on the premise of covenant, creation exists *coram Deo,* in the Presence of God, and the movement is vertical from above *toward* the creature. The Christological basis of theology rests upon the vertical movement and not the horizontal. Those who make Being the basis of theological reasoning have difficulty in incorporating the Christological dimension into their system, except by a departure from their basic premise. Ontological reasoning presupposes a self-contained monistic universe and carries within its structure a latent form of pantheism. On this basis a radical differentiation between God and creation is impossible. It is for this reason that metaphysicians show a decided preference for the doctrine of emanation: "in him we live and move and have our being" (Acts 17:28). This is not from the Old Testament but stems from a typically Stoic source.[2] Plotinus' whole structure of thought as outlined in the *Enneads* rests on a similar emanational assumption.[3] For a modern example of emanational theology we would suggest Hegel's metaphysical philosophy. There is little difference between Plotinus and Hegel except in vocabulary. According to Hegel's theory everything flows out of the Divine and strains to be reabsorbed into the Godhead.[4]

By contrast, the Bible presents us with a vertical dualism: God and creation remain eternally distinct. The whole

---

see James F. Anderson, *The Bond of Being,* 1949, pp. 49f; also George J. Klubertanz, *St. Thomas Aquinas on Analogy,* 1960, pp. 47ff; on the inadequacy of *analogia entis,* see Dorothy M. Emmet, *The Nature of Metaphysical Thinking,* 1946, pp. 169ff.

[2] The quotation from Epimenides of Crete is more a concession to his audience than an expression of Paul's theology. For this and similar quotations, see F. F. Bruce, *The Acts of the Apostles,* 1951, pp. 338f.

[3] For Plotinus Soul as Essence constitutes the internal unity of the universe; cf. *Enneads,* IV, 1.

[4] Cf. G. W. F. Hegel, *Philosophy of History,* 1901 trans.; cf. also Shinn, *Christianity and the Problem of History,* 1964, p. 116.

of creation exists not *in* Him but *before* Him. YHVH looks *down* upon the children of man (Ps. 33:13). But interestingly enough, YHVH does not only observe from above, He *comes* down to judge the earth with His righteousness and the nations in His faithfulness (Ps. 96:13).[5] It is this fact of God's coming into history that makes the covenant a historical category; it means that history takes place *before* God and in His presence. This creates many problems for theology, mainly because history is not visibly recognizable as under the ordered surveillance of a loving God.

1. THE TWO-DIMENSIONAL ASPECT OF HISTORY

It would seem that from a biblical perspective man moves in a two-dimensional universe. This is a definite dualistic proposition, though different from the Platonic dualism inherited by the Church Fathers.[6] Biblical dualism stems from the radical distinction between God and creation. As already observed, history in this context is conceived not as a process but as an act of will: God's will and man's will. Man wills and acts in the Presence of God, either with a "high hand" in defiance, or as a child of God within the covenant. The dualism therefore is not between spirit and matter but between right and wrong. It is at this point that *chronos* and *kairos* appear in all their dialectical tension: man can be caught up in the circular movement of *chronos* or else in the directional movement of *kairos*. In the first case he becomes subjected to the ebb and flow of nature. Here *systole* and *diastole*, contraction and expansion in the ceaseless rhythm of life and death, is the iron rule.[7] Within *chronos* history can produce nothing new, all that has been will be, there is no new thing under the sun (Eccl. 1:9). A blind mechanical force dominates nature in endless rotation. It is noteworthy that the writer of Ecclesiastes prefaces his view of the sameness of history with a reference to the circular movement in nature: the sun rises and the sun goes down

[5] *be'emūnāthô* is not just "truth," but faithfulness in reference to the covenant promises.

[6] Cf. Cherniss, *op. cit.*, pp. 61f.

[7] Cf. Goethe, "Über Naturwissenschaft," *Sämmtliche Werke*, 1868 (Taschenausgabe), XIII, 229; "Zur Wissenschaft im Allgemeinen," XXXVI, 192. Cf. also Friedrich Muckle, *Der Geist der jüdischen Kultur und das Abendland*, 1923, p. 17.

(1:5), so does the wind (1:6), so do the streams (1:7). Everything moves in a circle.

Though Ecclesiastes occupies a place in the Old Testament Canon, it does not represent a typical Hebrew point of view. Human life cannot be understood in terms of *chronos* only. Time becomes meaningful by events, acts, and decisions. The circularity of time is interrupted by the fact that God *comes* to man: God stands at the beginning and the end of man's life. Man lives in the Presence of God. The saga that tells of Jacob's dream at Bethel presents us with a typical biblical view of the universe: there is a division between heaven and earth but there is communication at the same time, though both are distinctly separate entities (Gen. 28:10ff). These two dimensions never fuse but constantly intersect. Here God is not part of nature but its Lord and Master. This dualistic frame of reference constitutes an offense to man, especially to scientific man;[8] but for theology there can be no choice: if God is at all other than the creature then we live in a two-dimensional world. Historians have tried to treat history on a par with nature and apply the same laws to both, but the results were never satisfactory. It is futile to pretend that man is a biological machine governed by mechanical laws. Hobbes tried to make out that life is merely the motion of limbs, that the heart is a kind of spring and that nerves are no more than strings attached to muscles.[9] But this is an intolerable oversimplification of the complexity of human life. It is contradicted by Hobbes's own observation that history turns upon "a perpetual contention for honour, riches and authority."[10] That the lust for power is man's greatest temptation disproves the mechanistic interpretation of man. Man always moves in *two* worlds: matter and spirit, *chronos* and *kairos*, appetite and moral decision; he moves in the cycle of time and in the realm of history.

Man's power-struggle would seem to exhaust the mean-

[8] Consider Einstein's life-long struggle to bring the gravitational and magnetic forces under one single principle by the Unified Field Theory. To allow for two structures in space he felt to be "intolerable to the theoretical spirit." Cf. Lincoln Barnett, *op. cit.*, p. 110; note also Shinn's remark, *op. cit.*, p. 270.

[9] Cf. Richard Peters, *Hobbes*, 1956 (Pelican ed.), pp. 64f.

[10] *Leviathan*, ed. Michael Oakshott, 1955, p. 460.

ing of history. All man glories in is wisdom, might, and riches (Jer. 9:23). But at a deeper level, at the point where *kairos* impinges upon *chronos,* we discover the covenantal aspect of history, namely that God also acts by practicing kindness, justice, and righteousness upon earth (Jer. 9:24). History is therefore the sphere of a double action: man's action and God's action. For this reason history is both rational and irrational at the same time. It is confusing and irrational on the large scale of *chronos* where man acts at cross-purposes. It is rational at the level of personal and moral decision where *chronos* is experienced as *kairos.* On this level even evil seems to become meaningful as it appears to serve positive ends.

2. THE PERSONAL AND IMPERSONAL ASPECT OF HISTORY

While there is no perceptible pattern to history on the large scale of time, there is a pattern to the personal story of every human being. Man as an individual cannot be integrated into the faceless mass of humanity. He has his own beginning and end; he belongs to a family, a people, a country, a culture. His life is intertwined with the lives of other human beings for better, for worse. He carries responsibility for others, and others are responsible for him. To live as an individual means to exercise one's freedom and to make responsible decisions. History, in the first place, is the result of decisions, choices, and responses on the part of individuals.[11] Even on the larger scale, the individual plays a decisive role. No group can manage to act unitedly without a leader. It is frequently the leader's motivation that ultimately decides about the turn of events.[12] History is forged in the clash of wills. The hidden motives behind man's decisions and deeds carry moral significance and transcend the purely biological rules. History never "happens"; it is the result of a complex of choices, struggles, and cross-purposes. A fatalistic view of

[11] Cf. Herbert Butterfield, *Christianity and History,* 1949, pp. 110f. Bultmann's insistence upon the importance of the individual, which he inherited from Kierkegaard, is essentially right, except that it lacks historic perspective and therefore sufficient frame of reference. Cf. Isaac C. Rottenberg, *Redemption & Historical Reality,* 1964, pp. 69ff.

[12] Cf. A. Richardson, *History Sacred and Profane,* 1964, pp. 62, 247ff.

history such as we meet it in the ancient world, governed by *Tyche, Fortuna,* and the *Moirae,* is the result of failure to attach moral value to personal decision. It stems from the conviction that history is circular and leads to no end. The blind, destructive force of *atē* dominates the fate of men and gods.[13] Only on the assumption that the gods do not meddle in human affairs was it possible to arrive at complete scepticism as in the case of the Stoics.[14]

The biblical view is different. Here the great issues of life hang upon decisions made in the human heart. Such decisions are determined not fatalistically but by man's responsible will. Yet God is no mere spectator of the human drama but His interference is of a peculiar nature: man is never a mere pawn on the checkered board of historic events. History is the very sphere where man is called upon to act in the Presence of God. Every historic situation presents man with the choice either to fall into the pattern of God's purpose, or else to pursue his own self-chosen ends. There is never a neutral position: man is either *with* God or against Him.

Because every individual is unique there can be no general rule for predicting man's decision in any given circumstances. The only approximation would be a statistical average of behavior derived from past experience. This would require a cyclical understanding of history. But history is not determined by the law of averages because it is irreversible. In the linear perspective of history no situation is repeatable; it will never occur again. We may try to learn from the past, but we can never know the future.[15]

The uncertainty of history is both a challenge and an offense to the philosopher. The contingent nature of history makes it irreducible to a rational system. We have noticed how Lessing deprecated the idea that general and timeless truths should be made dependent upon the accidents of history. Kant lays down the rule that "empirical principles are wholly incapable of serving as a foundation of moral laws."[16]

---

[13] For a discussion of the irrational aspects of μοῖρα and ἄτη see E. R. Dodds, *The Greeks and the Irrational,* 1957, pp. 37ff.

[14] Cf. Diogenes Laërtius, X, 84-116; Horace, *Epistles,* I, 6, 3-5.

[15] Cf. R. L. Shinn, *Christianity & the Problem of History,* 1964, pp. 14, 253.

[16] Immanuel Kant, *Fundamental Principles of the Metaphysic of Ethics,* 1916 trans., p. 73.

He contends that historical events can only serve as illustrations but never as demonstrations of truth. Chadwick quotes Fichte's dictum: "only the metaphysical can save, never the historical."[17]

The blame for confusing general truths with Christian revelation must be put at the door of the theologians. For centuries they have equated biblical revelation with general concepts of truth and by some strange lapse of logic have insisted that these universal truths are mediated by definite historic events. This is so great a contradiction that not even theological quibbling can resolve it. Either biblical revelation is self-evident and therefore nonrevelatory, or else it is unique and therefore outside the area of universal truth.

The biblical understanding of history must be taken seriously. Here events carry significance not because they express general principles but because they take place in the context of the covenant. All historic events ultimately derive from man's decision *before* God. Decisions can be made and remade but opportunities, situations, occasions, are unique and nonrecurrent, because time is irreversible. Outside the covenant therefore history can only appear as a demonstration of man's utter failure and helplessness. It can make no sense. But from within the covenant the situation looks different. It is at this point that God's providence over history becomes the decisive factor.

First, man's freedom is never absolute freedom. No man is free as God is free. Man's freedom is limited by his creatureliness. In his defiance of God's laws he can go thus far and no further. Second, man's freedom is circumscribed by his environment. No man can act without restraint from the outside: the more forceful his will the greater the opposition. It is a proven fact that no man, no matter how powerful, can translate to perfection his will into acts. There are always obstacles in the way that frustrate man's intentions. There is thus a gap between man's imagination and his achievement as there is between the artist's vision and his completed work.[18] Third, no man is entirely free of the laws of psychology so that he can overcome all his inhibitions and permanently divest himself of all inner scruples. If moral restraints cease to operate there is still reason and

[17] Henry Chadwick, *op. cit.*, p. 31.
[18] Cf. Shinn, *op. cit.*, p. 143 n. 3.

self-interest, which exert some sort of control over man's actions. Only at the point of madness does man act with complete freedom. This is why the Romans said: *quem vult perdere Jupiter prius dementat.* Lastly, we may point to the destructive nature of evil: it is an odd but remarkable fact that evil defeats its own ends. This may not be immediately evident, but in the wider perspective of history it becomes clear that the irrationality of evil avenges itself in that it results in utter futility. There is therefore a *Nemesis* of history which may be taken seriously, though this in no way redresses the wrongs of those who suffer at the hands of evil men.

But these are only hidden hints at God's providence, which faintly suggest some sort of a connection between the covenant and the ordering of God's purpose. We will have to probe deeper in order to discover the meaning of history in the covenant context.

3. HISTORY AS A MORAL TESTING-GROUND

Our difficulty in sorting out the complexities of history in order to discover a rationale that would endow events with meaning derives from the fact that we have to operate on two different planes: the universal and the particular. These interact and are inseparable but cannot be put under one denominator. In universal terms history seems to reveal no pattern, leads to no goal, serves no end, and makes no sense — it just continues from generation to generation. Because history seems to have no ultimate goal, man has to invent temporary goals in order to give a semblance of meaning to his existence. This is his problem: as a rational creature he finds himself engaged in an irrational concatenation of events. He thus needs provisional goals, such as the development of the human race, the improvement of society, the promotion of culture. This, however, only defers his problem. In the last resort, he knows, unless there is meaning to his being here that extends beyond his self-chosen ends, he is really deluding himself. Thus the question of the meaning of history resolves itself into the question as to the meaning of human life. There can be meaning to history in general only if there is first of all meaning to man's personal existence. Only if human life is meaningful is there sense in the general history of the human race. But the moment we touch upon the question of meaning we have already moved out of the area of historical inquiry and find ourselves back in theology.

There are here two questions that are interdependent and yet have to be treated separately: the question of man's existence and the question of history as the story of the human race. On the first question there can be no doubt from a biblical point of view: man exists by the will of God, who created him for fellowship with Himself and other creatures. This is the inner meaning of the covenant. Meaning, therefore, cannot be sought in one's own existence but in relation to others, primarily in relation to God.

Prof. Victor E. Frankl has shown from a purely psychological point of view the importance of meaning for man's will to live. Even a minimum of meaning is enough to provide some purpose to human life, but once all meaning is gone man cannot live.[19] Yet, though a minimum of meaning gives man the will to live, meaningful living requires more than the mere minimum. Man has to know what he is living for and what sense it makes. It is not the mere fact of suffering that is at the core of man's anguish but that his suffering serves no apparent purpose. Frankl's own recovery of the will to live began at the moment when he was able to endow suffering with meaning.[20] It is to be counted to Arnold Toynbee's special credit for endowing the element of suffering with positive significance in the drama of human history.[21] It is not suffering in itself that is important, but suffering that leads to deeper living and higher ends. There is positive meaning in suffering, of which the Cross of Jesus Christ is the supreme example. It brings back to us the fact of our responsibility before God and our inextricable involvement in the life of the community. But Christian suffering carries even greater significance in that it has a redemptive purpose: the Christian shares in the fellowship of suffering with his Lord. He suffers for the sake of Jesus Christ, for the sake of the Kingdom of God and His righteousness, for the sake of mankind.[22] His per-

---

[19] Cf. V. E. Frankl, *Man's Search for Meaning*, 1964 trans.; also *The Doctor and the Soul*, 1957 trans.; cf. also D. F. Tweedie, *Logotherapy and the Christian Faith*, 1961.

[20] Cf. Tweedie, *op. cit.*, p. 143.

[21] Cf. Shinn, *op. cit.*, pp. 231f and note 3; p. 238.

[22] For the positive aspect of suffering in the Christian context see

sonal sufferings as a sinner thus lead to the higher suffering as a saint.

In terms of the individual, history is certainly the testing-ground of man's humanity. "To be an individual," says Hugh Vernon White, "is both a fact and an achievement."[23] There can be no better place for man's training in human existence before God than the world in which we live. Seen in this way, Leibniz was perfectly right, this is the best of all possible worlds. Life in time is the God-given opportunity for man to become what he is called to be, namely a son of God. The problem of history does not arise at the point of testing but at the point of man's failure to stand the test. That *all* men *always* fail constitutes the puzzle of history.

Theologians therefore speak of a hidden meaning to history which cannot be assessed from within the drama as played out before our eyes.[24] At best it can only make sense as an opportunity for personal salvation, but it seems to make no sense on the larger scale where evil always appears to carry the victory. There is here a profound theological problem, namely the connection between history and redemption.

Jacques Maritain warns against an *a priori* position on the part of anyone who tries to comprehend the course of human history.[25] This is in keeping with the rule that data must be treated on their merit and not pressed into a preconceived mold. But at the same time it is admitted on every side that there is no approach to history without presuppositions.[26] For the theologian there can be no choice but to begin at the point of God's providence. Maritain has shown that no immanentist theory is sufficient to explain the meaning of history without contradiction.[27] For us the sovereignty of God is a basic theological supposition.[28] We

---

Merrill Proudfoot, *Suffering: A Christian Understanding*, 1964, pp. 34ff, 39f, etc.

[23] H. V. White, *Truth and the Person in Christian Theology*, 1963, p. 154.

[24] Cf. Shinn, *op. cit.*, pp. 177ff.

[25] Cf. Jacques Maritain, *On the Philosophy of History*, 1957, p. 30.

[26] Cf. Shinn, *op. cit.*, p. 242; cf. also Rottenberg, *op. cit.*, p. 61 (on Bultmann); cf. also A. Richardson, *op. cit.*, pp. 242ff, 250ff.

[27] Maritain, *op. cit.*, p. 162.

[28] Cf. Shinn, *op. cit.*, pp. 247ff. Cf. also Wm. Temple, "Christianity as an Interpretation of History," Wm. Ainslie Memorial Lecture, 1944.

therefore have to assume a connection, hidden or otherwise, between human history and God's ultimate purpose.

The importance of the covenant lies in the fact that such a connection is already established from the very beginning. Within the perspective of the covenant not only the individual but the history of mankind must be placed under the providence of Almighty God. But how does history with all its contingencies, failures, and brutalities fit into the benevolent scheme of God's purpose?

We can see why philosophers like Hegel, in order to endow history with meaning, had to fall back upon an evolutionary concept by which history itself becomes the vehicle of progress. On this premise, Hegel is able to announce ultimate achievement on the part of man:

> Humanity has now attained the consciousness of a real internal harmonization of Spirit, and a good conscience in regard to actuality — to secular existence. The Human Spirit has to stand on its own basis. In the self-consciousness to which man has thus advanced, there is no revolt against the Divine, but a manifestation of that better subjectivity, which recognizes the Divine in its own being; which is imbued with the Good and the True, and which directs its activities to general and liberal objects bearing the stamp of rationality and beauty.[29]

On reading the above passage one wonders in what kind of a world Hegel lived. The facts of history, as we know them, contradict almost every word in Hegel's description. For us, history is too terrible a story to be camouflaged by pretty words. It only goes to prove that philosophers are the least capable of coping with the crude and irreconcilable facts of life. To create order of the chaos we call history, they have to overlook the contradictions and idealize the facts. Those who take the facts seriously will not treat history as a vehicle of progress: history provides no solution but in itself constitutes a problem.[30]

The philosopher's approach to history fails because he

---

[29] G. W. F. Hegel, *Philosophy of History*, 1901 trans., p. 511. Those who talk about "man come of age" misunderstand Bonhoeffer (cf. K. Hamilton, *op. cit.*, p. 170), and move in a world of Hegelian illusion.

[30] Cf. Shinn's main thesis: *"History is not the solution of the human problem, but part of the problem demanding a solution"* (*op. cit.*, p. 201; Shinn's italics).

can only operate on the premise of universal rules. But history cannot be reduced to general rules for it presents us with no predictable pattern. In this respect the theologian has the greater advantage in that he is pressed to assume a linear concept of history that pays special attention to the irreversibility of time. From this point of view history loses much of its fortuitous character and becomes the area where man's decisions and responsibilities work themselves out in all concreteness. We oversimplify the dynamic of history when we try to apply to it the laws of nature. The biological principle of evolution does not easily fit the historical facts. The life of the individual, the life of nations, and the fact of culture, depend to a large extent upon human decisions, responses, and motives, which transcend the dynamics of natural evolution. In the sphere of history we have to reckon with moral forces, both positive and negative, which shape and mar human destiny. It is for this reason that the individual is of such importance in the overall story of humanity, for it is he who is concretely engaged in shaping history. There will never be another Moses, Elijah, David, Peter, or Paul. We must refrain from treating history as if it were a "something" apart from man, a kind of superforce. History is nothing else but the story of man's decisions, failures, strivings, and follies multiplied *ad infinitum*. Man makes his own history, but because he can only live in society he becomes caught up in the maze of the follies and decisions of others. In this sense man is the prisoner of history. There is no escape from the accumulative effect of the past. Not even the most violent revolutions can abrogate the burden we inherit.

There is, however, an inward escape that makes it possible for the individual to adjust himself to history. He may dissociate himself from the past and refuse to accept responsibility. He may regard it an injustice that while the fathers have eaten sour grapes his own teeth should be set on edge (Jer. 31:29f; Ezek. 18:2-4). But this is essentially an attitude of pride based on the conviction that he would have done better in similar circumstances. The other possibility derives from the Christian attitude: the burden of the past can only be effectively dealt with by redemptive living. Renewal from within is the answer to the problem of history. Jesus Christ associates Himself with the sins of the world and takes His place in solidarity with the sinner. Vicarious suffering, suffering on behalf of others, is the clue to history. There is no redemption without suffering. In this sense history is the moral testing-ground as far as the individual is concerned. He is challenged by the story of mankind to make the decision what to do with his life — to serve God's purpose, or his own ends.

4. THE COHERENCE OF HISTORY

To the superficial observer it may appear that the accidental character of historic events is devoid of all inner cohesion. The "ifs" of history seem so utterly fortuitous as to make no sense at all.[31] But this is only one way of looking at it. Though history may appear to have no observable pattern, there is a natural connection between cause and effect.[32] There is thus a hidden cohesion within events that make up the story of mankind. It is at this point that we may look for a deeper meaning of history in connection with God's gracious providence.

In this wider perspective history forms a coherent story in that it becomes the record of God's dealing with mankind. God *in* history is the God of providence who was known to our fathers before He was known to us. In the last resort, history can be understood only from within the story of revelation. Within this story the covenant is the overall "master metaphor" not only of the Bible but of the whole story of the human race.[33] From within the covenant God's dealing with mankind is not a sporadic, intermittent decision by which He intervenes from time to time. His Presence to His creatures is not a capricious act produced by emergencies. Revelation is a continuous act, which never ceases. God is always the same God, though the circumstances under which we meet Him may vary. It is for this reason that the dispensational divisions of history prove to be inadequate

[31] Cf. F. J. C. Hearnshaw, *The 'IFS' of History*, 1929.

[32] Hume questions the propriety of arguing from cause to effect (cf. his essay: "Of a particular providence and of a future state"), but it is difficult to take his contention seriously.

[33] Robert Worth Frank, President Emeritus of McCormick Seminary, describes the covenant as the "master metaphor of the Bible." He uses the expression "metaphor" not because the covenant is a fiction but only because it is in itself inadequate to convey the depth of God's faithfulness to His creation (cf. *McCormick Quarterly*, Jan. 1963, p. 4).

for a covenantal perspective. We misunderstand the story of revelation if we divide it up into segments: Old Covenant — New Covenant; Law — Gospel; Old Israel — New Israel. Such a disconnected approach rather suggests sporadic decisions on the part of God who is not quite sure of His own purpose. Once we treat God seriously we must assume that He does not step into history in order to withdraw again.[34] The idea of a history divided in dispensations with each age operating according to different rules casts a shadow upon the steadfastness of God's character. Dispensationalists not only divide history in segments but separate these according to strict rules. Behind the idea of distinct dispensations, Law — Gospel — Holy Spirit, is an effort to provide history with a progressive principle. Joachim of Flora (1132-1202) with his "apocalyptic spiritualism" has plainly worked into his Trinitarian scheme of history the principle of progressive evolution: from the dispensation of the law to the *ecclesia spiritualis*. His system has exercised endless fascination upon heretical sects,[35] but the orthodox have been equally affected.[36]

It is only when we recognize that history and revelation are not correlatives that the dispensational theory falls to the ground. The movement of sidereal time cannot be the determinant factor in the story of revelation. God is as present in the pre-Christian era as in the post-Christian era. The grace of God cannot be made dependent upon calendric chronology.

Our measurement of time is a social convenience but this in no sense determines our knowledge of God. Abraham may have known God more intimately than many a medieval Pope. It is a fallacy to assume that spiritual life is dependent upon history. In order to understand the coherence of history we will therefore have to distinguish the flow of sidereal time from the life of the individual *before* God.

God's covenant extends over history from beginning to end. Those before Christ, those under the law, those after Christ, are all under the same grace of God. Man's knowledge of the grace of God does not depend upon the era in

[34] Cf. John McIntyre, *The Christian Doctrine of History*, 1957, pp. 79f.

[35] Cf. G. H. Williams, *op. cit.*, pp. 18, 382, 858.

[36] Cf. *Baker's Dict. of Theology*, 1960, art. Dispensationalism; cf. also L. Berkhof, *Systematic Theology*, 1962, pp. 290ff.

which he lives. The individual has his own history: his movement within *chronos* and *kairos* is a matter between him and his Creator. But at the same time every man's life is determined by historic factors beyond his control. To live in the twentieth century is different from living in the second century B.C. By this we do not mean that the conveniences are different, or that the cultural amenities are different; this is not an essential point. The essential difference lies in relation to the End.

Without the eschatological perspective there can be no coherence of history. A story that has no end cannot be a coherent story, for the sequel is missing. But that there is an end at all, can only be seen from the covenant. Without the covenant we can only speak of a physical, geological or biological end. We can work out the end in terms of entropy, but in this case we can only see history as a story without meaning. The eschatological End relates to *apocatastasis,* to renewal, to ultimate fulfillment. Without this history is without coherence.

5. THE IMPORTANCE OF TIME

We have already spoken about the cyclic meaning of time in terms of *chronos*. We have said that *chronos* becomes eventful time at the point when it acquires personal meaning in the Presence of God. We now have to ask, What is the meaning of the *continuum* of time that makes up history?

We have to attach significance to the historic drama if we are to maintain biblical particularism as important to the story of revelation. It is the particularity of events in history that is of such importance to us. Herein we differ from classical philosophy and medieval theology in that we attach special significance not to the universal but to the particular.[37]

From a theological point of view time is the extension of grace not only for the individual but for the human race. This can only be understood if we take God's judgment over sin seriously. In fact judgment itself is a sign of grace. Without God's judgment history would end in utter destruction. Time therefore points to the sovereignty of God: time is God's time for man. In view of the Cross God's time for

---

[37] For the medieval stress upon the universal, see Shinn, *op. cit.*, p. 65 n. 2.

man is saving time. But the sovereignty of God in history is revealed in a paradox: in His weakness is His true strength. The reason for this is that God's sovereignty is inseparable from His love. Because love is the power proper to God, it can only be demonstrated in weakness.[38] But only in history is God's love manifested in weakness. Outside the area of human life God's sovereignty remains unchallenged. He is absolute Lord of creation enthroned in majesty. Only in relation to man is He revealed as Servant. This is both the glory and the offense of the gospel. We may therefore say that time has meaning not only to man but to God Himself. It is the sphere wherein God reveals Himself for what He really is: a loving Father.

It is at the point of God's love that time is lifted from mere spatial duration into the dimension of Eternity. The meaning of time must be linked to the *telos* of history: God's purpose with man as revealed in Jesus Christ. The whole drama would be senseless but for the fact that man is called to be a son of God. The moral and spiritual implications of this statement provide history with the dimension of beyondness that lifts *chronos* into the meaningfulness of *kairos*. It is within the dimension of *kairos* that the covenant acquires its fullest significance. It creates what Dr. Frank called "the open future." The covenantal relationship breaks the cycle of sidereal time; this means a break with blood and soil, with tribal ties and ancestral loyalties, with nature, culture, and past history.[39] Man is lifted out from mere existence into the Presence of God. We would venture the suggestion that it is only within time that the translation from *chronos* to *kairos* becomes meaningful. To the question why should man be put into *chronos* in the first place, there can be no answer, except that he would not be man if he were not a temporal creature. We can, however, say something about the moral significance of time.

The irreversible character of time provides urgency and meaning to man's choices. In a world where no choices are possible, good and evil, truth and falsehood, love and hate remain conceptual possibilities outside the realm of reality. It is only within the temporal order that motives

---

[38] Cf. Shinn, *op. cit.*, pp. 259ff.
[39] Robert Worth Frank, *op. cit.*, p. 4.

resulting in acts can carry moral meaning because they cannot be unmade.

Man has no control over time. Only He for whom past, present, and future are as one, holds time in His power. The Christian understanding of forgiveness is related to this fact. Because man can neither control nor reverse time forgiveness appears for what it is, namely the miracle of God's grace. What happened cannot be altered but it can be forgiven. Forgiveness, which is another aspect of the covenant, is yet another clue to history: without forgiveness human life becomes impossible. It is at the point of forgiveness that we come closest to the heart of God. Only those who know personally of God's forgiving grace are able to practice forgiveness themselves. The Cross is the token of God's willingness to forgive but the principle of forgiveness is as old as the human race. Humanity could not continue without it. It is in this context that we may see best the significance of time in relation to revelation: time provides the background for the exercise of God's love in all its concreteness; it removes it from the realm of mythology into the realm of event. That Christ died for sinners is not a beautiful thought but a bloody fact in history. Had God peopled the world with angels there would be neither time nor history. Angels are ministering servants who make no personal choices. But an angel can never become a son; it remains a servant. Time provides us with the opportunity of sonship.

6. THE IMPORTANCE OF EVENTS IN HISTORY

R. W. Hepburn raised the question all over again: how can events in time "speak of a God of eternity?"[40] His criticism is directed at theologians who notoriously stress the importance of history for the facts of faith. A case in point is the resurrection of Jesus Christ. Is the resurrection a historic fact? If we say that it is a matter of pure history, then the historian insists upon scientific investigation; if we say that it is a matter of faith, then why do we stress the importance of history?

The question of history in relation to faith has become a burning issue with the demythologizing school of Rudolf Bultmann.[41] Bultmann has tried to free theology from its

---

[40] Ronald W. Hepburn, *Christianity and Paradox*, 1958, p. 91.
[41] Cf. Rottenberg, *op. cit.*, pp. 37ff.

close association with "saving events in history" and substitute existential experience as the decisive factor of faith. But once historicity is surrendered all aspects of objectivity are lost and faith becomes a matter of a subjective mood. Hepburn subtly suggests that if it is only a question of a sense of Christ's Presence may it not be that the resurrection is nothing more than "the history of a stubborn illusion."[42] Bultmann has tried to extricate himself from the suspicion of sheer subjectivity by making a distinction between *Heilsgeschichte* and history, or *Geschichte* and *Historie*.[43] To return to the question of the resurrection: Bultmann explains that the resurrection is a matter of faith; as such it cannot be a historical event, for this would mean that we try to secure faith in the resurrection by faith in history:[44] "the Christian Easter-faith is not interested in the historical question."[45] But in this case we may well ask: did He rise or did He not? This is exactly Hepburn's point.

The way out of the difficulty is to spiritualize the resurrection, which is now a widely accepted practice.[46] But the question arises whether this is not in fact a subterfuge for demythologizing.

In the question of the resurrection we have an extreme case of the problem of history in relation to revelation. On the one hand we must take Shinn's warning seriously and refuse to divide history into secular and religious, or *Geschichte* and *Historie*;[47] on the other hand, the history of revelation, or *Heilsgeschichte*, does not easily fit into the mold of ordinary history for it does not stand the tests of verification. We cannot prove the resurrection; we can only believe it. Only on the principle that time is irreversible and that history does not repeat itself, is it possible to assert that the resurrection is a unique case and therefore without parallel. This is exactly what makes investigation impossible: there is nothing to compare it with, it is unprece-

---

[42] Hepburn, *op. cit.*, pp. 100f.

[43] The short treatise by Bultmann: "Neues Testament und Mythologie," in *Kerygma und Mythos*, 1948, gives the gist of Bultmann's theology. For criticism see James Barr, "Revelation Through History in O.T. and in Modern Theology," *Interp*, April 1963, pp. 199ff.

[44] Cf. *ibid.*, p. 49.

[45] *Ibid.*, p. 51.

[46] Cf. F. W. Beare, *The Earliest Records of Jesus*, 1962, pp. 240ff.

[47] Cf. Shinn, *op. cit.*, p. 56.

dented. It will also never occur again; there will never be another Jesus who was raised from the dead.

But assuming the resurrection to be a fact, though historically unverifiable, is the construction put upon it the only possible one? Had the resurrection occurred, say, in Athens and not in Jerusalem, would it have been interpreted in the same way and would theologians have arrived at the same conclusions? Hepburn objects to the idea that man should be made "the witness of a succession of ready-made events, complete with their 'meanings' " instead of fashioning history himself.[48] Without recourse to the covenant there can be no satisfactory answer to this question.

The story of revelation as depicted in the Bible is intimately linked to the history of a particular people. Not that the Bible reserves the knowledge of God to one racially defined group. Enoch walked with God (Gen. 5:22) long before there were any Hebrews; so did Noah (Gen. 6:9). A prophet in Israel tells us that "from the rising of the sun to its setting, God's Name is great among the nations, and in every place incense is offered to His Name" (Mal. 1:11). Biblical particularity must not lead to the conclusion that God had withdrawn from the rest of humanity. To read the Bible this way is to misread it. Hebrew history is not very different from the history of other nations in respect to idolatry, immorality, and lust for power. The difference between Israel and the nations is not in the quality of events but in the construction put upon them. The prophetic interpretation of Israel's history is orientated toward salvation and this only because of the covenant tradition.[49] The perspective under which the ordinary occurrences of history are viewed constitutes the difference between general history and *Heilsgeschichte*. Man is certainly the witness of a succession of events but the interpretation is his own. The "meanings" he himself has to supply. The prophets of the Old Testament and the writers of the New Testament interpret history, especially Israel's history, in the light of the covenant. A good example is Simon Peter's "sermon" on the day of Pentecost. Here the resurrection of the Lord Jesus (Acts 4:33) is not an isolated occurrence but the climax of God's dealing with His people under the covenant (cf. Acts

[48] Hepburn, *op. cit.*, p. 109.
[49] Cf. J. Jocz, *The Spiritual History of Israel*, pp. 118ff.

2:14ff): "For the promise is to you and to your children and to all that are far off, every one whom the Lord our God calls to him" (v. 39). A similar pattern we meet in the speech of Stephen (Acts 7). Under the perspective of the covenant, history becomes *Heilsgeschichte* and haphazard events assume a hidden meaningful pattern.

There is a definite connection between Israel's history and world history. The life of the Hebrews is molded by the historic happenings within the empires surrounding Palestine. These events bear in upon the spiritual life of Israel. No people lives in isolation. Religious syncretism, cultural assimilation, economic pressures, are forces from which no nation can escape. Knowledge of the covenant has not managed to isolate Israel from the rest of the nations, though such isolation was frequently attempted. What it did, however, was to provide a specific approach to history with a completely new orientation: it kept history open for the End.

The prophetic interpretation of history is, as it were, an esoteric lore. Every event in human life is patient of a variety of construction. The prophets developed their own historiosophy. For them events carried an *additional* meaning pointing toward God's ultimate triumph. This we may call the hidden side of history.

The birth, life, and death of Jesus were interpreted in the prophetic tradition. That Jesus rose from the dead could only strike the outsider as a strange superstition (cf. Matt. 27:64; Acts 17:18ff). The nonbeliever requires straightforward facts: "If thou be the Son of God come down from the cross" (Matt. 27:40). The Marcan version is even more explicit: "Let the Messiah, the King of Israel, come down from the cross, that we may see and believe" (Mark 15:32). But nothing happens; Jesus remains helpless in the face of ridicule. Yet to the believer His very helplessness becomes a sign of His Kingship. Who is right?

In this respect there is a modicum of truth in Bultmann's contention: faith in history and faith in the resurrection belong to two different orders and cannot be paired; and yet these cannot be separated. We cannot separate history from faith and faith from history without creating a phantom. It is only when we place both under the covenant that faith and history converge and carry the message of salvation. But we will have to admit that salvation-history and world history meet at the point of tension. Historic Israel is the extreme example of this fact. World history is challenged by salvation-history in the call to repentance. It is at this point that biblical particularity with its strange concentration upon Hebrew history acquires special significance. Israel serves as the paradigm of God's purpose for mankind. The drama of salvation with all its pitfalls is here played out in the historic life of a single people. Election, covenant, grace, on the one hand; rejection, rebellion, faithlessness, on the other hand, is the pattern we meet in the history of every nation.

7. CHRIST AS THE END OF TIME

A progressive view of history and the view that history is the vehicle of revelation are logically interconnected. There is a long tradition behind the evolutionary perspective. In a way it is already suggested by the New Testament when it appeals to the Old Testament for verification of the messianic hope. The whole theological structure of the church is built upon the idea of promise and fulfillment: what is promised in the Old Testament is fulfilled in the New Testament. We achieve thus a straight line of progression: the Law — the Prophets — the Writings — the gospel — the church. But this is a deceptive arrangement: there was church before the gospel; there is gospel in the Law; there were prophets before the Canon.

The question we have to ask is centered upon Christ in relation to time: is Jesus the Messiah the end-result of an evolutionary line or does He stand outside the sequence of the historical process?

The answer will depend upon the result of our exegesis of a crucial text. In Galatians 4:4 we read ὅτε δε ἦλθεν τὸ πλήρωμα τοῦ χρόνου, God sent forth His Son.... The RSV translates: "But when the time had fully come, God sent forth His Son...." The AV reads: "But when the fulness of the time was come, etc...." The latter is a literal rendering of πλήρωμα τοῦ χρόνου. Our problem is to decide what the Apostle meant by the "fullness of time."

Lightfoot takes the traditional line: fullness of time carries a double reference, first to the Giver and then to the recipient. As to the Giver, God Himself sets the time as indicated in verse 2: ἡ προθεσμία (*sc.* ἡμέρα) τοῦ πατρός.

But in respect to the recipient, fullness of time means that the world has now become ready to receive the gospel; the law has done its work and now it is being superseded by grace.[50]

But is it possible to credit Saul of Tarsus with such shortsighted idealism? He must have known better than anyone else how unwilling and unready the world was for the gospel. Even his own people seemed to be utterly unprepared. And does he really mean that man can now manage without the restraining influence of the law? There are too many contradictions involved in such a position to carry conviction.

Apologists for Christianity have taken two lines in explaining why Christ appeared at a particular time in history. One line puts a positive construction upon historic development in terms of progress: society had improved, righteousness was practiced, peace was established; in this way God had prepared the nations for the advent of Christianity. The universal rule of the Roman Empire Origen regards as a providential factor for the preaching of the gospel. He asks Celsus: how otherwise would it have been possible "to prevail throughout the world, unless at the advent of Christ a milder spirit had been everywhere introduced into the conduct of things?"[51] Eusebius argues in exactly the same manner: "Men as they lived in the olden days were unable to receive the all-wise and all-virtuous teaching of Christ." Only gradually, as the nations were "softened" by their lawgivers and philosophers and abandoned their fierce brutality for a "gentler mood," were they made fit to receive the gospel.[52] This progressive approach to history as *praeparatio evangelica* is Eusebius' basic answer to the question why Christ appeared when he did: God chose a time when human conduct "changed from its former wildness to something approaching to benignity."[53]

---

[50] Cf. J. B. Lightfoot, *St. Paul's Epistle to the Galatians*, 1902, p. 167: "The Gospel was withheld until the world had arrived at a mature age: law had worked out its educational purpose and is now superseded."

[51] Cf. Origen, *Contra Celsum*, II, 30. Roman roads and Greek culture were sometimes regarded as a precondition for Christianity; cf. Karl Löwith, *From Hegel to Nietzsche*, 1964 trans., p. 33.

[52] Eusebius, *Eccl. Hist.*, I, 2, 17ff.

[53] Eusebius, *Theophania*, II, 94. In fairness to Eusebius it must be

This progressive optimism finds its counterpart in the opposite view: Christ came at the time of man's deepest need. *The Epistle to Diognetus* by an unknown Christian writer of the second or third century takes this latter view. It is not moral development or cultural progress that marks the "fullness of time" for Christ's coming but rather the extremity of the human situation. The letter tells us that God endured the working of iniquity till the time "when our wickedness had reached its height": then God in His long-suffering took upon Himself "the burden of our iniquity" and graciously gave us His Son.[54] George Duncan follows the insights of the ancient document when he comments on the text of Galatians 4:4: "It was not man's progress which impelled God to act, but man's need." Duncan puts it down to a misunderstanding of the "schoolmaster" passage (Gal. 3:24), which gave rise to the idea "that man was now educated up to the stage to receive the Gospel."[55]

In view of the eschatological orientation of the New Testament there can be little doubt that *The Epistle to Diognetus* is more closely akin to the spirit of Pauline theology with respect to history than are Origen and Eusebius. For Paul "fullness of time" spells ultimate crisis and bankruptcy as far as history is concerned. Messianic time is the End of this aeon with all it stands for.[56] The parallel passage is I Corinthians 10:11: the things that happened in the past are for our warning "upon whom the end of the ages has come." Eschatologically speaking, Jesus Christ is for the Apostle the End of time. Another document of disputed authorship of the second or third century, the *Apocriticus* of Macarius Magnes, provides us with the proper interpretation of the End as carrying the meaning of "close at the door."[57] This is the Christian understanding of the *eschaton*. It is not so much the End as the beginning of the End. That history still continues is to the *Apocriticus*

---

added that occasionally he takes a more pessimistic line; cf. *ibid.*, II, 19; 52.

[54] *The Epistle to Diognetus*, 9.

[55] George S. Duncan, *The Epistle of Paul to the Galatians* (the Moffatt Series), 1934, p. 128.

[56] J. Y. Campbell remarks in reference to Gal. 4:4: "the idea of progressive infolding of God's plan in history may be in the writer's mind" (cf. *A Theol. Word Book*, *op. cit.*, p. 89).

[57] T. W. Crafer, *The Apocriticus of Macarius Magnes*, 1919, pp. 125f.

only a sign of God's mercy, who "delays the revolution of time which brings the end." The writer tells us that "we must find no difficulty in this lengthening of time. It is for us and for our benefit that the end has not yet come."

It is only because for us messianic time has lost its radical character in terms of judgment and grace that we find it difficult to adjust our thinking to New Testament eschatology. But once we endow the messianic event with the dimension of finality we immediately discover that the "fullness of time" spells out the end of history. Prof. Duncan's paraphrase of Galatians 4:4 is therefore correct: "When the time had fully expired, God sent forth His Son. . . ."[58] It is in the same sense that we must read Mark 1:15: ὅτι πεπλήρωται ὁ καιρός. The perfect indicative passive of πληρόω stands here for the ultimate completion of time: the End has come. Those who are puzzled by John's "realized eschatology" fail to pay attention to the fact that in a sense all New Testament eschatology is "realized" eschatology. The note of completion as a result of messianic fulfillment pervades all New Testament documents. Since the Messiah has come, the New Age has broken in; time is completed; the End has become visible. In this regard Bultmann's radical position in respect to eschatology must be taken seriously. Bultmann defines the message that Jesus preached: *Now has the time come! God's reign has broken in! The End is Here!*[59]

At the same time Bultmann refuses to identify the end of salvation-history with the end of world history, for obvious reasons.[60] We all know that world history is a continuing process and has never stopped. This creates a difficulty that was already an embarrassment to New Testament writers (cf. II Pet. 3:4).[61] It would be an easy way out to interpret the parousia in a spiritual sense and to say that Christ's Second Coming is fulfilled in the Advent of the

---

[58] G. S. Duncan, *op. cit.*, p. 127.

[59] R. Bultmann, *Theologie des Neuen Testaments*, 1948, pp. 4f (Bultmann's italics). Cf. also C. H. Dodd, *History and the Gospel*, 1938, p. 177.

[60] Cf. McIntyre, *op. cit.*, p. 66.

[61] According to Conzelmann the whole theology of the Lucan Gospel is an apologetic reconstruction due to the delay of the parousia (cf. Hans Conzelmann, *The Theology of St. Luke*, 1960 trans., pp. 131f, 135, 150f, etc.).

Holy Spirit to the believer and to the church.[62] On the other hand, it is suggested that the whole idea of a Second Advent is the result of an apologetic effort on the part of the church to explain the fact that history still continues and that the End is not yet.[63] But once we connect the covenant concept with salvation in time the situation becomes less embarrassing. In the covenant context the process of history and the gift of salvation are not chronologically interdependent: God always saves, for this is the very meaning of the covenant. Jesus Christ came to end history by introducing the Kingdom of God. The End came when Jesus Christ was raised from the dead.

The Second Advent must be seen as the ultimate completion of God's reign. McIntyre rightly observed that had Scripture not affirmed the Second Coming we would have been obliged to postulate it ourselves.[64] The parousia is only redundant to those who invest history with natural progress. But to us history reveals no such traits. Without the parousia history is left without ultimate purpose. It seems to us that McIntyre is essentially right in his insistence that the parousia is an integral part of the Incarnation and is not to be regarded as an afterthought. Christ's entry into history must not be limited to the short span of Jesus' life here upon earth. His Presence with humanity is the supreme fact in world history. He is the One who comes by the Holy Spirit into the lives and hearts of men. We must not conceive of the Second Advent as an event that will "happen" but as of a Person for whom the church waits.[65] The church is expecting not "something to happen" but Him whom she already knows by faith as her Lord and Savior.

Messianic time is the End of time and the beginning of the New Age. Since the Incarnation, history takes place under the signs of the Cross and the resurrection. In Jesus Christ the End has become visible. And this is the radical

---

[62] Conzelmann holds that Luke solves the problem of the delay by an appeal to the Presence of the Holy Spirit; see *ibid.*, p. 136 and note.

[63] This is essentially John A. T. Robinson's position; cf. *Jesus and His Coming*, pp. 182ff.

[64] McIntyre, *op. cit.*, p. 84.

[65] Cf. McIntyre, *ibid.*, pp. 88f. C. H. Dodd's emphasis upon "realized eschatology" fails to pay sufficient attention to the Second Coming as a N. T. hope. Cf. *History and the Gospel*, p. 171; cf. also *The Parables of the Kingdom*, 1935, pp. 107f.

difference between *ante et post Christum natum.* Not that God was absent before the Incarnation: "At every period therefore, in all ages of the world, He both looked and engaged Himself upon the things belonging to the earth; and gave freely in times of necessity . . . and so without upbraiding, evinced He the promptness of His providential care towards all men. . . ."[66] In other words, He is always the covenant-keeping God, loyal to His creation. It is this fact that makes it impossible for us to allow a break in the middle of history. For this reason, if for no other, we cannot in any sense speak of a "new" covenant unless we only mean by "new" the form and manner but not the substance. In this respect Calvin saw better than many a modern theologian: "God is never inconsistent with himself, nor unlike himself." The first covenant, Calvin explains, was inviolate; there could therefore be no other covenant: "He then who once made a covenant with his chosen people, had not changed his purpose, as though he had forgotten his faithfulness."[67]

Jesus the Messiah did not come to establish a "new" covenant but to fulfill and complete the covenant already established. But by doing so He brought history close to the End and inaugurated the New Age. Jesus Christ therefore stands at the end of history and therefore at the End of time.

8. THE NEW AGE

The End in God's providence spells out the new beginning. This process of renewal inaugurated by Jesus Christ is the new factor in history. It is important to notice how the concept of renewal underlies the whole structure of Pauline theology. There is nothing magical about it. God does not wave a wand to renew the human race, but by the slow and inexorable working of His Spirit effects renewal from within. The New Man, i.e. messianic Man, a hybrid as it were of Jew and Gentile (Eph. 2:15), is gradually emerging. The change is taking place by degrees as man advances from glory to glory in the process of being fashioned into

---

[66] Eusebius, *Theophania,* II, 85.

[67] Cf. John Calvin's Commentary on Jeremiah to 31:31; trans. John Owen, 1854, IV, 126f. By contrast cf. Leonhard Goppelt's views of the gospel as a totally new beginning (*Christentum und Judentum,* 1954, pp. 59f, 68f).

the likeness of the Messiah by the Spirit of God (II Cor. 3:17f). Messianic renewal, whereby the "old man" is abandoned and the new is put on, is the mark of the New Age (Col. 3:9f). The "new" covenant in Hebrews 8:13 and 12:24 directly relates to the hope of renewal in the Old Testament. II Corinthians 5:17 is perhaps the most eloquent expression of this experience of radical renewal: the old has passed away, behold all things are made new. To be saved means to be renewed, restored, refashioned. In Jesus Christ, God creates a new heaven and a new earth (II Pet. 3:13; Rev. 21:1). The new wine in the parable (Mark 2:22) is not just better wine as compared with Judaism but the *dynamis* of the breaking in of the Kingdom of God.

This new dimension that has entered history disrupts the circular involution of time and brings the End within sight: the night is far spent, the Day is at hand (Rom. 13:12). The decisive fact which radically alters the human situation is the resurrection of Jesus Christ. Here is the "integrative" principle which relates the past to the New Age.[68] The Messiah vindicates history in that He causes the *telos* of history to become visible: God's eternal purpose is now realized in Jesus Christ our Lord (Eph. 3:11).

Christ, as the End of time, is therefore the new beginning. This primarily applies in respect to the individual believer: he is God's "new creation" (II Cor. 5:17). Though on this side of history man has still to face sin and death, the fact that Christ identifies Himself with our human life places our earthly existence in a new light. In view of the resurrection of Jesus Christ death is no more the last word.[69] Though death may appear to be "our frontier," in Jesus Christ we discover that "God is the frontier even of our death."[70]

On the principle of the coherence of the human race, the miracle of renewal extends from the individual to the community. McIntyre defines holiness in terms of identification.[71] By this he means what Barth calls solidarity with sinners. Not only does Christ identify Himself with fallen

[68] McIntyre applies it to the Incarnation but this is only a formal difference (cf. *op. cit.*, p. 92).
[69] Cf. *CD*, III/2, 612.
[70] *Ibid.*, p. 611.
[71] McIntyre, *op. cit.*, p. 79.

man, but His followers can only prove their loyalty to the Master by identification with the world.[72] There can be no redemption in history unless personal redemption affects society. Salvation that does not impinge upon the life of the community is not salvation in the Christian sense. The missionary effort by the church is nothing if it is not the expression of God's renewal of the world. It is within this area of renewal that the covenant links eschatology with history and time. The problem of history, as we have seen, centers on the question of meaning. To vindicate history we have to discover ultimate purpose, i.e. purpose that goes beyond the historical. God's purpose for man is to raise him to sonship; he is thus the covenant partner from beginning to end. Even his failure to live up to his vocation is an integral part of the redemption story.

The covenant thus covers the totality of the historical venture. In the covenantal perspective history ceases to be a twisted skein of fortuitous happenings and acquires meaning and purpose. Christ Jesus, by becoming the first-born among many brethren (Rom. 8:29; cf. Heb. 2:11ff), vindicates not only history but also the Lord of history, who is the God of creation. The ingathering of the nations under the reign of God is the ultimate expression of covenantal grace.

---

[72] Cf. J. Jocz, *Christians and Jews: Encounter & Mission,* 1966, pp. 9ff.

BIBLIOGRAPHY

The following works are mainly those of contemporary writers. For ancient authorities, Josephus, Philo, Church Fathers, medieval theologians, rabbinic sources, etc., see footnotes and Index of Names. Other literature, especially journals, can be traced by names of writers as specified in the footnotes and listed in the Index.

Adler, Alfred. *Understanding Human Nature*, 1949.

Albright, Wm. F. *Samuel and the Beginnings of the Prophetic Movement* (Goldenson Lecture, 1961).

Aldwinckle, R. F. *Of Water and the Spirit*, 1964.

Anderson, J. F. *The Bond of Being*, 1949.

Annual of Swedish Institute, Vol. V, 1966/7.

Bailey, D. S. *Sponsors at Baptism and Confirmation*, 1952.

Baillie, D. M. *God Was in Christ*, 1958.

Baillie, John. *And the Life Everlasting*, 1934.

Bamberger, F. and S. Bernfeld, eds. *Lehren des Judentums nach den Quellen*, 1928/29.

Barnes, Hazel E. *The Literature of Possibility*, 1965.

Barnett, Lincoln. *The Universe of Dr. Einstein*, 1962.

Barth, K. *Church Dogmatics*, 1936-62.

———. *The Teaching of the Church regarding Baptism*, 1948.

———. *Die Protestantische Theologie im 19. Jahrhundert*, 1952.

———. *The Humanity of God*, 1960.

Battenhouse, R. W., ed. *Compendium to the Study of Augustine*, 1955.

Bavinck, J. H. *The Impact of Christianity on the non-Christian World*, 1949.

Beare, F. W. *The Epistle of Peter*, 1957.

———. *The Earliest Records of Jesus*, 1962.

Benjamin, S. and L. H. Hackstaff. *St. Augustine on Free Choice of the Will*, 1964.

Bentzen, Aage. *Introduction to the Old Testament*, 1948.

Bergson, Henri. *Creative Evolution*, trans. G. A. Mitchell, 1922.

Berkhof, L. *Systematic Theology*, 1962.

Berkouwer, G. C. *The Triumph of Grace in the Theology of Karl Barth*, 1956.

Bernfeld, S. and F. Bamberger, eds. *Lehren des Judentums nach den Quellen*, 1928/29.

Bethune-Baker, J. F. *An Introduction to the Early History of Christian Doctrine*, 1949.

Bett, Henry. *Johannes Scotus Erigena*, 1964.

Bible and the Ancient Near East, Essays in honour of Wm. F. Albright, 1961.
Black, M. *The Scrolls and Christian Origins,* 1961.
Blackman, E. C. *Marcion and his Influence,* 1948.
Blank, Sheldon H. *Jeremiah, Man and Prophet,* 1961.
Boman, Thorleif. *Das hebräische Denken im Vergleich mit dem griechischen,* 1952.
Bonhoeffer, D. *Act and Being,* 1956.
———. *Christology,* 1966.
Bonhoeffer, Thomas. *Die Gotteslehre von Aquin,* 1961.
Bonner, G. *St. Augustine of Hippo, Life and Controversies,* 1963.
Brasnett, R. *The Suffering of the Impassible God,* 1928.
Braude, Wm. G. *Jewish Proselyting,* 1940.
Brightman, E. S. *Is God a Person?* 1932.
Bruce, F. F. *The Acts of the Apostles,* 1951.
Brunner, E. *The Mediator,* 1947.
———. *Dogmatics,* 1952.
———. *Misunderstanding of the Church,* 1952.
Buber, Martin. *Moses,* 1946.
Bultmann, R. *Kerygma und Mythos,* 1948.
———. *Theologie des Neuen Testaments,* 1948.
Burckhardt, Jacob. *Force and Freedom,* 1955.
Buttenwieser, M. *The Psalms,* 1938.
Butterfield, Herbert. *Christianity and History,* 1949.

Camus, A. *The Fall,* 1957.
Chadwick, H. *Lessing's Theological Writings,* 1956.
Charles, R. H. *The Decalogue,* 1923.
Cherniss, H. F. *The Platonism of Gregory of Nyssa,* 1930.
Chorin, Shalom Ben and G. L. B. Sloan. *Das christliche Verständnis des Alten Testaments und der jüdische Einwand,* 1941.
Chwolson, D. *Das letzte Passamahl Christi und der Tag seines Todes,* 1892 (revised 1908).
Clements, R. E. *Prophecy and the Covenant,* 1965.
———. *God and the Temple,* 1965.
Conzelmann, Hans. *The Theology of St. Luke,* 1960.
Copleston, F. C. *Aquinas* (Pelican ed.), 1955.
Cross, F. L. *I Peter,* 1954.
Cullmann, O. *Christ and Time,* 1951.
———. *Salvation in History,* 1967.
Cunliffe-Jones, H. *The Book of Jeremiah,* 1960.

Daube, D. *The New Testament and Rabbinic Judaism,* 1956.
Delitzsch, F. and C. F. Keil. *Biblical Commentary on the Old Testament,* Vol. II, 1882.
Dembitz, Lewis N. *Jewish Services in Synagogue and Home,* 1898.
Dix, Dom G. *The Shape of the Liturgy,* 1945.
———. *Jew and Greek,* 1953.
Dixon, W. Macneile. *The Human Situation* (Gifford Lectures, 1935/37).
Doane, T. W. *Bible Myths and Their Parallels in Other Religions,* 1882.
Dodd, C. H. *The Parables of the Kingdom,* 1935.

———. *The Epistle to the Romans*, 1949.
———. *The Fourth Gospel*, 1953.
Dodds, E. R. *The Greeks and the Irrational*, 1957.
Dods, Marcus. *The Book of Genesis*, 1888.
Döllinger, J. J. I. *The Gentile and the Jew*, 1862.
Doniger, Simon, ed. *Nature of Man*, 1962.
Driver, R. S. *The Book of Genesis*, 1909.
Duncan, George S. *The Epistle of St. Paul to the Galatians*, 1934 (Moffatt series).
Dunkerley, R., ed. *Ministry and the Sacraments*, 1937.

Edersheim, A. *The Life and Times of Jesus the Messiah*, 1907.
Eichrodt, W. *The Theology of the Old Testament*, Vol. I, 1961.
Eisler, R. *The Enigma of the Fourth Gospel*, 1938.
———. *Man Into Wolf*, 1951.
Elmendorf, J. J. *Elements of Moral Theology*, 1892.
Emmet, D. M. *The Nature of Metaphysical Thinking*, 1946.
Every, G. E. *Lamb to the Slaughter*, 1957.

Farley, Edward. *The Transcendence of God*, 1960.
Farrar, F. W. *Sermons and Addresses delivered in America*, 1886.
Farrer, Austin. *A Study in Mark*, 1951.
Feifel, H., ed. *Meaning of Death*, 1959.
Finkenzeller, Josef. *Offenbarung und Theologie nach der Lehre des Johannes Duns Skotus*, 1961.
Foerster, W. *From Exile to Christ*, 1964.
Forsyth, P. T. *Christ on Parnassus* (n.d.).
Frankfort, Henri. *Kingship and the Gods*, 1948.
Frankl, V. E. *Man's Search of Meaning*, 1964.
Freud, S. *The Future of an Illusion*, 1949.
Fuchs, E. *Studies in the Historical Jesus*, 1964.

Garstang, John. *The Heritage of Solomon*, 1934.
Gilson, Etienne. *The Christian Philosophy of St. Augustine*, 1960.
Goethe, J. W. *Sämmtliche Werke*, 1868 (Taschenausgabe).
Goppelt, Leonhard. *Christentum und Judentum*, 1954.
Graham, Winston. *After the Act*, 1965.
Guilding, A. *The Fourth Gospel and Jewish Worship*, 1960.
Gunkel, H. *Einleitung in die Psalmen*, 1933.

Hackstaff, L. H. and S. Benjamin. *St. Augustine on Free Choice of the Will*, 1964.
Hamilton, K. *The System and the Gospel*, 1963.
Hanson, R. P. C. *Origen's Doctrine of Tradition*, 1954.
———. *Allegory and Event*, 1959.
Harrelson, Walter. *Interpreting the Old Testament*, 1964.
Harris, C. R. S. *Duns Scotus*, 1959.
Harrison, R. K. *A History of Old Testament Times*, 1955.
Hartshorne, Charles. *The Divine Relativity, A Social Concept of God*, 1948.
Hearnshaw, F. J. C. *The 'Ifs' of History*, 1929.
Hebert, G. *When Israel Went Out Of Egypt*, 1961.
Hegel, G. W. F. *Philosophy of History*, 1901.
———. *Die Germanische Welt*, 1920.

Hengel, M. *Die Zeloten*, 1961.
Hepburn, R. W. *Christianity and Paradox*, 1958.
Hertz, J. H. *Commentary to Pentateuch*, 1938.
———. *The Pentateuch and the Haftoras*, 1960.
Heschel, A. J. *God in Search of Man*, 1956.
———. *Who is Man?* 1966.
Hirsch, E. *Geschichte den neuern evangelischen Theologie*, 1960.
Hobbes, Thomas. *Leviathan* (ed. by M. Oakshott, 1955).
Hooft, W. A. Visser 't. *No Other Name*, 1963.
Hook, Sidney, ed. *Determinism and Freedom*, 1958.
Hooker, M. D. *Jesus and the Servant*, 1959.
Howard, W. F. *The Fourth Gospel in Recent Criticism and Interpretation*, 1955.
Hume, David. *Dialogues Concerning Natural Religion* (N. Kemp Smith, 1947).
Hunt, Leslie. *Principalities and Powers*, MS., Wycliffe College (n.d.).

Interpretationes ad Vetus Testamentum pertinentes Sigmundo Mowinckel, 1955.

Jacob, Edmund. *The Theology of the Old Testament*, 1958.
Jaeger, W. *The Theology of Early Greek Philosophers*, 1947.
James, O. E. *Christian Myth and Ritual*, 1933.
Jaubert, A. *La Date de la Cène*, 1957.
Jenson, R. W. *Alpha and Omega*, 1963.
Jeremias, Joachim. *The Eucharistic Words of Jesus*, 1955.
———. *Infant Baptism in the First Four Centuries*, 1960.
Jocz, J. *The Jewish People and Jesus Christ*, 1954.
———. *A Theology of Election*, 1958.
———. *The Spiritual History of Israel*, 1961.
———. *Christians and Jews: Encounter and Mission*, 1966.
Johnson, A. R. *The Vitality of the Individual in the Thought of Ancient Israel*, 1949.
———. *Sacral Kingship in Ancient Israel*, 1955.
———. *The One and the Many*, 1961.
Jung, C. G. *Psychology and Religion*, Bolligen Series, XX, 1958.

Kant, Immanuel. *Critique of Pure Reason*, trans. by T. K. Abbott, 1909.
———. *The Fundamental Principles of the Metaphysic of Ethics*, trans. by T. K. Abbott, 1916.
Keil, C. F. and Franz Delitzsch. *Biblical Commentary on the Old Testament*, Vol. II, 1882.
Kennett, R. H. *Ancient Hebrew Social Life and Custom*, 1933.
———. *The Church and Israel*, 1933.
King, H. C. *The Moral and Religious Challenge of Our Times*, 1911.
King, Magda. *Heidegger's Philosophy*, 1964.
Klausner, J. *Jesus of Nazareth*, 1926.
Klubertanz, P. *St. Thomas Aquinas on Analogy*, 1960.
Knight, G. A. F., ed. *Jews and Christians*, 1965.
Kraemer, H. *World Cultures and World Religions*, 1960.
———. *Why Christianity of All Religions?* 1962.
Küng, Hans, ed. *Christianity Divided*, 1962.

La Barre, Weston. *The Human Animal*, 1955.
Lagrange, M. J. *The Gospel of Jesus Christ*, 1938.
Langton, E. *Good and Evil Spirits*, 1942.
Le Grant, Wm. *Metaphysical Teachings*, 1963.
Leibniz, G. W. *Principles of Nature and Grace, Founded upon Reason*, 1714 (Everyman's Lib.).
Leivestad, R. *Christ the Conqueror*, 1954.
Lightfoot, J. B. *St. Paul's Epistle to the Galatians*, 1902.
Livingstone, R. W., ed. *Legacy of Greece*, 1921.
Lodge, R. C. *Plato's Theory of Ethics*, 1928.
Lods, A. *The Prophets and the Rise of Judaism*, 1937.
Loewe, H. and C. G. Montefiore. *A Rabbinic Anthology*, 1938.
Lorenz, K. *Das Sogenannte Böse*, 1963.
Löwith, Karl. *From Hegel to Nietzsche*, 1964.

MacIntyre, A. C. *Difficulties in Christian Belief*, 1959.
Maier, Johannes. *Vom Kultus zur Gnosis*, 1964.
Manson, W. *The Epistle to the Hebrews*, 1951.
Mantel, H. *Studies in the History of the Sanhedrin*, 1961.
Maritain, Jacques. *On the Philosophy of History*, 1957.
Marmorstein, A. *The Old Rabbinic Doctrine of God*, 1927.
Mascall, E. *Words and Images*, 1957.
Matchette, F. J. *Outline of Metaphysics*, 1949.
Maurice, F. D. *Theological Essays*, 1853.
McCabe, Joseph. *Evolution* (n.d.).
McIntyre, John. *The Christian Doctrine of History*, 1957.
McNeile, A. H. *The Book of Exodus*, 1917.
McRuer, J. C. *The Trial of Jesus*, 1964.
Mendenhall, G. E. *Law and Covenant in Israel and the Ancient Near East*, 1955.
Mentz, Hermann. *Taufe und Kirche*, 1960.
Minear, P. S. *Eyes of Faith*, 1946.
Montefiore, C. G. and H. Loewe. *A Rabbinic Anthology*, 1938.
Moore, G. F. *Judaism*, Vol. I, 1927.
Morgenstern, J. *The Ark, the Ephod and the Tent of Meeting*, 1945.
Morris, Leon. *The New Testament and the Jewish Lectionaries*, 1964.
Mowinckel, S. *He That Cometh*, 1956.
———. *The Psalms in Israel's Worship*, 1962.
Mozley, J. K. *The Doctrine of the Christian Incarnation*, 1936.
Muckle, Friedrich. *Der Geist der jüdischen Kultur und das Abendland*, 1923.

Newman, M. L. *The People of the Covenant*, 1962.
New Testament Essays in Memory of T. W. Manson, 1959.
Nias, J. C. S. *Gorham and the Bishop of Exeter*, 1951.
Niebuhr, Reinhold. *The Nature and Destiny of Man*, Vol. I, 1941.
North, C. R. *The Old Testament Interpretation of History*, 1946.
———. *The Suffering Servant in Deutero-Isaiah*, 1948.
Noth, Martin. *Überlieferungsgeschichte des Pentateuchs*, 1948.
Nygren, Anders. *This is the Church*, 1952.

Oehler, G. F. *The Theology of the Old Testament*, 1883.
Oesterley, W. O. E. and T. H. Robinson. *The Hebrew Religion*, 1930.

Oosterzee, J. J. van. *Christian Dogmatics*, 1873.
Orlinsky, H. M. *The So-Called Suffering Servant in Isaiah 53* (Goldenson Lecture, 1964).
Orr, James. *The Christian View of God and the World*, 1897.
———. *Sin as a Problem Today* (n.d.).
Owens, Joseph. *The Doctrine of Being in the Aristotelian Metaphysics*, 1957.
———. *An Elementary Christian Metaphysics*, 1963.

Pedersen, Johs. *Israel*, 1926.
Peters, A. *Realpräsenz*, 1960.
Peters, Richard. *Hobbes*, 1956 (Pelican ed.).
Pfeiffer, R. H. *The Books of the Old Testament*, 1967.
Philp, H. L. *Jung and the Problem of Evil*, 1958.
Powis, J. M. *The Origin and History of Hebrew Law*, 1960.
Proudfoot, Merrill. *Suffering: A Christian Understanding*, 1964.

Rad, Gerhard von. *Das formgeschichtliche Problem des Hexateuchs*, 1938.
———. *Genesis*, 1956.
———. *Old Testament Theology*, Vol. I, 1962.
Ramsey, Wm. M. *A Historical Commentary on St. Paul's Epistle to the Galatians*, 1899.
Rashdall, H. *The Idea of Atonement in Christian Theology*, 1919.
———. *The Theory of Good and Evil*, 1924.
Reisel, M. *The Mysterious Name Y.H.W.H.*, 1957.
Richardson, A. *An Introduction to the Theology of the New Testament*, 1958.
———. *History Sacred and Profane*, 1964.
———, ed. *Theological Word Book*, 1950.
Ringgren, H. *The Messiah in the Old Testament*, 1956.
———. *Sacrifice in the Bible*, 1962.
———. *Israelite Religion*, 1966.
Roberts, D. E. *Psychotherapy and a Christian View of Man*, 1950.
Robinson, J. A. T. *Jesus and His Coming*, 1957.
Robinson, H. Wheeler. *The Religious Ideas of the Old Testament*, 1938.
Rosenzweig, Franz. *Der Stern der Erlösung*, 1954.
Rottenberg, Isaac C. *Redemption and Historical Reality*, 1964.
Rowley, H. H. *The Discovery of the Old Testament*, 1945.
———. *The Old Testament Interpretation of History*, 1946.
———. *The Biblical Doctrine of Election*, 1950.
———. *The Unity of the Bible*, 1953.
Russell, B. *The History of Western Philosophy*, 1946.

Sartre, Jean-Paul. *The Devil and the Good Lord*, 1960.
Scheler, Max. *Man's Place in Nature*, 1961.
Schlatter, A. *Der Evangelist Johannes*, 1930.
Schmithals, W. *Paul and James*, 1965.
Schopenhauer, A. *Die Welt als Wille und Vorstellung*, 1847.
Schrenk, G. *Gottesreich und Bund im älteren Protestantismus*, 1923.
Schweizer, E. *Church Order in the New Testament*, 1961.
Scott, E. F. *The Epistle to the Hebrews*, 1922.
Scott, R. B. Y. *The Relevance of the Prophets*, 1944.

Segal, J. B. *The Hebrew Passover*, 1963.
Shinn, R. L. *Christianity and the Problem of History*, 1964.
Simon, U. E. *A Theology of Auschwitz*, 1967.
Simpson, G. Gaylord. *The Meaning of Evolution*, 1951.
Sloan, G. L. B. and Shalom Ben-Chorin. *Das christliche Verständnis des Alten Testaments und der jüdische Einwand*, 1941.
Snaith, N. H. *The Distinctive Ideas of the Old Testament*, 1944.
Spinoza, B. *Ethics*, trans. by R. H. M. Elwes (n.d.).
Stamm, J. J. *Der Dekalog im Lichte der neueren Forschung*, 1962.
Stern, Karl. *The Third Revolution*, 1955.
Studies on Psalms, Deel XIII, Leiden, 1963.
Such, S. T. *Justification*, MS., Knox College, Toronto, 1965.

Teilhard de Chardin, P. *The Phenomenon of Man*, 1959.
Thackery, St. John. *The Septuagint and Jewish Worship*, 1923.
Tillich, P. *The Protestant Era*, 1951.
———. *Courage to Be*, 1952.
———. *Love, Power and Justice*, 1954.
———. *Systematic Theology*, 1957.
Torrance, T. F. *The Doctrine of Grace in the Apostolic Fathers*, 1948.
Tournier, P. *Guilt and Grace*, 1962.
Toynbee, A. *The Study of History*, Vol. VI, 1939.
———. *Christianity Among the Religions of the World*, 1957.
Tresmontant, Claude. *A Study in Hebrew Thought*, 1960.
Tweedie, D. F. *Logotherapy and the Christian Faith*, 1961.

Unger, Erich. *Das Problem der mythischen Realität*, 1926.

Vahanian, G. *The Death of God*, 1961.
Vriezen, Th. C. *An Outline of Old Testament Theology*, 1958.
———. *The Religion of Ancient Israel*, 1967.

Weber, Max. *Ancient Judaism*, 1952.
Weber, Otto. *Ground Plan of the Bible*, 1959.
Weiser, A. *The Psalms: A Commentary*, 1962.
Westcott, B. F. *The Gospel According to St. John*, 1908.
White, H. V. *Truth and the Person in Christian Theology*, 1963.
Widengren, George. *Sakrales Königtum im Alten Testament und im Judentum* (Franz Delitzsch lecture, 1952).
———. *Muni and Manichaeism*, 1961.
Wildberger, Hans. *Jahwes Eigentumvolk*, 1960.
Williams, G. H. *The Radical Reformation*, 1962.
Williams, N. P. *The Ideas of the Fall and of Original Sin*, 1927.
Windelband-Heimsoeth. *Lehrbuch des Geschichte der Philosophie* 1948.
Winter, P. *On the Trial of Jesus*, 1961.
Witte, J. *Die Christus-Botschaft und der Religionen*, 1936.
Wright, Sir Almroth E. *Prolegomena to the Logic which Searches for Truth*, 1941.

Zimmerman, P. A., ed. *Darwin, Evolution and Creation*, 1959.

INDEX OF SUBJECTS

INDEX OF NAMES

INDEX OF TEXTS